D1789210

Categories in Context

International Studies in Social History
General Editor: Marcel van der Linden,
International Institute of Social History, Amsterdam

Published under the auspices of the International Institute of Social History, Amsterdam, this series offers transnational perspectives on labour and working-class history. For a long time, labour historians have been working within national interpretive frameworks. But interest in studies contrasting different national and regional experiences and studying cross-border interactions has been increasing in recent years. This series is designed to act as a forum for these new approaches.

Recent volumes:

Volume 31
Categories in Context: Gender and Work in France and Germany, 1900–Present
Edited by Isabelle Berrebi-Hoffmann, Olivier Giraud, Léa Renard and Theresa Wobbe

Volume 30
What Is Work? Gender at the Crossroads of Home, Family, and Business from the Early Modern Era to the Present
Edited by Raffaella Sarti, Anna Bellavitis and Manuela Martini

Volume 29
Laborers and Enslaved Workers: Experiences in Common in the Making of Rio de Janeiro's Working Class, 1850–1920
Marcelo Badaró Mattos

Volume 28
Labour, Unions and Politics under the North Star: The Nordic Countries, 1700–2000
Edited by Mary Hilson, Silke Neunsinger and Iben Vyff

Volume 27
Rescuing the Vulnerable: Poverty, Welfare and Social Ties in Modern Europe
Edited by Beate Althammer, Lutz Raphael and Tamara Stazic-Wendt

Volume 26
The History of Labour Intermediation: Institutions and Finding Employment in the Nineteenth and Early Twentieth Centuries
Edited by Sigrid Wadauer, Thomas Buchner and Alexander Mejstrik

Volume 25
Bread from the Lion's Mouth: Artisans Struggling for a Livelihood in Ottoman Cities
Edited by Suraiya Faroqhi

Volume 24
Bondage: Labor and Rights in Eurasia from the Sixteenth to the Early Twentieth Centuries
Alessandro Stanziani

Volume 23
Migration, Settlement and Belonging in Europe, 1500–1930s: Comparative Perspectives
Edited by Steven King and Anne Winter

Volume 22
Alienating Labour: Workers on the Road from Socialism to Capitalism in East Germany and Hungary
Eszter Bartha

For a full volume listing, please see the series page on our website:
http://www.berghahnbooks.com/series/international-studies-in-social-history

Categories in Context

Gender and Work in France and Germany, 1900–Present

Edited by

Isabelle Berrebi-Hoffmann, Olivier Giraud,
Léa Renard and Theresa Wobbe

First published in 2019 by
Berghahn Books
www.berghahnbooks.com

Library of Congress Cataloging-in-Publication Data

Names: Berrebi-Hoffmann, Isabelle, editor.
Title: Categories in context : gender and work in France and Germany, 1900-present / edited by Isabelle Berrebi-Hoffmann [and three others].
Description: New York : Berghahn Books, 2019. | Series: International studies in social history ; Volume 31 | Includes bibliographical references and index.
Identifiers: LCCN 2018056279 (print) | LCCN 2019000038 (ebook) | ISBN 9781789201888 (ebook) | ISBN 9781789201871 (hardback : alk. paper)
Subjects: LCSH: Women--Employment--France--History. | Women--Employment--Germany--History. | Sex discrimination in employment--France--History. | Sex discrimination in employment--Germany--History.
Classification: LCC HD6134 (ebook) | LCC HD6134 .C38 2019 (print) | DDC 331.40943--dc23
LC record available at https://lccn.loc.gov/2018056279

British Library Cataloguing in Publication Data

A catalogue record for this book is available from the British Library

ISBN 978-1-78920-187-1 hardback
ISBN 978-1-78920-188-8 ebook

Contents

Charts, Tables and Graphs

Charts

Tables

Graphs

Acknowledgements

This has been a collaborative endeavour from the beginning, and we are grateful to the German National Science Council (WO 550-6-2) and the French National Research Agency (ANR-11-FRAL-0012) for funding our French-German research project 'The Metamorphosis of Equality' from 2011 to 2016. Olivier Giraud and Theresa Wobbe also thank the Käthe Hamburger International Centre 'Work and Human Lifecycle in Global History' (re: work), Humboldt University of Berlin, for its support during their fellowship years 2012–13 and 2014–15. Isabelle Berrebi-Hoffmann thanks the Department of History of Harvard University for its invitation and support during her two visiting years 2015–17. Further, Theresa Wobbe is very grateful to the Fritz Thyssen Foundation for funding the Conference 'International Labour Organization as Producer of Statistical Knowledge' in February 2016. We are deeply grateful to Juergen Kocka for his support.

The editors thank the Centre Marc Bloch, the University of Potsdam, the Conservatoire national des arts et metiers (cnam) in Paris, and the Gender Research Group of the Laboratory for Research in Economic Sociology (Lise), at the French National Center for Scientific Research (CNRS). Without the project members, our research assistants and our colleagues, this book would not have come into existence. We warmly express our thanks to Pamela Wehling for her contribution to the project, and to Leora Auslander, Sigrid Betzelt, Hans-Georg Haupt, Karin Hausen, Tamar Herzog, Milena Kremakova, Lydia Malmedie, Catherine Marry, Manuela Martini, Valeska Korff, Marie-Thérèse Letablier, Régis Schlagdenhaufen, Ursula Rust, Nikola Tietze, Raf Vanderstraeten, Sigrid Wadauer, Bernard Zarca and Bénédicte Zimmermann for their helpful comments. We thank the research assistants Charles-Eric Adam, Theresa Adenstedt, Max Fröbel, Ivan Getmancev, Emil Herrling, Susanne Kalka, Antonia May, Theres Matthieß, Bianca Nagel and Max Schultz for their steady support and enthusiasm. Finally, a word of gratitude to Chris Chappell and two anonymous referees for their editorial guidance, as well as to Anne Gillet for her editing support.

Introduction

Categories of Gender and Work in Context
Ways Towards a Research Agenda

Isabelle Berrebi-Hoffmann, Olivier Giraud, Léa Renard and Theresa Wobbe

This book aims to bring a new understanding of the fabric of categories of gender and work and their impact on different groups of actors. It focuses on the circulation and transformation of categories, through distinct institutions – such as language, science and research, statistics, law, social policies – and on the dynamics of social conflicts and resistance which over time have led to the institutionalization of specific categories.

Despite broad research regarding the gender–work nexus, surprisingly little is known about modes of classification and transformation over time (see, e.g., Allen and Eby 2016; Jeanes, Knights, and Martin 2011; Powell 1999). This book brings together a range of chapters on the categorization of gender and work from a historical-sociological perspective (Clemens and Cook 1999; Zimmermann 2015). Our aim has been to provide a fresh analytical perspective on long-term transformations in two national contexts, France and Germany. Both were European colonial powers facing multiple tensions of empire (Cooper and Stoler 1997). We argue that they are increasingly embedded within and between the transnational and the global while eliciting different understandings of that embedment.

The ten chapters are based on case studies conducted in France and Germany, by a team of sociologists, political scientists and historians who have worked together on an integrated research project over a period of four years. They examine gender categorization and labour regulation while citing numerous examples of their institutionalization and transformation: the dynamic of legal and statistical categorization of female labour in the context of the family business; professional gender equality through the lens of statistical classification and remuneration; contested legal categories of women's night work; struggles over women's employment quotas on the boards of large firms; as well as shifting family policy measures, such as parental leave schemes.

By viewing gender and work as institutionalized cultural structures and forms of knowledge, the case studies presented here illustrate how work has been a major field in the restructuring of gender relations, while gender has increasingly determined and limited access to and status in the world of employment in the course of the twentieth century. This world of work, at the same time, was embedded in colonial structures and discourses about civilization (Zimmermann 2016a, 2016b, 2018). Suspecting categories and categorization to have a particular hand in these social processes, and elaborating just as much on their social as on their contingent quality, the chapters emphasize a sociological way of taking categories and categorization seriously. Actors engage in serious debates about and with categories; categories are at the basis of their struggles and they reveal contradictory ways of viewing the interactions between work and gender.

Taking Classification and Categories Seriously

With this book and our empirical studies, we aim for a sociological comprehension of classification as a social practice, embracing both everyday categorization and technical-scientific classification. Classification encompasses the ordering of objects into groups or sets on the basis of their assumed relationships as similar or different (Starr 1987), or a set of boxes into which people and things can be put (Bowker and Star 1999: 10; Hacking 1986). Classification informs the processes of making distinctions between things entailing two dimensions, that is, 'lumping and splitting', a process in which, on the one hand, entities are lumped in distinct clusters and, on the other, separated into different entities (Zerubavel 1996; see also Czarniawska and Sevon 1996). The recognition of both similarity and difference is at the core of self- and collective identification (Jenkins 2000; Jepperson 2001). Put differently, categorizations that are used on a daily basis across various social fields touch on elementary social operations, as they rest upon social conditions and cultural expectations (Berger and Luckmann [1966] 1991). They gain their authority as they are collectively produced, sustained and enforced (Douglas 1986; Durkheim and Mauss 1903; Fourcade 2016).

Interrogating the social order of sexual classification together with that of 'work' and its categorical framework constituted the very beginning of women's and gender studies. The reclassification of 'sex' and 'gender' itself, and the controversies it initiated, were the outcome of throwing new light on the arrangement between the sexes and its cultural representation (Scott [1988] 1999a). In her book on *Deceptive Distinctions*, Cynthia Epstein Fuchs (1988) explored the conceptual boundaries that define the categories of sexual difference, which are both symbolic and social in the world of work. Furthermore, historians (Bock and Duden 1976) and sociologists (Lopata 1971; Oakley 1974) redefined housework as 'work' rather than 'love', a 'natural' female disposition or a residue of 'tradition'. The emergence of modern housework was put into the context of social transformations, namely the rise of market-oriented 'gainful employment', which, around 1900, also triggered the classification of homework. However, global labour history offers a more nuanced global picture of the various kinds of domestic, care-giving and wage work (Van Nederveen Meerkerk, Neunsinger, and Hoerder 2015). As the dichotomous distinction between market-related and home-related work shows, categorization flags the social territories of belonging, which in turn matter for social status (Canning 1996; Epstein 1989; Wobbe and Renard 2017; for methodological elaboration see Goertz and Mazur 2008). Following Erving Goffman (1977: 302), sex-class placement provides an exemplary case, 'if not a prototype, of social classification'. As Cecilia Ridgeway shows, sexual categorizations often function as cultural 'super-schemes' to make sense of persons in the workplace so that we are framed 'before we know it' (Ridgeway 2009: 145, 2011).

Over recent decades, economic sociology has also been concerned with classifications, but mostly with product and market mechanisms of classification. This interest later led to broadening the span of research objects of market sociology to 'populations of would-be customers' (Fourcade and Healy 2013) and thus to investigating 'market classifications' in a broader sense, that is, 'various forms of sorting, categorizing and valuating of economic subjects and objects' (Krenn 2017: 7). Following the French approach of economics of conventions (Diaz-Bone 2017; Diaz-Bone and Didier 2016) and studies in (historical) sociology of quantification and statistics (Desrosières 1998, 2011; Espeland and Stevens 2007, 2008; Heintz 2010, 2012, 2016; Porter 1995), this research field focuses on the mechanisms through which markets are ordered, value is attributed to objects and objects are ranked. By doing so, it highlights the production of hierarchies in markets by technical and thus highly social procedures of classification and comparison, such as credit and university rankings (Espeland and Sauder 2007; Fourcade and Healy 2013). However, if classification dynamics bring hierarchies among those who are classified, they also exclude or include over time different kinds of activities and groups from the visible economic activity and state statistics. They also engender a process of framing and eventually a process of definition of identities and social groups.

Another field of sociological research has turned to the cultural and discursive dimensions of categories touching on unsettled and transgressing identities of individuals and groups, on their politics of difference and differentiation (for overviews, see Brubaker 2015, 2016; Lamont and Molnár 2002; Lamont et al. 2016). This focus on 'identity' and 'group' has been challenged by perspectives beyond 'groupism' (Brubaker 2002; Lamont et al. 2016) and 'identity' (Brubaker and Cooper 2000) to take categories as culturally contingent phenomena instead of essential and fixed properties. More recent debates underscore the need to reconnect cultural processes to social inequality to explore how inequality is produced through the mobilization of common categories and classification systems (Epstein 2007; Lamont, Beljean, and Clair 2014).

Building on both approaches, we propose to look at classifications as collective representations of gender and work, how they configure and reflect the boundaries of categories that manifest in the structures of institutions, such as occupational classification, legal categories, recruitment schemes or branches (Anderson 1994; Rudischhauser 2017; Wobbe 2012; Zimmermann 2006). We understand categorization as the result of definition and differentiation of social groups in political and legal institutions through technical-scientific procedures of ordering (ibid.).

Our ten cases show that even in different national contexts, the categorization of gender and work is always a double process. The first process is one of substantive co-definition. Whether discussing women's night work laws throughout Europe, or equality labour laws, controversies refer to women's social, economic and private roles. Similarly, controversies in both countries led to the assessment of new definitions of work and labour. This is what we call a process of 'substantive co-definition'. The second process we have highlighted is the definition of boundaries as a 'dynamic-relational process'. Through time, since the nineteenth century, categorization processes have led to an evolution of boundaries between private and public spheres as well as an evolution of boundaries with regard to the gender division of labour. At the same time, these boundaries are unstable and reveal the attribution of certain work activities performed by women at the intersections between these fields to 'grey zones', as a way of stabilizing the emerging system. Our common understanding of the categorization process consequently builds on this double process of co-definition of, on the one hand, substantive categories and, on the other, dynamic frontiers of work, through the comparative approach of our case studies.

With this book, we aim to broaden the research by exploring categorization and its transformation in the world of work over a longer stretch of time, namely from around 1900 up to the present. This approach allows for exploring the emergence, alteration and decline of categories, which reveals a complex interplay of durability and change. For example, the category of gainful employment, institutionalized around 1900, would not become only one type of work among others. Rather, it came to be the standard and norm of market-related paid work, closely coupled with a gendered coding of labour, which is still with us in certain sectors (Folbre 2001; Topalov 2001; Wobbe 2012; Wobbe and Renard 2017).

Comparison in Context: Ways Towards a Historical-Sociological Comparative Approach

In the following chapters, we try to take categorization processes in the long term seriously and highlight differences and similarities between two national contexts. By doing so, we aim to combine historical sociology with French-German comparison. We assume that comparison between contexts, as a heuristic tool, can help to shed light on critical processes, which a single case study would have missed out. In this enterprise, we can build on a long and productive tradition of intellectual relations and historical comparative analysis between France and Germany, specifically in the domain of work and forms of labour mobilization. At first centred on the nation viewed as a contained entity and as the most relevant frame for comparative analysis, this bilateral comparative perspective has been opened up to other spaces of social interaction including concepts of 'work' and 'unemployment' (Zimmermann 2006) and gender in the world of work (Lallement et al. 2015; Wobbe, Berrebi-Hoffmann, and Lallement 2011).

In the 1980s, the comparative tradition between France and Germany was marked by an approach in terms of 'societal effect' (Maurice, Sellier, and Silvestre [1982] 1986). In order to account for the differences between the two models of work organization, according to these authors, it was necessary to look for meaningful differences both in the nature of the industrial relations systems and in the structure of the education system of both countries. These results made the case for a fruitful comparative approach apprehending cases as entireties and as separate entities. Focusing on the embeddedness of the compared objects in their national contexts, the compared objects were related to a large set of social domains, institutions, actors and so on in each national context in order to identify meaningful relations between variables. This ensured a comprehensive analysis of the case in line with the Weberian tradition of comprehensive sociology. By extending the search for relevant social mechanisms to various domains and mechanisms in society, it demonstrated the variety of causal relations between one social phenomenon and various elements of its national social context. This view of (multiple) co-variation led directly to the central argument of institutional complementarities that has been at the core of the institutional approaches of the 1990s and 2000s (e.g. Hall and Gingerich 2009) and is also mostly in line with the dominant approaches in the field of comparative history (Haupt and Kocka 2009), which frequently relays to detailed case studies (e.g. Frader 2008; Rudischhauser 2017). They are intrinsically idiosyncratic and consider multiple inferences.

However, from the 1990s onwards, a crucial turn emerged in the field of social history, away from the comparative analysis of closed systems towards the comparison of related entities in which the concepts of transfers (Espagne 1994; Osterhammel 2001), circulations (Kaluszynski and Payre 2013), entanglements (Conrad 2008) and *croisements* (Werner and Zimmermann 2006) have been key. Gender history in a transnational perspective is going beyond interstate relations to discover obscured biographies, networks and institutions (see, e.g., chapters in Janz and Schönpflug 2014), conceiving in contrasting ways the nature of the relations between cultures or countries, the importance of the transnational spaces or, conversely, of the nation. These approaches propose to further broaden the apprehension of the contexts of the historical phenomenon to be compared by considering their connections and mutual construction, which are not 'coloured by methodological nationalism' (Wimmer and Glick Schiller 2002: 302).

The common integration of France and Germany into the context of the European Union (EU) and their strong level of attention to the normative framework of international organizations like the International Labour Organization (ILO) have created an increasingly important further shared context between these two countries. The research on knowledge circulation stresses the embeddedness of national pathways in a transnational framework, which goes far beyond European supranational policies and international organizations. By doing so, a renewed approach in historical sociology attempts to pass over the 'occlusion of the global and transnational' in historical-sociological studies: 'The issue is that, for too long, comparative historical sociology has failed to look beyond, through, or across national processes and international systems to explore *trans*-national and global dynamics: that is, connections, relations, and processes that traverse conventional state boundaries' (Go 2014: 122–23). According to Go, one of the main reasons comparative historical sociology has long occluded transnational processes is situated in the search for causal explanations when comparing separate cases (2014: 127–30). The global and transnational matter not in a causal way to explain national pathways of change, but because they are intertwined in coalitions of actors and configurations of meanings, which, together, can provide us with explanations for mechanisms. Thus, the analysis of the specific channels and mechanisms and the relations between national objects and transnational dynamics are crucial elements of our comparative approach.

In her book on *Economists and Societies*, Marion Fourcade (2009) deploys a similar approach, which she considers a critical organized comparison. Accordingly, we have to reflect the categories used in the comparison as contingent, culturally defined terms and to explore how they 'combine into fairly coherent constellations' (ibid.: 13). In order to investigate the historical and social conditions that enabled the concepts of gender and work across national contexts, we connect the comparative perspective with the historical one. The period around 1900 provides a point of departure, since only then did 'work' come to be classified as gainful employment, together with the sexual distinction between market-related and home-related work. During the twentieth century, particularly its second part, reclassifications of gender distinctions took place.

Against this backdrop, we propose a comparative approach that we call 'comparison in context' in order to combine two research lines in historical sociology. First, it considers the compared objects as embedded in specific social and historical contexts (Werner and Zimmermann 2006). The *histoire croisée* approach emphasizes the historization of the objects and categories of analysis, 'with the processes back to the temporal and spatial interactions that make up the category' (ibid.: 44), which is contextual itself. In line with the comparative-historical analysis perspective, the various chapters ground their demonstration in a thorough knowledge of empirical situations making up the contexts at stake (Mahoney and Thelen 2010: 13) and enabling us to make use of 'empirical mechanisms' to elucidate the cases under scrutiny (ibid.: 15).

Second, our approach focuses on the dynamics of transnational mechanisms (Conrad 2002; Go 2014). We believe that valuing the idiosyncrasy of a specific situation neither hinders the capacity to compare, nor implies restriction of the analysis to the national frame. Due to the ontological peculiarities of the social, George Steinmetz (2004: 372) suggests seeing case studies and so-called small-N comparisons 'as privileged forms of sociological analysis', as our only access to underlying structures is via the empirical event. Comparison in context analyses how a context, made up of various possible spaces or scales of social interaction, relates to the comparative object, and how the specific logic of embeddedness of each case is to be put in perspective with that of the other cases, in a manner inspired by Michael Burawoy's 'extended case method' (Burawoy 1998; Crozier [1964] 2010). While studying the process of categorization through deep case studies in comparison, we deal with a level of deep granularity – local, historical moments, actors, power struggles, political conflicts, language of labour and conceptions of gender and equality – as well as a global and transnational level of analysis. We argue that this allows us to contribute genuinely to ongoing issues of equality and identity in different contexts and at different levels today.

Cognitive Options, Driving Forces, Coalitions of Actors, Scales

Our comparison is carried out with the help of a series of case studies. Both teams of French and German researchers elaborated integrated analytical and methodological frames of analysis and engaged in empirical study. As we assume that categories are at the basis of social controversies between actors, we selected four debates at the intersection between work and gender: (1) women's night work and its legal regulation; (2) the categorization and legal regulation of the work of family workers; (3) legal categories of employment equality; and (4) quotas for women on company boards.

Combining a historical perspective with analytical tools stemming from the sociology of public controversies, the sociology of knowledge and of institutions, our case studies focus on critical issues touching upon the recognition of women's labour or the structuring of genderized power relations in regard to labour. As a consequence, the studies are rooted in the systematic and compared analysis of the semantic scripts underlying the – mostly competitive or even contentious – process of institutionalizing categories. The role of social actors in the formation and imposition of categories is at the centre of our analysis. But interactions between social actors systematically refer to the sociohistorical context made up of cultural repertoires, institutions or socioeconomic conditions. In order to make sense of the tension between contextual elements such as culture or institutions and the interplay of actors in relation to a specific issue, all case studies are structured around two (or more) sequences, with the genesis of categorization and its institutional formation organizing a form of social order. We thereby build on the sociological tradition of neo-institutionalist research (Jepperson 1991; Thelen 1999) and especially focus on 'critical junctures' (Collier and Collier 1991) as moments of crystallization in which mechanisms of redefinition and reinterpretations of categories become salient. This allows empirical insights about historical ruptures and continuities in the way public problems are formulated. Thus, the focus of the comparative analysis is on the various problematizations of issues related to gender and work, which could be similar or different according to specific contexts and settings (Clemens 2007; Haydu 1998).

In order to uncover the mechanisms responsible for institutional changes from an inductive, empirical perspective, our analytical framework articulates four main elements. First, the chapters examine dominant semantic scripts about gender and their specific articulation in the social spheres at hand. Mainly, these articulations are related to structuring oppositions such as work/non-work, work/family, tradition/modernity, equality in values/equality in rights, and so on. These cognitive options inform the apprehension of the analysed objects, as well as the multiple dimensions for reframing in terms of norms, discourses, regulatory forms and so on. Second, our case studies look at driving forces. These are context-related social transformations and cultural concepts, such as globally shifting social and economic rationales like the internationalization of labour law after World War I, the United Nations Decade for Women, the feminist agenda since the 1960s and the agenda of work flexibility since the 1980s; they contributed to destabilizing former collective representations of gender roles in the social field of labour. Third, actors and actors' coalitions play an important role in the phrasing of social, political and economic issues that have influenced the structuring of the domains in which our comparative research objects are embedded. Finally, scales are explored as spaces of social interactions and, more precisely, as areas for the formulation and circulation of categories, social mobilization and institutional regulation. The analysis of rescaling processes – both up- and downscaling – helps us to understand the tensions and transformations of discourses, expertise and statements regarding a social phenomenon at different stages of circulation between the various spaces of social interaction.

Structure of the Book

The book is structured in two parts. The case studies in the first part relate to similar comparative objects in the two national contexts, the genesis and transformation of which can be read in the mirror of each other. The second part provides four individual chapters that address national and transnational changes in equality concepts. The ten chapters cover this topography in the following manner.

Part I: Shifting Categories from a Comparative Relational Perspective

Olivier Giraud and Léa Renard explore the shifting categorization of family members working in family businesses in France and Germany. Giraud demonstrates how the category of family work became a reference for a social movement of spouses of independent workers in France after 1945. In her chapter, Renard examines the statistical and social placing of 'family workers' in Germany (1880–2010), showing both the emergence of the category in the field of statistics and its shifting meaning over time. Michel Lallement and Theresa Wobbe and Katja Müller deal with the emerging categorization of 'women's night work' as both an international phenomenon and a national protective measure around 1900 and its dissolution in the late twentieth century. Their chapters suggest that the deinstitutionalization of that category is shaped by similar transformations in the European labour market in France and Germany, even though it is embedded in different cultural trajectories and political breaks such as National Socialism. The last chapters of Part I show different semantics and driving forces shaping the controversy on women's quotas on corporate boards during the early 2000s in both countries. For the French debate, Anne-Françoise Bender, Isabelle Berrebi-Hoffmann and Philippe Reigné reveal the reconfiguration of actors' constellations and power relations in a national space strongly embedded in a transnational environment. They highlight the tensions between the logic of anti-discrimination present in European laws and the French definition of equality and parity. Katja Müller analyses the discourse on females' human capital (and its potential waste as a threat) in the German debate on quotas. In comparison to the French case, she points to a very different coalition of actors anchored in national legal and economic spheres.

The comparative results exposed in this part show strong national trajectories and, at the same time, ongoing processes of convergence since the 1970s. Among other similarities, a new way of articulating social justice and economic productivity in equality discourses is common to both national contexts. Compared to protective measures around 1900, it reveals a transformation in the patterns of gender difference – based not only on moral but also on economic arguments. The results gathered in Part II give some lines of explanation, embedded first in the European integration and second in the process of globalization.

Part II: Transnational Interplay of Categorization

The four individual chapters presented in Part II explore altering models of gender equality, its semantics, driving forces, struggles over classification, and rescaling. Arnaud Lechevalier starts with the question of how gender regimes in France and Germany have changed over the past decades and how these changes can be explained, while both gender regimes have been considered very different during the twentieth century. Exploring the reform of parental leave in Germany, Theresa Wobbe, Maike Bussmann, Carolin Höroldt and Léa Renard discuss the discontinuities of German family policy, in particular its shifting configurations and rescaling in the frame of human capital and flexibility. Finally, the last two chapters address the quest for 'equal pay for equal work' in the national context, the EU and the ILO. Departing from the interwar years, Theresa Wobbe, Carolin Höroldt and Maike Bussmann exemplify two German legal cases on equal pay (1950–1980s) in a transnational legal field of debate on equal employment rights within the ILO. Ferruccio Ricciardi explores the practical challenges of the EU's early equal pay norm in relation to job evaluation schemes in the member states.

Our results show a variety of transnational networks of actors and categorizations, both within and beyond national structures and international organizations. The introduction of quotas for women on company boards in France, for instance, cannot be understood without taking into account the role of economic actors and multinational corporations. The institutionalization of the principle 'equal pay for equal work' has been a result of struggles and redefinition processes, involving civil society, national, supranational and international actors. Thus, the space of categorization in the field of gender equality at work seems to be a transnational one.

As Sonya O. Rose (2010) put it, if gender and work are categories, they not only have a specific history, but they also *are* history. The chapters in this book show that more work remains to be done on exploring the historicity of gender and work. Our goal has been, through this collective research and book, to show how this conflicting fabric of gender and work categories is intertwined with political and social change, and embedded both in historical domestic contexts and global movements and regulations.

Isabelle Berrebi-Hoffmann is a research faculty member in sociology at the French National Center of Scientific Research (CNRS) and a member of the Lise-CNRS. She has led several international research projects on the transformations of work and the history of equality and gender. Her recent publications include a collective edited volume on the politics of intimacy at work since the nineteenth century (*Politiques de l'intime: Des utopies sociales d'hier aux mondes du travail d'aujourd'hui*, La découverte, 2016) and a book (with M.-C. Bureau and M. Lallement) on the makers' movement and the digital economy (*Makers: Enquête sur les laboratoires du changement social*, Seuil, 2018).

Olivier Giraud is Research Director at the Lise-CNRS, Paris. He is a specialist in comparative policy analysis, specifically in the domains of social policies (long-term care policies) and gender regimes. He has recently coordinated a research project on the remuneration of family care-givers in the context of cash for care benefits in France. Together with Stefanie Börner and Silke Bothfeld, he edited in 2017 an issue of the journal *Zeitschrift für Sozialreform* on the concept of autonomy in contemporary social policy-making, entitled 'Sozialstaalichkeit und Autonomie: Historische, soziologische und wohlfahrtsstaatsheoretische Perspektiven'.

Léa Renard is a PhD candidate in sociology and political science at the University of Potsdam (Germany) and the University of Grenoble Alpes (France). She worked for the project 'Metamorphoses of Equality II (1945–2010)' (Potsdam/CNAM-Lise Paris), co-founded by the Agence Nationale de la Recherche and the Deutsche Forschungsgemeinschaft, on family workers and statistical classification. Her PhD project explores shifting statistical categories of migration and nationality in France and Germany over time (1880–2010).

Theresa Wobbe is Professor Emerita of Sociology at the University of Potsdam, and fellow of the Margherita von Brentano Centre for Gender Studies at the Free University of Berlin. She specializes in historical sociology, sociology of knowledge, institutionalist gender analysis, and sociology of classification. Her research focuses on long-term transformations of gender and work, international statistics as an instrument of globalization, and the making of gender as a global category of comparison. Her current projects deal with the ILO discontinuities in the notion of forced labour, 1919–2017, and the conceptional history of gender in global political institutions.

References

Allen, T.D., and L.T. Eby (eds). 2016. *The Oxford Handbook of Work and Family*. Oxford: Oxford University Press.

Alonso, W., and P. Starr (eds). 1987. *The Politics of Numbers*. New York: Russell Sage.

Anderson, M. 1994. '(Only) White Men Have Class: Reflections on Early 19th-Century Occupational Classification Systems', *Work and Occupations* 21: 5–32.

Arrow, K.J. 1973. 'The Theory of Discrimination', in O. Ashenfelter and A. Rees (eds), *Discrimination in Labor Markets*. Princeton, NJ: Princeton University Press, pp. 3–33.

Berger, P.L., and T. Luckmann. [1966] 1991. *The Social Construction of Reality: A Treatise in the Sociology of Knowledge*. London: Penguin Books.

Bock, G., and B. Duden. 1976. 'Arbeit aus Liebe – Liebe als Arbeit: Zur Entstehung der Hausarbeit im Kapitalismus', in Gruppe Berliner Dozentinnen (ed.), *Frauen und Wissenschaft, Beiträge zur Berliner Sommeruniversität für Frauen*. Berlin: Courage Verlag, pp. 118–99.

Bowker, G.C., and S.L. Star. 1999. *Sorting Things Out: Classification and Its Consequences*. Cambridge, MA: MIT Press.

Braun, L., and E. Hammonds. 2012. 'The Dilemma of Classification', in K. Wailoo, A. Nelson, and C. Lee (eds), *Genetics and the Unsettled Past: The Collision of DNA, Race, and History*. New Brunswick: Rutgers University Press, pp. 67–80.

Brubaker, R. 2002. 'Ethnicity without Groups', *European Journal of Sociology* 43(2): 163–89.

________. 2015. *Grounds for Difference*. Cambridge, MA: Harvard University Press.

________. 2016. *Trans: Gender and Race in the Age of Unsettled Identities*. Princeton, NJ: Princeton University Press.

Brubaker, R., and F. Cooper. 2000. 'Beyond "Identity"', *Theory and Society* 29(1): 1–47.

Burawoy, M. 1998. 'The Extended Case Method', *Sociological Theory* 16(1): 4–33.

Canning, K. 1996. *Languages of Labor and Gender: Female Factory Work in Germany, 1850–1914*. Ithaca, NY: Cornell University Press.

Clemens, E.S. 2007. 'Toward a Historicized Sociology: Theorizing Events, Processes, and Emergence', *Annual Review of Sociology* 33: 527–49.

Clemens, E.S., and J.M. Cook. 1999. 'Politics and Institutionalism: Explaining Durability and Change', *Annual Review of Sociology* 25: 441–66.

Collier, R.B., and D. Collier. 1991. *Shaping the Political Arena: Critical Junctures, the Labor Movement, and Regime Dynamics in Latin America*. Princeton, NJ: Princeton University Press.

Conrad, S. 2002. 'Doppelte Marginalisierung. Plädoyer für eine transnationale Perspektive auf die deutsche Geschichte', *Geschichte und Gesellschaft* 28(1): 145–69.

________. 2008. *Deutsche Kolonialgeschichte*. Munich: C.H. Beck Wissen.

Conrad, S., and S. Randeria (eds). 2002. *Jenseits des Eurozentrismus: Postkoloniale Perspektiven in den Geschichts- und Kulturwissenschaften*. Frankfurt: Campus.

Cooper, F., and A.L. Stoler (eds). 1997. *Tensions of Empire: Colonial Culture in a Bourgeois World*. Berkeley: University of California Press.

Crenshaw, K. 1995. *Critical Race Theory: The Key Writings that Formed the Movement*. New York: New Press.

________. 2011. 'Race, Reform, and Retrenchment: Transformation and Legitimation in Antidiscrimination Law', in 'Critical Legal Thought: An American-German Debate – Republication [with a New Introduction] Twenty-Five Years Later', Part 3: The State, Liberal Rights, and Social Movements, *German Law Journal* 12: 247–84.

Crozier, M. [1964] 2010. *The Bureaucratic Phenomenon*. Chicago: Chicago University Press.

Czarniawska B., and G. Sevón. 1996. 'Introduction', in B. Czarniawska and G. Sevón (eds), *Translating Organizational Change*. Berlin: Walter de Gruyter, pp. 1–12.

Desrosières, A. 1998. *The Politics of Large Numbers: A History of Statistical Reasoning.* Cambridge, MA: Harvard University Press.

________. 'Words and Numbers: For a Sociology of the Statistical Argument', in A.R. Saetnan, M. Lomell, and S. Hammer (eds), *The Mutual Construction of Statistics and Society.* London: Routledge, pp. 41–63.

Diaz-Bone, R. 2017. 'Classifications, Quantifications and Quality Conventions in Markets: Perspectives of the Economics of Convention', *Historical Social Research* 42(1): 238–62.

Diaz-Bone, R., and E. Didier. 2016. 'The Sociology of Quantification: Perspectives on an Emerging Field in the Social Sciences', *Historical Social Research* 41(2): 7–26.

Douglas, M. 1986. *How Institutions Think.* Syracuse, NY: Syracuse University Press.

Durkheim E., and M. Mauss. 1903. 'De quelques formes primitives de classification', *L'Année sociologique* 6: 1–72.

Epstein, C.F. 1988. *Deceptive Distinctions. Sex, Gender, and the Social Order.* New Haven, CT and New York: Yale University Press and Russell Sage Foundation.

________. 1989. 'Workplace Boundaries: Conceptions and Creations', *Social Research,* 56(3): 571–90.

Epstein, S. 2007. *Inclusion: The Politics of Difference in Medical Research.* Chicago Studies in Practices of Meaning. Chicago: University of Chicago Press.

Espagne, M. 1994. 'Sur les limites du comparatisme en histoire culturelle', *Genèses: Sciences sociales et histoire* 17: 112–21.

Espeland, W.N., and M. Sauder. 2007. 'Rankings and Reactivity: How Public Measures Recreate Social Worlds', *American Journal of Sociology* 113(1): 1–40.

Espeland, W.N., and M.L. Stevens. 2007. 'Commensuration as a Social Process', *Annual Review of Sociology* 24: 313–43.

________. 'A Sociology of Quantification', *European Journal of Sociology* 49: 401–36.

Ferree, M.M., and A.M. Tripp (eds). 2006. *Global Feminism: Transnational Women's Activism, Organizing, and Human Rights.* New York: New York University Press.

Folbre, N. 2001. *The Invisible Heart: Economics and Family Values.* New York: The New Press.

Folbre, N., and M. Abel. 1989. 'Women's Work and Women's Households: Gender Bias in the US Census', *Social Research* 56(3): 545–69.

Fourcade, M. 2009. *Economists and Societies. Discipline and Profession in the United States, Britain, & France, 1890s to 1990s.* Princeton, NJ/Oxford: Princeton University Press.

________. 2016. 'Ordinalization', *Sociological Theory* 34(3): 175–95.

Fourcade, M., and K. Healy. 2013. 'Classification Situations: Life-Chances in the Neoliberal Era', *Accounting, Organizations and Society* 38: 559–72.

Frader, L.L. 2008. *Breadwinners and Citizens: Gender in the Making of the French Social Model.* Durham, NC: Duke University Press.

________. 2016. 'Gender, Ethno-racial Difference, and the "Languages of Labor" in 20th Century France', *Industrielle Welt, Semantiken von Arbeit: Diachrone und vergleichende Perspektiven* 91: 167–89.

Frank, R. 2015. 'Back to the Future? The Emergence of a Geneticized Conceptualization of Race in Sociology', *The ANNALS of the American Academy of Political and Social Science* 661(1): 51–64.

Go, J. 2014. 'Occluding the Global: Analytic Bifurcation, Causal Scientism, and Alternatives in Historical Sociology', *Journal of Globalization Studies* 5(1): 122–36.

Goertz, G., and A.G. Mazur (eds). 2008. *Politics, Gender, and Concepts: Theory and Methodology.* Cambridge: Cambridge University Press.

Goffman, E. 1977. 'The Arrangement between the Sexes'. *Theory and Society* 4: 301–31.

Hacking, I. 1986. 'Making up People', in T. Heller, M. Sosna, and D. Wellberry (eds), *Reconstructing Individualism.* Stanford, CA: Stanford University Press, pp. 222–36.

Hall, P.A., and D.W. Gingerich. 2009. 'Varieties of Capitalism and Institutional Complementarities in the Political Economy: An Empirical Analysis', *British Journal of Political Science* 39(3): 449–82.

Haney-Lopez, I. 2014. *Dog Whistle Politics: How Coded Racial Appeals Have Wrecked the Middle Class*. Oxford: Oxford University Press.

Haupt, H.-G., and J. Kocka. 2009. 'Comparison and Beyond: Traditions, Scope, and Perspectives of Comparative History', in H.-G. Haupt and J. Kocka (eds), *Comparative and Transnational History: Central European Approaches and New Perspectives*. New York: Berghahn Books, pp. 3–5.

Haydu, J. 1998. 'Making Use of the Past: Time Periods as Cases to Compare and as Sequences of Problem Solving', *American Journal of Sociology* 104(2): 339–71.

Heintz, B. 2010. 'Numerische Differenz: Überlegungen zu einer Soziologie des (quantitativen) Vergleichs', *Zeitschrift für Soziologie* 39(3): 162–81.

_______. 2012. 'Welterzeugung durch Zahlen: Modelle politischer Differenzierung in internationalen Statistiken 1948–2010', *Soziale Systeme* 18: 7–39.

_______. 2016. '"Wir leben im Zeitalter der Vergleichung": Perspektiven einer Soziologie des Vergleichs', *Zeitschrift für Soziologie* 45(5): 305–23.

Janz, O., and D. Schönpflug (eds). 2014. *Gender History in a Transnational Perspective: Networks, Biographies, Gender Orders*. New York: Berghahn Books.

Jeanes, E., D. Knights, and P.Y. Martin (eds). 2011. *Handbook of Gender, Work and Organization*. Chichester, UK: Wiley-Blackwell.

Jenkins, R. 2000. 'Categorization: Identity, Social Process and Epistemology', *Current Sociology* 48(3): 7–25.

Jepperson, R.L. 1991. 'Institutions, Institutional Effects, and Institutionalism', in W. Powell and P. DiMaggio (eds), *The New Institutionalism in Organizational Analysis*. Chicago: University of Chicago Press, pp. 143–63.

_______. 2001. *The Development and Application of Sociological Neoinstitutionalism*. San Domenico/Firenze, Italy: European University Institute, Robert Schuman Centre.

Kaluszynski, M., and R. Payre (eds). 2013. *Savoirs de gouvernement: circulation(s), traduction(s), réception(s)*. Paris: Economica.

Krenn, K. 2017. 'Markets and Classifications – Constructing Market Orders in the Digital Age: An Introduction', *Historical Social Research* 42(1): 7–22.

Lallement, M. et al. (eds). 2015. Kategorien des Geschlechts in der Arbeitswelt/Catégories de genre et mondes du travail. *Trivium. Deutsch-Französische Zeitschrift für Geistes- und Sozialwissenschaften* 19.

Lamont, M., et al. 2016. *Getting Respect: Responding to Stigma and Discrimination in the United States, Brazil, and Israel*. Princeton, NJ: Princeton University Press.

Lamont, M., S. Beljean, and M. Clair. 2014. 'What Is Missing? Cultural Processes and Causal Pathways to Inequality', *Socio-Economic Review* 12(3): 573–608.

Lamont, M., and V. Molnár. 2002. 'The Study of Boundaries in the Social Sciences', *Annual Review of Sociology* 28: 167–95.

Lopata, H.Z. 1971. *Occupation: Housewife*. New York: Oxford University Press.

Mahoney, J., and K. Thelen. 2010. 'A Theory of Gradual Institutional Change', in J. Mahoney and K. Thelen (eds.), *Explaining Institutional Change: Ambiguity, Agency, and Power*. New York: Cambridge University Press, pp. 1–36.

Maurice, M., F. Sellier, and J.J. Silvestre. [1982] 1986. *The Social Foundation of Industrial Power: A Comparison of France and Germany*. Boston, MA: The MIT Press.

Minow, M. 2013. 'Brown v. Board in the World: How the Global Turn Matters for School Reform, Human Rights, and Legal Knowledge', *The San Diego Law Review* 50(1): 1–28.

Molnár, V., and M. Lamont. 2002. 'Social Categorization and Group Identification: How African Americans Shape their Collective Identity through Consumption', in K. Green et al. (eds), *Interdisciplinary Approaches to Demand and Its Role in Innovation*. Manchester: Manchester University Press, pp. 88–111.

Oakley, A. 1974. *The Sociology of Housework*. London: Penguin Books.

Osterhammel, J. 2001. *Geschichtswissenschaft jenseits des Nationalstaats: Studien zu Beziehungsgeschichte und Zivilisationsvergleich*. Göttingen: Vandenhoeck & Ruprecht.

Porter, T.M. 1995. *Trust in Numbers: The Pursuit of Objectivity in Science and Public Life*. Princeton, NJ: Princeton University Press.

Powell, G.N. (ed.). 1999. *Handbook of Gender and Work*. Thousand Oaks, CA: Sage.

Ridgeway, C. 2009. 'Framed Before We Know It: How Gender Shapes Social Relations', *Gender & Society* 23(2): 145–60.

_______. 2011. *Framed by Gender: How Gender Inequality Persists in the Modern World*. Oxford: Oxford University Press.

Roberts, D. 2011. *Fatal Invention: How Science, Politics, and Big Business Re-create Race in the Twenty-First Century*. New York: New Press.

Rose, S.O. 2010. *What is Gender History?* Cambridge: Polity.

Rudischhauser, S. 2017. *Geregelte Verhältnisse: Eine Geschichte des Tarifvertragrechts in Deutschland und Frankreich 1890–1918/19*. Vienna: Böhlau.

Scott, J.W. [1988] 1999a. 'Gender: A Useful Category of Historical Analysis', in J.W. Scott, *Gender and the Politics of History*. New York: Columbia University Press, pp. 28–50.

_______. [1988] 1999b. 'A Statistical Representation of Work: La statistique de l'industrie à Paris', in J.W. Scott, *Gender and the Politics of History*. New York: Columbia University Press, pp. 113–38.

Star, S.L., and M. Lampland (eds). 2009. *Standards and Their Stories: How Quantifying, Classifying, and Formalizing Practices Shape Everyday Life*. Ithaca, NY: Cornell University Press, pp. 35–53.

Starr, P. 1987. 'The Sociology of Official Statistics', in W. Alonso and P. Starr (eds), *The Politics of Numbers*. New York: Russell Sage, pp. 7–57.

Steinmetz, G. 2004. 'Odious Comparisons: Incommensurability, the Case Study, and "Small N's"', *Sociological Theory* 22(3): 371–400.

Strang, D., and J.W. Meyer. 1993. 'Institutional Conditions for Diffusion', *Theory and Society* 22: 487–511.

_______. 1994. 'Institutional Conditions for Diffusion', in R.W. Scott and J.W. Meyer (eds), *Institutional Environments and Organization: Structural Complexity and Individualism*. Thousand Oaks, CA: Sage, pp. 100–12.

Thelen, K. 1999. 'Historical Institutionalism in Comparative Politics', *Annual Review of Political Science* 2: 369–404.

Thelen, K., and J. Mahoney. 2015. 'Comparative-Historical Analysis in Contemporary Political Science', in J. Mahoney and K. Thelen (eds), *Advances in Comparative Historical Analysis*. Cambridge: Cambridge University Press, pp. 3–36.

Topalov, C. 2001. 'A Revolution in Representations of Work: The Emergence over the 19th Century of the Statistical Category "Occupied Population" in France, Great Britain, and the United States', *Revue Française de Sociologie* 42: 79–106.

Van Nederveen Meerkerk, E., S. Neunsinger, and D. Hoerder (eds). 2015. *Towards a Global History of Domestic and Caregiving Workers*. Leiden: Brill.

Werner, M., and B. Zimmermann. 2006. 'Beyond Comparison: Histoire croisée and the Challenge of Reflexivity', *History and Theory* 45(1): 30–50.

Wimmer, A., and N. Glick Schiller. 2002. 'Methodological Nationalism and Beyond: Nation-State Building, Migration and the Social Sciences, *Global Networks* 2(4): 301–34.

Wobbe, T. 2012. 'Making up People: Berufsstatistische Klassifikation, geschlechtliche Kategorisierung und wirtschaftliche Inklusion um 1900 in Deutschland', *Zeitschrift für Soziologie* 41: 41–57.

Wobbe, T., I. Berrebi-Hoffmann, and M. Lallement (eds). 2011. *Die gesellschaftliche Verortung des Geschlechts. Diskurse der Differenz in der deutschen und französischen Soziologie um 1900.* Frankfurt/New York: Campus.

Wobbe, T., and L. Renard. 2017. 'The Category of "Family Workers" in International Labour Organizations Statistics (1930s–1980s): A Contribution to the Study of Globalized Gendered Boundaries between Household and Market', *Journal of Global History* 12: 340–60.

Zerubavel, E. 1996. 'Lumping and Splitting: Notes on Social Classification', *Sociological Forum* 11(3): 421–33.

Zimmermann, B. 2006. *Arbeitslosigkeit in Deutschland: zur Entstehung einer sozialen Kategorie.* Frankfurt: Campus.

_______. 2015. '*Socio-Histoire* and Public Policy Rescaling Issues: Learning from Unemployment Politics in Germany (1880–1927)', in S. Börner and M. Eigenmüller (eds), *European Integration, Processes of Change and the National Experience.* Basingstoke: Palgrave Macmillan, pp. 121–46.

Zimmermann, S. 2016a. 'Night Work for White Women and Bonded Labour for "Native" Women? Contentious Traditions and the Globalization of Gender-Specific Labour Protection and Legal Equality Politics, 1926 to 1939', in S. Kimble and M. Röwekamp (eds), *New Perspectives on European Women's Legal History.* New York: Routledge, pp. 558–90.

_______. 2016b. 'The International Labour Organization, Transnational Women's Networks, and the Question of Unpaid Work in the Interwar World', in C. Midgley, A. Twells, and J. Cartier (eds), *Women in Transnational History: Connecting the Local and the Global.* London: Routledge, pp. 33–53.

_______. 2018. 'Globalizing Gendered Labour Policy: International Labour Standards and the Global South, 1919–1947', in E. Boris, D. Hoehtker, and S. Zimmermann (eds), *Transnational Networks, Global Labour Standards and Gender Equity, 1900 to Present.* Leiden: Brill, pp. 227–54.

I

Shifting Categories from a Comparative Relational Perspective

Chapter 1

Making Sense of Women's Labour in the Context of the French Family Business

From Domestic Labour to Recognized Work

Olivier Giraud

In their comprehensive study of the transformation of the petite bourgeoisie in Europe between 1780 and 1914, Geoffrey Crossick and Heinz-Gerhard Haupt (1995) mention three types of family photographs that artisans and merchants would have taken in order to showcase their family and their business in the early twentieth century. Most artisans liked to pose at the very centre of the picture, relegating wife, children and employees to the background. Sometimes, merchant couples would appear united in the foreground of the picture with their children, in front of their shop and wearing their work clothes. And some artisan or merchant families would ostensibly pose in the residential area of the business, wearing 'smart clothes', gazing through the window at the family shop, demonstrating the separation between domestic and work life, and consequently their belonging to the (petite) bourgeoisie of the time (Crossick and Haupt 1995: 96–98). Compared in this manner, such photographs depict the variety of power relations within the couples and families and the tense relations between the domestic/private and the business/public spheres in this time of transition for family businesses. In some cases almost absent from the photo, and in some cases represented as equals, the diverse situation of women in these pictures illustrates the uncertainty of their position in the family business of the early twentieth century. They could play cumulatively the roles of spouses, workers and mothers, or just be proudly displayed at the heart of the private family interior.

In France, the uncertainty of women's position in the context of the family business is reflected by the long-lasting lack of institutional recognition of the labour they would perform as spouses of self-employed artisans and merchants. In a nutshell, women's labour in family businesses was at first classified as domestic labour and has only more recently been recognized as regular productive work, subject to collective or public regulations and related to specific social rights. As has been demonstrated for other contexts (Wobbe 2012), the categorization of women's labour depends more frequently on gender identity than on the nature of the work performed. In this chapter, I will argue that the specific situation of women's labour in the family business relates both to the situation of the independent business and to the family in the general social and political context of the country. The progressive integration of the family business into the realm of public regulation and the step-by-step individualization of the conception of the family are, at least in the case of France, key transformations in the long-lasting process of recasting the very nature of female labour activities in independent businesses.

In order to follow such an argument, I will argue that women's positions at the intersection between family and enterprise in both instances are themselves embedded in and revealed by cultural and institutional codes relating to the role of the family and of small businesses in the French society and economy. The trajectory of spousal labour recognition in family businesses in France appears to be characteristic of the political, social and cultural transformations that work was undergoing at the time, combining recognition of fundamental individual rights with the socialization of social functions, the most important being social solidarity and protection.

On a theoretical level, the process of institutional recognition of women's labour in the context of the family business illustrates the tension between self and group identification on the one hand and social categorization on the other. Distinctly elaborated by Richard Jenkins, this tension is formed by a series of interactions between the individual order producing the 'point of view of selfhood', the group or interactional order relating to the 'co-presence and relationships' between individuals, and lastly the institutional order relating to the 'world of patterned, organized and symbolically-templated "ways of doing things"' (Jenkins 2000: 7).

Three 'critical junctures' of the sort described by Kathleen Thelen (1991, 1999) have marked the long-term process of recasting the category attached to women's labour in the context of the family business. The period following the French Revolution represents a first key step in the making of the status of women's labour in the case of artisans' and merchants' wives. Family business was defined in this period as the cornerstone of French society, both in the economic and political dimensions, but also of social solidarity. The second critical juncture took place between the 1920s and the 1960s. During this time, on the one hand, the fundamental role of the family business in France began to be contested by the development of bigger economical units and by the progressive imposition of public regulation. On the other hand, the conception of the family would start to become progressively more individualized. These transformations would begin to influence the situation of women's labour in family businesses. However, only the far-reaching structural transformations and important social mobilizations that appeared from the late 1960s have triggered a third and decisive change. This last step eventually led to the formal and institutional recognition of women's labour in the context of family businesses. These three critical junctures will shape the structure of this chapter.

In order to analyse this multidimensional transformation process, I will first consider, for each time period, the structural dimension of the position of family and the family business in the French national context. Second, I will explore the consequences of these developments for the situation of women working in family businesses by analysing the legal regulation and the statistical categorization of female work in that context. For the last and crucial critical juncture, I will also look at the role of the social mobilization of spouses of artisans and merchants, which began to develop from the early 1970s, as these developed a form of 'interactional' group identification that has decisively influenced categorization.

Social Invisibility of Women's Labour in the Family Business from the Nineteenth to the Mid Twentieth Century

During the *ancien régime*, the semi-public regulation by the corporations moderated the influence of family regulation of the independent artisan and merchant workshop. Being first and foremost a bourgeois revolution, the French Revolution emancipated the family business from corporative rule and reshuffled the structure of social status in society. The family – marriage strategies, kinship and gender relations – became the key regulator of the family business. Simultaneously, the abolition of serfdom made the cleavage between independent and dependent social positions a key principle of social structuration. In this context, domestic workers became the only population that did not fully benefit from the general emancipation from serfdom. Likewise located in the domestic sphere, women's labour became partly assimilated to this domestic work.

In the political sphere, women did not benefit from the rights associated with post-revolutionary citizenship. Men held citizenship in the name of their entire family (Verjus 2010). The family was in turn socially and politically recognized both as the elementary unit of society and as the basic economic unit of the time. According to the Civil Code promulgated by Napoleon in 1803, women became a disenfranchised group (Daune-Richard 2004: 69). They could not dispose of their own income or enter into contracts without the consent of their husbands. Finally, the principle of mutual aid within the couple codified in Article 214 of the Napoleonic Code addressed the issue of power relations within the couple in terms that apply equally to the family business: 'If matrimonial contracts do not address the contributions of spouses to the cost of the household, they [are to] contribute in proportion to their respective skills. If one spouse doesn't fulfil his obligations, he/she may be compelled by the other in the manner provided in the Code of Civil Procedure'.[1]

Deemed incapable of entering into contracts or disposing of their own income, consigned to the domestic sphere, considered non-productive, not recognized as 'active' on the labour market and, finally, beholden by the duty of spousal support, spouses of artisans and merchants were caught in a web of socially codified principles underlying social, economic and political activities that guaranteed their institutional invisibility.

The first classifications of work in France proposed by physiocrat economists, even before the revolution of 1789, would focus on the nature of personal wealth (property, agriculture, business activity, etc.), and then later, in the nineteenth century, on the business activity conducted by the head of the household. In this general framework, individual positions and work were not originally distinguished. The set of people living off a given productive unit was assimilated with that unit (Chélini 2008). The *a priori* non-material and intangible character of female activities, as well as their assigned location in the domestic sphere, reduced women's labour in family businesses to the category of 'inactivity'. This category would persistently cast a shadow over women's work and directly affect the status of the women working in family businesses for decades to come.

Progressively, over the course of the nineteenth century, the parties that held an interest in family businesses – bakeries, retails shops and so on – would become distinguished as employers, servants, clerks and so on. Within this increasingly individualized attempt to categorize work, however, the situation of women would remain poorly defined and practically unchanged. Women would have to actively declare an occupation that differed completely from that of the family business in order to be acknowledged as an active worker. In its categories and survey forms, the French bureau of statistics would try, from the late nineteenth century onwards, to differentiate between productive work activities and domestic labour (Topalov 1998). The criterion chosen to that end was the granting of remuneration. Both the declaration of a professional activity by women non-related to the family business and the remuneration of non-domestic female labour supposed that the families would understand and be able to identify themselves with those external categories. This was by this time only occasionally the case (Amossé 2004). In 1906, the first systematic labour statistical analysis of the country transformed the categorization of spousal labour in the family business. Representing 28.5% of the female labour force, women performing labour in the context of the family business were classified together with their husbands in the category of 'head of the establishment' (Maruani and Meron 2012: 172).

The social understanding of women's situation in the family context also began to evolve and to be reflected by public regulation. The law of 'free wages' of married women (11 July 1907) recognized the right of the wife to dispose of the 'products of her own labour and economic gain from it'. Nonetheless, legal commentaries noted that the law did not imply a right to the free choice of occupation for women. The situation of the spouses of the self-employed is in this case the object of a particularly explicit treatment:

> Take note beforehand that insofar as the wife takes care of household matters or helps her husband in the course of his business, industrial or commercial, it may not have an effect on the wife's earnings. This is not a salaried person, an employee or a worker of her spouse. She cannot participate in the profits unless she is associated by pecuniary regime to the enterprise. In the absence of such an association, she contributes freely her assistance to her husband, as a sort of extra dowry. The question about the products of labour of a woman does not arise if she has a separate industry or occupation. (Le Courtois and Surville 1908: 2)

First Developments from the Aftermath of World War I to the 1960s

After World War I, the lines would move further as the alternatives and debates about female labour would take new forms. While women's growing demands for citizenship continued to go unanswered, the family, and notably the family business, would start to become destabilized by the growing trend towards salaried employment and economic concentration. Increased state intervention in socioeconomic life (including the development of tax regimes and social protection, and later, in the 1930s, the eight-hour day, paid leave, higher wages, etc.) challenged the central and autonomous position of the family business in French society. In the aftermath of World War I, artisans and merchants generally succeeded in avoiding income taxes through the mobilization of their business associations and through the work of parliamentary deputies. In the 1930s, business associations sought to reproduce this success, though more vigorously and with a more extreme political character in order to oppose new state attempts to integrate family businesses into the tax and social security systems (Zalc 2012: 58–59). In general, the interwar period in France witnessed a shift to the right in the politics of family businesses, which sometimes tended towards sympathies with fascist organizations. This points to a general loss of centrality of the world of independent business in the French political landscape.

Until the interwar period, recognition for the work done by spouses of the self-employed remained at a standstill, notably because of the lack of change in the systems of work classification. Spousal work remained confined within its family help ('aide familial') status, which was, especially in the case of France, poorly defined and unstable. The work done by women in family businesses was still considered to be an extension, into the economic world, of their spousal role as wives. Long considered as a long-lasting dowry, or as a contribution to household welfare, feminine work in family businesses was not seen as a regular, gainful, recognized and protected work activity.

After World War II: The Marginalization of the Family Business Leaves Women's Labour on the Wayside

In the aftermath of World War II, France underwent a series of radical and sudden modernizations, which sought to make amends for its delayed evolution. First, women's right to vote was granted through a simple order issued on 21 April 1944 by the provisional French government in Algiers. This decision did not give rise to any public debate. Second, the construction of the French social security system as part of a compromise between Gaullists, communists and Christian Democrats, before the end of the war, was handled in a similar way. Third, beyond the development of the social security system, the construction of a norm of salaried employment was established via the restoration of collective agreements, the introduction of representatives for working forces, and the nationalization of large companies used by the state as leverage for the enforcement of employment standards or the implementation of minimum wages in 1950 (Lallement 1999).

Mostly aimed at regulating wage labour, these important reforms triggered the resumption of significant tensions and protests in the family business milieu. Furthermore, the 1948 modernization of the tax system resulted in the quasi-cancellation of exemptions enjoyed by merchants and artisans. Tax audits were also modernized and were specifically targeted at these sectors from the early 1950s (Zalc 2012: 61). Organizations representing crafts and small businesses strongly opposed their integration into the national social protection system. They fuelled right-wing protests against new taxation schemes proposed by the government. Pierre Poujade, a populist leader, capitalized on resentment among the members of the Union for the Defence of Shopkeepers and Artisans (UDCA), and went on to place fifty-two deputies in the National Assembly in 1956. His party had received 2.4 million ballots, more than 11% of the vote. However, in socioeconomic terms, the space occupied by craftsmen and small businesses shrank rapidly. The number of self-employed fell in France from more than 6.6 million in 1954 to less than 2.4 million in 1968 (Maruani and Meron 2012: 52). This sudden collapse also encompassed and signalled the rapid decline of the agricultural sector during this period, as well as indicating the profound transformation of the craft sector, and even more so of the retail industry.

Finally, besides the transformation of the political location of the family business in the French context, and women's access to political suffrage, the law of 13 July 1965, which reformed the matrimonial regime, indicates that the understanding of the family had evolved towards greater individualization. This new law granted women the right to administer and manage all their property (Colomer 1966). It changed the status established in the reform of the marriage law of 1907, which gave women control only over the income from their own work. Nonetheless, this law was not a statute of emancipation as it continued to assert a status quo in which both spouses must decide together on most social and patrimonial issues. This was especially true with regard to real estate and other assets owned in common, including craft and commercial enterprises (Terré 1965).

The categorization of the labour provided by female spouses in the context of the family business did not progress in this context. On the contrary, the official employment statistics, which introduced socio-professional categories in 1954, no longer counted the spouses of the self-employed as active employees, and even less as heads of the establishment, according to the category of 1906 (Maruani and Meron 2012: 44). Besides the fact that this decision accounted for the sudden disappearance of nearly one million women from the official employment statistics, it also expressed the fact that the state expected a continuous increase of wage earners. This further indicates the process of the casting out of independent business in the country.

The family business encountered a deep crisis in the first decades of the post-war period, that did not favour the transformation of the status of the working spouses. The radical resistance emanating from the craft and trade sectors against the movements towards increasingly salaried workers and the standardization of employment for the general population may be its cause and is most certainly its expression. The situation of the family in this configuration did not significantly change but instead raised tensions about issues related to different forms of taxation and social contributions, which the self-employed had to pay. None of this heralded a swift transformation in the situation of the spouses of the self-employed.

The Institutionalization of Women's Labour in the Family Business: State Support and Social Mobilization

Recognition of women's labour performed in the family business as a regular type of work, subject to regulation and with rights and protections attached, began to be achieved in France in the early 1970s. As had previously been the case, the situation of small independent businesses in French society and the situation of women in the family context also played a role in this period.

First, the position of the family business in the French political and socioeconomic context remained critical. The state project to carry on with the incorporation of family businesses into the realm of regular social protection gave rise, from the late 1960s onwards, to a new wave of strong contention. Since 1969, Gérard Nicoud, a restaurateur established in the department of Isère, has trumpeted his position through the French media. He provokes the public administration through the occupation of public spaces, acts of rebellion, calls for fiscal disobedience and so on. Nicoud founded the CID (Centre d'Information et de Défense) and, following this, the CID-UNATI (Confédération Intersyndicale de Défense et d'Union Nationale des Travailleurs Indépendants) as a way of defending a hard-line position against social contributions and to push a populist right-leaning approach akin to the Poujadist movement of the post-war period. However, this movement did not suffer from the xenophobic and racist inclinations of its predecessor. The success of Nicoud's energetic strategy destabilized the traditional organizations representing artisan and retail interests in the Chambres des Métiers as well as in the regular business and professional associations (Zarca 1993b: 66).

The second issue that encapsulates the matter of recognition of women's labour in family businesses concerns the place of the woman in the family order, where the family is understood to be the pillar of society. In this respect, a key role was played by the sudden and forceful advent of feminist discourse in the public sphere during the 1960s. The events of May 1968 would spread the words of women in France into the public space and contribute to signalling the subversion of the hegemony of conservative values and associated conformism built during the 1940s and 1950s.

However, feminist struggles throughout the 1960s and 1970s took place in a divisive and conflictive context between feminist organizations and the labour movement. Women's associations that had occupied the spotlight in debates about gender before 1968 – for instance in the context of the reform of marital rights in the middle of the decade (Terré 1965: 7) – were either close to the Communist Party (Union des Femmes Françaises) or affiliated with the Christian social movements (Union Féminine Civique et Sociale). Nothing indicates that these movements or their networks participated in the formulation of the issues or the promotion of public debate about the situation of the spouses of the self-employed. After 1968, the tendency to fuse class struggle with gender struggles under radical Marxism became more significant, for instance in the bosom of the MLF (Mouvement de Libération de la Femme), one of the dominant feminist movements of the time. However, the relation between the feminist movements and the labour movements remained weak. On the one hand, women's struggles in France focused on abortion rights (Mouvement de Libération de l'Avortement et de la Contraception, MILAC) and on matters of emancipation, which made targets of the traditional family configuration and the favourable position of men in the power relationships internal to a couple. On the other hand, feminist leaders – often intellectuals like Simone de Beauvoir, Christine Delphy and Antoinette Fouque, lawyers like Gisèle Halimi or even businesswomen like Elisabeth Badinter – were openly attacked and singled out as 'bourgeoises' by the (mostly male) left-wing leaders of the time (Delphy 1977). The development of feminist positions at the core of the labour movement would only take full force towards the end of the 1970s, and this principally by way of the Confédération Française Démocratique du Travail, a relatively moderate and modernizing labour union. Merchants and artisan business associations, however, emanating from essentially traditional milieus, did not support feminist discourses either. Given that the overlap between feminism and labour struggles in family business was hardly visible, no explicit coalition existed between the feminist movement and female labour in the construction of a public debate in relation to the situation of the spouses working in merchant and artisan businesses.

Consequently, the explicit formulation as a public problem of the situation of women working in family businesses took place in the 1960s and 1970s outside the world of labour and feminist movements. Instead, it was imposed in two specific but related ways: through the intervention of the state and through the social mobilization of the women concerned.

Expanding Social Citizenship: The Continued State Project

It was principally at the beginning of the 1970s that the public administration began to specifically take notice of the until then little-known case of the spouses of the self-employed. The public administration's persistent desire to integrate the entire population into social protection schemes was the principle motive for the consideration of this specific population.

For instance, the law of 29 December 1973 permitted the spouses of business owners participating in professional activity in the context of the family business to contribute voluntarily to a system of insurance for pensions and invalidity (Sicard 1982). Beyond the construction of a public agenda to be treated in the public space, the specialized services of the state had already included these questions in their own specialized agendas.

Later in the 1970s, the Ministry of Commerce and Crafts and the Secretariat of State for Women's Affairs (Secretariat d'Etat à la condition féminine) jointly commissioned a report on the situation of women working in family businesses. Written by a member of the Court of Auditors,[2] Madame M.-T. Claudé, and released in May 1976, this report presented a complete analysis of the situation of the spouses of the self-employed grounded in statistical data and a large number of interviews with officials and representatives from the independent business sector (Claudé 1976).

This official expertise also gave significant space and legitimacy to the first claims and pressures exercised by – at first small and informal – feminine groups directly organized by spouses of independent workers (Zarca 1993a: 94). The importance of these emerging collective female actions, anchored in the milieu of artisans and retailers, was already documented in the Claudé report itself (1976):

> For some years now, women seek to escape this isolation, mostly in the craft sector where they are grouped in 'women's clubs' with the aim of promoting collective reflection concerning their common difficulties. These clubs, which are formed either in the context of the labour organizations or in the context of the trade chambers, have rapidly received the attention of those interested and their growth in numbers has not subsided. They face, however, the overt or covert hostility, even the derision of male leaders, who fear that women will

> take a major part in professional bodies, an assumption that may not be fully rejected given how great is their willingness to think and modernize....
>
> Thus organized, women do not present themselves as 'suffragettes'. Their intention is to be brought out of invisibility (oblivion) where they were kept thus far even within their social or professional categories. They wish to prove that their cooperation and participation are essential to their profession and they hope that their reflection will contribute to the modernization of their business.

Speaking on Their Own Behalf: The Social Mobilization and Interactional Categorization of Spouses of Independent Workers

The organization of spouses of artisans and retailers was mostly rooted in the chambers of crafts (Chambres des métiers). These chambers began, from the 1960s onwards, to propose management, book-keeping, administration and other professional training courses specifically destined for spouses of artisans and merchants. Implicitly acknowledging the professionalization of women's labour in family businesses, these courses gave an opportunity to the women working in family businesses to share their experiences and difficulties. Some specifically harsh situations, such as divorces or the early death of a husband, could plunge married women working in family businesses, as well as their families, into destitution. Such tragic cases led to local solidarity and to the expression of anger in the face of developments perceived as intolerable in the context of the time.[3] These events increased awareness of these women's fragile situation. Sharp division among the (male-dominated) retail and craft associations triggered support for the initial mobilization of these women, but in a divided and conflicting manner.

At first, traditional business associations provided, at the local level, some organizational support to the original groups of women who had decided to enter into an action of advocacy about their situation. More or less simultaneously, in 1975, two women's movements were encouraged by concurring regular crafts and retail organizations. The tone of the discourse of the craft and commercial women's associations was based, first and foremost, upon the claims for recognition of work and the minimal necessary social protections that ought to come with it.

On the one hand, in the department of Isère (Alps, Grenoble), the radical CID-UNATI supported the development of the ADEAC (Association des épouses d'artisans et commerçants). Members had focused their demands on several issues such as the 'possibility of a transference of the family patrimony to the individual patrimony ... the simplification of the domestic cooperation system through measures such as the "presumption of mandate" … the recognition of women's work by awarding the wife maternity benefits … and substitution benefits, without neglecting, however, the issue of pension rights, which at the time took on growing importance' (Zarca 1993a: 94). The ADEAC's agenda was geared towards obtaining permanent solutions for women, in order to better serve the family business but without seeking to challenge the power relationships within the familial economic unit. The ADEAC quickly liberated itself from the support of the male-dominated CID-UNATI, which tended to be rather obtrusive and controlling, and whose radical orientation was not in line with their repertoires of action and mobilization.

On the other hand, in the Vaucluse (Provence, Avignon), the head of the local Chamber of Crafts gave support to a local group of women working in the family business context. This second group developed a more radically feminist agenda. In 1975, this network gave birth to an association, the ACTIF (Association des Conjoints de Travailleurs Indépendants de France). This association focused its claims on the issues of retirement and gave priority in its organizational agenda to radical independence from male-dominated organizations. The claims of the ACTIF were geared towards the recognition and award of personal rights that did not necessarily derive from retirement rights, and were more directly defined by feminism: 'to demand a social redistribution destined to level the situation of female workers in different social conditions and categories in a more equitable manner … to claim personal retirement rights returns to a gender struggle', which could go so far as to expose the tensions at the very bosom of conjugal life (Zarca 1993a: 96).

An example of the public discourse spread by the more radical organization, the ACTIF, can be found in an editorial piece written by Lucienne Weber, president of the ACTIF, in the first bulletin of the association in January 1979, entitled 'Out of the Shadows!':

> The wife of the artisan is now someone in the company! The wife of the merchant is someone behind the counter! We are collaborators, office workers, drivers, salespeople, managers, operators, delivery persons, assistants in the workshop and yet we are counted as jobless (with no known profession) and although we work 10, 12 or 14 hours a day, we have no legal recognition.
>
> Prove your will to act effectively in the public interest. We *must* obtain *juridical status* and *recognition for our work*. This legal status which will give us precisely our own rights, income, social and professional rights … *This is the objective of our association.*
>
> We are not: a feminist movement.
>
> But we are: joint artisans and traders aware of our problems.

> ... The status of the employee as an entrepreneur will be submitted to the National Assembly during the legislative session of the spring. However, you must save free choice at all costs: *either the association* or the *collaboration* or the *wage*, depending on the specific role of the wife in the company. However, our legal recognition, social and fiscal, is critical. (Weber 1979: 3–4, emphasis in original)

This editorial piece is representative of the ambiguous situation in which the spouses of the self-employed found themselves. On the one hand, they explicitly emphasized their divorce from feminist ideas, but on the other hand they claimed for themselves their own rights and particularly the rights of social protection, as women. Moreover, if the couple and the family space were not apparent in Weber's editorial, they were central notions in the status of the national federation ACTIF.[4] This status was defined as a 'normative' publication: 'The national federation ACTIF is not a feminist protest movement. It pursues honourably the promotion of the professional unity of the couple'. Under their long-term objectives, the document claimed the organization's goal to be 'the reform of the company where the place and function of the spouses must be defined in an equitable manner. The National Federation ACTIF insists on the family-based character of the enterprise. The company is the business of the *couple* in whose bosom will be determined: a juridical status and a social status which will grant proper rights to each of the spouses – revenues, social and professional rights'.

Structured in two national associative networks, these movements spread across the entire country, taking on a more political form and formulating clearer agendas at around the same time as M.T. Claudé released her report in the mid 1970s. At the local level, the meetings and activities of both associations were vocal and well organized. However, at the grassroots level, the competition between the two associations could become vitriolic. This is shown in the words of a local leader of the ADEAC in Brittany:

> Madame L. used to come to our meetings ... at the beginning ... and she always used to ask questions about how we were organized, which contacts we would have to these or those people, and the like. And once, she even tried to present the agenda of the ACTIF and to convince our members ... There, I had to put a stop to this. I said to her in front of everybody: 'Madame L., I know you are a member of the ACTIF and what you are doing here is just not fair ...'. One week later, she launched an ACTIF section in our city.[5]

At the national policy level, the influence of both these associations was important. From 1976 onwards, after the publication of the Claudé report and the constitution of both associations at the national level, their leaders would regularly be invited to Paris both for general contacts and in order to participate in official hearings, at the Secretariats of State for the Crafts and Trades, and for Women's Affairs. Both associations benefited from strong recognition, even at the highest level of the state apparatus, and demonstrated a real political ability:

> There, on this photo, you see me with Anne-Aymone Giscard d'Estaing[6] ... On this one, there's me, Madame B., the president of the Republic, his wife again ... Oh yes, they were all very friendly with us. They knew we represented something. They wanted to show they were doing something for us.... In the preparation of the 1981 presidential election, Chirac got in touch with us as he wanted us to officially join his supporting committee. I was not president of the association anymore at that time, ... but I remember very well how I said during the bureau's session [of the ACTIF]: 'We never should accept such a thing. If we go with the politicians, I am telling you ladies: we are finished!'[7]

Beyond division and competition, the shared claims were clearly formulated and fixed upon the idea of the recognition of work, of the plurality of statuses and of the free choice of the family entities in favour of one or other of its statutes. To some degree they determined the outline of the law, which would be promulgated in 1982.

Institutionalizing a Status for the Spouses of the Self-Employed

The process of institutionalization of the juridical status for the spouses of the self- employed was initiated by the presentation of Claudé's report to the government. The report led to a field investigation and multiple meetings with professionals and industry representatives, which helped to more systematically formulate the problems faced by the spouses of the self-employed: double labour days for women, absence of any recognition, great vulnerability in the face of risks such as illness, death of a spouse or divorce, and facing the onset of economic risks such as company bankruptcy (Claudé 1976). The report also took note of a number of options for reform in terms of the law, as well as in relation to ways of managing the family business in order to address the recognition of women's work and their need for social protection. These proposals would feed into the process of institutionalization, which, however, the governments led by the moderate conservative *Giscardist* majority in the late 1970s did not achieve. This was partly due to divisions in both majority parties but more especially the divisions among the various business associations of the retail and craft sectors. There was a sharp contrast between those who were fiercely opposed to any increase in social contributions for individual businesses and those who thought it necessary to better establish the status and social protection as well as the employment rights of the spouses of the self-employed. Additional mechanisms that could have improved the situation of these women – for example, the maternity insurance benefits of 1978 – were not successful due to administrative lags. The decree for the implementation of the maternity insurance scheme for spouses of independent workers was never published (Sicard 1982: 25).

During the reform process itself, the Secretary of State for Women's Affairs grew closer to the ACTIF movement as it expressed clearer feminist claims, which were more in line with the position of the left-wing government. The feminist position of the ACTIF was a further inspiration for the newly elected socialist-communist government coalition of the early 1980s.

> At some point, Mrs. Yvette Roudy gave me a private appointment. We met in a café and she asked me: 'What are the points that really matter to you?' You can believe me or not, but at the end of the day, we wrote the core of the law together there.[8]

The legislative process revived during the presidency of François Mitterrand by the parliamentary coalition of socialists and communists, beginning with the parliamentary report by the socialist deputy Odile Sicard, released in April 1982. Besides the ministers in charge of the dossier, the members of the commissions of the permanent assembly of representatives of the chambers of commerce and industry and of the chambers of crafts as well as the representatives of the bureaus of the associations of the spouses of the self-employed (ACTIF and ADEAC) and the leaders of the UPA (Union Professionnelle Artisanale) were interviewed in the context of the parliamentary process.

The review of the minutes of the parliamentary debates of 8 and 13–14 April concerning the law is not particularly surprising. MPs from the left defended the law. Members of the French Communist Party defended independent business as a response to the large retail companies through which capitalism was advancing. Members of the Socialist Party (PS) mostly upheld the feminist line of discourse with an anti-capitalist undercurrent, which singled out and demanded a regulation, which would 'make-up for the inequalities caused by [the] capitalist society to the victims of the victims: the woman' (Minutes of the Debate Assemblée Nationale, Raymond Douyères, MP PS[9]). The conservative camp was divided between supporters of additional protection for women and those who were completely opposed to the increase in social security.

Finally, the National Assembly unanimously adopted the legislation defining the first status for the spouses of the self-employed in France on

13 July 1982 after several days of fairly intense debates and discussions. The text grants to these women the choice of three statuses. The first is as associate partner. Through simple registration with the trade or crafts registry, any spouse who does not hold any other professional activity can have recognition of her own activity, can act on behalf of the company and is allowed to share the pension and insurance contributions and will have open access to maternity insurance. The second is the status of employee-spouse, which allows any partner to join the business through a standard employment contract. This, however, indicates a relationship of subordination, which, though problematic for the couple, permits the payment of social security contributions and the full enforcement of labour laws. The last status is the spouse partner, which allows the spouse of the self-employed to share equal rights and responsibilities in the family business.

Conclusion

In France, the long march towards recognition of spousal labour in the context of the family business provides an example of the cognitive oppositions that regularly structure the dynamics of categorization. In this case, the intellectual operations are organized around the cleavages between domestic labour and wage work; the independent company – specifically autonomous vis-à-vis the state – and an organized company, responsible for the social situation of its employees; a conception of the family as an intangible social unit and a conception of the family as the union of individuals; and lastly, a family-based form of social protection and a collective social protection regime, organized and supervised by the state.

Thus, the requalification of women's labour is of at least two different orders. First, the economic dimension of labour carried out within the family unit shifted from a domestic order to a professional one. This shift in categorization is associated with the progressive integration of the family business in the general realms of publicly supervised social protection and social citizenship. Second, the family lost its capacity to determine identity, forms of social protection, and the substance of the labour carried out by women. Women were therefore able to benefit from a shift towards individualized treatment. This also contributed greatly to the weakening of the gender dimension in the categorization of labour, to the benefit of the professional dimension of work.

Several driving forces account for both the orientation and the form taken by the dynamic of recognition of women's labour in family businesses in the French case. Most of these forces are related and complementary to each other: the institutionalization of a public form of social protection; the salarization of work; the sharp decline in the economic, social and political centrality of the independent business to the benefit of a model of socially integrated, bigger enterprises; the generalization of labour rights; the individualization of the family conception; and last but not least, the generalization of social rights, accessible at the individual level.

The dynamics of recognition of women's labour in family businesses also implied complementary transformations located at various scales of action. The national scale is important in the case of France, as the decision to integrate the whole working population into the realm of a standardized form of social protection has played a key role in that respect. Transnational logics of economic development – the ones that so dramatically weakened the position of family businesses, for instance – but also shifts in values, for example the wave of feminism that influenced the mostly conservative milieus of the family business in an ambivalent way, have triggered important transformations too. Finally, the logics of local solidarities and mobilizations of spouses of independent workers, which in the most recent years have become organized at the national level, have completed the dynamics and could set in motion a decisive institutionalization dynamic that was not to happen in the case of Germany before the start of the twenty-first century (see Renard's chapter in this book).

Finally, the tension between the various mechanisms of social categorization as they are displayed by Richard Jenkins (2000) provides strong insights into the case of women's labour in family businesses in France. The inherited logic of categorization of women's labour as domestic labour integrated in the spousal and family duties was supported by institutional categorization – the Civil Code of 1803 for instance – but equally in the self-perception that women had of their role and activities (Martini 2014). In the same vein, the idea of radical independence of the family business, key to the French Revolution's legacy, was both reflected in legislation – the tax exemption regime, for instance – and supported by social organizations until the 1970s with regards to the integration of the collaborators in family businesses into the national social security system. Finally, the transformation of the self-perception of the spouses of independent workers, from the 1960s onwards, eventually led to the development of social mobilization – the interactional order, in the words of Jenkins – and to the formulation of alternative collective expectations and claims that supported the shift in categorization in a decisive manner.

The historically grounded analysis of the logics of the embeddedness and relations of specific cognitive scripts – 'female labour equals domestic labour', for instance – to individual, interactional and institutional forms of categorization depicts in a comprehensive but differentiated manner the complexity of the social processes at stake.

Olivier Giraud is Research Director at the Lise-CNRS, Paris. He is a specialist in comparative policy analysis, specifically in the domains of social policies (long-term care policies) and gender regimes. He has recently coordinated a research project on the remuneration of family care-givers in the context of cash for care benefits in France. Together with Stefanie Börner and Silke Bothfeld, he edited in 2017 an issue of the journal *Zeitschrift für Sozialreform* on the concept of autonomy in contemporary social policy-making, entitled 'Sozialstaalichkeit und Autonomie: Historische, soziologische und wohlfahrtsstaatsheoretische Perspektiven'.

Notes

1. https://www.legifrance.gouv.fr/content/download/1950/13681/version/3/.../Code_22.pdf (last accessed 21 November 2018).
2. This refers to the Cour des Comptes, the office of public administration in charge of overseeing public expenditure.
3. Interview with the leader of the Association of Spouses of Independent Workers (ADEAC) in the mid 1970s, Brittany region (17 March 2016).
4. Statutes published in the first *Bulletin for the Wives of Artisans and Retailers of Alsace (personal archive of an interviewee).*
5. Interview with the leader of the ADEAC in the mid 1970s, Brittany region (17 March 2016).
6. The wife of the President of the Republic.
7. Interview with a high-ranking leader of the ADEAC in the mid 1970s at the national level (25 June 2013).
8. Ibid.
9. http://archives.assemblee-nationale.fr/7/cri/1981-1982-ordinaire2/008.pdf (last accessed 21 November 2018)

References

Amossé T. 2004. 'Professions au féminin: représentation statistique, construction sociale'. *Travail, genre et sociétés* 11: 31–46.

Chélini, M.-P. 2008. 'L'évolution des catégories socioprofessionnelles dans l'entreprise en France et en Allemagne depuis 1850. Approche comparée'. *Working paper IRHIS*, Université Lille 3.

Claudé, M.-T. 1976. 'Situation of Women in the Retail and Craft Sectors'. Report for the Ministry of Commerce and Craft and for the Secretary of State of the Condition of Women, Paris.

Colomer, A. 1966. 'Le nouveau régime matrimonial légal en France', *Revue internationale de droit comparé* XVIII(1): 61–78.

Crossick, G., and H.-G. Haupt. 1995. *The Petite Bourgeoisie in Europe 1780–1914: Enterprise, Family and Independence*. London: Routledge.

Daune-Richard, A.-M. 2004. 'Les femmes et la société salariale: France, Royaume-Uni, Suède', *Travail et Emploi* 100: 69–84.

Delphy, C. 1977. 'Nos amis et nous: les fondements cachés de quelques discours pseudo-féministes', *Nouvelles Questions Féministes* 1(1): 20–49.

Jenkins, R. 2000. 'Categorization: Identity, Social Process and Epistemology', *Current Sociology* 3(48): 7–25.

Lallement, M. 1999. *Les gouvernances de l'emploi: Relations professionnelles et marché du travail en France et en Allemagne*. Paris: Desclée de Brouwer.

Le Courtois, J., and F. Surville. 1908. *La loi du 13 juillet 1907 sur le libre salaire de la femme mariée et la contribution aux charges du ménage*. Paris: Librairie de la Société du Recueil J.-B. Sirey et du Journal du Palais.

Martini, M. 2014. 'When Unpaid Workers Need a Legal Status: Family Workers and Reforms to Labour Rights in Twentieth-Century France', *International Review of Social History* 2(59): 247–78.

Maruani, M., and M. Meron. 2012. *Un siècle de travail des femmes, 1901–2011*. Paris: La Découverte.

Sicard, O. 1982. *Rapport fait au nom de la commission spéciale chargée d'examiner le projet de loi (n°730) relatif aux conjoints d'artisans et de commerçants travaillant dans l'entreprise familiale*. Assemblée Nationale, n°748, Paris.

Terré, F. 1965. 'La signification sociologique de la réforme des régimes matrimoniaux', *L'Année sociologique* XVI: 3–83.

Thelen, K.A. 1991. *Union of Parts: Labor Politics in Postwar Germany*. Ithaca, NY: Cornell University Press.

________. 1999. 'Historical Institutionalism in Comparative Politics', *Annual Review of Political Science* 2: 369–404.

Topalov, C. 1998. 'L'individu comme convention: Le cas des statistiques professionnelles du xixe siècle en France, en Grande-Bretagne et aux Etats-Unis', *Genèses* 31: 48–75.

Verjus, A. 2010. *Le bon mari: une histoire politique des hommes et des femmes à l'époque révolutionnaire*. Paris: Fayard.

Weber, L. 1979. 'Out of the Shadows!', *Women Artisans and Merchants: Bulletin of the Association of Women Artisans and Merchants of Alsace* 1: 3–4.

Wobbe, T. 2012. 'Making up People: Berufsstatistische Klassifikation, geschlechtliche Kategorisierung und wirtschaftliche Inklusion um 1900 in Deutschland', *Zeitschrift für Soziologie* 41 (1): 41–57.

Zalc, C. 2012. 'Les petits patrons en France au 20e siècle ou les atouts du flou', *Vingtième Siècle* 114: 53–66.

Zarca, B. 1993a. 'Indépendance professionnelle, relations entre les sexes et mobilisations collectives', *Sociétés contemporaines* 16: 77–109.

________. 1993b. 'L'artisanat. La plus populaire des classes moyennes?', *Vingtième Siècle* 37: 55–68.

CHAPTER 2

THE GREY ZONES BETWEEN WORK AND NON-WORK

Statistical and Social Placing of 'Family Workers' in Germany, 1880–2010

Léa Renard

Introduction

In the last decades, historical-sociological research has investigated wage and market-based work as a narrow and contextualized understanding of work that became dominant at the end of the nineteenth century (Topalov 1994; Vanderstaeten 2006; Wadauer 2008; Wobbe 2012; Zimmermann 2001). These exclusive conceptions of work interacted with patterns of gender difference and built a gendered labour order (Hausen 2000). This chapter argues that the categorization undertaken by both the state and interest groups reflects the shift in the interpretation of work and gender that occurred in twentieth-century Germany. To focus on the categorization of the occupation of farmers' and artisans' wives and children sheds light on shifting concepts of work and the increasing standardization of market-based, gainful employment. German statisticians have named this specific group *Mithelfende Familienangehörige* (literally: 'helping family members'; in the following text: 'family workers'), although this denomination does not correspond with any legal category.[1] Even if male children are also included, women strongly dominate in numbers: in 1950, 32% of the gainfully employed women in West Germany worked in a business owned by a family member, while the proportion of family workers in the male active population reached only 4.5% (Quante 1961: 107). Thus, the metamorphoses of the identification and categorization of family workers have to be interpreted against the background of gender and labour history.

Today, the category of 'family workers' is one of five that constitute the nomenclature entitled 'occupational status' (*Stellung im Beruf*). This subcategory is part of national, European and international statistical standards (Wobbe and Renard 2017). Whereas family workers have been recognized as part of the active population since the very first German occupation census in 1882, the category only appeared as an autonomous class for the nomenclature in 1925. While on the one hand the term endured throughout the political changes of the twentieth century, even after 1945, its meaning and boundaries have been an object of permanent redefinition, redraft and repositioning within the nomenclature. After 1945, social placement of family workers and their social rights were discussed and addressed in the political arena in (West) Germany. This is related to two crucial social processes of the second part of the twentieth century: first, the progressive inclusion of all types of workers in the welfare state; second, the inclusion of women as both workers and individuals (Weinbach 2002).

Analysing the emergence and changes in the category of family workers, I argue, points to multiple grey zones between work and non-work, which are altering over time. In the case of family workers, we have a multiplicity of grey zones, both in everyday life and in statistics and legislation. First of all, at the level of legislation, family workers lay in the grey zone of regulation. In the eyes of the early twentieth-century legislation, not labour law but family law seemed to be responsible for regulating the situation of family workers. This changed at the turn of the twenty-first century. Second, in everyday, statistical and legal classifications, family workers were at the intersection between household, family and business, between unpaid work and gainful employment, between self-employed and employees (Supiot 2000: 142). Last but not least, these tensions triggered conflicts between different actors but also opened a zone of negotiation.

The two parts of this chapter describe two non-simultaneous processes of categorizing family workers in two different arenas. The first section is dedicated to historical changes in classification in the German census between 1882 and 1925. A corpus of published reports from the Imperial Statistical Office (Kaiserliches Statistisches Amt) and articles in statistical journals[2] have been analysed qualitatively according to content analysis. The discussions regarding the classification of family workers around 1900 highlight how statistics contribute to the (re)production of a gendered labour regime that differentiates between family and business. Labour statistics helped to establish standards and norms of work, such as gainful employment and the central distinction between independent workers and employees. Unpaid family workers constituted a challenge for these structures of classification. In the end, the solutions determined by the statisticians reproduced this classification order instead of inventing a new system.

In the second section, this contribution examines the tensions and negotiations between legal and social categorization for family workers in (West) Germany after 1945, beginning with the claims of craft organizations in the field of tax policies in the 1950s–60s. In the 1980s, organizations of women in craft and agriculture proposed alternative categories and discourses that emphasized their affiliation to the economically active population (just like ACTIF in France; see Giraud's chapter in this volume). I have chosen to focus on one specific organization for women in craft, the UFH ('UnternehmerFrauen im Handwerk'), because of its role in bringing a clarification of the legal status of family workers onto the political agenda around 2000. The results of the qualitative analysis of documents they produced reveal a specific and concrete arrangement between social justice and economic effectiveness in the German case: the claims for professional acknowledgement through training and insurance are embedded in a larger discourse about family business, in which conservative values and managerial patterns are intertwined.

This chapter investigates how different actors in different arenas categorize differently and how categories are infused with social meanings. One and the same object can take on different meanings and can be represented in different categories. In the case of family workers in Germany, the statistical category we focus on between 1882 and 1925 does not have a legal equivalent at that time. Later, the legal conception does not match the self-entitlement formulated by interest groups after 1985. Thus, this contribution develops a 'social pragmatics of categories' that focuses on the historical contexts in which categories are rooted (Zimmermann 2001: 4).

Family Workers in German Occupation Statistics: Shifting Conceptions of Work and Gender in the *Kaiserreich* and Weimar Republic

How to Define Occupation? The Genesis of Stellung im Beruf *(1850–1925)*

At the end of the nineteenth century, 'occupation' (*Beruf*) underwent a change of meaning, from the ethics-based conception of 'vocation'

(*Berufsethos*), inherited from Martin Luther (Weber 2011: 64), to an economically oriented definition that matched both the new industrial world and the old order of corporations (Zimmermann 2001: 19; see also Tooze 2001). A core attribute of the emerging employment model was the division between employed and self-employed people, between dependent (with a work agreement) and independent persons. This dividing line is constitutive for the emergence of the category of (artisan and industrial) 'workers' (*Arbeiter*) at the General German Workers' Congress in 1848 (Zimmermann 2001: 23). This social division is also logged into the 'handcraft registers' (*Handwerkertabelle*) of 1846 Prussia[3] prior to German unification. Prussian statistics differentiated in these registers between masters and apprentices, and then between employers and employees (Engel 1870: 172); however, these tables were designed to provide insights only into the structure of the workshop. For the 1867 Prussian census, this nomenclature was also used in the population census, as strongly requested by the head of the Prussian office, Ernst Engel. From now on, the focus was on the entire industrial landscape and the 'whole population' (ibid.: 173), that is, each individual, and no longer on the microcosm of the workshop.

The nomenclature 'occupational status' (*Stellung im Beruf*) was introduced in the first German occupation census of 1882. The nomenclature contained the subcategory 'family workers' from the start, but under a restricted definition: in 1882 (see Table 2.1), only paid family workers were included in the active population, according to the idea at the time that wage should be the core criterion for differentiating between active and inactive people (Müller, Willms, and Handl 1983: 20). Paid family workers were incorporated as a subcategory under the general term 'workers' (*Arbeiter*). The nomenclature was meant to be the basis for future public action (Zimmermann 2001: 47). The new workers' insurances (1883, 1884, 1889) only included persons with employment agreements and working on a regular basis, 'leaving out workers evolving

Table 2.1 Occupational status, census 1882.

Self-employed persons
Self-employed persons in home industry (*Hausgewerbetreibende*)
Self-employed persons in agriculture
Employees
Workers (other assistants, apprentices, factory workers, wageworkers, day labourers, **family workers**)

Source: Fritz 2001: 161.

Table 2.2 Occupational status, censuses 1895 and 1907.

a. Self-employed persons
b. Employees
c. Workers and **family workers**
c.1. Family workers
c.2. Skilled workers
c.3. Unskilled workers

Source: Kaiserliches Statistisches Amt 1900: 33.

on the margins of poverty, work and non-work' such as unpaid family workers (Zimmermann 2001: 45).

In 1895 (see Table 2.2), after the economic recession which led to a crisis in the industrial labour market in 1892 (Zimmermann 2001: 27), the entire active population was classified into just three categories, resulting in a reinforcement of hierarchical structures between dependent and independent work: (a) self-employed persons (corresponding to the first three categories in the nomenclature of 1882); (b) employees; and (c) 'workers and family workers' (together in one category) (Fritz 2001: 17). In comparison to the classification of 1882, family workers are no longer treated as a subcategory, merely a specification of the general label 'workers', but instead as a separate entity that must be specifically mentioned. Workers and family workers are counted together but named separately, emphasizing the specificity of family workers.

The definition and criteria of the statistical category 'family workers' also changed in the censuses of 1895 and 1907. German statisticians took not only the type of wage earning into account but also the regularity of the activity, so as to determine who fit in the active population and who did not (Müller, Willms, and Handl 1983: 20f). The goal of this further differentiation was the capacity to more stringently distinguish between household and business activities (for example farming activities, in the case of family workers in agriculture). For this purpose, the statisticians provided strict recommendations on the census forms: 'the procurement of household matters should not be seen as gainful employment' (ibid.). The more the category opened up to unpaid family workers, the more the boundary making (Lamont and Molnár 2002) between domestic activities and business activities intensified. Only the second were recognized as gainful employment. Thus, the more statisticians integrated various types of work into the category of gainful employment, the more they designated domestic work to be non-work. This led to the institutionalization of a strong differentiation between domestic/household work and gainful employment/business in occupational statistics and labour relations in general in most European countries (Aulenbacher 2010: 301; Kocka and Offe 2000: 10). Statistical nomenclatures of employment that arose at the end of the nineteenth century strictly differentiated between people who worked for domestic and familial purposes and those who worked for their living in a (family) workshop or business. Whereas economic purposes were attributed to the second, the first were excluded from economic life.

This process took place in a 'context of redefinition of the artisan community' (Romero-Martín 2016). For the case of handcraft in Barcelona, Juanjo Romero-Martín describes how (female) family members used to work outside of the family workshop before the crisis of the guilds system (which regulated the transmission of the workshop not only on the basis of family bonds) in the first half of the nineteenth century:

> After centuries of open workshops, from 17th century onwards, depending on the country, women were progressively expelled from artisan workshops. Guilds, threatened by the expansion of markets and by competition, modified their policies and women's labour in their small workshops became informal. The strategy of artisan family women working in businesses different from their family ones changed too. Therefore, the defensive strategy of artisan families implied the withdrawal of family women from the labour market and their return to the household economy, out of the industrial labour market. (ibid.)

These appearing standards and strategies contributed to the allocation of a wide range of working people to a grey zone of informality and non-regulation within the domestic and familial sphere.

In the case of poor artisan workshops, wives and daughters worked without receiving any salary or regular payment for their work. In the case of wealthier artisan families, women worked for the family profit, without any specific personal income. Artisan economy was a family-based economy where all members worked on behalf of the group under the control of the head of the family, who managed the economic resources of the family business (Romero-Martín 2016).

This new economic model based on the familial community conflicted with the purposes of an occupation census based on the individual, such as the Prussian census in 1867 and the Imperial census after 1882. The individualization triggered by census practices (e.g. individual census forms) thus placed family workers into a zone of statistical negotiation. As a result, the emerging nomenclature under the *Kaiserreich* can be analysed as a compromise between picturing the new industrial order and, at the same time, integrating the metamorphoses of agrarian and artisan communities. The state elite at the head of German ministries and statistical offices contributed to forming a national economic space that constitutes an 'original synthesis' between conservative and liberal views (Zimmermann 2001: 70).

1925: A Turning Point in the Context of the Weimar Republic

After the political and social changes during the war and the revolution, the German state underwent crucial transformations under the Weimar Republic as a result of the institutionalization of 'the national economy for the first time as a regular object of government' (Tooze 2001: 77). The development of labour law resulted in the formalization and contractualization of employers/workers relationships and in the redefinitions of the boundaries between these (now) legal categories (Zimmermann 2001: 190–91). In this context, official statistics was required to adapt (Tooze 2001: 43). This led again to a phase of redefinition of occupation (*Beruf*) by distancing the meaning one step further from its religious connotation (vocation).

In a speech for the Society of Social Reform (Gesellschaft für Soziale Reform) in Berlin, the national economist (*Nationalökonom*) and statistician Rudolf Meerwarth, a member of the Prussian statistical office, elaborated on an 'economic-based' ('wirtschaftlich orientiert') definition of occupation in contrast to an ethics-based one, explicitly referring to Max Weber (Meerwarth 1925: 28). It was not one's 'life purpose' (*Lebenszweck*) but one's 'living' or 'means of subsistence' (*Lebensunterhalt*) that defined this new conception of work and, thus, had to be recorded by occupational statistics (ibid.: 29). Living is decoupled from one's life purpose but connected with earning (*Erwerb*) and wage (*Entgelt*) (ibid.: 28). At this time, gainful employment gained another central connotation: according to the definition of Georg von Mayr, the head of the Bavarian statistical office, occupation stood for a 'permanent chance of earning a living' ('dauernde Erwerbschance') (Mayr 1926: 191; ibid.: 28).[4] Thereby, wage and stability in time acquired a crucial value in the so-called 'modern' – meaning 'economic-based' – definition of employment, now conceived as gainful employment, which continued to dominate economics and economic statistics in Germany even after 1945.

In his speech, Rudolf Meerwarth also referred to the recurrent debate on the status of housewives throughout the twentieth century (Fürst 1929; Lange and Bäumer 1902). In the Weimar Republic, housewives' associations demanded the recognition of housewife as an occupation.[5] During the preparation of the 1925 census (Fürst 1929: 6), the debate recurred in the statistical community. According to the idea of a 'permanent' occupation, Rudolf Meerwarth argued that only domestic workers, not housewives, could be considered part of the active population (Meerwarth 1925: 29f). In the opposite camp, Gerhard Fürst, head of division at the Imperial Statistical Office, recognized the economic value of housewives' work: He argued that the 'living, food and clothes' that women receive in exchange for their household work should be assimilated to remuneration in kind (Fürst 1929: 6f). Thus, he called for a definition of occupation based on wage, in a broader sense, on the one hand, and, on the other hand, also on the *actual* activities performed, regardless of the familial affiliation. In the end, the German statisticians decided against the inclusion of housewives in the active population, in contrast to the Austrian statisticians, for example (Hiess 1931: 175). This exemplifies the fact that it was not the activities themselves that were subject to classification as work or non-work, but it was the economic purpose implied by one's activities that stood for gainful employment from that point on and thereby redefined work. Housewives' activities were hence excluded from this definition.

As a result of these debates and the modernization of German administration, the categorization of family workers under the label 'workers' was strongly criticized in the occupation census of 1925. According to the statisticians at the time, the goal of this classification schema was to elucidate the 'social stratification' (*soziale Schichtung*), namely the internal differentiation, of the industrial society (Burgdörfer 1925: 45f). For this reason, Franz Zizek (professor of statistics at the University of Frankfurt on the Main) and Rudolf Meerwarth argued that family workers could not be compared to workers, as they do not belong to the working class but their 'permanent interest' lies with the 'self-employed class' (Meerwarth 1925: 92; Quante 1961: 92). According to Zizek and Meerwarth, family workers were situated at the intersection between dependent workers and self-employed persons. In that sense, they enjoyed an 'exceptional' position among the gainfully employed population (Birkner 1960: 41). Thus, the differentiation between employees and self-employed persons seemed inappropriate for the circumstances of family workers; they were considered an 'exception' to the category of gainful employment. This example illustrates to what extent gainful employment and the distinction between employees and self-employed persons had become standards for defining work in the first thirty years of the twentieth century.

In this debate, patterns of both gender and social difference played a crucial role. The *Reich* statisticians strongly distinguished between male and female family workers in order to determine the economic purpose, now defined as a criterion of classification. A male family worker, as a farmer's son or a craftsman's son, was expected to become the 'future owner' of the farm or the business, 'even though he only replaces by his activities an employee or a farmhand' (Fürst 1929: 20f; see also Meerwarth 1925: 92). Conversely, female family workers, namely wives and daughters, were seen as only 'interested' in the finances of the firm as their livelihood depended on the success of the business (Fürst 1929: 20f). Again, this example shows that occupation status is defined not on the basis of performed activities but of economic purposes, as ascribed by statisticians. Yet, unlike male family workers, female family workers always remained in a dependent position according to the German statisticians. Daughters were not expected to become self-employed persons, but rather spouses, and therefore they would remain family workers for life. It is noteworthy that the same person, Gerhard Fürst, argued for a differentiated interpretation of daughters' and sons' work, strongly elaborating on patterns of gender difference and, in the same article, defended recognition of the economic value of housewives' work (Fürst 1929). However, this kind of rationale did not lead to a differentiation between male and female family workers in the statistical classification but was used, instead, to emphasize the absurdity of assimilating farmers' and artisans' sons to workers.

For the occupation census of 1925, at the behest of Gerhard Fürst, the Imperial Office decided indeed to remove family workers from the category 'workers' and to create a specific, statistical category (see Table 2.3). In addition, the stronger separation from domestic workers in the nomenclature points to a clear dividing line between family members working in familial business and those external persons engaged in domestic activities. Again, class ascription played a crucial role here. This decision contributed thus to producing new forms of differentiation within the category of gainfully employed population. Though

Table 2.3 Occupational status, census 1925.

Self-employed persons
Employees and civil servants
Workers
Family workers
Domestic workers

Source: Fritz 2001: 19.

family workers remained in this classification schema, their specificity is emphasized.

As a consequence, both the schema and the classification criteria changed in the 1925 occupation census. According to the new definition, all family members of a farming or artisan business who 'regularly' helped were considered family workers, insofar as they did not declare another activity (for example, 'co-owner') (Birkner 1960: 43). As in 1895 and 1907, the regularity of the economic activity was taken into account so as to define what work was (and was not). However, in 1925, the definition was much more inclusive: every family member was presumed to help and, thus, to be part of the gainfully employed population. This means that help *as such* could be considered work.[6]

The introduction of a specific category in 1925 and the inclusive definition led to a quantitative increase of the active population in agriculture (Quante 1961: 93). Because of the growing differentiations triggered by industrialization (employees/self-employed persons, household/business), family workers as a statistical category were attributed an exceptional status at the intersection of these binary schemata of interpretation. Thus, the decisions taken by the German official statisticians between 1882 and 1925 reinforced the standardization of work as gainful employment. On the other hand, the challenges to integrate this category into a model designed for the industrial world constantly triggered redefinitions of the boundaries of gainful employment: from an activity-oriented conception to wage earning, then to a regular, economic activity.

After 1945, the statistical category of family workers endured in both German states. In the Federal Republic, from 1957, the micro-census question on employment systematically specified that family workers were considered by statistics to be gainfully employed and, as a result, were to be declared as such (1990–95: 'Have you been in gainful employment this week – full-time but also only part-time, or helping in family business?' [Schmidt 2010: 18]). By specifying this, the statisticians of the Federal Office anticipated false self-identification. From 1996, the questionnaire also asked those who declared that they were not gainfully employed if they had been working in the business of a family member, in order to rectify such declarations. This proved the degree to which self-categorization could diverge from statistical categorization.

This is where the second part of the story begins. Contrary to the first part, it does not occur in the field of official statistics but in the political arena of social movements, lobbying and policies. In this regard, the case study of family workers in Germany illustrates the strong divide between statistical, legal and social categorization.

Table 2.4 The statistical evolution of family workers in Germany (1925–2001).

	Family workers (% of the active population)
1925[(a)]	19.6
1933[(a)]	18.8
1939[(a)]	18.4
1950[(a) (b)]	14.4
1957[(a) (b)]	11.3
1960[(b)]	10.1
1970[(b)]	6.4
1980[(b)]	3.6
1990[(b)]	2.0
2001	1.2

Sources: 1925–57, Birkner 1960: 44; 1960–2001, Abraham 2005: 40.
[(a)] Without Saarland and Berlin
[(b)] For the German Federal Republic only

Social and Legal Categorizations in Tension (1950–2010)

It is of interest to note that the population statistically classified as family workers decreased drastically over the course of the second half of the twentieth century (see Table 2.4). The statistical definition used in micro-censuses only included 'helping' family members (*mithelfend*), that is, those without wage and work agreement, not 'co-working' family members (*mitarbeitend*) who were classified as employees or as self-employed depending on their legal status (Deutscher Bundestag 2005: 10–11).[7] Indeed, formal and contractual working relationships (partnerships or employment agreements) had increasingly become the most common form of work in a family business, and thus replaced informal work. As a result, the decrease in numbers only reflects a loss of relevance for this work form, though, astonishingly, not triggering the disappearance of the category in occupation statistics (Abraham 2000: 36; Abraham 2005: 37; Willms 1980: 102). This shift in the organization of work in small family businesses in craft, trade and agriculture has to be interpreted with regard to the more general context of the loss of legitimacy for non-contractual working relationships relative to other types of employment relationships in the second half of the twentieth century (see Kocka and Offe 2000: 11).

The following section analyses the social conditions and historical circumstances that led to a recurrent problematization of the legal status of family workers (understood as a social group from this point on, no longer a statistical category).

Tax Policies and Craft Organizations in Western Germany (1953–62)

In the 1950s, organizations that represented the interests of medium-sized businesses in craft (most notably the Deutsche Mittelstandsbund [DBM] and Hauptverband des Deutschen Einzelhandels [HDE]) placed the issue of tax exemption for family businesses on the political agenda, in the context of 'small' (1953), 'big' (1954) and income tax (1956, 1958) reforms of the German tax system (Scheybani 1996: 336). In 1954, tax exemption for the couple was increased by 100 DM, whereas in 1956, a tax exemption of 300 DM for the co-working spouse was introduced. In 1958, the introduction of tax division for married couples (*Ehegattensplitting*), supported by the HDE (HDE 9. Arbeitsbericht 1956, in ibid.), created the possibility for married couples to split their total income into two equal parts. For craft organizations, this financial exoneration was a matter of economic fairness and competitiveness for small and medium businesses compared to larger ones, and was not a matter of gender equality at all. Tax splitting has been strongly criticized for promoting the male breadwinner model (Oertzen 1999: 194).

In 1962, the question of the legal status of spouses and its consequence for taxation was placed into the judiciary arena. The Constitutional Court had to decide whether spouses with work contracts should be assimilated with associates (as the government argued) or with employees in order to determine taxation (BVerfGe 24 January 1962 – 1 BvL 32/57). Regarding the government's argumentation, one finds the same patterns as those that led statisticians to create a specific category for family workers in 1925: spouses had 'the same interests as persons involved in business capital' (ibid.). They had an 'entrepreneur-like position' ('eine unternehmergleiche Stellung') and could be compared with a 'silent partner' ('stiller Gesellschafter'). As a result, work agreements between spouses were illegal. Conversely, the court's decision affirmed that family bonds should not be taken into account when qualifying work relationships. Spouses' status was not specific but comparable with the status of other employees. This decision breaks with the pattern of specificity due to family bonds that had shaped official discourse on family workers since the creation of a statistical category in 1925. However, although this legal case marks the entry of family workers into the general legal framework with regard to taxation, this is not the case concerning social insurance.

'UnternehmerFrauen': Promoting Managerial Skills and Securing Social Rights (1985–2010)

In France, few family workers declared a professional status after the 1982 law had introduced three possible official statuses to choose from (associate, employed, and collaborating) (Martini 2014: 264; see Giraud's chapter in this volume). In Germany, however, the case was exactly the opposite. Although there was no official status recognized by law, many family workers considered themselves employed and, therefore, paid the corresponding contribution to pension and unemployment insurance funds. In many cases, however, the responsible authorities denied their status as employees when it came to welfare benefits.

The UFH ('UnternehmerFrauen im Handwerk', with a double meaning of 'Entrepreneurs' Wives' and 'Female Entrepreneurs in Craft') is an interest group founded in 1988 in West Germany.[8] They put this issue on the political agenda at the turn of the twenty-first century. This organization represents only family workers in craft, yet aims at a more general legal clarification that would be applicable to all family workers, including those in trade or in the agricultural sector.[9] This example highlights three dimensions in the interactions between self- and state categorization: first, the political dimension of claiming recognition as subjects of the welfare state; second, the symbolic dimension of semantic choices; and third, the professional dimension, focused on qualification and skills training.

The UFH engaged in political and legal struggles, claiming transparency and binding decisions with regard to the legal determination of their occupational status and corresponding social benefits. They focused on the legal coding of family workers' statuses as well as the securing of their rights. At the beginning of the twenty-first century, more and more spouses were refused social benefits by official authorities, despite the fact that they paid social contributions for years according to their self-determination as employees. Official authorities, however, classified them as self-employed, arguing that their working conditions equated to those of joint venturers (Dött 2004: 5).[10] Once again, the case of family workers illustrates the divergence between self-categorization and official categorization. At the federal level, Marie-Luise Dött, deputy of the conservative party, supported their position and demanded the introduction of an official determination and clarification of their status (Dött 2004: 2). Some of their leaders also directly lobbied the federal government (Deutscher Bundestag 2005: 10; Dohle 2013).

The status regulation for co-working family members was introduced in 2005 in the framework of the reform of the *Sozialgesetzbuch*, the so-called Hartz-IV legislation, and in the broader context of the European

Employment Policy. As a result, family workers were required to submit a prior assessment of their status as an employee or entrepreneur in order to be incorporated into the corresponding systems of social security and health care (§7a Abs.1 Satz 2 SGB IV).[11] A further judgement in 2010 created the possibility for co-working family members who were already engaged in working relationships before 2005 to request an official examination of their status by authorities afterwards (Deutsche Rentenversicherung Bund 2010). The recognition of the employee's status thereby tends to highlight the hierarchical relationships between the spouses, while the state categorized them as equal partners. In fact, other logics may have played a role: whereas the German state has been afraid of 'silent' (undeclared) partnership since the 1950s, spouses apprehended this official categorization as co-owner as an injustice with regard to the social benefits they were denied. Unlike the French condition, this compulsory status examination was based on the official categorization by authorities, not on self-declaration. Whereas the French spouses' associations defended the freedom to choose their own status out of three (see Giraud's chapter in this book), the German organization demanded the external settlement of their status by the administrative authorities as a matter of security and stability. Furthermore, the informal status of German family workers was replaced and made commensurate with existing legal notions of the employee and the entrepreneur within the labour code, without challenging this division, a condition also at the core of the German social insurance system.

In addition to this political action, the UFH also became involved in symbolic redefinitions of the family workers' social placing. The name, 'UnternehmerFrauen', maintained a semantic ambiguity between wives of entrepreneurs and female entrepreneurs (*Frau* meaning both wife and woman), and these were the two target groups of the organization. In the documents edited by the association, one notes a preference for the lexical field of 'collaboration' over that of 'assistance' and 'help' (as in the statistical term), which connotes devaluation of work. This semantic preference corresponds with one of the main activities of the organization with regard to wives working in small and medium businesses: to promote professionalization through commercial and management training in business administration (e.g. the certificate 'Fachwirtin im Handwerk' – female business administrator in craft). This instrument supported competences and skills development and aimed to increase the legitimacy and recognition of wives' performance within family businesses. It is of interest to explore the arguments for a better qualification of women in small businesses. The promotion of the individual and professional development of women is deeply intertwined with economic arguments: better skilled employees could support the economic development of the enterprise. The economic and moral value of family business played a crucial role in this line of argumentation. In fact, the discourse tended to make the destiny of women, like the queen in a game of chess, inseparable from that of family businesses: 'We are important motors of business's life and of our family's life too! The modern female entrepreneur/wife of entrepreneur [*Unternehmerfrau*] in craft is skilled, informed and a factor of success in craft management' (UFH 2010: 1). Defined as a 'modern' and thus contemporary avatar of national economy in 1920s statistical discourse, managerial language is convoked both in the field of business and in the familial sphere. Spouses are regarded as 'family manager[s]' (*Familienmanagerin*). This permanent interconnectedness between the two roles challenges the division between family and business. At the same time, these groups refused to be seen as a women's organization. Though they supported women's professional lives, they also defended a conservative model based on familial values and gender difference:

> Today, thanks to technical innovations, jobs in craft aren't as physically demanding as was the case a few years ago. Furthermore, small businesses offer attractive working conditions. Women can rely on flexible working hours and thus can reconcile working and family life. (Kluth 2012)

To summarize, the UFH's discourse interwove professionalism and economic valuation, as well as the recognition of women managing activities as the heads of (family) businesses with traditional representations of family and gender relationships. Thus, this dynamic is closer to that of the French ADEAC than to the ACTIF (see Giraud's chapter in this volume).

Conclusion

At the end of the nineteenth century, the standardization of work through statistics made some activities visible (those of family workers) while leaving others invisible (those engaged in housework; see also Hausen 2000: 346). At the same time, new census practices (e.g. individual census forms) triggered the individualization of statistical recording and, thus, the necessity to classify every single person in one nomenclature. This process opened up a (grey) zone of negotiation where different conceptions (those of feminist organizations, housewives' organizations as well as different opinions among the statisticians) conflicted. The statistical practices of categorization in France and Germany could not have been more different: whereas French family workers were sometimes considered inactive, and sometimes classified under the category of the head of the household (see Giraud's chapter in this book), the German category placed individuals both in the active population and in a specific irregular situation. As one can see over the course of the time period in question, the changes in statistical classification, census after census, resulted not only in huge fluctuations in numbers but also in shifting boundaries between work and non-work. 'Family workers', as a category, is a marker of this movable line over time.

This chapter has addressed some turning points in the history of gender, work and statistical classification. It argues that official categorization supported social representations regarding work and gender that can be challenged by self-categorization. The focus on classification (redefinition of categories, introduction of new categories) gives access to shifting conceptions of work and the labour market. The changes in statistical nomenclatures reveal the social transformations of an industrializing society towards the individualization of rights, salarization and the contractualization of labour relationships, both in France and Germany, though different national pathways were highlighted (see Giraud's chapter in this book for the French part). The German case clearly points to a shift towards individualized rights instead of social and economic protection provided on the basis of family bonds, and towards a redefinition of family business as an economic entity carried on by qualified professionals. The work of family members moved from its informal character and the field of family law to a concrete clarification of their legal status aligned on labour law. Whereas they had been addressed as wives and children under the scope of family law, they are now recognized as workers in the field of labour law. At the turn of the twenty-first century, family workers were gradually included in the institutions of the welfare state, their status being less exceptional, removing them from the grey zone.

This case study offers an illustration of the interconnectedness as well as the gap between official (statistical and legal) categorization and self-categorization determined by social groups (interest groups in our case). It is argued that categorization, at these two levels, played a crucial role around 1900 in the establishment and, after 1945, in the reproduction of a gendered labour market based on shifting definitions of occupation (Wobbe and Renard 2017; Wobbe, Renard, and Müller 2017). The transformations in categorization, social placement and legal status reflect the metamorphoses of the patterns of interpretation of work after 1945.

Léa Renard is a PhD candidate in sociology and political science at the University of Potsdam (Germany) and the University of Grenoble Alpes (France). She worked for the project 'Metamorphoses of Equality II (1945–2010)' (Potsdam/CNAM-Lise Paris), co-founded by the Agence Nationale de la Recherche (ANR) and the Deutsche Forschungsgemeinschaft (DFG), on family workers and statistical classification. Her PhD project explores shifting statistical categories of migration and nationality in France and Germany over time (1880–2010).

Notes

Special thanks to Theres Matthieß for her support, especially in fieldwork. Warm thanks go to Caroline Arni, Sabine Rudischhauser, Sigrid Wadauer, Theresa Wobbe and the WIPCAD fellows for their comments.

1. In the following, this expression is translated with the term 'family workers', which is the corresponding term used in the British census, as well as in international statistics. However, this translation does not render the semantic richness of the German concept. Where the Anglo-Saxon term addresses the people in question as workers, the German one emphasizes the familial character of their working condition, while, at the same time, devaluing their economic performance by calling it 'help' and not 'work'.
2. The articles analysed are from the *Allgemeines Statistisches Archiv* and the *Zeitschrift des Königlich Preußischen Statistischen Bureaus.*
3. Business counts (*Gewerbezählungen*) of 1846, 1861, 1867.
4. However, it is a controversial issue to determine whether and how this rigid conception influenced the statistical recording of occupations around 1900. Regarding this debate, see Schneider 2013: 375; Tooze 2001: 52–53.
5. Regarding housewives' associations in the Weimar Republic, see Reagin 2007.
6. The occupation census of 1939, which took place under the national-socialist regime, defined family workers as follows: 'all family members of farming households between 14 and 60 years … are classified as family workers' (Birkner 1960: 44).
7. In 1933, one can already find the following indication on census forms: family workers who paid compulsory contribution (*Pflichtbeiträge*) into employees' insurance (*Angestelltenversicherung*) had to be classified as 'employees' (Willms 1980: 34).
8. The first local group was founded in Koblenz in 1985; local groups then gathered in 1988 under the auspices of the 'Federation of Entrepreneurs' Spouses in Craft' (*Bundesverband Unternehmer-Frauen im Handwerk*).
9. Organizations of women in agriculture (e.g. *LandFrauen*) formulated similar demands concerning social protection of widows and separate income from the head of the business/family.
10. Authorities based their judgements on the following criteria: higher hierarchical position within the enterprise, extra hours on Sundays and public holidays, entrepreneurial risk, decision-making, and accounting competences (Dött 2004: 5).
11. https://www.gesetze-im-internet.de/sgb_4/__7a.html (last accessed 21 November 2018).

References

Primary Sources

Birkner, H. 1960. 'Die statistische Erfassung der mithelfenden Familienangehörigen', *Allgemeines Statistisches Archiv* 44: 41–48.

Bundesverfassungsgericht [24 January 1962] 1 BvL 32/57.

Burgdörfer, F. 1925. 'Die Volks-, Berufs- und Betriebszählung 1925', *Allgemeines Statistisches Archiv* 15(1): 7–78.

Deutsche Rentenversicherung Bund. 2010. 'Statusfestellung von Erwerbstätigen', *Summa Summarum* 2: 14–15. Retrieved 27 January 2017 from http://www.deutsche-rentenversicherung.de/cae/servlet/contentblob/204664/publicationFile/11695/2010_2_zeitschrift.pdf.

Deutscher Bundestag. 2005. Antwort der Bundesregierung auf die Kleine Anfrage der Abgeordneten Marie-Luise Dött, Hartmut Schauerte, Maria Michalk, weitere Abgeordnete und der Fraktion der CDU/CSU – Drucksache 15/5171.

Dohle, A. 2013. Letter addressed to the Chair of Gender Sociology of the University of Potsdam, 17 June, personal file.

Dött, M.-L. 2004. *Sozialversicherungspflicht für mitarbeitende Familienangehörige*. Berlin: Deutscher Bundestag, 2 December. Retrieved 27 January 2017 from http://www.marie-luise-doett.de/daten/downloads/sozialversicherungspflicht.pdf.

Engel, E. 1870. 'Die Notwendigkeit einer Reform der volkswirtschaftlichen Statistik', *Zeitschrift des königlich preußischen statistischen Bureaus* 10(3): 143–232.

Fürst, G. 1929. 'Zur Methode der deutschen Berufsstatistik', *Allgemeines Statistisches Archiv* 19: 1–29.

Hiess, F. 1931. *Methodik der Volkszählungen*. Jena: Verlag von Gustav Fischer.

Kaiserliches Statistisches Amt. 1900. 'Statistisches Jahrbuch für das Deutsche Reich: Die Deutsche Volkswirtschaft am Schlusse des 19. Jahrhunderts'. Berlin: Verlag von Puttkammer & Mühlbrecht.

Kluth, H. (interview with). 2012. 'Wohin steuern die Unternehmerfrauen?', *Handwerk.com*, 19 November. Retrieved 22 April 2016 from http://handwerk.com/wohin-steuern-die-unternehmerfrauen/150/651/58684/.

Lange, H., and G. Bäumer. 1902. *Handbuch der Frauenbewegung: Die deutsche Frau im Beruf*. Erlangen: Fischer Verlag.

Mayr, G. von. 1926. *Statistik und Gesellschaftslehre. II. Band: Bevölkerungsstatistik*. Tübingen: J.C.B. Mohr.

Meerwarth, R. 1925. *Nationalökonomie und Statistik: Eine Einführung in die empirische Nationalökonomie*. Berlin: Walter de Gruyter & Company.

Quante, P. 1961. *Lehrbuch der praktischen Statistik: Bevölkerungs-, Wirtschafts-, Sozialstatistik*. Berlin: Walter de Gruyter & Company.

UFH. 2010. 'Unternehmerfrauen im Handwerk (UFH) sind Erfolgsfaktor für die Unternehmen', press release, May.

Secondary Sources

Abraham, M. 2000. 'Die Rolle des (Ehe-)Partners für kleine und mittlere Unternehmen', in D. Bögenhold (ed.), *Kleine und mittlere Unternehmen im Strukturwandel – Arbeitsmarkt und Strukturpolitik*. Frankfurt/Main: Peter Lang Verlag, pp. 33–50.

________. 2005. 'Mitarbeit statt Mithelfende Familienangehörige: Ein Vorschlag zur Ergänzung des Standardinstruments für die Erhebung der beruflichen Stellung', *ZUMA-Nachrichten* 29(56): 37–48.

Aulenbacher, B. 2010. 'Rationalisierung und der Wandel von Erwerbsarbeit aus der Genderperspektive', in F. Böhle, G. Voß, and G. Wachtler (eds), *Handbuch Arbeitssoziologie*. Wiesbaden: Verlag für Sozialwissenschaften, pp. 301–28.

Desrosières, A. 2010. *La politique des grands nombres: Histoire de la raison statistique*. Paris: La Découverte.

Fritz, W. 2001. *Historie der amtlichen Statistiken der Erwerbstätigkeit in Deutschland. Ein fragmentarischer Abriß: Darstellung, Quellen, Daten, Definitionen, Chronik*. Cologne: Zentrum für Historische Sozialforschung.

Hausen, K. 2000. 'Arbeit und Geschlecht', in J. Kocka and C. Offe (eds), *Geschichte und Zukunft der Arbeit*. Frankfurt: Campus Verlag, pp. 343–61.

Heintz, B. 2012. 'Welterzeugung durch Zahlen: Modelle politischer Differenzierung in internationalen Statistiken, 1948–2010', *Soziale Systeme* 18(1–2): 7–39.

Kocka, J., and C. Offe (eds). 2000. *Geschichte und Zukunft der Arbeit*. Frankfurt: Campus Verlag.

Lamont, M., and V. Molnár. 2002. 'The Study of Boundaries across the Social Sciences', *Annual Review of Sociology* 28: 167–95.

Martini, M. 2014. 'When Unpaid Workers Need a Legal Status: Family Workers and Reforms to Labour Rights in Twentieth-Century France', *International Review of Social History* 59(2): 247–78.

Müller, W., A. Willms, and J. Handl. 1983. *Strukturwandel der Frauenarbeit 1880–1980*. Frankfurt: Campus Verlag.

Oertzen, C. von. 1999. *Teilzeitarbeit und die Lust am Zuverdienen: Geschlechterpolitik und gesellschaftlicher Wandel in der Bundesrepublik, 1948–1969*. Göttingen: Vandenhoeck und Ruprecht.

Reagin, N.R. 2007. *Sweeping the German Nation: Domesticity and National Identity in Germany, 1870–1945*. Cambridge: Cambridge University Press.

Romero-Martín, J. 2016. 'Craftswomen in Times of Change: Artisan Family Strategies in Nineteenth Century Barcelona', *Mélanges de l'École française de Rome: Italie et Méditerranée modernes et contemporaines* 128(1). Retrieved 7 March 2016 from https://journals.openedition.org/mefrim/2445.

Scheybani, A. 1996. *Handwerk und Kleinhandel in der Bundesrepublik Deutschland: Sozialökonomischer Wandel und Mittelstandspolitik 1949–1961*. Munich: Oldenburg.

Schmidt, S. 2010. *Erwerbstätigkeit im Mikrozensus: Konzepte, Definition, Umsetzung*. ZUMA-Arbeitsbericht 2000/01. Mannheim: Zentrum für Umfragen, Methoden und Analysen.

Schneider, M. 2013. *Wissensproduktion im Staat: Das königlich preußische statistische Bureau 1860–1914*. Frankfurt: Campus Verlag.

Supiot, A. 2000. 'Les nouveaux visages de la subordination', *Droit social* 2000(2): 131–145.

Tooze, A.J. 2001. *Statistics and the German State, 1900–1945: The Making of Modern Economic Knowledge*. Cambridge: Cambridge University Press.

Topalov, C. 1994. *Naissance du chômeur: 1880–1910*. Paris: Michel.

Vanderstraeten, R. 2006. 'Soziale Beobachtungsraster: Eine wissenssoziologische Analyse statistischer Klassifikationsschemata', *Zeitschrift für Soziologie* 35(3): 193–211.

Vormbusch, U. 2012. *Die Herrschaft der Zahlen: Zur Kalkulation des Sozialen in der kapitalistischen Moderne*. Frankfurt: Campus Verlag.

Weber, M. 2011. *Die protestantische Ethik und der Geist des Kapitalismus*, 3rd edn. Munich: C.H. Beck.

Weinbach, C. 2002. 'Systemtheorie und Gender: Überlegungen zum Zusammenhang von politischer Inklusion und Geschlechterdifferenz', *Soziale Systeme* 8(2): 307–32.

Willms, A. 1980. *Die Entwicklung der Frauenerwerbstätigkeit im Deutschen Reich: Eine historisch-soziologische Studie*. Nuremberg: Beiträge zur Arbeitsmarkt- und Berufsforschung.

Wadauer, S. 2008. 'Vazierende Gesellen und wandernde Arbeitslose (Österreich, ca. 1880–1938)', in A. Steidl, T. Buchner, W. Lausecker, A. Pinwinkler, S. Wadauer, and H. Zeitlhofer (eds), *Übergänge und Schnittmengen: Arbeit, Migration, Bevölkerung und Wissenschaftsgeschichte in Diskussion*. Wien: Böhlau Verlag, pp. 101–31.

Wobbe, T. 2012. 'Making Up People: Berufsstatistische Klassifikation, geschlechtliche Kategorisierung und wirtschaftliche Inklusion um 1900 in Deutschland', *Zeitschrift für Soziologie* 41(1): 41–57.

Wobbe, T., and L. Renard. 2017. 'Gendered Boundaries between Household and Market as a Globalized Distinction: The Category of 'Family Workers' in International Statistics (1930s–1980s)', *Journal of Global History* 12(3): 340–360.

Wobbe, T., L. Renard, and K. Müller. 2017. 'Wirtschaften mit der Differenz: Deutungsmodelle des Geschlechts im Spiegel arbeitstatistischer und -rechtlicher Kategorisierungsprozesse von Arbeit (1882–1994)', *Soziale Welt* 68: 63–85.

Zimmermann, B. 2001. *La constitution du chômage en Allemagne: entre professions et territoires*. Paris: Maison des sciences de l'homme.

Chapter 3

Night Work for Women in France in the Last Two Decades before 2000

Regulations, Discourse and Gender Issues

Michel Lallement

Introduction

According to the French Ministry of Employment, between 1991 and 2008, the number of people working occasionally or habitually between midnight and five in the morning increased from 2.5 million to 3.6 million (Alvaga 2014). As reported in 2010 to the Economic and Social Council, 'it is particularly for women that the increase during this period has been most marked, with numbers more than doubling, from 495,000 to 994,000. Non-salaried workers were also concerned since 570,000 were doing night work in 2008. Overall, habitual night work increased more than occasional night work. It was often combined with other forms of atypical schedules, mainly for women' (Edouard 2010: 8). Despite this somewhat alarmist observation, the debate rebounded in 2013 when the media relentlessly reported that some stores were being made to close their doors at night and on Sundays. Once again, in the name of employment, many protagonists swung into action to demand more 'flexibility' in the use of night work. This study does not focus on the recent period but rather, for reasons that I will explain, on the last two decades before 2000. As the century came to an end, we could see significant change in terms of statistics. During the 1980s, the proportion of employees working at night remained stable. However, in the following decade, things changed. The 'Working Conditions' survey by the French Ministry of Employment (Bué, Coutrot and Puech 2004) produced the following estimate: in 2001, 14.3% of employees were doing night work (20.3% men and 7.3% women). Ten years earlier, these figures were 13%, 18.7% and 5.8% respectively.

The priorities adopted for action following the 1990s were not insignificant. At that time, as the rate of female working continued to rise and women's work began to be valued, at the European level at least, calls began for revision of the ban on night work for women. The period also corresponds to a particularly intensive time of reconfiguration in the organization of work in French companies. For both these reasons, the end of the 1990s was conducive to strong discursive activity in favour of revising the rules on night work for women in France. I have therefore chosen to focus on this pivotal period by asking what the transformations brought about by such activity can teach us about gender representations. In doing this, the theory defended here is that, after breaking away from the frame of reference that predominated at the time of canon law on women's work in 1892, we witnessed a double shift in the course of the 1990s, with a cognitive impact that cannot be seen simply by examining the statistics.

In methodological terms, this study is based on the examination of many texts: parliamentary debates, laws, conventions and agreements, internal working papers from organizations closely involved in debates, press articles and academic articles. To understand how and why women's night work is an interesting subject enabling us to grasp empirically the cognitive categories that structure our collective gender representations, the procedure adopted is the following. I first give a brief review of the main stages in the debates and the regulations surrounding night work for women in France before going on to examine the regulatory split in more detail, with the laws of 1987 and 2001 forming the two extreme limits. Next, I consider the discourse strategies used during the debates that punctuate this two-decade period.

The Main Stages in the Debates and Regulations Covering Night Work for Women in France

In France, night work for women has been the subject of many controversies and regulations. The starting point can be found as the nineteenth century was drawing to a close. To counter the most harmful consequences of rampant industrialization, French legislators proposed a minimum degree of legal protection for the benefit of those categories deemed to be weak and incapable, in other words, women and children. It was in this context that the question of women's night work was considered. The ten-year debate leading up to the law of 2 November 1892 revealed some highly contradictory interests and positions. In the name of free competition and the risk of perverse effects (women would no longer be able to enter certain professions), liberals showed the greatest reservations about regulating night work according to gender. On the left, the socialists advocated the ban, arguing the merits of fighting against the exploitation of women. Trade unionists, for their part, held to their more conservative positions: women should remain at home and certainly not compete with men in a world – the world of business – which, to their eyes, was naturally masculine. In truth, however, by exempting women workers from working conditions judged too tiring and even dangerous, it was France's demographic capital that was being preserved and, even more so, the reserve army of workers that industry would soon be clamouring for.

In spite of many differing points of view and the Senate's rejection of bills proposed in 1889 and 1891, the 1892 law resulted in legislation that defined the night as being between 10pm and 5am. The law forbade women from working during this time period in factories, manufacturers, mines and quarries, building sites, workshops, and their dependencies, of any sort whatsoever, whether public or private, secular or religious, even when these were professional teaching or charitable establishments. It also applied to public and ministerial offices, professional establishments, non-commercial companies, professional societies and associations of any kind.

Over the years, many exemptions have emerged to broaden the range of occupations accessible to women at night (Bué and Roux-Rossi 1993). The law of 25 January 1925 allowed for two exceptions. The first concerned industries producing perishable goods. The second was in the event of unemployment resulting from an accidental interruption or force majeure. On 2 January 1979, the rule was once again revised to allow night work for women in managerial posts or in technical positions with responsibility. Again in 1982, the order of 16 January provided the possibility of moving the time limits set by the law by two hours. In addition, the Labour Code authorized exemptions for certain professions. Before the 1987 law, the labour inspectorate was able to grant dispensations in exceptional circumstances in national defence establishments and it was stipulated that the prohibition did not apply to night supervisors in boarding schools and cultural establishments constituted as associations.

It was in this same spirit of exemption that the law of 19 June 1987 was promulgated. It was directly inspired by the 17 July 1986 agreement with the metal and mining industries, which laid down three conditions to override the old 1892 law: it should only be applied in exceptional circumstances and in cases of national interest, on the understanding that, in the mind of the legislator, the circumstances referred to may fall within the economic sphere; the law only covered shift work; the introduction of night work must be subject to two-fold negotiations – an industry-wide agreement and a company convention or agreement.

The gradual march towards contractual authorizations was the result of non-legal interests that constantly undermined the effectiveness of the legal rules. A century after the adoption of the landmark law on night work for women, the liberal nineteenth-century arguments were taken up by a left-wing government to reverse the priorities; the production imperative now prevailed over that of reproduction. This situation soon bordered on contradiction. Officially, French law did indeed continue to prohibit night work (Article L-213-1 of the Labour Code) but this rule was overridden by community law, which authorized it in the name of the principle of gender equality. French legislation eventually complied with the supranational law by officially authorizing night work for women. At the beginning of 2001, fifty-five thousand women worked nights in industry. A year and a half later, as a result of the new regulation, there were already fifteen thousand more women working. Alongside the plastics industry, the pharmaceutical industry, canning industries and so on, metallurgy was one of the first sectors to negotiate a sector-wide agreement to offer compensation to the female employees concerned. Overall, as can be seen from Table 3.1, at the end of the twentieth century there was a shift towards a new discourse repertoire.

Table 3.1 From one discourse repertoire to another.

	End of nineteenth century	End of twentieth century
Reasons put forward to justify regulating women's work	Woman = not as strong Woman = wife Woman = mother Woman = guarantees dynamic demographic (productivity and military issues) Woman = potentially competing against men in the labour market	Accumulation of exemptions for non-legal reasons: health and hygiene interests, food processing interests, production interests, interests of economic efficiency …, then gender equality argument
Principle used to define and classify the genders	Natural and functional differentiation	Equal rights but keeping specific differences (childbirth, childcare, conciliation, etc.)

1980–2001: The Time of Change

The 1980s were therefore a time of major change, which saw the gradual emergence of a new discursive and normative paradigm. Regarding the regulation of night work for women, two rulings from the Court of Luxembourg (the Stoeckel ruling of 25 July 1991 and the Levy ruling of 2 August 1993) proved to be particularly significant. The first, which is also the one that had the most impact, was the result of a contradiction. On the one hand, the French Labour Code stipulates – in Article L-213-1 – that women cannot be employed for night work (i.e. between 10pm and 5am) in industrial establishments, mines, quarries, building sites, public and ministerial offices, professional establishments, non-commercial companies, associations and professional societies of any kind. Commercial establishments, on the other hand, are not affected. In the same way, women in managerial and technical posts (positions carrying responsibility) are not affected by the rule, nor are those working in health and welfare services and who do not normally carry out manual labour.

On the other hand, Community Directive EC/76/207 of 9 February 1976 is unambiguous in imposing equal treatment for men and women as regards access to employment, vocational training and promotion and working conditions. There are only three exceptions to this rule. Different regulations can be applied to men and women's work and employment in activities where the nature or the conditions of the work make the sex of the worker a determining factor; specific provisions can be made concerning the protection of women, particularly as regards pregnancy and maternity; and finally, measures can be adopted to reduce unequal opportunities between the sexes. In addition, Article 5 obliges member states to take the necessary measures for national rules and regulations to be adapted to these principles. Social partners should also, if necessary, adjust their contractual corpus along the same lines. The *Official Journal of the European Union* of 14 February 1976 stipulated that member states should make changes to their regulations within four years.

France did not play the game. The non-compliance with the directive came to light with the Stoeckel and Levy rulings, which followed on from decisions by police courts in the towns of Illkirch and Metz. The first considered that French law was contrary to the principle of gender equality since there was no similar prohibition applied to men. The second concluded that if a law on the prohibition of night work for women, enacted nationally, arose from the application of an international convention adopted before the Treaty of Rome of 1957 came into force, then the judge must apply this law nationally. Thus, the Court of Luxembourg provided arguments to structure the regulatory orders: community law takes precedence over national law when national law is the result of the country's own national rules or international rules adopted after the Treaty of Rome came into force. In the French case, the situation quickly unravelled. After the Stoeckel ruling, the European Commission warned governments, including France, to denounce International Labour Organization (ILO) Convention no. 89, which prohibits night work for women. The French government complied on 17 February 1992 and, given the delay of one year in force for this type of denunciation, this resulted in a challenge to the principle of prohibiting night work for women effective from 17 February 1993.

The Ministry of Employment was first to recognize that Article L-213-1 of the Labour Code had become invalid. In response to written question no. 5291 presented on 7 July 1994 by Deputy Pierre-Christian Taittinger, the government stated that, 'while the provision prohibiting night work is still included in the Labour Code, it has no legal effect and does not prevent women from having jobs in industry'.[1] However, since the Code had not been specifically amended regarding this subject, this did not suffice. The proof of this came when Directive EC 93/104 of 23 November 1993 set a new deadline for compliance of national legislations on aspects of the organization of working time by 23 November 1996. Because France turned a deaf ear, the Court of Justice of the European Communities condemned it on 13 March 1997, 'for violation of the principle of equal treatment for men and women'.[2] To avoid paying a financial penalty of 142,425 euros per day, applicable from 30 November 2000, France took a small step forward in the direction of bringing the law into compliance with supranational norms. On 28 November 2000, an amendment to the law on professional equality removed the principle of prohibiting night work for women in France.

A short while later, law no. 2001-397 of 9 May 2001, on professional equality between men and women, redefined the notion of night work (which now referred to the time between 9pm and 6am), affirming that its use should remain exceptional, and referred to the convention or collective industry-wide agreement, or the company or establishment agreement on introducing night work, on the understanding that each agreement should contain explanations justifying the use of night-time working as well as clauses relating to the compensations to be granted to the employees concerned.

Political Discourse, Trade Union Discourse, Expert Discourse, Academic Discourse

In less than two decades, as we have seen, the regulations covering night work for women shifted from prohibition in principle (combined with many exceptions) to common law practice, accessible to men and women (subject to some non-binding conditions, enacted by the law). To understand this shift, we can hypothesize that the discourse repertoires that underpin the way in which institutions think and classify have also evolved and that the dynamics of this change have contributed actively to the construction of new rules and collective representations. We can also put forward a second hypothesis, namely the existence of discourse struggles involving participants who use figures of rhetoric, which although varied are finite in number, in order to impose their views. The aim here is to construct a repertoire of the arguments put forward in the 1980s and 1990s to justify or, conversely, to prevent the lifting of the ban on night work for women.

To test these hypotheses, I use three different types of material to go back over different times and look in detail at arguments put forward. First, I consider the report by the Catholic right-wing deputy, Etienne Pinte, for the 1986–87 ordinary session of the National Assembly (the report is appended to the session of 30 April 1987) (Pinte 1987), debates in the National Assembly (30 April and 12 May 1987) on the draft bill relating to the duration and organization of working time, and finally the information report presented by Nicole Bricq, socialist deputy, on professional gender equality (Bricq 2000). Next, I am interested in looking at the position of the trade unions on night work, as found in the internal notes of the two main French unions (the French Democratic Federation of Labour [CFDT] and the General Confederation of Labour [CGT]). Finally, I look briefly at where international experts and the few French legal and sociological experts who have considered and worked on the subject stand in relation to night work for women.

The Method Used

The method consists in identifying the different arguments in the material used and then numbering them. It is a question of identifying affirmations that result in the defence of a position (maintain the prohibition, lift the prohibition, regulate differently). If the same argument recurs, but in a slightly different form and/or spoken by another participant, I assign the same number but preceded by an upper-case letter to identify the author of the statement: P1, for example, refers to argument #1 found in the Pinte report. The code used is as follows: P for the Pinte report, D for the left-wing deputies hostile to the Pinte report, B for the Bricq report, F for the CFDT, G for the CGT, E for the ILO (and other bodies that use experts) and A for articles signed by researchers. Finally, I assign lower-case letters to the number (e.g. P3a) to indicate a type of argument that derives from a higher-level argument (P3 in this case). Once the corpus has been created, I then define each brick in the argument according to simple criteria: nature of the argument, form of argument (if ... then ...; it contradicts ...; etc.), implication for position taken in debates, and figure of rhetoric used.

The Pinte Report

The Pinte report mobilizes many arguments to justify transforming the rules of the economic game in order to adapt the labour market and the rules of labour law, the ultimate objectives being to fight against unemployment, to win the economic war and to facilitate innovations. From the outset, the deputy mentions in his report the unemployment rate, the energy crisis, international monetary disorder, the transformation of international trade, and France's technological backwardness. To create jobs, adds Pinte, policies to stimulate global demand had their limitations. 'Unemployment is largely due to the rigidities of the labour market, which because of anticipating the cost of jobs, have slowed hiring' (Pinte 1987: 8). This is why the organization of working time, where night work is an ingredient of choice, is a good solution. It will (P1) extend the time that equipment is in use, adapt the employees' work to economic fluctuations and promote the optimal use of productive capacities.

Among the arguments used to justify such wishful thinking are the following:

- P2. Since the late 1970s, there has been an increase in the number of employees (male and female) working regularly or occasionally at night. Approximately 70% of the women concerned (i.e. 280,000) are government employees: doctors, nurses, hospital workers, post office workers.
- P3. The ban on night work for women in industries where the workforce is highly feminized and which are most severely exposed to international competition results in dismissals or threats of dismissal, which only increase the disparities between men and women, where more and more women are becoming victims, and so on.

Using another entire arsenal of arguments, which will not be described in detail here, the draft bill brought by Pinte suggests putting an end to certain restrictions on women's work. In particular, it removes the ban on employing women in actual work for ten hours a day without interrupting this work with one or more breaks.

The debates taking place in the National Assembly on the basis of these proposals are equally instructive. Asked in April about the sector-level agreements signed with no legal basis to allow exemptions for night work by women, P. Séguin, then Minister of Social Affairs and Employment, reported ninety-two agreements reached since 1 September 1986, of which forty-six were signed by the CGT.[3] He concluded that the law will permit the legalization. Taking the opposite view, Deputy Gérard Collomb noted that the law will allow companies to take all productivity gains linked with organizing working time. Other arguments, linked more directly with the question of night work for women, were put forward by the socialist opposition, such as the fact that it is contradictory to require a sector-level agreement to authorize night work for women and to authorize them to work continuously if this condition is presented, for an adjustable hours agreement, as a blocking element (D7). This list was based on the discursive material found in the minutes of the session at the National Assembly when Pinte returned to the draft bill on working time.

The switch that happened in the period under consideration ended in 2001. The counterpart to the Pinte report, which in 1987 signalled the opening of a political debate and a desire for reform, was the Bricq report of 2000, which for its part was committed to ending the dispute. In the name of gender equality, this report advocates women's full access to night work. Some of the arguments used were as follows:

- B20. The good reasons that were used in the past to justify the ban are no longer valid today. The ban on night work for women corresponded to the predominant representation of women inspired by a paternalistic, or even patriarchal viewpoint. In addition, it created competition with men who received attractive bonuses when doing night work. The same is not true today.
- B21. French legislation has to be brought into line with the European directive of 9 February 1976 on the principle of equal treatment for men and women.
- B13. Night work disrupts biological rhythms of men and of women, it also causes cognitive disorders, problems with mood and sleep, it lowers alertness and increases the risk of workplace accidents, it upsets the nutritional balance, and so on. So that it must be used only in case of necessity, but both by men and women.

I now deal with a slightly different kind of material as these are notes that are internal to the CFDT, and more peripherally to the CGT. The former are taken from confederation and interfederation archives; most of the latter consist of declarations and letters to departmental federations and unions in 1992 and internal arguments on the confederation positions regarding relations between French law and international standards. At the end of the 1970s and the beginning of the 1980s, both confederations held basically the same position. From 1981, following discussions at the ILO at which the CFDT was represented, the confederation nevertheless put forward some elements of analysis that were less unilaterally opposed to the removal of the ban. For the CFDT, some of the main arguments were as follows:

- F28. Removing the ban on night work for women will lead to an increase in shift work.
- F29. Equal rights for men and women means restricting night work for all.
- F11b. It is antisocial to seek to extend exemptions for women's night work.
- F30. Women already have a double workload, it would therefore penalize them even further if they were made to work at night, and so on.

For the CGT, we do not see a similar swing in their argument. At the end of the 1970s, the dominant position was that night work for women was a necessity that should be restricted to public service jobs or jobs in sectors with technical requirements (G41). In the report on night work for women published in 2001 in the journal *Travail, genre et sociétés* (Laufer et al. 2001), we see an even more concise argument for the positions adopted by the two main French trade union confederations as the debate that had begun two decades earlier was about to come to an end. Unsurprisingly, the points of view are more or less the same.

In the context of expert opinion, there were two main characteristics in the production of arguments. First, it was less well developed; second, it was produced earlier, with specialists in law, economics, health and so on being consulted beforehand, which helped in different ways to prepare the ground for political sparring. At the start of the 1980s, the question of night work for women was put to experts subsequent to the law of 13 July 1983 on professional gender equality, which chose to maintain the provisions of the Labour Code that were specific to women. In an attempt to remove the contradiction, Yvette Roudy, Minister for Women's Rights, appointed a commission to produce a report looking at the 'specific provisions of the Labour Code that are not directly linked with maternity'

(Junter-Loiseau, Gentilhomme, and Pone 1985).[4] Within this framework, eight experts were heard – three doctors, an epidemiologist, a lawyer, two administrative officials and an expert in the organization of work from the ILO. During these sessions, the experts first pointed out 'the permanence of the special measures relating to work by women, despite a series of amendments to national and international regulations', and 'the apparent contradiction between maintaining special measures and introducing the concept of professional equality into national and international regulations' (E21). The ILO expert further emphasized the fact that the organization she represented originally wanted to promote the protection of women in their reproductive capacity and in terms of the protection of the family. From now on, the ILO promotes gender equality (E40).

In France, the few learned articles and studies on night work are in general even more measured in their arguments than the experts. There is perhaps only William Grossin, a well-established specialist in working time, who has clearly stated his opposition to night work because of its harmful effects on employees' health and living conditions (A13), men and women alike (Grossin 1996). For the rest, researchers are generally less radically affirmative, although this does not mean that their thoughts or their work are not based on substantive arguments. For example, we note the position taken by Jennifer Bué and Dominique Roux-Rossi, which corresponds to the position of the CFDT from the 1980s onwards. For these two researchers, 'taking a stance for or against a ban on night work for women, for men, for everyone, seems to us to be a false debate. The real question, in our view, concerns the working and living conditions of night workers. Night work cannot, in any circumstances, be considered as a commonplace form of work or a type of working time flexibility, because it can have harmful effects for health, as experts have established. However, the principle of prohibiting night work does not seem to solve the problem' (Bué and Roux-Rossi 2001: 151). Argument A54 is based primarily on examples taken from field surveys. We can therefore learn from the overall results (A54a) or simply from a monograph that is considered relevant (A54b) in order to deduce that night work is dangerous for health.

A similar option was chosen by Margaret Maruani who, when questioned on the principle of prohibiting night work for women, suggested two positions, 'both of which make sense': that of equality, which tends to favour access to night work for women (A26), and that of health and working conditions, which encourages us to adopt the opposite position (A13) (Maruani and Sebilotte 1999: 13). Yet another way of taking a stand, which is also qualified, is to look beyond the voluntary/non-voluntary aspect, and explain, supported by field surveys, that an in-depth analysis of a case study shows that women who work at night are forced volunteers (A54). Any notion of choice would therefore be false (Carteron 2008).

From Rhetoric to Reconfigurations by Category

To treat the repertoire of arguments established above in a more analytical fashion, tools derived from the rhetoric, and more specifically those developed by Chaïm Perelman, are particularly heuristic. Perelman's main thesis is that 'the purpose of argumentation is not like demonstration, to prove the truth of the conclusion from premises, but rather to transfer to the conclusion the *adherence* accorded to the premises' (Perelman 2002: 41, emphasis in the original). In other words, Perelman insists on one crucial point, which is that in order to be convincing, one has to adapt to one's audience and choose as the premise of the argumentation theories that they accept.

Perelman distinguishes three major rhetorical strategies to which can be added others that are used less frequently. The first consists in using quasi-logical arguments. The aim of this strategy is to convince by taking advantage of the relationship of the argument with formal reasoning. However, since natural language does not have the rigour of formal logic, quasi-logical arguments may come up against obstacles that a logician would describe as logical fallacies but which, in reality, the art of social actors and institutions is able to drive out, to temper, to ignore, to circumvent. Among the main obstacles that interest us directly for our study, three should be mentioned: contradictions and incompatibilities (autophagy), unclear definitions, and finally the relative nature of any comparison (where strength lies in the standard of measurement used).

The second strategy invites us to use arguments based on the structure of reality. In this instance, 'most arguments based on reality rely on liaisons of succession, such as the relationship of cause and effect, or liaisons of coexistence, such as the link between a person and his actions' (Perelman 2002: 95). In the former case, we see a typical pragmatic argument which reduces the value of a cause to that of its consequences and where one of the main limitations is that it is not easy either to 'stop in the indefinite chain of consequences that result from an action', or to impute to a single cause the consequences that result most often from many events. There is also a problem in that in some cases the consequences of means are contrary to what was expected when they were implemented,[5] and sometimes the means transform into ends (as in the case of love or avarice), and so on. The second case, liaisons of coexistence, associates people with their actions and their images. In this context, one figure is particularly interesting to look at: that of the double hierarchy. The argument consists in deriving a hierarchy of behaviours from a hierarchy of beings. For example, if we consider the superiority of adults over children, we deduce that being reasonable involves acting like a 'grown-up' and not like a child.

The third rhetorical strategy consists in argumentation by example and by illustration. The use of the example only makes sense if we assume that there are regularities of which the examples are tangible manifestations. Illustration has a slightly different function, however, as its main purpose is to 'strike the imagination', to use Perelman's words. The model and the anti-model can also be used for similar ends. To conclude this brief presentation of Perelman's rhetoric, we should also note the strategies of analogy and metaphor, which do not concern us much at present, and finally that of dissociation of ideas, which is more interesting. This involves inverting the primacy in pairs of ideas (individual/universal, means/end, action/person, etc.) or going beyond apparent incoherencies by reinterpreting one of the terms so that it provides a new meaning with a strong persuasive value.

I used the categories defined above to classify the arguments identified previously. What do we see when proceeding in this way? First, that the first observation is the simplest. Different rhetorical figures are mobilized, and not only the perverse effect, in order to convince of the desirability of extending exemptions, maintaining the ban imposed by the law or regulating night work for women in a different way. Here are some examples of the categorizations carried out to order the argumentations listed above.

- *Quasi-logical arguments*
  Contradictions and incompatibilities: 'easing the ban on women's night work is contradictory to the policy of reducing social security costs' (14).
  Unclear definitions: the way that concrete uses of women's night work are defined is unclear, for example positions of responsibility. It would therefore be better to relax the ban (18).
  Relative nature of the definition: 'Night work is a societal choice. Every society must choose between producing and protecting the producers' (48).
- *Arguments based on the structure of reality*
  Positive, negative or perverse effects: 'Night work for women promotes increased economic performance' (1), 'night work is harmful to health' (13), 'allowing night work for women will lead to

compensation policies working against them, blocked career development' (47).
Cause: A majority of employees are in favour of night work for women in the private sector (3).
Coexistence: Women do not have any particular special characteristics, especially physical ones, in comparison with men (26).

- *Examples and illustrations*
  Example: Field surveys show the harmful nature of women's night work (54).
  Illustration: The case of company X reveals how dangerous women's night work can be (54).
- *Dissociation of ideas*
  Improvements in working conditions are such that women can work at night, just like men (37).

When we classify all the arguments listed previously using Perelman's categories, it appears that arguments based on the structure of reality prevail (87.7%), well ahead of quasi-logical arguments (20.37%) and a long way ahead of the other types of figure. On its own, the logic of effects represents more than 42% of argumentations, which although it does not fully confirm the thesis of Albert Hirschman (1991), nevertheless fully reflects his meaning. It is no great surprise that we see that the rhetoric of negative effects is most used by actors who refuse any project to regulate night work for women, whereas those who promote the need for a new regulation mobilize more arguments through causes. However, this does not mean that the same figure of rhetoric cannot be used to reach conclusions on different recommendations. Sequential sorting comes up with further interesting indications. Figures for negative effect and perverse effect were mainly used in response to the projects for additional exemptions (at the beginning of the 1980s), when the motivation behind incorporating new provisions for night work for women was first and foremost economic and largely ignored concerns about professional equality (Table 3.2).

Gender is another criterion that warrants consideration (Tables 3.3 and 3.4). We see that the arguments that refer to gender are usually mobilized to justify abandoning the principle of prohibition while campaigning mainly in favour of greater regulation. This confirms the hypothesis mentioned earlier. This type of argument gives an indication of the powerful upswing of a frame of reference which, in the course of the 1990s, marked a structural rupture from the differentiated protection paradigm of the nineteenth century. One of the effects that this change had in shared representations is that, at the end of the 1990s and especially at the beginning of the 2000s, it became more obvious

Table 3.2 Figures of rhetoric and regulatory recommendations.

	Exempt	Prohibit	Regulate	Total
Contradiction and incompatibility	25%	50%	25%	100%
Definition (unclear, relative in nature)	33.3%	0%	66.7%	100%
Positive effect	33.3%	0%	66.7%	100%
Negative effect	50%	37.5%	12.5%	100%
Perverse effect	100%	0%	0%	100%
Cause	33.3%	0%	66.7%	100%
Coexistence	0%	0%	100%	100%
Illustration and examples	50%	0%	50%	100%
Dissociation	25%	25%	50%	100%
Total	*40.74%*	*20.37%*	*38.89%*	*100%*

Table 3.3 Gender argument and regulatory recommendation.

	Exempt	Prohibit	Regulate	Total
Gender	20%	10%	70%	100%
Non-gender	52.9%	26.5	20.6%	100%
Total	*40.74%*	*20.37%*	*38.89%*	*100%*

Table 3.4 Figures of rhetoric and gender arguments.

	Gender	Non-gender	Total
Contradiction and incompatibility	12.5%	87.5%	100%
Definition (unclear, relative in nature)	33.3%	66.7%	100%
Positive effect	33.3%	66.7%	100%
Negative effect	25%	75%	100%
Perverse effect	50%	50%	100%
Cause	41.7%	58.3%	100%
Coexistence	100%	0%	100%
Illustration and examples	0%	100%	100%
Dissociation	100%	0%	100%
Total	*37.04%*	*62.96%*	*100%*

for most actors that prohibiting night work for women would simply increase gender inequalities rather than mitigate them. Yet another result: the gender variable is the one most mobilized in the register of structures of reality. Dissociation and coexistence come next. Conversely, this means that quasi-logical arguments count for little when the gender variable is used. In general, they concern only the formal rationalization of the law and, hence, problems related to conflicts in standards.

A simple correspondence analysis of the small sample of data is used to synthesize the results and link them with the discourse strategies of those involved. The respective weight of the axes is 0.44 and 0.3. The first opposition, on the vertical axis, opposes a register of argumentation based on reality using two major figures of rhetoric: cause and perverse effect. Here, as in right-wing discourse, the focus is on the imperative of flexibility or the actual increase in women's work, which must inevitably lead to playing the exemption card (rhetorical strategy through cause). There are also trade union discourses, produced first by the CGT, which aim to show, using rhetoric, the perverse effect that an exemption could have: women evicted from work, a weakening of trade unionism and so on. In contrast, the central argument is that of regulations: we see that French law is opposed to supranational rules. This discourse tended to be used more by experts and the left wing in the 2000s, but it uses the rhetorical thread of contradiction in the first instance. It is not prohibited to look at this first opposition as the expression in the discourse of a typically Weberian tension between material rationalization (affirmation of extra-legal interests) and formal rationalization (requirement of legal coherence). Gender is not central in this opposition, or it serves only as a secondary pretext in the argumentation.

On the horizontal axis, we see an opposition between a 'non-gender' strategy in the argumentation at the end of the 1980s, which aimed to facilitate the extension of exemptions for women's night work, and a strategy that conversely uses the figures of coexistence and dissociation to take gender issues into account when regulating night work (this will be the final switch at the beginning of the 2000s). It was indeed quite late that social actors did away with the reflex of reasoning by effect and, by using other figures of rhetoric, integrated more considerations based on the inanity of the protection mindset, the differences (if any) in physical stamina at work, the social roles of men and women, but also on the new 'gender' risks, or the importance of conciliation, which carries more weight on the female side than on the male side. To summarize, a consensual condemnation of night work because of its harmful effect (this is the only argument shared by all actors at the same time), a condemnation based on the rhetoric of the negative effect, conflicts with a discourse

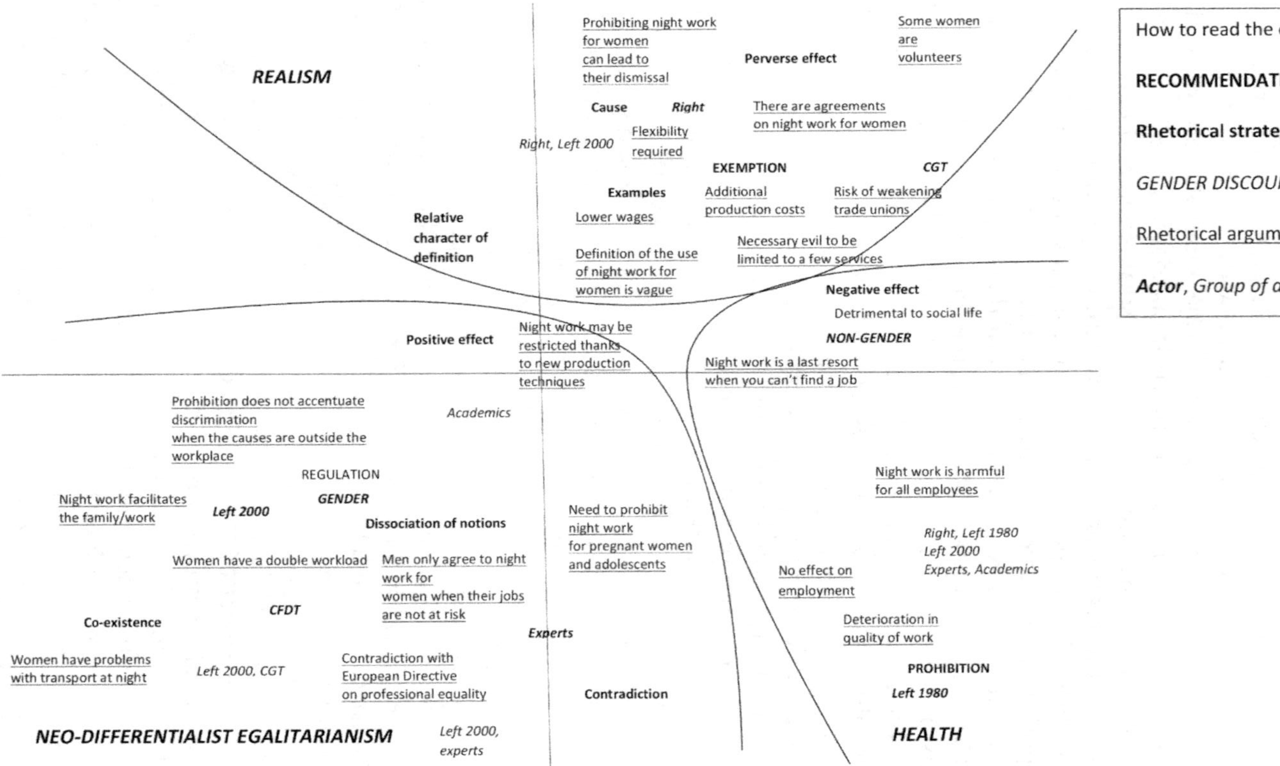

Graph 3.1 Area of discourse registers on night work for women in France in the 1980s and 1990s. Graph created by author.

that is not aiming for prohibition but for regulation. This carries with it arguments that may seem contradictory. Nevertheless, they have a point in common in that they rely on the figure of coexistence and place gender at the centre of the discussion: the affirmation that there are no specific differences between men and women, which means that women can be mobilized in just the same way as men in the world of production (provided that night work is regulated); emphasis on a principle of professional equality; an affirmation that there is a requirement to reconcile professional life and family life, which weighs more heavily on female shoulders; and awareness of the existence of material problems associated with night work and which are likely to affect women more directly (which is another reason to call for regulation).

In total, we can distinguish three discourse registers that mobilized actors to varying degrees, each having its own impact, evolving in different ways over the course of the 1980s and 1990s. The first discourse type, *health*, highlights the deleterious effects of night work for all employees, advocating a campaign in favour of banning it. Next, the *realist* discourse gives prominence to economic and social 'realities', opening the debate on whether or not to develop exemptions. These two discourse types coexisted and occupied the main space for discussion in the 1980s. Towards the end of this decade a new type of discourse emerged (*neo-differentialist egalitarianism*), which mobilized gender explicitly as a major argument, both to affirm equal rights at work and at the same time to suggest that there may be gender differences that require vigilance in terms of regulations. As we can see, the old adage of equality through difference has not yet had its day.

Conclusion

The aim of the approach adopted here was two-fold: first, to point out the importance of the decades of the 1980s and the 1990s in the way the regulation of night work for women in France changed; and second, to highlight the strength of the battles of words that were fought in various arenas to put an end once and for all to the ancient concept of the gender divide. From the end of the nineteenth century, and for many decades later, a structural homology could be seen in the legislation governing night work, which associated men with production and women with reproduction. At the end of the twentieth century, collective representations had evolved, legal contradictions had been honed, and the space given over to symbolic struggles was no longer the same, with the result that standards of justice, as applied by Perelman (1963), were no longer the same either. The study of the rhetorical arguments mobilized by the different stakeholders involved in regulating night work enables us to identify three discourse repertoires that overlap in part, but their historicity clearly shows that the ways in which we think of gender in relation to work have changed significantly.

To support such an outcome, it could be further substantiated by producing elements that can help in our understanding of the shift we have observed. There are several possible options. The first is to work on the finer points of the social conditions in which the different discourses used as source material were produced. In any case, it is not insignificant to observe that, from one space of action to another and from one discourse to another, the implications are not the same: on the subject of night work for women, men are more present in the political arena, while women are mobilized more in circles of expertise and academic knowledge. The second option is comparative. It is striking to observe that in France, as in Germany, similar arguments (mainly relating to health) have been mobilized to justify the type of night work regulation to be applied and ultimately to legitimize changing conceptions of gender relations. However, the historical culture, the procedures and the historicity that form the background against which these changes have taken place are by no means comparable. Given this observation, we can understand that the congruence of legal changes is not a sufficient argument to help us understand how gender representations and the relevant regulations have evolved in the two countries. From this point of view, too, much still remains to be done.

Michel Lallement is Professor of Sociology at the CNAM (Conservatoire national des arts et métiers), Paris, France. His research affiliations are with the Lise-CNRS. He has written numerous articles and books on work and the history of sociology, including *Le Travail: une sociologie contemporaine* (Gallimard, 2007), *Tensions majeures: Max Weber, l'économie, l'érotisme* (Gallimard, 2013), *Logique de classe: E. Goblot, la bourgeoisie et la distinction sociale* (Les Belles Lettres, 2015) and, with I. Berrebi-Hoffmann and M.-C. Bureau, *Makers: Enquête sur les laboratoires du changement social* (Seuil, 2018).

Notes

I am grateful to Isabelle Berrebi-Hoffmann, Olivier Giraud, Arnaud Lechevalier, Marie-Thérèse Letablier, Léa Renard, Ferruccio Ricciardi and Theresa Wobbe for their many comments and suggestions. In particular, I would like to thank Ferruccio Ricciardi for his decisive help in researching and compiling the material on which this study is based.

1. http://www.assemblee-nationale.fr/rap-info/i2703.asp (last accessed 21 November 2018).
2. Judgment of the Court (Fifth Chamber), 13 March 1997. In Case C-197/96. https://publications.europa.eu/en/publication-detail/-/publication/902dbd92-8f77-4758-b707-840a613c2c00/language-en (last accessed 21 November 2018).
3. Assemblée Nationale, compte-rendu de la première séance du mercredi 13 mai 1987. http://archives.assemblee-nationale.fr/8/cri/1986-1987-ordinaire2/037.pdf (last accessed 21 November 2018).
4. This quotation and those that follow are taken from this report, which is not paginated.
5. This is the theme of the composition effect, whose 'perverse effects' are well known in sociology, notably through the work of R. Boudon. A. Hirschman (1991) shows how often this figure of rhetoric has been used in France, by both the right and the left, to challenge the adoption of reforms.

References

Alvaga, E. 2014. 'Le travail de nuit en 2012', *Dares Analyses* 62: 1–8.

Bricq, N. 2000. *Rapport d'information fait au nom de la Délégation aux droits des femmes et à l'égalité des chances entre les hommes et les femmes sur la proposition de loi (n° 2604), modifiée par le Sénat, relative à l'égalité professionnelle entre les femmes et les hommes.* No. 2703. Paris: National Assembly, 15 November.

Bué, J., T. Coutrot, and I. Puech (eds). 2004. *Conditions de travail: les enseignements de vingt ans d'enquêtes.* Toulouse: Octarès.

Bué, J., and D. Roux-Rossi. 1993. *Le travail de nuit des femmes.* Paris: La documentation française.

________. 2001. Contribution to the issue 'Le travail de nuit des femmes', *Travail, genre et sociétés* 5(1): 150–54.

Carteron, H. 2008. 'Volontaires pour la nuit: des ouvrières de l'industrie matière', in D. Linhart (ed.), *Pourquoi travaillons-nous?* Toulouse: éditions érès, pp. 239–64.

Edouard, F. 2010. *Le travail de nuit: impact sur les conditions de travail et de vie des salariés.* Paris: Report to the Economic, Social and Environmental Council.

Grossin, W. 1996. *Pour une science des temps: introduction à l'écologie temporelle.* Paris: Octarès.

Hirschman, A. 1991. *Deux siècles de rhétorique réactionnaire.* Paris: Fayard.

Junter-Loiseau, A., M. Gentilhomme, and C. Pone. 1985. *Rapport final de la Commission Mesures particulières.* Paris: Mission for Professional Equality, Ministry for Women's Rights, July.

Laufer, J., M. Maruani, R. Silvera, M.-H. Zylberberg-Hocquard, M.-T. Lanquetin, J. Bué, D. Roux-Rossi, G. Ximenes, and M.-F. Boutroue. 2001. 'Le travail de nuit des femmes', *Travail, Genre et Sociétés* 5(1): 135–160.

Maruani, M., and L. Sebilotte. 1999. 'L'emploi féminin aujourd'hui: contrastes et paradoxes', *Lunes* 8: 6–15.

Perelman, C. 1963. *Justice et raison.* Brussels: Presses universitaires de Bruxelles.

________. 2002. *L'empire rhétorique: rhétorique et argumentation.* Paris: Vrin.

Pinte, E. 1987. *Rapport fait au nom de la Commission des affaires culturelles, familiales et sociales sur le projet de loi, rejeté par le Sénat, après déclaration d'urgence relatif à la durée et à l'aménagement du temps de travail.* Paris: National Assembly, second ordinary session 1986–87.

CHAPTER 4

'WOMEN'S FACTORY NIGHT WORK' IN GERMANY

Changing Classification Schemes in Varying Environments, 1891–1994

Theresa Wobbe and Katja Karolin Müller

Introduction

Since the nineteenth century, the regulation of working time has been a fundamental dimension of the emerging labour market system. The distinguishing of work and non-work into separate social fields reveals the system's external differentiation, while the various arrangements of working hours are connected to the system's internal differentiation across Europe. As early as 1839, when the Prussian state started to regulate labour conditions, child labour (under nine years) was banned, while juveniles' working time in factories was restricted to ten hours, since working for longer periods ruined the young men's health, making them unfit for the army. These legal provisions would become the starting point of the history of the regulation of working time in Germany, a process which in the late nineteenth century resulted in the introduction of social security and protective measures administered by welfare institutions. In 1891, the revision of the Industrial Code also included a prohibition on female factory night work, and it restricted the length of the working day for women workers to a maximum of eleven hours (§137). By addressing female workers with responsibilities for the household, the codification also provided for half an hour's break in addition to the mealtime (ibid.).

Even though legislation for women was connected to (international) competition rules and the effort to protect male workers' wages against the 'cheaper' wages of female workers, the Industrial Code did point to lurking sexual dangers that could be inflicted on health or morals (§139a). At the same time, women factory workers were categorized along with young workers and children as 'non-adults' who were 'in practice or by law incapable of making decisions on their own behalf' (Brentano 1873: 17), consequently requiring state intervention. They were excluded by their age or gender category from the right of association, whereas the revision of the Industrial Code in 1891 granted male industrial workers freedom of association (Canning 2006; Wobbe 2012; for Europe, North America and Australia, see Wikander, Kessler-Harris, and Lewis 1995).

One hundred years later, when the regulations on working time were restructured and standardized, the ban on female factory night work was abolished. Today, however, night work and its twin – 'evening work' – constitute an important and steadily growing portion of the labour market. According to the German Statistical Office, the share of gainful workers in evening work (between 6pm and 11pm) grew from 15.5% in 1992 to 25.2% in 2016. Over the same period, the share of night workers (between 11pm and 6am) increased from 7.6% to 8.5%. Men work at night nearly twice as often (10.8%) than women (5.8%).[1] Across the European Union (EU current composition), the portion of the total employed population usually in night work declined from 7.5% in 2007 to 5.4% in 2017.[2]

Meanwhile, the concept of time itself underwent a fundamental change. During the 1990s, the use and coordination of time became an issue of employees' individual flexibility and management. International competition has prevailed, although changing categories, classification systems, rights and key terms – flexibility, mobility, equal treatment and non-discrimination – have taken centre stage. They reflect the internal differentiation of the modern labour market system, its mechanisms of inclusion and exclusion, but also changing structures, social problems and economic expectations (see Wobbe's, Bussmann's, Höroldt's and Renard's chapter in this book).

In this chapter, we will use the example of 'women's factory night work' in German labour law to discuss the transformations indicated by these issues. Since gender and work are institutionalized cultural models, legal categorization can provide instructive insight into how classifications inform our perception of reality in specific ways, rather than merely reflecting it. In studying the issue of women's factory night work, we investigate to what extent classifications of work, over the course of the twentieth century, played a significant role in the restructuring of gender relations, while gender was in turn determining, limiting and changing who was included in the labour market system.

We argue that the twentieth century experienced two significant transitional periods of legal categorization as regards working time. The first is marked by the establishment of sexually coded classification schemes around 1900, and the second is marked by its abandonment in Germany and other European countries over the 1990s. When compared, the two periods appear to indicate different cognitive possibilities in regard to work and gender, different constellations of actors and different driving economic forces – not unlike night work in France (see Lallement's chapter in this book). Nevertheless, this is by no means a self-evident or determinate development. In the German context, the National Socialist classifications of work, working time and gender are distinct both from the older and the subsequent legal categorizations because of the enforcement of a racial taxonomy (Bock 1993; Hachtmann 1998; Schulz 1998).

This chapter is organized in two parts. In the first part, the two transitional periods and the break that occurred during National Socialism will be analysed with respect to the classification systems for time regulation (1). Against this backdrop, we will discuss the findings concerning the changes between the respective periods. Among other questions, we ask whether reiterated problem solving (Haydu 1998) can be observed, and in what kind of social regime the second transitional period begins (2). In the following, we do not take an underlying continuity or persistence of gender designations for granted, but instead explore gender's contingent configurations.

The source materials consulted include labour law codifications, European and international law, including case law, parliamentary debates and recommendations from public actors such as employer organizations, trade unions, feminist lawyers and so on. In methodological terms, this material was elaborated with respect to the reference system of interpretations and concerning the guiding categorical distinctions within the respective classification system.

Regulating Working Time in Varying Classification Systems

Around 1900, women's factory night work came to be codified in the national labour laws of European states as a means of protective labour legislation. We will discuss this historical moment of institutionalization, and then investigate the National Socialist classifications of work, working time and gender. In the last section of this part, we will discuss how and why the night ban on women's factory work was abrogated, along with the remaining National Socialist regulation, in 1994. Finally, we will discuss the category by which both schemes were replaced.

Regulating Working Time: 'Protecting' Women's Factory Night Work around 1900

With the founding of the German Empire as a nation-state in 1870–71, a national framework was established for responses to the 'social question'. In this new frame of reference, social policy-oriented university professors and civil servants founded the Verein für Socialpolitik, the Social Policy Association (1872–73) (Gorges 1980). They strove to apply their expertise to the task of advancing responses to the 'social question' in politics and scholarship. The founding of the nation provided both official statistics and the social sciences with completely new stimuli to regulate the social. Two aspects of this deserve emphasis. First, the emergence of the social brought with it a new domain of phenomena and problems, a field of specific 'trans-individual structures, identities, culture and social needs and risks' (Steinmetz 1993: 1). Second, because this new field posed a threat to order, it raised 'the "social question" or, rather, a series of social questions' (ibid.: 2; for more detail, see ibid.: 55ff.).

Three phases of the debate can be distinguished. Between 1848 and 1880, the problem of pauperism came to be superseded by the *Arbeiterfrage*, the 'worker question'. Between 1885 and 1900, the second phase, social reform and social policy came to the fore. The 'social question of women's work' now became 'a volatile public controversy' (Canning 2006: 144). The last phase, between 1900 and 1914, was marked by endeavours to deal with the problems that had arisen since 1884. As Kathleen Canning (2006: 141; 1996) has shown, this concern for social order was deeply marked by interpretive patterns based on gender binaries: if measures directed at male workers were determined in the semantic field of law and insurance, at the heart of measures directed at female workers was a discourse of protection. The mechanisms of social safety nets – especially for male industrial workers – took shape in the social insurance laws of 1883, 1884 and 1889, and in terms of labour legislation in a revision to the Industrial Code granting freedom of association (see Ritter 1998). In the debates around protective labour legislation, female factory workers were the target group for measures aiming to restrict their access to the labour market and to place their health as women under state protection.

The efforts of the Verein für Socialpolitik to regulate women's industrial labour belong to the second period, too. In the course of the association's first hearings in 1872, social scientist Lujo Brentano addressed the question of labour protection, claiming that Germany, unlike England, suffered from a lack of knowledge about the internal life of the factory.[3] Factory inspectors should therefore be charged with acquiring knowledge of industrial working conditions and reporting back to the Reichstag.

For Brentano, the state thus has no business intervening 'in the working hours of adult male workers' (Brentano 1873: 17), whereas in the case of what he calls 'non-adults' (the children, youngsters and women) state intervention is necessary in the field of regulating working time (ibid.). His distinction between the male worker, independent in labour law, and the female worker, in need of protection, is based on the priority of their distinct role obligations in marriage and the family.

While invoking a principle by which the role of women's gainful work is irreconcilable with that of motherhood, he argues: 'And in what frame of mind would a mother directly participating in battles against her employers raise her children? Truly, to leave woman to look after herself ... would mean poisoning the springs of the family and society' (Brentano 1873: 18). Female workers are conceived of as the ones bearing primary responsibility for the family context in which male workers exercise their personal rule as the breadwinner and head of the household. In this arrangement of family, gender and work, the very existence of female employment is considered a problem. In the course of these social policy debates and enquiries, the 'woman worker' became a visible and problematic discursive figure with a specific social definition of its behaviour (Scott 1993).

Around 1900, special laws regulating women's factory work were passed in all European countries as well as in North America and Australia. Due to the regulation of international competition rules and the efforts to protect male workers' wages against lower female workers' wages, intergovernmental conferences were held between 1890 and 1914. At their basis, these amounted to a restriction or prohibition of factory work, combined with various measures for maternity protection; in Europe, the prohibition of women's night work formed the focus of such legislation (Wikander, Kessler-Harris, and Lewis 1995).[4]

In Germany, the first steps were taken with the 1878 reform of the Industrial Code. In the wake of the Kaiser's 'new course' in social policy and the repeal of the Socialist Laws, in 1891 a further revision of the Industrial Code was carried out,[5] adding detail to the prohibition on night work and setting the maximum length of the working day for women at eleven hours (§137). The definition of night work encompassed the period from 8.30pm to 5.30am as well as on Saturday and the eve of festive days from 5.30pm. It also imposed a four-week ban on work for new mothers, to be extended for a further two weeks if no medical certificate could be provided; in addition, for those female workers over sixteen 'who have a household to care for' (§137), a one-hour midday break was to be provided, which could be extended by a further half hour upon application. Differently from the French regulation, the German codification prohibited the night work of female factory workers. Within the legal text, this measure constitutes a part of the section regulating the relations between industrial workers.

Finally, the revision aimed to ensure that the sexes were spatially separated as much as possible (§120b). The obligation to undergo training at state-recognized continuation schools, already applicable to male workers, was extended to female workers, in this case at schools 'teaching female handiwork and housework' (§120). The establishment of housekeeping schools allowed the state to institutionalize two separate models of training. On the one hand, the legal framework imposed a practical household training and, as Canning puts it, 'certified the improvement of working women's domestic skills as a long-term solution for the new social question of female factory work' (Canning 1996: 127). On the other hand, it created a firm legal basis for vocational training, which taught young men writing, technical drawing and arithmetic as well as commercial knowledge and related subjects (see Canning 2006: 154). The legal restriction of women's work was spelled out, and the partial separation by gender categories was delineated in more concrete terms.

What is remarkable is how few women were actually affected by working time restrictions. By the middle of the 1880s, four thousand women out of one and a half million female wage workers performed regular night work all year round or worked nights on an irregular basis due to overtime in the textile industry or as seasonal workers (Ayaß 2000: 195). Moreover, according to the Reich's enquiry of 1899, only 28% of female wage workers were married (ibid.: 206). By contrast, the majority of gainfully occupied women in the German Empire worked as family workers (see Renard's chapter in this book), in domestic services, in farming, in smaller manufacturing firms and in the service industry (Hausen 1997: 721; Willms 1983). Across Europe, the debates about women's night work all dealt with the issues of nation, race and reproduction (Bock 2002; Wikander, Kessler-Harris, and Lewis 1995). In this respect, the ban on female night work gained a highly symbolic function for the gendered coding of the labour market as such. While only affecting female factory workers, it evoked the designation of 'all women' in assigning them primary responsibility for family, health and reproduction (Berkovitch 1999; Wobbe, Renard, and Müller 2017).

It cannot go without notice that in the same period, around 1900, the socio-structural conditions for the separation of the sexes were gradually crumbling. The proportion of female industrial workers doubled between 1882 and 1925, while the number and visibility of women in commerce and in the service industries increased enormously. At the same time, young single women were abandoning the field of domestic service (see Willms 1983: 48ff.; ibid.: 47, Figure 3).

To sum up, this section has addressed a period of transition during which the emerging labour system's internal differentiation manifested a gender-coded regulation of working time. The Industrial Code granted the right of association to male factory workers (§134d) without reducing their working time, which then was a core issue of the labour movement. By contrast, female workers' time was restricted on the basis of their primary duty to the family, even while women were classified as non-adults and placed in the same category as children and juveniles (Berkovitch 1999; Wobbe 2012).

The Classification System of Race and Nation in the National Socialist War Economy

From 1924 to 1994, the *Arbeitszeitordnung* (AZO, Working time regulation) constituted the regulative framework of German labour law – first in the Weimar Republic, then during National Socialism, and finally in both the Federal Republic of Germany (FRG) and the German Democratic Republic (GDR). Over the seventy years of its existence, the AZO displayed radical discontinuities, but also incorporated some of the directives of the different political systems it served, especially during the Nazi period (Hachtmann 1998).

By the last years of the Weimar Republic, labour rights and the eight-hour day had already been partially undone. When the Nazis came to power, whatever rights still remained were rescinded. The first law they introduced targeted Jewish civil servants (they were all dismissed) and political enemies in the civil service. This law did not yet include workers on the shop floor, but many employers nonetheless took it as an invitation to get rid of their Jewish employees (Majer 1987: 193). A year later, the *Gesetz zur Ordnung der Nationalen Arbeit* (AOG, Law regulating national work) enabled systematic state regulation and a radical reorganization of the shop floor.

The establishment of the Nazi *Führer*-principle in the workplace enabled a synchronization of economy and work with the state. Imposed as the firm's Führer, the boss made the decisions while the workers, organized as a 'firm community' (§1 AOG), had to obey him for the sake of the

Volk and the Nazi state. In this way the private character of the firm as well as individual and collective labour rights were abolished. The firm's leader was invested with unrestricted power, while the workers were subordinated in a fiduciary relationship without any contractual basis (§2 AOG). Basic labour rights ceased to exist (Hachtmann 1998: 41).

The Nazi Führer-principle uprooted the relationship that had existed between employers and employees. Their relationship now rested on the racial category of the *Volksgemeinschaft* (Community of the Volk) (Majer 1987: 193). This category by no means conceived of society as the entire realm of the social, but instead denoted a racist community that per definition excluded people classified as 'non-Aryan' (ibid.). Jews, Sinti, Roma and *Fremdvölkische* (foreigners) thus found themselves on the outside.

Not only did the notion of Volk represent a racist ideology, it was also a legal category. While excluding foreign workers (foreigners), socially non-conformant people (thieves and prostitutes) and political opponents, it applied protective measures at work only to German *Volksgenossen* (comrades of the Volk) (Hachtmann 1998: 28). More laws followed suit. They abolished the citizenship and marriage rights of Jews, Sinti and Roma and prohibited them from marrying 'people of German or similar blood'. From now on, German nationality was for 'people of German or similar blood' who moreover 'had given proof to be willing and fit to serve the German Volk'.[6]

A new regulation on working time (AZO) introduced in 1938 pushed the concepts of Führer and *Volksgemeinschaft* even further. It no longer treated employer and employee as contractual categories, but established a core category of *Gefolgschaftsmitglieder*, workers with an allegiance to the boss. The heightened protective measures for women (§16–21 AZO) now addressed these *Gefolgschaftsmitglieder* exclusively and left all other women out (for maternity protection, see Wobbe's, Bussman's, Höroldt's, and Renard's chapter in this book). Therefore, time regulations, in particular protective measures, addressed 'German' women following the racial meaning of the notion *Gefolgschaftsmitglieder*. The ban on factory night work was extended to all sectors. At the outbreak of the war, working time measures for men were suspended altogether, and for women in part. The ban on night work was abrogated (Hachtmann 1993: 343). From 1939, another time regulation was introduced. In order to mobilize 'German' women for industrial labour, the NS regime extended part-time work. The regime also succeeded in keeping women in full-time work by introducing factory kindergartens, additional social provisions and twice monthly days off for washing and housework (ibid.: 346f.; Sachse 1994).

After the outbreak of war, Jews became subject to the Imperial Administration and the Security Police (SS) (Majer 1987: 196). The 'closed work unit' ordinance of 1938, issued after the November pogroms, initially stipulated obligatory labour only for Jewish males, while the 'closed work unit' decree of 1939 introduced forced labour for all Jews. From 1941 until 1943, they were deported from the forced labour camps to death camps (Gruner 1997). Also after the outbreak of war, 'non-Aryan' female and male workers (ibid.), particularly war prisoners and forced labourers from the occupied countries as well as civilian *Fremdarbeiter* (foreign workers), were forced to do heavy work in the arms, electricity and machine industries (Hachtmann 1993: 348f.).[7] From 1940 to 1944, the share of foreigners in the total workforce of these industries rose from between 1 and 2% to between 23 and 40% by mid 1944 (ibid.: 348). Altogether, the consumer goods industry remained a domain of 'German' women while the share of foreign women was minimal (ibid.; Table 6: 366).

In 1943, the day off for housework was incorporated in the Nazi leisure time order (*Freizeitanordnung*). As in the case of the 1938 AZO, the order of 1943, according to its racialized rationales, excluded Jewish women and forced labour workers (Sachse 1994: 35–47). One-third of female workers in the war industry, namely 'fremdrassige' (foreign races) forced labour workers and prisoners of concentration camps, were excluded from the day off regulation (ibid.: 47).

Forced labourers were subjected to a racist hierarchy in which Northern and Western Europeans found themselves at the top, Russian and Polish workers were treated as inferior, and Jewish workers were trodden upon (Hachtmann 1993: 349). No protective measures or time regulations applied to any of these workers, including pregnant women and mothers. The National Socialist rise to power marked a radical change in the labour market system and in labour law. A racial taxonomy of 'inferior' and 'superior' human beings legitimized particular laws and forced labour. The previous categories of female and male workers, as well as the working time regulation and protective measures for pregnant women, women in childbirth and mothers, no longer applied.

Regulating Working Time in the Classification System of Economic Efficiency, Flexibility and Equal Treatment

It is noteworthy that the AZO remained in force in FRG labour law until the early 1990s, even though the German constitution (1949) had introduced human rights principles of non-discrimination, and the regulations of the NS secretary of labour had been repealed in 1951 (Drucksache Nr. 2952). The 1993 draft of the law for a new regulation of working time aimed at standardizing protective health measures for all workers according to the equal treatment principle while also abolishing the ban on women's night work. 'At the same time', the AZO of 1938 was to be replaced on the grounds that 'the whole labour law has to be liberated from NS terminology' (Drucksache 12/5888: 2020). When the new law on working time became effective one year later, it also incorporated the European Equal Treatment Directive (76/207/EEC) of 1976 as well as the decision of the German Constitutional Court to dissolve the ban on night work for women factory workers (BVerfGE 85, 191: 206).

In 1981, the German parliament took up the reform of working time regulations. Both parties, the Christian Democrats and the Social Democrats, agreed that heavy manual labour had declined since the interwar period and given way to an increase in lighter work. Therefore, protective measures for women had to be evaluated with regard to their appropriateness to current factory conditions, on the one hand, and to their discriminatory potential, on the other (Plenarprotokoll 9/22). The Christian Democratic Party advocated repealing the night ban since it restricted employment opportunities for women, whereas the Social Democrats favoured its retention along with protections for both women and men workers (ibid.: 979–983). In any case, the criteria for further legislation had to be interrogated with respect to the changed technological conditions of work and health. An ergonomic study was requested, which ended up constituting the first decisive thread on the path to new legislation.

According to the findings of the study, night work affected both women's and men's health in similar ways (Rutenfranz, Beermann, and Löwenthal 1987). The report only identified differences in the effects of night work on men and women with respect to the sleep deficit between females and males. In particular, women with toddlers were expected to experience more sleep problems, which in turn could result in greater health risks for them. The report stated that the phenomenon did not relate directly to the strain of labour, but was instead a result of the different distribution of social roles between the sexes in the private sphere. The experts' conclusion appears ambivalent in indicating that there were no 'assured findings' regarding differing effects of night work on men and women, indicating instead only a 'well-grounded suspicion' that women, due to their social obligations, are more vulnerable during night work than men (ibid.: 56). The umbrella organization of the trade unions recommended retaining protective measures on the basis of women's particular burden regarding family responsibilities (DGB 1988).

Changing technological conditions, labour market relations and Germany's competitive position in the emerging internal market (including high unemployment figures in Germany and across Europe) formed the second basis for legal revision. During the 1970s, the Fordist production and time regime underwent fundamental changes, which became manifest in the deregulation between state and market (Offe, Hinrichs, and Wiesenthal 1982). As the micro-census figures for 1989 suggest, the demand for night work overall had increased from 1975 to 1989 (64.5%) in Germany, for men (82.9%) and for women (56.2%) (Schiek 1992: 86). According to a survey carried out by the European Commission in 1989, night work was performed by 14% of the gainfully occupied population in the European Community (twelve member states) (ibid.: 91). In 2016, 43% of employers and 24% of employees worked during the evening, and 8.9% over the night in Germany.[8] From the 1950s, the demand for part-time work increased because of the post-war growth economy. By the 1960s this time working scheme became accepted as a scheme for married women and mothers (see Wobbe's, Bussmann's, Höroldt's and Renard's chapter in this book).

These shifts were reflected in the new notion of flexibility, which placed working time in an altogether different reference system (Promberger 2005: 28). In promoting competitive advantage, flexibility also legitimized the reduction of jobs. The Christian Democratic government insisted on the deregulation of barriers to flexibility, and argued that restrictions were justified only on the basis of 'the framework of health requirements to be defined by collective agreements' (Plenarprotokoll 11/53, 1988: 3736). According to the Christian Democrats, more flexibility would also result in more individual self-determination (ibid.: 3737). In the early 1980s, employers' organizations had started demanding flexible working times in collective agreements in order to ensure they could better adjust to market dynamics (Promberger 2005). The Social Democrats in turn argued that the state has a social policy and family policy responsibility to constrain flexibility to a minimum, instead of undermining already achieved standards (Plenarprotokoll 11/53, 1988: 3739).

The legislation also aimed to adapt to the equal treatment principle and to make German labour law consistent with the European Equal Treatment Directive of 1976. Particular protective measures were only to be maintained as necessary to 'protect against gender-specific exposures' (Drucksache 11/360: 1–2). This legislative process resulted in the working time law (ArbZRG 1994), which aimed at the standardization and flexibilization of the working time right. To this end, it introduced minimal protective health and security standards for *all* workers and employees (for the first time) according to the European equal treatment principle. The day off for housework was abolished (ArbZRG 1994, Art. 19) along with the protective measures (on the day off for housework from 1939 to 1994, see Sachse 1994). Simultaneously, particular measures for pregnant women and women in childbirth were excluded from this law and transferred to maternity regulations.[9]

The timing and the language of the national working time legislation are, thus, embedded in a European and international field of legal norms, which constitutes a third component of the reclassification. Beginning in the 1970s, International Labour Organization (ILO) member states abolished the night ban or made a multitude of exemptions (ILO 1989a). Due to economic rationales, member states found it difficult to retain the night ban and announced a recall of the existing ILO Convention No. 89 (1948) (ibid.: 85). In the course of drafting the revision of that convention, it became clear that almost all member states asked to increase the flexibility of the working time regulation (ILO 1989b). This was also true for the European Commission and member states. Many member states had already abolished the night work ban or had instituted exemptions (Schiek 1992).

In 1991, when the European Court of Justice (ECJ) decided in Stoeckel/Tribunal de police d'Illkirch[10] that national provisions forbidding women's night work were inconsistent with the principles of the Equal Treatment Directive (76/207/EEC), the French and Italian governments argued that the prohibition protected women. The ECJ, however, considered women's exclusion from work as a source of discrimination.[11]

The French government claimed that night work exposed women to the risk of violence and resulted in more and extra work in addition their family responsibilities. The ECJ, on the other hand, emphasized that according to its understanding of equal treatment, 'with regard to working conditions … men and women are to be offered the same conditions without discrimination of sex' (Art. 5 ETD 76/207). With respect to sexual assault and women's family work, the ECJ argued against general protections for women. In the event that the risks for women exceeded those for men, employers were required to take measures. As far as family responsibilities were concerned, the court strictly refused to intervene.[12] In 1992, the EU passed its directive (93/104/EC) concerning the organization of working time for all workers by providing 'minimum safety and health requirements for the organization of working time' (Art. 1).

German courts dealt with litigations concerning women's factory night work from the 1960s to the 1990s. In 1992, the German Constitutional Court decided that the night ban violated both the EU principles of equal treatment and the German constitution's equal opportunity principle

(Art. 3 German Constitution) and the free choice of profession principle (Art. 12 GG) (BVerfGE 85, 191). From this perspective, the protective measure discriminated against women factory workers not only as compared to males, but also with respect to female clerical workers and civil servants (ibid.).

Previous approaches to regulation and protection based on the eight-hour day had aimed to reduce the amount of time worked overall. Flexibility indicated a reorganization and reclassification of working time in terms of duration, location and distribution. Flexibility meant the decoupling of workplace and working time, and thus the dissolution of the presumed normalcy of the eight-hour day (Klenner and Pfahl 2005; Promberger 2005).

Discussion of the Findings

In this chapter we have investigated the classification schemes of working time and the significance of the regulation of working time for the restructuring of gender relations, while gender was in turn determining, limiting and changing who was included in the labour market system.

The example of women's factory night work evinces three different classification systems during the twentieth century (see Table 4.1). Around 1900, the working time of (wage) workers was classified according to sexual difference. The notion of women's factory work was situated on the outer edge of the inclusion range, while the category of work, that is, largely male industrial work, was placed at the emerging centre of wage work inclusion (Wobbe 2012). During the 1990s, the category of working time spanned all sectors as well as all gainfully employed by introducing minimum standards of health and safety for them. The previous sexually coded taxonomy was replaced by a more abstract scheme transgressing former particular categories. Now, the notion of the worker became the core personnel category of the labour force, which was distinguished from categories in other social systems such as the pupil and the university student in education, and the voter in the political system. The labour market system's internal differentiation, thus, indicates an increasing self-referentiality. Together with this, the guiding classifications became gender neutral and more inclusive in that former particular categories had been dissolved. The altered concept of the worker incorporates a diversity of dimensions such as gender, age, migration, disability, nationality and so on.

In contrast to these transitional periods, the scheme under National Socialism was fundamentally different. Its guiding categories were race and nationality, which rest upon the classification system of 'inferiority' and 'superiority'. This taxonomy of racial policy became institutionalized not only in the fields of economy and work, but instead permeated every area of society (such as science, sport, polity, law etc.), superimposing sexual difference.

Finally, the discussed classification systems indicate reiterated problem solving (Haydu 1998) inasmuch as the challenge of social reproduction and the issue of economic competition prevail, although institutional constellations have changed. The case of the day off for housework exemplifies the delicate issue of social reproduction. From 1871, work time regulation reflected this social problematic in the emerging welfare state, whereas in National Socialism it became the issue of racial policy. When in 1994 the day off was abolished, the problematic of social reproduction disappeared from the context of working time schemes and was transferred to individual arrangements in gender relations. This case illuminates the paradoxes of gender-neutral working time regulation, pointing to both its impact on everyday gender relations and its consequences for social reproduction (see Rai, Hoskyns, and Thomas 2014).

The issue of economic competition also prevails, even though the social conditions and actor configurations have changed. Measures around 1900 referred to competition between national states resulting in, among other things, working time regulation. Together with social provisions of the welfare state, the institutional model of the male breadwinner

Table 4.1 Shifting legal classification schemes.

	Around 1900	**NS 1933–45**	**Since 1990s**
Guiding classification	(Male) industrial worker vs. the woman worker	'Inferior' vs. 'superior' 'German' vs. 'non-Aryan'	Worker (gainfully occupied) vs. not (gainfully occupied) worker
Labour market	Formation period of national labour market	War economy	Established (trans) national labour markets
State/market	Foundation welfare state	Synchronization *Gleichschaltung*	Deregulation state and market
Expertise	Social reform, social sciences	Eugenics	Economic and medical knowledge
Rationales	Social prevention, gender-coded treatment	'Unequal value, unequal rights'	Economic efficiency, flexibility, equal treatment
→ Reiterating problematic of social reproduction and economic competition			

emerged wherein social reproduction was predominantly assigned to the economically dependent wife. From the 1980s, in the course of economic globalization and competition, state-market and gender relations (see Orloff 1996) underwent a shift. Ever since, more tasks of social reproduction have been both commodified and privatized due to deregulation and cutbacks in social provisions. Competition at a European and global level, thus, reflects the welfare state's deregulation within a dense net of transnational economic regimes and legal codifications.

Furthermore, our findings suggest a shift in cognitive possibilities between the first and the second transitional periods. During the first period, a binary scheme of sexual difference played a role in factory working time regulation, whereas in the 1990s this scheme was replaced by the notions of flexibility and competitiveness. Within the latter model, the rationales of the production system (utilization of shifting technological infrastructures etc.) together with the promotion of competitiveness come to the fore. Importance is placed on the availability of workers and their capacity to be flexible, along with their health and the security of the work environment. In contrast to the period around 1900, the gendered coding of work and working time was abandoned. This does not automatically imply social equality between the sexes, since different conditions prevail, such as the large share of women in part-time work (see Lechevalier's chapter in this book) and the 'doing domestic time' (Wajcman 2015) responsibility for social reproduction (see Wobbe's, Höroldt's, Bussmann's, and Renard's chapter in this book). Thus, the cessation of gendered measures does not automatically bring about equal opportunities for both sexes. As the discontinuation of the day off for housework in the legislation of 1994 illuminates, the wicked problem of sharing the housework between the sexes stays with us.

The first transitional period is indicative of the formation of the labour market system, whereas the second period documents a self-reference to that already established market system within a transnational economic field and legal order. As the night work example shows, both of them display new characteristics. While women were considered second-class workers around 1900, and their inclusion was thus limited by sexual difference, today they are considered both human capital and persons with individual rights to the same extent as men. Their share in atypical employment, in contrast to regular and full-time work, has increased from 23 to 31% over the period from 1991 to 2016 (Statistisches Jahrbuch 2017, Arbeitsmarkt: 358). The case of working time regulation therefore suggests that inequality between the sexes is reproduced by structural inequalities such as that between full-time work and part-time work while the impact of social reproduction on gender relations persists.

Conclusion

In this chapter, we have raised the example of the working time regulation of women's factory night work to explore the implied transitions that have taken place since the period around 1900. By putting legal categorization as institutionalized cultural models we enquired to what extent they both reflect and push the restructuring of gender relations. From a historical-sociological perspective we studied the long-term entanglements and short-term configurations (Zimmermann 2006: 23ff., 254ff., 2015) of 'women's factory night work', which reframed the notions of working time regulation and gender. While classical welfare state research (Esping-Andersen 1990) focuses on the second part of the twentieth century, the methodological strategy of this chapter was to follow the category over a long-term period. By doing so we reconstructed the historicity of the controversies and discovered shifting meanings in institutional configurations. The altering legal classification schemes show two transitional periods with respect to the labour market, state/market, expertise and driving rationales around 1900 and since the 1990s. The Nazi racial taxonomy was fundamentally different. During the 1990s, female labour-specific categories were dissolved and replaced by gender-neutral classifications. One case in particular – the day off for household work – documents the impact of deregulation on gender relations. It exemplifies the costs of individualization and gender-neutral categories with respect to social reproduction.

The chosen research design broadens the focus not only in time, but also with respect to cases in comparison. Since the working time regulation was explored in another study for France over the same period (see Lallement's chapter in this book), the German example could be put in perspective. We find that in the evolution of German legal categories during the twentieth century, the classification schemes that were used were different from those on which the French working time regulation was based. By taking the discontinuities in the German history of working time regulation into consideration, we identified various schemes. From the conventional national comparative perspective of social policy literature, the German case is considered an example of a particular 'conservative' welfare model after 1945 (Esping-Andersen 1990). Turning to an intra-national perspective, focusing only on the history of German working time regulation brings various types of social policy into view (Hockerts 1998), providing evidence for different arguments about categories.

Nevertheless, working time regulation in the French and German contexts shares some significant patterns. Around 1900, problems of international competition in labour were resolved by restricting working time for a particular group of women workers who were viewed as competing with male workers. From this view, the ban or restriction of women's work was understood as an improvement of male workers' social situation. In this context, the state took on a paternalistic role, partially replacing the position of the husband (Schiek 1992).

However, our results do not suggest a German *Sonderweg*. On the contrary, they point to historically contingent breaks and discontinuities that became decisive for the regulation of working time. The second transitional period is a historically specific outcome of the world's restructuring after World War II, the outcome of which was not clear even by 1941. Against this background of shifting cultural concepts and social transformations, our findings also point to changed constellations of actors and rescaling processes. Between the first and second transitional periods, national labour market systems and legal categories were increasingly embedded in and affected by transnational structures. As we have shown here, arguments about the night work ban were closely connected to Germany's location within the emerging internal market as well as in international and European labour law. Thus, over the twentieth century, the creation and re-creation of categories itself underwent a substantial transformation that, in turn, was closely tied to changes in the distinctions generated by legal classifications, and in this respect also to the internal differentiation of the economic and labour market system.

Theresa Wobbe is Professor Emerita of Sociology at the University of Potsdam, and fellow of the Margherita von Brentano Centre for Gender Studies at the Free University of Berlin. She specializes in historical sociology, sociology of knowledge, institutionalist gender analysis, and sociology of classification. Her research focuses on long-term transformations of gender and work, international statistics as an instrument of globalization, and the making of gender as a global category of comparison. Her current projects deal with the ILO discontinuities in the notion of forced labour, 1919–2017, and the conceptional history of gender in global political institutions.

Katja Karolin Müller MA is a PhD candidate at the University of Potsdam (Germany) and Lecturer in Sociology and Gender Studies at Humboldt-Universität zu Berlin and at the University of Potsdam. Her research focuses on the sociology of gender and work and the major significance of gender categorization and ascription for institutional effects in the labour market. She worked for the Agence Nationale de la Recherche (ANR) and the Deutsche Forschungsgemeinschaft (DFG) project 'Metamorphoses of Equality II (1945–2010)' (Potsdam/CNAM-Lise Paris). She has recently published, with Theresa Wobbe and Léa Renard, 'Nationale und globale Deutungsmodelle des Geschlechts im arbeitsstatistischen sowie arbeitsrechtlichen Klassifikationssystem: Ein vergleichstheoretischer Beitrag (1882–1992)' in *Soziale Welt* (2017).

Notes

1. DESTATIS, Qualität der Arbeit. Geld verdienen und was sonst noch zählt, Wiesbaden, p.26. https://www.destatis.de/DE/Publikationen/Thematisch/Arbeitsmarkt/Erwerbstaetige/BroschuereQualitaetArbeit0010015179004.pdf?__blob=publicationFile (accessed 10 November 2018).
2. Eurostat, Employed persons working at nights as a percentage of the total employment, by sex, age and professional status (%) (https://ec.europa.eu/eurostat/web/products-datasets/product?code=LFSA_EWPNIG (accessed 8 November 2018).
3. Among the reasons Brentano gives for the deficits in Germany is 'the nature of the organs that are supposed to carry out the monitoring' (Brentano 1873: 9), namely the local police authorities, who often collaborated with the factory owners and failed to fulfil their task of providing information on working conditions.
4. Night work was prohibited in Switzerland in 1877, in Britain and Germany in 1878, in France in 1892, in Sweden in 1909, in Spain in 1912, in Russia in 1905 and in the Soviet Union in 1918. In Britain, women's working hours were restricted to twelve hours in 1844 and to ten hours in 1847, in France to eleven hours in 1892, in Italy to twelve hours in 1902, and similarly in twenty states of the USA between 1909 and 1917 (Bock 2002).
5. Gesetz betreffend Abänderung der Gewerbeordnung vom 1. Juni 1891 (Law on the Revision of the Industrial Code, 1 June 1891).
6. Reichsbürgergesetz und Gesetz zum Schutze des deutschen Blutes und der deutschen Ehre ['Nürnberger Gesetze'], 15 September 1935, *Reichsgesetzblatt* 1935 I, p. 1146, and the two implementation regulations, 14 November 1935, *Reichsgesetzblatt* 1935 I, p. 1333.
7. As Hachtmann (1993, 1998) underscores, the distinction between the categories of 'civilian' and war prisoners broke down.
8. DESTATIS, 'Qualität der Arbeit: Dimension 3: Arbeitszeit, Ausgleich von Beruf und Privatleben', https://www.destatis.de/DE/ZahlenFakten/GesamtwirtschaftUmwelt/Arbeitsmarkt/_Doorpage/Indikatoren_QualitaetDerArbeit.html?cms_gtp=318944_slot%253D3 (accessed 6 June 2018).
9. In 1997, the maternity protection regulation (MuSchArbV) was adopted (BGBl. I p. 782), then, in 2002, the maternity protection law was adopted (BGBl. I p. 2318). Also, a general labour law protection (Arbeitsschutzgesetz) was adopted in 1996 regulating altogether measures beyond the time regulation (BGBl. I p. 1246).
10. Case 345/89 Stoeckel/Tribunal de police d'Illkirch [1991] ECR.
11. Ibid., 19.
12. Ibid., 17.

References

Primary Sources

Federal Law on Working Time Law

Draft Law

Drucksache Nr. 2952 – 1951: Entwurf eines Gesetzes über die Aufhebung von Vorschriften auf dem Gebiete des Arbeitsschutzes.

Drucksache 11/1617 – 1988: Gesetzentwurf der Fraktion der SPD, Entwurf eines Arbeitszeitgesetzes (ArbZG).

Statements

DGB (1988) – Stellungnahme zum Entwurf eines Arbeitszeitgesetzes, Typoskript in Auszügen veröffentlicht in: Archiv Arbeit im Betrieb.

Law

Gesetz, betreffend Abänderung der Gewerbeordnung (*Order of Trade*), *Reichsgesetzblatt* Bd. 1891, No. 18, pp. 261–90.

ArbZRG (1994): Gesetz zur Vereinheitlichung und Flexibilisierung des Arbeitszeitrechts (Arbeitszeitrechtsgesetz – ArbZRG) (*Working Time Law*), 6 June 1994, in *Bundesgesetzblatt* Part I, pp. 1170–83.

Minutes of Plenary Proceedings (Plenarprotokolle)

Plenarprotokoll 9/22 – 18 February 1981.

Plenarprotokoll 11/5 – 19 March 1987.

Plenarprotokoll 11/53 – 15 January 1988.

Plenarprotokoll 12/108 – 25 September 1992.

Plenarprotokoll 12/110 –8 October 1992.

Plenarprotokoll 12/183 – 22 October 1993.

Official documents (Drucksachen)

Drucksache 11/360 – 1987.

Drucksache 11/1188 – 1988.

Drucksache 11/1617 – 1988.

Drucksache 12/2412 – 1992.

Drucksache 12/5888 – 1993.

Judgements

BVerfGE 85, 191 – Nachtarbeitsverbot.

BVerfGE 5, 9 – Frauenarbeitszeit.

Secondary Sources

Ayaß, W. 2000. '"Der Übel größtes": Das Verbot der Nachtarbeit von Arbeiterinnen in Deutschland (1891–1992)', *Zeitschrift für Sozialreform* 46: 189–220.

Berkovitch, N. 1999. *From Motherhood to Citizenship: Women's Rights and International Organizations*. Baltimore, MD: Johns Hopkins University Press.

Bock, G. 1993. 'Gleichheit und Differenz in der nationalsozialistischen Rassenpolitik', *Geschichte und Gesellschaft* 19(3): 277–310.

________. 2002. *Women in European History*, trans. Allison Brown. Oxford: Blackwell.

Brentano, L. von. 1873. 'Referat. Fabrikgesetzgebung', in Ständiger Ausschuss des Vereins für Socialpolitik (eds), *Verhandlungen der Eisenacher Versammlung zur Besprechung der socialen Frage am 6. und 7. Oktober 1872*. Leipzig: Duncker & Humblot, pp. 8–29.

Canning, K. 1996. *Languages of Labor and Gender: Female Factory Work in Germany, 1850–1914*. Ithaca, NY: Cornell University Press.

_______. 2006. *Gender History in Practice: Historical Perspectives on Bodies, Class and Citizenship*. Ithaca, NY: Cornell University Press.

Esping-Andersen, G. 1990. *The Three Worlds of Welfare Capitalism*. Cambridge: Polity Press.

Gorges, I. 1980. *Sozialforschung in Deutschland 1872–1914*. Schriften des Wissenschaftszentrums Berlin, vol. 14. Meisenheim: Hain.

Gruner, W. 1997. *Der geschlossene Arbeitseinsatz deutscher Juden: Zur Zwangsarbeit als Element der Verfolgung 1938–1943*. Berlin: Metropol.

Hachtmann, R. 1993. 'Industriearbeiterinnen in der deutschen Kriegswirtschaft 1936 bis 1944/45', *Geschichte und Gesellschaft* 19(3): 332–66.

_______. 1998. 'Arbeitsverfassung', in H.G. Hockerts (ed.), *Drei Wege deutscher Sozialstaatlichkeit. NS-Diktatur, Bundesrepublik und im Vergleich*. Munich: R. Oldenbourg Verlag, pp. 27–54.

Hausen, K. 1997. 'Arbeiterinnenschutz, Mutterschutz und gesetzliche Krankenversicherung im Deutschen Kaiserreich und in der Weimarer Republik: Zur Funktion von Arbeits- und Sozialrecht für die Normierung und Stabilisierung der Geschlechterverhältnisse', in U. Gerhard (ed.), *Frauen in der Geschichte des Rechts: Von der Frühen Neuzeit bis zur Gegenwart*. Munich: Beck, pp. 713–43.

Haydu, J. 1998. 'Making Use of the Past: Time Periods as Cases to Compare and as Sequences of Problem Solving', *American Journal of Sociology* 104(2): 339–71.

Hockerts, H.G. (ed.). 1998. *Drei Wege deutscher Sozialstaatlichkeit: NS-Diktatur, Bundesrepublik und DDR im Vergleich*. Munich: R. Oldenbourg Verlag.

ILO. 1989a. *International Labour Conference 76th Session 1989 Report V (1), Night Work*. Geneva: ILO.

_______. 1989b. *International Labour Conference 76th Session 1989 Report V (2), Night Work*. Geneva: ILO.

Klenner, C., and L. Pfahl. 2005. 'Stabilität und Flexibilität: Ungleichmäßige Arbeitszeitmuster und familiale Arrangements', in H. Seifert (ed.), *Flexible Zeiten in der Arbeitswelt*. Frankfurt: Campus Verlag, pp. 9–39, pp. 124–68.

Kocka, J. 1990. *Arbeitsverhältnisse und Arbeiterexistenzen: Grundlagen der Klassenbildung im 19. Jahrhundert*. Bonn: Dietz.

Majer, D. 1987. *Grundlagen des nationalsozialistischen Rechtssytems: Führerprinzip, Sonderrecht, Einheitspartei*. Stuttgart: Kohlhammer.

Offe, C., K. Hinrichs, and H. Wiesenthal (eds). 1982. *Arbeitszeitpolitik: Formen und Folgen einer Neuverteilung der Arbeitszeit*. Frankfurt/New York: Campus.

Orloff, A. 1996. 'Gender in the Welfare State', *Annual Review of Sociology* 22: 51–78.

Promberger, M. 2005. 'Wie neuartig sind flexible Arbeitszeiten? Historische Grundlinien der Arbeitszeitpolitik', in H. Seifert (ed.), *Flexible Zeiten in der Arbeitswelt*. Frankfurt: Campus Verlag, pp. 9–39.

Rai, S.M., C. Hoskyns, and D. Thomas. 2014. 'Depletion: The Cost of Social Reproduction', *International Feminist Journal of Politics* 16(1): 86–105.

Ritter, G.A. 1998. *Soziale Frage und Sozialpolitik in Deutschland seit Beginn des 19. Jahrhunderts*. Opladen: Westdeutscher Verlag.

Rutenfranz, J., B. Beermann, and I. Löwenthal. 1987. *Nachtarbeit für Frauen: Überlegungen aus chronophysiologischer und arbeitsmedizinischer Sicht*. Stuttgart: Gentner.

Sachse, C. 1994. *Der Hausarbeitstag: Gerechtigkeit und Gleichberechtigung in Ost und West 1939–1994*. Göttingen: Wallstein Verlag.

Schiek, D. 1992. *Nachtarbeitsverbot für Arbeiterinnen: Gleichberechtigung durch Deregulierung?* Baden-Baden: Nomos.

Schulz, G. 'Soziale Sicherung von Frauen und Familien', in H.G. Hockerts (ed.), *Drei Wege deutscher Sozialstaatlichkeit: NS-Diktatur, Bundesrepublik und DDR im Vergleich*. Munich: R. Oldenbourg Verlag, pp. 117–49.

Scott, J.W. 1993. 'The Woman Worker', in Geneviéve Fraisse, and Michelle Perrot (eds), *History of Women in the West*, vol. 4. Cambridge, MA: Harvard University Press, pp. 399–425.

Steinmetz, G. 1993. *Regulating the Social: The Welfare State and Local Politics in Imperial Germany*. Princeton, NJ: Princeton University Press.

Wajcman, J. 2015. *Pressed for Time: The Acceleration of Life in Digital Capitalism*. London: University of Chicago Press.

Wikander, U., A. Kessler-Harris, and J. Lewis (eds). 1995. *Protecting Women: Labour Legislation in Europe, the United States, and Australia, 1880–1920*. Champaign: University of Illinois Press.

Willms, A. 1980. *Die Entwicklung der Frauenerwerbstätigkeit im Deutschen Reich: Eine historisch-soziologische Studie*. Nuremberg: Beiträge zur Arbeitsmarkt- und Berufsforschung.

________. 1983. 'Grundzüge der Entwicklung der Frauenarbeit, 1880–1980', in W. Müller, A. Willms, and J. Handl (eds), *Frauenerwerbstätigkeit im Lebenslauf*. Frankfurt: Campus, pp. 25–54.

Wobbe, T. 2012. 'Making up People: Berufsstatistische Klassifikation, geschlechtliche Kategorisierung und wirtschaftliche Inklusion um 1900 in Deutschland', *Zeitschrift für Soziologie* 41(1): 41–57.

Wobbe, T., L. Renard, and K. Müller. 2017. 'Nationale und globale Deutungsmodelle des Geschlechts im arbeitsstatistischen sowie arbeitsrechtlichen Klassifikationssystem: Ein vergleichstheoretischer Beitrag (1882–1992)', *Soziale Welt* 68(2): 63–85.

Zimmermann, B. 2006. *Arbeitslosigkeit in Deutschland: Zur Entstehung einer sozialen Kategorie*. Frankfurt: Campus.

________. 2015. '*Socio-Histoire* and Public Policy Rescaling Issues: Learning from Unemployment Politics in Germany (1880–1927)', in S. Börner and M. Eigenmüller (eds), *European Integration, Processes of Change and the National Experience*. Basingstoke: Palgrave Macmillan, pp. 121–46.

Chapter 5

Women on Company Boards in France

French Republican Equality and Anti-discrimination Laws Conflicting Logics, 2006–13

Anne-Françoise Bender, Isabelle Berrebi-Hoffmann and Philippe Reigné

Introduction

A public debate over the presence of women on corporate boards of directors emerged in France in 2006. It brought together management organizations, unions, professional organizations, feminist networks, political parties and major French corporations, and drew them towards positions that would progressively evolve towards consensus in 2009–10. The law, which was adopted on 27 January 2011, imposed a female membership quota of 40%. It was the first time that the French legislature had imposed an obligatory quota within the area of corporate and business law. Surprisingly, the consensus for a law that significantly constrained corporations was able to garner support both from management organizations (most notably 'le mouvement des entreprises de France', MEDEF) and representative professional organizations.

These observations give rise to the following questions:

- What occurrences between 2006 and 2009–10 caused a relative consensus to emerge in the French national space, and what caused the continued opposition of some of the most respected voices in French legal academia?

- What occurrences led to the adoption of a law promising an impact on the gender diversity of boards of directors that would materialize more swiftly than the impact promised by previous French laws relating to workplace equality, such as the Génisson law adopted in 2001?
- What factors might explain how – contrarily to all preceding French laws relating to workplace equality, including the Génisson law of 2001 – the adoption of the 2011 law had a relatively swift impact on board diversity (see below)?
- What factors might explain how the 2011 law appeared relatively quickly in France, while similar legislation was deferred or amended in other countries that were nonetheless more accustomed to quotas (such as the United Kingdom and Germany)? France had to modify its constitution before any such laws could be adopted, and even then the use of quotas was initially limited to the political sphere (constitutional amendment in 1999, and then adoption of the law on gender parity in 2000) before spreading into the economic sphere (constitutional amendment in 2008, and then the 2011 law relating to the balanced representation of women and men on corporate boards of directors and supervisory boards, and to workplace equality).

We defend a thesis according to which it is necessary to consider two contextual variables in order to understand the strategic positions taken by key actors in France. The first external explanatory variable is the set of international legislative transformations occurring at the time, especially in the United States where the Sarbanes-Oxley Act was adopted in July 2002. This law (also designated by neologisms such as SOX and Sarbox) had extra-territorial effects. Between January 2005 and 2009, it incited major publicly traded French corporations to put anti-discrimination policies into place and to develop indicators for measuring internal diversity. The ratios and percentages thus measured were then published in publicly available annual reports of social data, which were made obligatory and which provided an eventual means for financial analysts to attribute social ratings to each corporation. These analyses and ratings had a potential impact on stock prices in financial markets that were growing increasingly weary of social risks in the wake of the Enron and Worldcom bankruptcies, followed by the financial and moral crises of 2008–9. As diversity, and the means necessary to measure it, became one of the elements that could have an impact on financial markets, they also became a source of concern for stockholders generally, and for those serving on corporate boards particularly. However, the obligations of the Sarbanes-Oxley Act – along with its impact on private corporate behaviour in France – remain the object of little study in French scholarship relating to corporate workplace equality.

The second variable is the clash of cultures that occurred between, on the one hand, the logic of anti-discrimination, which arrived in France by way of the European Union, and, on the other hand, the particularly French conception of 'equality', over which a set of national-level academic and legal actors could claim specialized expertise.

To treat these two questions, it will be necessary to look at some of the debates and some of the research results that arose out of two distinct fields of expertise. The Sarbanes-Oxley Act and its effects on French corporations would be predominantly debated in the fields of management and finance, in reviews and reports that rarely address gender issues, quotas or workplace equality. In a sense, the following analysis is, in and of itself, also a result of this phenomenon in which corporate law, finance, management, the sociology of firms, gender studies, and academic debates over notions of direct and indirect discrimination all converge.[1]

The two variables cited above lead us furthermore to push the scale of our analysis beyond the limits of national space, so as to link phenomena observed at the national level with those observed at a transnational level in which many of France's large private corporations are active. We argue that the positions taken up by the various actors, along with the timing of consensus formation, become easier to understand when both of these levels of observation are analysed. Whether actor concern for indirect discrimination was greater or lower than concern for the French doctrine of republican equality tended to depend upon whether the actor in question was engaged in activities on a transnational level or on a strictly national level. The controversy was therefore illustrative of tension between two contradictory normative cultures with regard to gender equality. This tension was a characteristic of cultural and institutional transformations underway in France.[2]

The French Law of 2011 and French Jurists: Tension Evident between Two Normative Logics

The French republican model excludes, as a matter of principle, any differentiation resulting from affirmative action measures (*la discrimination positive*). The Conseil constitutionnel, which is the governmental body tasked with deciding whether laws passed by the French legislature conform to the French constitution, has on several occasions struck down measures that attempted to instate legal quotas. Until 1999, for instance, the Conseil systematically struck down all quota-based initiatives – however modest – favouring gender parity in civil service. On 18 November 1982, the Conseil struck down a measure according to which the candidate lists for municipal elections in large cities could not consist of more than 75% of candidates of the same sex. The Conseil considered that the constitution did not permit such gender-based discrimination among candidates. Because of that decision, it would take nearly twenty years for any new initiative to appear along the same lines, as it first became necessary to clear the hurdle of constitutional reform, according to Noëlle Lenoir, member of the Conseil since 1992. She explains that once the constitution was revised in 1999, the *loi Jospin* of 2000 could open the way for more diversity in political elections.

In 2006, Marie-Jo Zimmermann, Head of the Delegation to Women's Rights and Gender Equality at the French Parliament proposed imposing a 20% quota for women on corporate boards. Her proposal was subsequently adopted by the legislature; however, it was ultimately struck down by the Conseil constitutionnel. A Norwegian law adopted in late 2003, imposing a quota of 40% and enforceable as of January 2006, had already provoked debate throughout Europe.[3] In 2005, women accounted for 6% of board members among corporations listed on the CAC 40, a figure that had France lagging behind most other Organization for Economic Cooperation and Development (OECD) countries.

In 2006, the Institut Français des Administrateurs (IFA) denounced this situation and recommended an initiative to reach 20% female membership, entrusting IFA member and corporate CEO Agnès Touraine with the leadership of a working group dedicated to that purpose; Touraine went on to become the executive director of the IFA in 2013 (Lebègue and Picard 2006). In summer 2008, a constitutional amendment proposed by Marie-Jo Zimmermann was successfully adopted, creating the principle of equal access to professional and social responsibility in the commercial and social sectors. This constitutional reform was followed in March 2009 with a new legislative proposal including a 40% quota, following Norway's example. According to an article published in the French weekly news magazine *L'Express*, Brice Hortefeux, who had just begun his tenure as Minister of Labour at the time, characterized the proposal as 'utopian'; as a stalling tactic, Hortefeux ordered Brigitte Grésy, who was the Inspector General of Social Affairs, to prepare a report on workplace equality. However, in July 2009, Grésy's widely read report would help raise public awareness of gender inequalities with respect to salary and career progression. A journalist from *L'Express* would subsequently wonder, if women represented 41% of management-level employees in France, why should they not henceforth account for 40% of the country's board members? Furthermore, the journalist continued, women represented merely 10% of the corporate advisors serving the CAC 40 and 8% of those serving France's five hundred largest corporations, a situation that had not changed over a period of five years. The Conseil constitutionnel struck down, as we saw above, the 20% quota proposed by Marie-Jo Zimmermann in 2006. A new constitutional amendment was adopted in 2008, and Zimmermann's second attempt was successfully adopted in 2011, clearing the path for the implementation of a quota system affecting corporate management and shareholder representation on the board of directors.

> The law of 27 January 2011, relating to the balanced representation of women and men on corporate boards of directors and supervisory boards, and to workplace equality (*La Loi du 27 janvier 2011 relative à la représentation équilibrée des femmes et des hommes au sein des conseils d'administration et de surveillance et à l'égalité professionnelle*):
> The law was promulgated on 27 January 2011. It was published in the *Journal Officiel* on 28 January 2011. The definitive text of the legislative bill was adopted without modification at second reading by the Assemblée nationale on 13 January 2011. The modified text was adopted at first reading by the Senate on 27 October 2010. The first legislative draft brought before the Assemblée nationale on 3 December 2009, by Jean-François Copé, Marie-Jo Zimmermann, Christian Jacob and Michèle Tabarot, along with several of their colleagues, was adopted at first reading on 20 January 2010.
>
> *What did the law do?*
> The text provided for the progressive implementation of quotas as a way of assuring a more balanced representation of women in the decision-making organs of large corporations.
> The measure affects membership on the board of directors and the supervisory board (not the executive committee) of any public or publicly traded corporation.
> Implementation was to proceed progressively, in respect of the following two thresholds:
> - Within three years of the law's promulgation, 20% of the membership of affected corporate decision-making organs had to be women. Boards of directors without a single woman member at the time of the law's promulgation had six months to name one.
> - Within six years of the law's promulgation, 40% (not 50%) of the members of affected corporate decision-making organs had to be women. Failure to abide by this quota would henceforth result in the annulment of any and all nominations to the board except nominations of women. An amendment adopted by the Assemblée nationale, but later deleted by the Senate, also provided for the annulment of board deliberations in the event of such failure. Furthermore, financial penalties included a potential suspension of the payment of director fees.[4]

Beginning in 2006, the prospect of legally imposed quotas gave rise to controversy in the world of corporate law. There was constant protest leading up to the Assemblée nationale's vote in 2010. One of the most striking examples was perhaps the position defended by François-Xavier Lucas, professor of law at Université Paris I – Panthéon Sorbonne. In a disparaging editorial (Lucas 2009), he began by observing that while corporate law had already known its share of useless laws, it was now coming under the threat of idiotic ones. Citing Jean-François Copé's unveiling of a new legislative bill that would impose a 40%, and eventually a 50%, female membership quota upon corporate boards of directors, Lucas expressed his alarm that the French commercial code stood to include such an inept and heinous law, characterizing the bill as 'pitiful' (*misérable*) and refuting the notion that 5% female membership on corporate boards of directors was indicative of discrimination. Even if it were evidence of discrimination, Lucas maintained that such discrimination would not have been inadmissible since board members were elected by stockholders, and since the latter needed to remain free to exercise their full discretion, unfettered by any obligation to justify themselves, when choosing their representatives. If any operative criterion might be considered to exist, according to Lucas it would be that of competence, as any other criteria would be superfluous; furthermore, he argued, the quota system stood to compromise stockholder property rights. For these reasons, the eminent professor considered that communitarian demands for affirmative action measures stood to undermine the republican principle of equality and should have no place in a meritocratic society.

Finally, after characterizing Jean-François Copé's project as 'Orwellian', Lucas reached the following conclusion:

> Upon passing a quota on the number of women to be included on corporate boards of directors, the flood gates would inevitably be thrown open for all the wretched of the earth to come streaming forward with their litany of compassionate whining, passing their hats around for director's fees. One could easily imagine the number of other similar feel-good laws waiting to be passed, so as to impose quotas benefitting transsexuals, the obese, dwarfs, or perhaps even whirling dervishes – all of which were categories presently under-represented on corporate boards but which would stand to gain their rightful place in the future thanks to Jean-François Copé's brilliant idea. (Lucas 2009: 945)

After the law was promulgated, other academic jurists would also express strong criticism, similar in substance but formulated in more moderate terms than those chosen by Lucas in his editorial. This later round of criticism often denied the hypothesis that there existed any systematic discrimination against women, while presenting the quota mechanism as a form of legal suspicion directed towards men. Thus, according to Renaud Mortier, professor at Université de Rennes I, efforts to characterize the under-representation of women on corporate boards as the result of odious discrimination were too easily reduced to a simple logical step, which many seemed all too happy to take, sometimes with a tone of voice that one could just as easily attribute to an indignant virgin. Mortier considered that the situation was on the whole rather insulting to men and, paradoxically, also to women, who obviously harboured no ill will against women (Mortier 2011). With the possibility of systematic discrimination thus being denied, the quota-based anti-discrimination measures adopted by the legislature appeared to these authors to be a rather clear case of 'frontal discrimination': Mortier reasoned that the law should not make access to a given right dependent upon the presence or absence of a physical characteristic with which the right had no direct relation, especially when the physical characteristic in question was gender; in doing so, the law would be providing cover for frontal discrimination, in violation of the principle of equality that figures so prominently in the national motto (ibid.). Adrien Mairot, doctor in law, reached a similar conclusion, reasoning that for the principle of equality to be preserved, nominations to corporate boards had to be founded upon an individual's personal and professional qualities, rather than upon physical characteristics of whatever sort (Mairot 2011).

The implementation of legal quotas for women generally made the above-cited authors fear the creation of a slippery slope, with numerous other categories of people in turn demanding to benefit from other similar quotas. This fear, which we already saw evoked by Lucas above, was echoed by others. For Mairot, the Zimmermann law constituted an open door for the creation of all sorts of contingents. If recourse to affirmative action measures came to be admitted, then he predicted that nothing would justify limiting the use of such measures to issues relating to gender fairness. Quotas relating to other characteristics (ethnic origin, geographic origin, social conditions, sexual orientation, etc.) stood to be implemented as well (Mairot 2011). Mortier was of the same opinion, arguing that there was no effective way to justify that measures used to benefit one category deemed deserving of protection (women) should not be available for other categories that seemed just as deserving: youth, homosexuals, ethnic minorities and so on (Mortier 2011). The fear of a dismantling of the principle of equality, in the above remarks, was concomitant with a desire to maintain the status quo.

The criticism articulated by some academic jurists was logically aimed at the use of quotas and affirmative action measures generally, and not merely at their use in relation to the place of women as members of corporate boards. Mortier, for example, considered that the crusade for affirmative action, while undertaken for a worthy cause, could potentially bring about a number of undesired effects, gender war being first and foremost among them; by trying to bring men and women together, these measures would unwittingly reinforce their opposition to each other. This line of criticism was susceptible to masculinist turns. With a play on words (*cantonner le mâle, c'est cantonner le mal*), Mortier observed that confining 'the male' (*le mâle*) seemed to be becoming an acceptable means for confining 'evil' (*le mal*), that it was thus becoming increasingly acceptable to heap shame upon a large portion of humanity because of its gender, and that these phenomena demonstrated that positive and negative discrimination were merely two sides of the same coin. Hence, according to him, measures designed to benefit women only were necessarily designed to operate to the detriment of men (Mortier 2011).

The Conseil constitutionnel failed to provide the barrier that Lucas hoped it would provide. However, radical resistance among academic jurists against the logic of affirmative action – anchored as it was in the constitutional principle of equality and in the social ideal of meritocracy – proved to be vigorous and full of imagery, even if along the way readers had to bear thoroughly sexist and phallocratic stereotypes, as was pointed out by Philippe Reigné, law professor at the Conservatoire National des Arts et Métiers, in an article he wrote in response to Lucas (Reigné 2010).

The law ultimately had a surprisingly swift impact on the diversity of corporate boards. By January 2012 (merely one year after the law's promulgation), the number of women serving as members of corporate boards had already more than doubled, passing the 20% threshold on average. Beyond the realm of private enterprise, similar rules were diffused throughout national public corporations, as well as public sector organizations, as a result of the law of 12 March 2012.

Women Members of Boards of Directors: Effects of the Law of 2012

The law of 27 January 2011, relating to the balanced representation of women and men on corporate boards of directors and supervisory boards, and to workplace equality, requires the board of directors and the supervisory board of qualifying corporations to respect a membership quota, according to which the proportion of women – and also the proportion of men – cannot be less than 40%. The law applies to limited liability corporations and limited stock partnerships (*sociétés en commandite par actions*) which are publicly traded or which both employ at least five hundred permanent employees and which benefit from total revenues of at least 50 million euros. For publicly traded corporations, a 20% quota was imposed as of 2015 as a transitory measure.

Since promulgation of the law of 12 March 2012, relating to access to post incumbency and to the improvement of working conditions for temporary civil service employees, similar rules apply to national public corporations, to public industrial and commercial firms, to hybrid firms operated by the state with employees subject to the rules of private law, and to public administrative firms.

The rate of women's membership of boards of directors among the largest publicly traded corporations increased dramatically, estimated at 35% by the end of 2015. By comparison, among corporations figuring among the CAC 40, the rate of women's membership was at 10.8% in 2008 (Moulin and Point, 2012) and 4.4% in 2003 (Maclean and Harvey, 2008). The proportion of women serving in executive roles that report directly to boards of directors also increased, reaching 14% by the end of 2015, compared to 7.7% in 2009.

Professor Lucas' strong reaction could be seen as symptomatic of surprise at the way in which France chose to proceed in implementing reform. Indeed, when compared with other similar initiatives undertaken previously in France or elsewhere in Europe, there were significant differences. France effectively became one of the first countries to choose the imposition of obligatory measures (an obligatory quota enforced by stiff penalties) rather than merely aspirational ones (incentives for self-regulation) such as those seen in the United States and the UK. Other European countries had nonetheless adopted similar legislative or regulatory measures.

The controversy among jurists had relatively little impact on the larger public debate in France. Our analysis reveals a general consensus surrounding the proposed law.

The Public Debate: An Apparent Consensus among Business, Government and Professional Organizations

Drawing upon French press archives dating from 2009 and 2010, we can distinguish two group of actors, who adopted converging positions and played important, sometimes central, roles while advancing similar arguments in favour of adopting a binding law.

Table 5.1 Chronology of legislative or regulatory initiatives undertaken in Europe.

Date	Country	Measure	Notes
1980s–90s	Finland	Regulatory measures for creating balance among men and women on boards of directors and other decision-making bodies.	
1990s	Denmark	Regulatory measures for creating balance among men and women in public corporations.	
December 2003	Norway	Law setting a 40% quota for the representation of women.	The quota became obligatory on 1 January 2006.
22 March 2007	Spain	Organic law on gender equality, which encouraged at least 40% representation of each gender.	Recommendation; no penalties.
27 January 2011	France	Law setting a quota of 40% representation for each gender by 2017.	Applicable to publicly traded companies having at least 500 employees, and to public companies (about 2,000 companies total); financial penalties; non-compliant nominations rendered legally null.
1 March 2011	European Union	European Commission's *Women on the Board* pledge initiative.	The EU called upon European companies to voluntarily pledge to reach the 30% mark by 2015.
14 March 2011	Austria	Administrative decision by the Council of Ministers to gradually introduce quotas.	
6 June 2011	Netherlands	Law on 'balanced representation' (at least 30% for each gender).	Applicable to large public and private firms; temporary measures providing for sanction were set to expire in 2016.
12 July 2011	Italy	Law establishing representation quota equal to at least one-third for each gender.	Applicable to publicly traded firms (monitored by the National Commission of Stock-Market Operations) and public firms.

Date	Country	Measure	Notes
28 July 2011	Belgium	Law establishing representation quota equal to at least one-third for each gender.	Modification of corporation law as applicable to publicly traded companies.
14 November 2012	EU	European Commission, proposed directive, representation of women on corporate boards should reach at least 40% by 2020.	Reduced penalties compared to initial text.
March 2015	Germany	Law establishing representation quota equal to at least one-third for each gender.	Applicable to limited corporations and joint stock partnerships employing more than 2,000 employees in the German private sector.

Government and Institutional Politicians

First, Marie-Jo Zimmermann's initiative over ten years largely contributed to the advancement of gender equality in public executive decision-making bodies at the regional and local levels, including penalties for any such body that did not assure that women made up 50% of the candidates presented during legislative elections, the addition of professional equality to the constitution, and the implementation of a 40% quota for boards of directors in large corporations in 2009. This initiative was described in the following terms by Anne-Marie Rocco, a journalist writing for the economic weekly *Challenges*:

> Marie-Jo Zimmermann, a former history and geography teacher said that she became aware of the 'glass ceiling' when she started tracking the career paths of girls who had been in her class. Lower salaries than their male counterparts, professional disengagement at around age 35, exclusion from social circles where decisions are made, affecting even those students who had been admitted into prestigious universities. 'That is what made me want to fight' … Beginning in 2000, she was entrusted with two tasks which fed into her thinking as it related to this fight: in 2002, she was both Official Recorder for the Observatoire de la parité, and President of the delegation on women's rights and equal opportunity at the French National Assembly. There, she acquired the conviction that corporate executive boards were at the heart of the system.[5]

There was nonetheless divergence within the government with respect to the best way to implement the measures in question. Valérie Lion, a journalist for *L'Express*, wrote:

> Marie-Jo Zimmermann's first proposition sought to impose a rule whereby women would constitute 50% of the membership of the boards of directors of publicly traded companies within five years! Last week, advisors at Matignon flatly rejected adopting such a radical perspective, at least until they were later at least partially reassured: in the Commission des lois, the quota was brought down to 40%, with a six-year horizon for implementation (which was more compatible with the duration of the mandates of board members) and the only penalty would be the nullification of nominations, and not the more general nullification of deliberations, which threatened to compromise ongoing business. 'Too rigid and uniform' replied Xavier Darcos, Minister of Labour, who preferred proportional representation based on the larger presence of women within the company, so as not to impose unattainable obligations upon sectors with high proportions of male workers, such as the construction sector. (Lion 2010)

The law was ultimately adopted with support from both the Union pour la Majorité Présidentielle and the Parti Socialiste.

On the institutional side of things, the French Autorité des Marchés Financiers (AMF), an agency in charge of monitoring the financial markets, officially supported the measure. Its director, Jean-Pierre Jouyet (who had an affinity for the Parti Socialiste), stated: 'I am in favour of quotas, since self-regulation has failed. Only 10% of board members are women. That places Europe on the same level as Turkey. Nevertheless, we should remain watchful, so that any penalties for the violation of these new rules remain proportionate and do not impede companies from functioning normally' (Lion 2010).

Feminist Networks, Consultancy Firms and Corporate Executives

The consequential activity of feminist networks composed of women managers and women executives must be emphasized. These networks produced studies and issued statements that were systematically diffused through the economic press and news media (Blanchard, Boni-Le Goff, and Rabier 2013). These networks were at the origin of various conferences of relevance, including a conference entitled 'Comment accélérer l'accès des femmes aux conseils d'administration', organized by the IFA, the European Professional Women's Network (EPWN) and the Observatoire sur la responsabilité sociétale des entreprises (ORSE) on Tuesday, 15 September 2009. During that conference, Daniel Lebègue,

Table 5.2 Main actors in the public debate in 2009–10.

Politics/high civil service	Marie-Jo Zimmermann, Member of Parliament for the Union pour la Majorité Présidentielle, Head of the Delegation to Women's Rights and Gender Equality at the French Parliament Jean-François Copé, President of French Parliamentary Group Union pour la Majorité Présidentielle Brigitte Grésy, Chief Auditor at the French Social services
Institutional actors/ world of finance	IFA: Institut Français des Administrateurs AMF: Autorité des Marchés Financiers
Representatives of the corporate world	MEDEF: Laurence Parisot Association Française des Entreprises Privées : Maurice Lévy Accenture and McKinsey
Feminist networks	Women's Forum at Deauville European Professional Women's Network Grandes Ecoles au Féminin
Personalities/ corporate executives	Carlos Ghosn, Renault-Nissan Véronique Morali, Terrafemina Mercedès Erra, Euro RSCG

President of the IFA, declared that his organization was in favour of a law imposing a certain number of representatives of each gender, at least equal to 40%. This legal obligation would apply to all publicly traded companies, as well as to all companies above a certain size – at least a thousand employees, for example – thus including public and mutualist firms as well. The fact that nothing had happened over the past four years was cited as a motivation for taking such a measure. In 2005, Agnès Touraine, President of Act III consultants, Administrator of the IFA and a corporate leader in France and abroad, had undertaken a study on the presence of women on corporate boards. She succeeded Daniel Lebègue as President of the IFA and declared in 2010 in an interview that nothing would change if no law was passed. Companies had already been gently incited to diversify their board membership for five years, and the situation had not changed. Consequently, the time had come to recognize that these previous measures had failed.[6]

Another example of such public positioning involved Véronique Morali, President of Fimalac Développement and of Terrafemina.com, who stated in the press that it had become apparent that new measures would be required to change the situation, and that even if quotas were not an ideal solution, they had become necessary within the context of a cultural revolution that would trigger a virtuous circle. It would be up to us to find the right balance necessary to introduce certain elements of affirmative action, as already known in the English-speaking world, while also adhering to the particularly French ideal of equality.[7] We should also cite the impact of the annual Women's Forum organized at Deauville, which was instrumental in spreading these messages.[8]

Other major actors included international consulting firms such as McKinsey, which took a leading role with its famous 2009 report showing a positive correlation between the presence of three or more women on a firm's board of directors and the successful performance of the firm.[9] The French periodical *Les Echos* picked up on another report showing that one out of every two women still considered that her job responsibilities were below her skill level.[10] We should add that actors in the field of education and professional training – including for example Ecole Supérieure des Sciences Economiques et Commerciales, the IFA, lawyers, accountants – proposed learning opportunities for women who wanted to work in administrative capacities and therefore promoted administrative careers among women managers, consultants and professionals.

Two common arguments put forward by these actors were systematically reported upon by the French press.

The Inescapable Observation that the Number of Women Present on Corporate Boards of Directors Had Changed Very Little since 2006

As Valérie Lion (2010) wrote, one after the other, Jean-François Copé, leader of the UMP in the French parliament, Xavier Darcos, Minister of Labour, and Laurence Parisot, President of MEDEF, were coming out in favour of the introduction of quotas as a means for reinforcing women's place within decision-making bodies, marking a turning point after years of merely trying to raise awareness among employers. Measures aimed at mere awareness-raising, the journalist explained, had only produced limited effects, and impatience eventually won out as women who were initially sceptical about the use of quotas increasingly came to support their use, given the glass ceiling's apparent solidity.

Even personalities like Laurence Parisot, who once opposed formal legal measures, preferring a soft-law approach instead, eventually recognized that legal constraint was proving necessary. She came out in favour of a 40% quota benefitting women, which would enter into effect in six years, thus leaving enough time for the mandates of current board members to expire. Parisot added that large corporations would need to be exemplary; as she had been suggesting since 2005, CAC 40 companies should significantly increase the number of women serving on their boards (Lion 2010).

Women Add Value

A second but more discreet argument found in the French press, mainly when citing statements made by certain business leaders such as Alliance Renault-Nissan President Carlos Ghosn, was that women leaders add value. In *Echos*,[11] he came out in favour of voluntary quotas and expressed his pride in Renault France because over 20% of its managers were women. Ghosn was also cited by *L'Express* as stating that legislation relating to the presence of women on corporate boards seemed reasonable to him, that attempts to resolve the issue would never move beyond the level of mere rhetoric without clear numerical objectives, and that the success of a global enterprise depended on its ability to understand the diversity of the society around it, which he considered to be a source of business performance (Lion 2010).

This line of reasoning was disseminated through the media by feminist networks, including EPWN. An article in *Le Monde* evoked studies identified in a report published by the IFA, EPWN and ORSE, proving that firms with stronger female representation in their decision-making structures also perform better (Kahn 2009).

The financial crisis of 2009 also provided an opportunity to call the performance of (mostly male) financial market actors into question, given the apparent recklessness and greediness of their behaviour. The actors in place were not as effective as they had previously appeared to be, and the introduction of diversity within corporate boards offered the prospect of better control over company strategies, given the link, as suggested by certain economic and financial theories, between board member diversity and improved corporate governance. Valérie Lion thus wondered whether it was the financial crisis that had weakened the masculine model of leadership, noting that the initiative to integrate more women into corporate boards thereafter spread well beyond the small activist circles that usually sustained it, and also noting that governance experts were increasingly supportive, including Daniel Lebègue, President of the IFA, who expressly supported the idea of quotas (Lion 2010).

This argument, which represented board member diversity as a path towards better governance, would reappear in the opening parliamentary debates over the law of 2011.

Arguments for Adopting the Law of 27 January 2011

The proposed law was justified mainly by two lines of arguments. The first one related to democratic representation. Although women had come to occupy a large portion of the workforce, they remained under-represented among the highest-ranking decision-makers. Balanced representation at the highest levels being a necessary condition for democratic society, the law cited European Union objectives in order to make that link clear.

The second one related to economic performance. An argument relating to competence was evoked, according to which it was no longer conceivable for companies to continue depriving themselves of the experience and skill that qualified women could bring to corporate decision-making bodies. Another similar argument related to governance. The law emphasized the importance of corporate governance being in phase with the society in which the underlying business was developing. Additionally, an end to the endogamy of recruitment into corporate boards was needed. This law would bring about greater diversity in candidate profiles and raise *de facto* the issues of cumulating mandates and cumulating functions as a means for ending this endogamy.[12]

The main counter-arguments mobilized by the rare opponents or sceptics evoked the relatively small number of women who had the required skills. However, this argument was quickly refuted by networks of women managers and in the press. Valérie Lion raised the following points in her article in *L'Express* (2010). Given that, according to Marie-Jo Zimmermann, it would be necessary to find 1,350 women with two mandates each, or 550 with five mandates each (the maximum allowed), to respect the quota, the issue became whether this task would be feasible. Lion acknowledged that the right people would not be readily found on any street corner, but also pointed out that Françoise Gri, the former CEO of IBM France and current President of Manpower France, had been integrated into corporate boards in Norway but never in France. The journalist went on to cite Véronique Morali, a board member for Fimalac, Havas, the Compagnie financière Edmond de Rothschild and Coca-Cola enterprises, who opined that the talent pool existed but that companies would need to stray from the beaten path in order to find the right candidates. To facilitate the task, Morali created a French branch of the Women Corporate Directors network, based in the United States. Also, Lion noted that the IFA was in the process of preparing, along with the EPWN, a programme called 'Women on Board'.

For Valérie Lion, the most emblematic initiative, which hitherto had been undertaken in the shadows but was revealed by a feature in *L'Express*, was that undertaken by Marie-Claude Peyrache, a former senior manager at Orange, and by Véronique Préaux-Cobti, Director General of the consulting firm Diafora. Drawing inspiration from a programme originating in the UK five years earlier with respect to the FTSE-100, the pair imagined 'Board Women Partners', an initiative in which corporate executives agreed to mentor women from another company identified by one of their peers. Anne Bouverot, Service Director at Orange and currently a board member for Groupama, participated in the British programme.

In fact, considering the large number of women in France working in management positions and entrusted with important responsibilities, the notion that there was not enough talent among women candidates for board positions did not receive significant attention during parliamentary debates.[13]

Finally, there was a certain consensus among institutional actors in the business world with respect to the need to increase the number of women serving on corporate boards. Thus, according to Olivier Auguste, a journalist from *Le Figaro*, MEDEF and AFEP changed their code of governance in 2010, for the express purpose of cutting the grass from under the feet of the Copé-Zimmermann Law.[14] However, MEDEF and AFEP nonetheless supported the stated objectives of the law. During parliamentary debates, AFEP's initiative was even evoked to demonstrate that the corporate world supported the spirit of the law.[15]

Olivier Auguste recalled when Maurice Lévy, CEO of the Publicis Group and the new President of AFEP, asked his MEDEF counterpart to consider changes to their common code of corporate governance that would encourage parity. Henceforth the text would recommend that corporate boards include at least 20% women within three years' time, and 40% within six years' time. These time periods would, according to Auguste, allow corporations the time to act gradually as existing board mandates expired. These recommendations corresponded, as Auguste pointed out, with those voted upon by the French Assemblée Générale.

However, Auguste added that the proposed legislation provided for punitive measures, including the nullification of board member nominations, in cases where the rule was not respected, and that no such punitive measures were contained in the AFEP-MEDEF code, which instead followed the 'comply or explain' principle. The journalist reported that Maurice Lévy thought that the use of 'comply or explain' in this situation would prove effective, that it would force boards to justify non-compliance in their annual reports, and that this was the strongest possible measure that could be imposed upon a board. Even though Lévy considered that in any case the law was not an imposition, and even though Marie-Jo Zimmermann acknowledged that she was very happy to see the corporate world showing its willingness to move forward, she nonetheless hoped to see her law continue to move forward as well, considering that it was her Sword of Damocles that got things moving in the first place.[16]

In order to understand how and why over time French economic actors began to change their positions, which for a long time were unmoved by any desire for gender equality (Bender 2004), we propose to consider events in the economic world on a larger scale from the 1990s onwards, particularly in the United States.

The American Sarbanes-Oxley Act of 2002 and Its Extra-Territorial Effects

Contrary to François-Xavier Lucas (2009), who considered that the law ran contrary to the shareholders' best interests, we suggest that large corporate boards in Europe were motors for debate within the larger corporate world and encouraged measures in favour of diversity, including quotas, within corporate decision-making structures generally. As early as 2004, after the passing of the Sarbanes-Oxley Act in the United States, American shareholders represented in French corporations with shares traded on the American stock market became increasingly sensitive to diversity.

The Sarbanes-Oxley Act was adopted in the United States on 1 July 2002. It would later be designated in professional literature – even in French – under neologisms such as 'SOX', 'Sarbox' or 'SOA'. Its purpose was to reform corporate governance in the wake of major corporate scandals involving Enron, Worldcom and Arthur Andersen. Touted as the largest federal economic reform measure since the 1930s and the New Deal, the Sarbanes-Oxley Act had extra-territorial effects impacting, for example, all European companies with stock traded on an American stock exchange. This law, and the considerable constraints it imposed – production not only of quarterly accounting and financial reports in line with the new norms that were to be put in place, but also social reports on the organization, labour relations, ethnic and social diversity and gender equality, an obligation to put in place an 'ethics code' and indicators for measuring its application, the introduction of whistleblower protection, penalties of ten or twenty years in prison for directors who failed in their obligations or were clearly cheating, and the creation of internal and external independent control committees and actors – opened the way for an intense and rapid reform (in less than three years) of American capitalism. It also created a new market for actors in auditing and consultancy, which the major American consultancies immediately seized upon, especially – and this is not the least ironic part of this recent economic history – the Big Four.[17] The 66-page law is comprised of eleven sections. Section 404, along with certain articles in sections 300 and 800, applies to foreign corporations with stock traded through the New York Stock Exchange (NYSE) or with branches or other interests in the United States. While American corporations had three years to implement SOX compliance measures, foreign corporations had four years. The deadline was therefore 31 July 2006 for corporations with stock traded on NASDAQ, and 31 August 2006 for corporations with stock traded on the NYSE.

While compliance costs were widely discussed in the United States, in Europe it was the law's extra-territorial impact that was at the centre of debate.[18] Additionally, in France, there was concern about potential conflicts with the Loi de sécurité financière (LOLF) voted in August 2003, as evident in the numerous commentaries and Senate reports produced by the AMF. In particular, the provisions relating to whistleblowing seemed difficult to reconcile with national norms and rules of law.[19] The 'Commission Nationale de l'Informatique et des Libertés' (CNIL), the commission which controls and enforces private rights laws, and personal data use's regulations in France, was opposed to the SOX whistleblowing provisions, as were Danone and Bouygues Telecom. Danone would eventually withdraw from the NYSE in 2007, considering that compliance with SOX was going to be too costly and that the company would have to concede too much power to the Securities and Exchange Commission (SEC).

However, between 2005, the year during which the law entered into effect for United States companies, and 2006, institutional funds and American investors represented on corporate boards in France began to demand that French corporations comply with these requirements. HR directors and financial directors were summoned, called upon first to account for the current state of affairs, with respect to the implementation of an ethics code, the system of internal control, and also to provide social indicators relating to gender, disability and ethnicity. Thus, the financial aspect of this new reporting structure was accompanied by a social aspect relating to diversity.

From that time onwards, alongside the right to equality (the Génisson law of 2001 for example), it is important to open up academic research to an entirely different field relating to corporate governance in France as a vehicle for transformation of workplace equality following the 1995 Vienot report.[20] Particularly with respect to the present controversy, corporate boards during this period were profoundly marked by successive reforms. Between 1993 and 1997, there was a period of privatization associated with Edouard Balladur's term as Prime Minister,[21] as well as the beginning of a deep reform of the French system of cross-shareholdings.[22] It was also the period that economists would come to refer to as bank disintermediation. From 1995 onwards, companies could intervene directly in global finance markets (stock markets in London, New York, Paris, Frankfurt, etc.), whatever their nationality, and securitize their debt obligations. They could go on to increase their capital outside their national territory and without going through a financial intermediary, something which until then had been compulsory. These intermediaries – the banks – now lost their key role of supporting companies wanting to use the markets to finance themselves. At the same time, a company's share price also became a means of buying or buying back other companies directly on the markets. The share price became a strategic asset that may or may not enable them to develop policies for national and international growth, and acquisitions.

These transformations during the 1990s and early 2000s were accompanied by a change in the composition of shareholders for French companies. There were three major reasons for this. First was the withdrawal of the state or the end of its role as majority shareholder (privatization). Second, there was a wave of fast fusions and acquisitions that resulted in the construction of large multinational groups (the pharmaceutical sector, for example, saw the emergence of groups like Sanofi Aventis, and the automobile sector saw the emergence of Renault-Nissan). Third, the arrival of investment funds from the UK and US among the shareholder community and even among the community of corporate board members in France modified the functioning and the culture of the French corporate world through the mid 2000s. Board members had a more international profile than before, often including members from the English-speaking world, and state actors were less present. Business reports were now published in English, and executive compensation was disclosed therein, along with social reporting, including diversity figures. At the same time, financial markets in London and New York were creating social indexes[23] and a new profession was created – social financial analysts, who rate the risk (corruption, bankruptcy etc.) of corporations, using specific indicators. These ratings stood to influence share value.

It is in this context that attention must be drawn to the extra-territoriality of the Sarbanes-Oxley law, as experienced in French corporate boards. And beyond the French financial world, among an administrative and political elite that was enthusiastic about new public management and globalization, a need for foreign expertise and international consultancy and audit firms emerged (Berrebi-Hoffmann and Grémion 2009).

In view of the preceding chronology concerning the Sarbanes-Oxley Act and the LOLF, which then becomes inspirational, it is interesting to revisit the chronology of the equality agreements that have developed rapidly in France, especially from 2005, in which anti-discrimination and diversity vocabulary appears alongside equality and then equity (Laufer and Silvera 2004). The vocabulary of the agreements evolves from equality and equity to the use of the term 'diversity' in the wake of the 2004 Charter of Diversity and the fight against discrimination (Bender 2006;

Garner-Moyer 2006). Moreover, among the companies that signed the diversity charter in January 2005, by publicizing their approach, there are many CAC 40 companies that are listed abroad (Bender and Pigeyre 2010).

From 2005 onwards, an additional variable can be taken into account in the evolution of enterprise equality policies: the demand, directly emanating from boards or boards of directors, to rapidly increase the number of women in managerial positions when this was much lower than the rest of the sector, so that the first social reports made mandatory by the Sarbanes-Oxley Act did not reveal a too high a difference with the sector average which would mechanically result in a negative impact on the share price.

Law and European Politics: An Approach via Discrimination

The European approach since the Lisbon Treaty has introduced and valued the so-called 'integrated' or gender mainstreaming approach to gender equality following certain member countries (Sweden and Norway, for example). As early as 2006, as part of the social inclusion policies developed by the Union, the European Commission played an important catalytic role in the field of disability (UN Convention 2006) and gender equality (Beijing Action Plan) in favour of an integrated approach. Gender mainstreaming is thus defined by the Council of Europe: 'Gender mainstreaming is the (re) organization, improvement, evolution and evaluation of decision-making processes, in order to incorporate the perspective of equality between women and men in all fields and at all levels, by the actors generally involved in the implementation of policies'.[24] The reference is the approach adopted in the field of disability, since the 2005 law, where the reasoning moves from a reasoning in terms of categorization of the disability and in terms of quotas towards a reasoning in terms of opposable right (in terms of 'employment', for example, it is for companies to prove that they have not discriminated against hiring, subject to 'reasonable accommodation' of the workplace) and non-discrimination. In France, the integrated approach was making its entry into government policy (inter-ministerial committee) from 2012 onwards. In practice, since May 2012, France has embarked on the implementation of this new approach through the creation of a number of tools. A 'senior official in charge of equal rights' has been appointed in each ministry. This person is responsible for defining and implementing the ministry's policy on gender equality. A referent on the issue of gender inequalities has been appointed within each ministerial cabinet to facilitate the conduct of inter-ministerial work. The Ministry of Women's Rights has set up awareness-raising activities for all ministers, enabling them to generate reflection and contribute to their awareness of the direct and indirect consequences of stereotypes. A mechanism for systematic evaluation of the impact of legal texts on gender equality was set up by the Prime Minister's Circular of 23 August 2012 on the inclusion in the preparation of legislative and regulatory texts of their impact in terms of equality between women and men. And Decree No. 2013-8 of 3 January 2013 established the High Council for Gender Equality to conduct an evaluation of policies on women's rights and gender equality.[25]

> *The European Community Framework*
> The very substantial Community achievements in the field of gender equality draw on the current Article 157 TFEU, which gives the Community competence to intervene in the field of equal pay.
> ...
> Of the fifteen directives on the scope of equality, seven have been recast in a single text: Directive 2006/54/EC of the European Parliament and of the Council of 5 July 2006, equal treatment in employment. In accordance with this text, direct or indirect discrimination between men and women, which concerns the conditions of recruitment, access to employment or self-employment, dismissal, training and promotion, and affiliation to workers' or employers' organizations, is prohibited. A difference in treatment between men and women can only be justified on account of the nature of the occupational activities concerned and whether the measures taken are legitimate and proportionate. Women and men should be treated equally within the framework of occupational social security schemes, in particular as regards the scope and conditions of access to schemes, contributions and the calculation of benefits, in particular concerning increases, the conditions of duration and maintenance of rights. Member states must establish remedies and take measures to protect workers from unfavourable treatment when a complaint is made at company level or in the course of legal proceedings.
> Three instruments also play a structuring role in national equality policy:
> *The Strategy for Gender Equality* with a five-year horizon (2010–2015) supports the implementation of the Europe 2020 strategy. It is based on the following five priorities:
> – equal economic independence for women and men,
> – equal remuneration for work of equal value,
> – equality in decision-making,
> – dignity, integrity and end of gender-based violence,
> – promotion of equality between women and men in the EU's external policy.
> *The Women's Charter based on the same five priorities* was presented on 5 March

> 2010. It aims to integrate equal opportunities within the Commission's policy mix for the period 2010–2015.
> *The Pact for Gender Equality,* which is aimed at member states, is an instrument to accompany them in the implementation of the new Strategy for Equality 2010–2015. (Sénat 2013)

In 2012 and 2013, in line with Community policy, the executive introduced measures and decrees based on reasoning in terms of indirect (and therefore systemic) discrimination. The tensions with the logic of 'Republican equality' and the actors who bear it are undoubtedly to come, especially in the public sectors recently concerned, and will open other places of observation of the confrontation between the two logics that make up the present study.

Conclusion

The case of the Act relating to corporate boards of directors in France illustrates a process of evolution of French reform elites towards a logic of indirect discrimination and quotas. The positions gradually taken by the actors around the controversy about the utility, legality or the perverse effects of the introduction of a binding quota for companies on their boards of directors testify either to a form of ambivalence (government, French feminist movements and feminists) or a determined opposition (some of the most recognized academic lawyers). We wanted to reveal these positions, through a sociology of the action of each of the identified groups of actors. The analysis of both the transnational circulation of norms and the contradictions that may arise between norms of French Republican equality and anti-discrimination norms and reasoning in terms of gender mainstreaming, highlights different actors' strategies in a space of cultural and normative action. In this sense, the arguments developed by the actors, as we have described, are at once a symptom of a normative position to be interpreted and an operator in a discursive and normative space of action. The arguments of indirect discrimination are gradually becoming more legitimate and familiar in public debates and among political and economic elites – despite their contradictions with Republican equality – as a result of reforms in corporate governance, financial globalization and the Sarbanes-Oxley Act, on the one hand, and the new public management policies and European directives on the other. It seemed to us that the case of the law on business boards called for reflection in terms of method as well. The analysis that we conducted led us to think together of the social construction of the groups of actors and the social construction of categories of analysis of public action (justice, equity, equality). Finally, beyond the analysis of discourse, it is necessary to situate the space of action of each actor in its scope and thickness. Distinct spaces of analysis such as the evolution of corporate governance and the rules governing boards of directors, as well as the transnational environment in which the space of action, strategy and functioning of large groups now resides, on top of other binding legislative frameworks for companies (US law) and of new reasoning circulations carried by Europe, consultants and audit firms, public and private reform elites or certain French laws (the LOLF) had to be considered simultaneously. The 'local/global' articulation is then thinking less in terms of imports or the conversion of the national space to global or sometimes Anglo-Saxon logics, and thinking more at a more intermediate level (sometimes referred to as 'meso' in sociology) of reorganization of the actors in relations of force internal to the national space. Actors close to a global logic and those who remain close to a local logic are opposed by conviction, by interest and according to the semantic, cognitive and economic fields in which they operate. The long history of debates and controversies on equality between men and women in France also makes it possible to better understand the possible turning point of the law. Taking the typical French tradition of republican equality seriously, one sees clearly the lines of tension, with a definition of equality as 'non-discrimination' carried by Europe and the Western world today. At the end of the nineteenth century in France, a transnational controversy, which was then called 'the question of women', was for more than ten years, at the core of a public dispute between jurists, scholars and politicians. Durkheim had interfered in this by proposing a formula, that of 'equality in difference' (Berrebi-Hoffmann 2011), which nourished essays and debates for more than a century. As early as the nineteenth century, the tension between republican equality and difference was an intellectual concern. The present case can thus also be read in the mirror of a long French history made up of normative tension and contradiction around equality, hierarchies between the sexes and the apprehension of difference.

Anne-Françoise Bender is Assistant Professor at CNAM Paris, where she teaches human resource management and organization theory. A researcher at Lise-CNAM CNRS, her research fields are career management, women's careers, gender equality and diversity management. She coordinates a special interest group on Diversity and Gender at the Francophone Research Association in Human Resource Management (AGRH) and has recently written many articles on women on corporate boards in France.

Isabelle Berrebi-Hoffmann is a research faculty member in sociology at the French National Center of Scientific Research (CNRS) and a member of the Lise-CNRS. She has led several international research projects on the transformations of work and the history of equality and gender. Her recent publications include a collective edited volume on the politics of intimacy at work since the nineteenth century (*Politiques de l'intime: Des utopies sociales d'hier aux mondes du travail d'aujourd'hui*, La découverte, 2016) and a book (with M.-C. Bureau and M. Lallement) on the makers' movement and the digital economy (*Makers: Enquête sur les laboratoires du changement social*, Seuil, 2018).

Philippe Reigné is Chair Professor of Business Law at the CNAM (Conservatoire des Arts et Métiers) and a member of the Lise-CNRS. He holds an MA in Business Law and Economic Law, a Certificate of Proficiency in Law, an MA in Criminal Law and Criminal Sciences, and a PhD in law. His fields of research and expertise cover in particular corporate law, the law of liberal professions, the law of sex and gender and animal rights.

Notes

1. The empirical elements cited here are based, on the one hand, on the authors' earlier research into professional equality, the circulation of norms and expertise, corporate governance and business law, and on the other hand on a specific treatment of various types of material: reports published since 2004 on equality in France and Europe, a qualitative analysis of the discourse of the national press and the specialized press, and the results of a survey conducted by one of the authors in 2005 on the corporate board of a major French group (Danone). In addition, Philippe Reigné was one of those involved in the legal controversy.
2. On this methodological point, see, for example, Berrebi-Hoffmann 2013.
3. See Table 5.1 for a chronological summary of measures taken by European countries on this matter. For example, at the same time, a draft law was being discussed in Spain.
4. République Française, Direction of legal and administrative information, retrieved from http://www.vie-publique.fr/actualite/panorama/texte-vote/loi-relative-representation-equilibree-femmes-hommes-au-sein-conseils-administration-surveillance-egalite-professionnelle.html.
5. Anne-Marie Rocco, 'La victoire de Marie-Jo', Blog/femmes, *Challenges*, 14 January 2011, https://blog.challenges.fr/femmes/la-victoire-de-marie-jo/.
6. Interview by Cécile Daumas, 'Davantage de femmes à la table des patrons', *Libération*, 20 January 2010.
7. 'Les quotas ne sont plus tabous', *Les Echos* no. 20547, 6 November 2009, 5.
8. Anne Bauer, 'Au Women's Forum, les femmes s'impatientent', *Les Echos* no. 20535, 21 October 2009, 14, IDEES.
9. Muriel Jasor, 'La parité hommes-femmes, beaucoup de paroles, peu de résultats', *Les Echos* no. 20520, 30 September 2009, 12.
10. 'Les quotas ne sont plus tabous', *Les Echos* no. 20547, 6 November 2009, 5.

11. 'Les quotas ne sont plus tabous', *Les Echos* n° 20547, 6 November 2009, 5.
12. Bill no. 2140 'relative à la représentation équilibrée des femmes et des hommes au sein des conseils d'administration et de surveillance et à l'égalité professionnelle' (relating to the balanced representation of women and men on corporate boards of directors and supervisory boards, and to workplace equality), Assemblée Nationale, 3 December 2009, http://www.assemblee-nationale.fr/13/propositions/pion2140.asp.
13. The report on the bill to the Senate contained the following: 'Most of the people heard did indeed state that there was no problem of finding a "pool" of competent women; at the most the problem would be one of training and experience, for women who had not yet held the highest management positions in their company, on corporate boards and executive committees'. Report to the Senate on the bill relating to the balanced representation of women and men on corporate boards of directors and supervisory boards, and to workplace equality, by Marie-Hélène Des Esgaulx, 13 October 2010, http://www.senat.fr/rap/l10-038/l10-0381.html#toc5.
14. 'Les grandes entreprises promettent la parité' [Major companies promise equality], *Le Figaro*, Economie, L'entreprise (Archives), Olivier Auguste, updated 19 April 2010. http://www.lefigaro.fr/entreprise/2010/04/19/05011-20100419ARTFIG00680-les-grandes-entreprises-promettent-la-parite-.php.
15. Report to the Senate on the bill relating to the balanced representation of women and men on corporate boards of directors and supervisory boards, and to workplace equality, by Marie-Hélène Des Esgaulx, 13 October 2010, http://www.senat.fr/rap/l10-038/l10-0381.html#toc5.
16. 'Les grandes entreprises promettent la parité', *Le Figaro*, Economie, L'entreprise (Archives), Olivier Auguste, updated 19 April 2010. http://www.lefigaro.fr/entreprise/2010/04/19/05011-20100419ARTFIG00680-les-grandes-entreprises-promettent-la-parite-.php.
17. The Big Five were the five largest accounting, legal and tax audit firms worldwide: PriceWaterHouse Coopers, Deloitte Touche Tohmatsu, Ernst & Young, KPMG and Arthur Andersen. Following the collapse of Andersen in 2002, the Big Five became the Big Four.
18. See Senate report by Philippe Marini, Senator, http://www.senat.fr/rap/r03-431/r03-4315.html (last accessed 29 November 2018).
19. 'Article 301-4 of the SOX requires that American companies, their subsidiaries and all companies quoted on the New York Stock Exchange, put in place a procedure enabling any employee to report any criminal act concerning accounting malpractice. "Each audit committee should establish procedures for: (A) the receipt, retention and treatment of complaints received by the issuer regarding accounting, internal accounting controls or auditing matters, and (B) the confidential, anonymous submission by employees of their concerns regarding questionable accounting or auditing matters." Article 806 of the SOX forbids the use of any retaliatory measures against employees who report wrongful accounting activity, and, in the event of a violation of this prohibition, the right to take legal action against the employer who has taken reprisals. The protection of whistleblowers, which is at the heart of the system, is guaranteed by the commitment on the part of companies to protect the anonymity of disclosures. It is especially ensured by the addition of a new article to the US Penal Code, since retaliation against a whistleblower is now a crime punishable by a large fine or even up to ten years in prison' (Didier 2009: 3).
20. This private report to the French government was the historical first step of the regulation of corporate governance in France. It is available at http://www.ecgi.org/codes/documents/vienot1_fr.pdf (last accessed 29 November 2018).
21. Following nationalizations in 1982, the state controlled a large part of industrial activity in France, including almost half of the energy sector, the steel industry, chemicals, armaments,

artificial fibres and wires, aeronautics and virtually all of the banking sector. In 1982, the public sector included almost three thousand companies employing 9% of the active population, or 1.9 million people. From 1986, a disengagement of the state as shareholder began, through three massive waves of privatizations of major groups. The first wave was between 1986 and 1988, when more than 1,100 companies, employing just under 500,000 staff, were privatized, including CCF, BTP, CGE, Havas, Matra, Paribas, Société Générale, Bull, Suez, TF1 Thompson and Saint Gobain. This movement continued into the 1990s: BNP, Rhone Poulenc, Elf Aquitaine, UAP, SEITA, Usinor Sacilor and Pechiney were sold between 1993 and 1997. The state then gradually withdrew from the last public companies (Air France, GAN France Telecom, etc.), while the last state monopolies (EDF, SNCF, La Poste, etc.) were opened up to competition, as a result of European directives on competition.

22. Following on from the privatizations, from the beginning of the 1990s the state adopted a policy which, in the words of Balladur, would establish a 'hard core'. It was at this point that cross-shareholding developed: a hard core of companies bought each other's shares to stabilize share ownership and the decisions of the main French firms. In short, we found the same people – mainly CEOs of banks and large industrial companies (like the CEO of what would become BNP-Paribas, Michel Pébereau) – on the executive boards of the major companies. Hence the terms 'hard core' and 'cross-' shareholding.
23. The best known of these are the index created in London, the FTSE KLD 400 Social Index (formerly the Domini Social Index 400, launched in 1990) and the New York Stock Market social index, the Dow Jones Sustainability Global Index (DJSGI) (http://www.sustainability-index.com/), created in 1999. Companies are therefore also quoted 'socially' on the stock markets. In addition, the SOX provides social financial analysts with even more new data and on a more regular basis, in order for them to 'quote' companies.
24. *Projet de loi pour l'égalité entre les hommes et les femmes, Etude d'impact, Sénat, 1er juillet 2013*, http://www.senat.fr/leg/etudes-impact/pjl12-717-ei/pjl12-717-ei.pdf (last accessed 29 November 2018).
25. 'Gender Equality Bill', Impact Assessment, Senate, 1 July 2013, 12–13.

References

Bender, A.-F. 2004. 'Egalité professionnelle ou gestion de la diversité: quels enjeux pour l'égalité des chances?', *Revue Française de Gestion* (June/August): 205–17.

________. 'Les politiques de gestion de la diversité', in *La gestion des ressources humaines*, coll. Cahiers Français n°333. Paris: La documentation française, pp. 11–13.

Bender, A.-F., and F. Pigeyre. 2010. 'Mieux conceptualiser la diversité: un enjeu de gestion', in I. Barth and C. Falcoz (eds), *Nouvelles perspectives en management de la diversité*. Paris: Economica, pp. 83–100.

Berrebi-Hoffmann, I. 2011 'Gleichheit und Differenz bei Emile Durkheim am Falle der Geschlechterbeziehungen', in T. Wobbe, I. Berrebi-Hoffmann, and M. Lallement (eds), *Die gesellschaftliche Verortung des Geschlechts: Diskurse der Differenz in der deutschen und französischen Soziologie um 1900*. Frankfurt am Main: Campus, pp. 21–46.

________. 'Penser le changement au-delà des acteurs et des institutions', *Socio, nouvelle revue de sciences sociales* 1: 119–40.

Berrebi-Hoffmann, I., and P. Grémion. 2009. 'Elites intellectuelles et réforme de l'Etat: Esquisse en trois temps d'un déplacement d'expertise (1980–2009)', *Cahiers Internationaux de Sociologie* 126: 39–60.

Blanchard, S., I. Boni-Le Goff, and M. Rabier. 2013. '"Une cause de riches?" L'accès des femmes au pouvoir économique', *Sociétés contemporaines* 1(89): 101–30.

Didier, C. 2009. 'L'alerte professionnelle en France: un outil problématique au coeur de la RSE'. http://halshs.archives-ouvertes.fr/halshs-00768469.

Garner-Moyer, H. 2006. 'Gestion de la diversité et enjeux de GRH', *Revue Management et Avenir* 7: 23–42.

Kahn, A. 2009. 'Les administrateurs favorables à une loi sur des quotas de femmes dans les conseils', *Le Monde Economie*, 16 September, https://www.lemonde.fr/economie/article/2009/09/16/les-administrateurs-favorables-a-une-loi-sur-des-quotas-de-femmes-dans-les-conseils_1241232_3234.html.

Laufer, J., and R. Silvera. 2004. *Accords sur l'égalité professionnelle suite à la loi du 9 mai 2001: premiers éléments d'analyse*. Paris: Emergences.

Lebègue, D., and J.-P. Picard 2006. 'La révolution discrète des conseils d'administrations', *Le journal de l'école de Paris du management* 5(61): 8–15.

Lion, V. 2010. 'Conseils d'administration: Où sont les femmes', *L'Express*, 13 January. https://lexpansion.lexpress.fr/actualite-economique/ou-sont-les-femmes_841709.html.

Lucas, F.-X. 2009. 'La "modernitude" s'invite dans les conseils d'administration', *Le Bulletin Joly Sociétés*, November, 945.

Lucci, J.-P. 2003. 'Enron: The Bankruptcy Heard Around the World and the International Ricochets of Sarbanes-Oxley'. *Albany Law Review* 67(211).

Maclean M., and Harvey C. 2008. 'Women on Corporate Boards of Directors: The French Perspective', in S. Vinnicombe, V. Singh, R. Burke, D. Bilimoria and M. Huse (eds.), *Women on Corporate Boards of Directors: International Research and Practice*, Cheltenham: Edward Elgar, pp. 47–56.

Mairot, A. 2011. 'La féminisation des conseils d'administration et de surveillance légalement imposée', *Droit des sociétés*, March, alert no. 9.

Mortier, R. 2011. 'La féminisation forcée des conseils d'administration', *Droit des sociétés*, April, commentary no. 75.

Moulin, Y., and S. Point. 2012. 'Les femmes dans les conseils d'administration du SBF120: qualités féminines ou affaires de famille?', *Revue de gestion des ressources humaines* 83: 31–44.

Rapport 'Grésy'. 2009. *Rapport préparatoire à la concertation avec les partenaires sociaux sur l'égalité professionnelle entre les femmes et les hommes*. Brigitte Grésy, Member of social affair's general inspection, 7 July. http://travail-emploi.gouv.fr/IMG/pdf/Rapport_egalite8-07-09.pdf.

_______. 2011. *Inspection générale des affaires sociales RM2011-084P: Rapport sur l'égal accès des femmes et des hommes aux responsabilités professionnelles et familiales dans le monde du travail*. Etabli par Brigitte Grésy, with Philippe Dole and Francois-Xavier Chivot, June. http://www.ladocumentationfrancaise.fr/var/storage/rapports-publics/114000300/0000.pdf.

Reigné, P. 2010. 'Les femmes et les conseils d'administration: Réponse à un éditorial de M. Francois-Xavier Lucas', *JCP/La semaine juridique: édition entreprise et affaires* 3: 27–29.

Sabbagh, D. 2003. *L'égalité par le droit: Les paradoxes de la discrimination positive aux Etats-Unis*. Paris, Economica.

Sénat. 2013. 'Projet de loi: pour l'égalité entre les hommes et les femmes', Impact study, 1 July. http://www.senat.fr/leg/etudes-impact/pjl12-717-ei/pjl12-717-ei.pdf.

Stoltenberg, C. 2005. 'A Comparative Analysis of Post-Sarbanes-Oxley Corporate Governance Developments in the US and European Union: The Impact of Tensions Created by Extraterritorial Application of Section 404', *The American Journal of Comparative Law* 53(2): 457–491.

Chapter 6

Women on Company Boards in Germany

A Result of Constancy and Change in Gendered Categorizations, 1980–2013

Katja Karolin Müller

Introduction

In March 2015, the 'Law for the equal participation of women and men in leadership positions in the private and the public sector' was passed by the Bundestag and the Bundesrat. This law stipulates 30% quotas on members of supervisory boards in all limited corporations and joint-stock partnerships employing more than two thousand employees in the German private sector. If these requirements are not met, the so-called 'vacant chair' sanction comes into effect, and those positions designated for the under-represented gender remain vacant by force of law. France had adopted the law in January 2011, although the debates started in both countries in 2006 (see Bender, Berrebi-Hoffmann, and Reigné's chapter in this book). In France, therefore, consensus was achieved more quickly, and a higher quota of 40% was imposed (ibid.). Germany, with a 30% quota, is an exception, and was one of the last countries in Europe to implement the quota.

The years from 2006 until the law's enactment in 2015 saw intensive debates and a swell of mobilization efforts by scientific, political and advocacy group actors, closely followed by the media. The present study gathers a wide range of materials that represent the discourse as it played out from 2000 to 2013, in the political arena in particular.[1] Focusing on the parliamentary discursive arena allows me to represent the culmination of several strains of discourses and arenas in the enactment of a law, and thus in a legal regulation. Legal regulations play a substantial role in the construction of reality and take part in the establishment of cultural interpretative schemes and the production of perceptions of normality (Fuchs and Berghahn 2012; Rehbinder 2009). From a historically oriented, social-constructivist perspective that inquires after the construction of knowledge and the relevance of social categorization and classification, the introduction of a quota for private German enterprises is not self-explanatory. Instead, this event in particular reflects shifts in the cultural conceptions of social interpretative and explanatory schemes related to the category of gender, which have long been formative for the structuration of the labour market. In its theoretical foundations, this event displays the significant impact of gender norming, categorization and ascription on institutionalized effects on the labour market, specifically on so-called vertical segregation (Gottschall 2010). This labour market structure is a component of the social organization of western societies rooted in the nineteenth century (see Berkovitch 1999; Scott 1994; Wecker 1996; Wobbe 2012). The study of the construction and development of this structure proceeds not least from the premise that gender differences are discursively produced and concomitantly reinforced by institutional practices (Bublitz 1998; Honegger 2011; Laqueur 1992).

This chapter aims to ask to what extent traditional gendered knowledges and traditional classifications of gender and work either disappeared, underwent changes or found application in the political, economic and scientific discourses that led to the introduction of a law stipulating quotas for supervisory board positions. The analysis focuses on the various, in part competing, social orders of knowledge and their associated classifications. Simultaneously, this approach will enable us to understand the new legal norm as the result of discursive struggles over classifications (Barlösius 1997) and definitory or interpretative power (Stückler 2014: 295), which ultimately culminated in a particular knowledge about gender in the context of work prevailing over others.

The number of women in leadership positions in the private sector tells an unambiguous tale: equal education, equal qualification and legal equality still do not add up to a reasonable chance of overcoming vertical segregation (Achatz 2008; Gottschall 2010). Despite the fact that they make up 42% of employees in private enterprises, with only 26% occupying top management positions, women are significantly under-represented in Germany (Holst and Kirsch 2016a: 13). They are still under-represented on corporate company boards, with 6% representation on executive boards and 20% on supervisory boards (ibid.: 15f.). This indicates an increase of less than one percentage point on executive boards and an increase of over one percentage point on supervisory boards against the previous year of 2014. In addition to this small increase, 56% of female supervisory board members were employee representatives, but in this respect the shareholders are catching up (ibid.: 15).

Furthermore, while the figures for women's participation on corporate boards in the financial sector indicate a slight increase, 'men still call the shots' (Holst and Kirsch 2016b: 27). For more than fifteen years, the financial sector in Germany (large banks, savings banks and insurance companies) has employed more women than men (57–59%). Nevertheless, the share of women on executive boards in the top one hundred banks and savings banks remains approximately 8%, one percentage point higher than in 2014. At the end of 2015, women occupied 21% of seats on supervisory boards, corresponding to an increase of three percentage points (ibid.).

For decades, the phenomenon known as vertical segregation has been intensively discussed, particularly in women's and gender studies, which focus on the disadvantaging of women seeking access to attractive positions in the labour market. On the one hand, segregation phenomena linked to gender have been explained as an effect of gender as a structural category (Gottschall 1995: 126ff.). Other explanations have focused on the establishment in the nineteenth century of an 'order of the sexes' as a social construction with specific classifications. The order of the sexes was conceived as a 'natural' order (Honegger 1991) and connected to polarized gender characteristics derived from nature (see Hausen 1976). On the basis of a postulated 'order of nature', such gender classifications allowed 'male labour power to be categorized, in an imagined or factual relation to female labour power, as fundamentally leading as opposed to carrying out, as principally working as opposed to partly or additionally working, as qualified as opposed to unskilled labour power; areas of men's work could thus be classified as more valuable than areas of women's work, and on this basis a gender-hierarchical differential was built into the supposedly merit-based income pyramid' (Hausen 2000: 352).

Since the nineteenth century, the construction of gender difference has thus constituted the basis for declaring women's work a categorical special case, thereby justifying the limited inclusion of women in the employment system.

However, studies have empirically demonstrated a transformation in gender relations, with the result that the breakdown or maintenance of gender differentiations and hierarchies has become increasingly dependent upon context. Recent studies of the transformation of gender relations thus speak of a new 'dis-order of the sexes' (Heintz 2008), of continuities and breaks (Frey et al. 2010), of increasing equality alongside ongoing inequality (Gottschall 2010), of the contextual contingency of gender difference (Aulenbacher 2007; for organizations Wilz 2002), and of a 'deinstitutionalization of gender difference' (Heintz and Nadai 1998). At the same time, international and supranational organizations such as the International Labour Organization (ILO) and the EU play an important role (see Wobbe's, Höroldt's, and Bussmann's chapter in this book). In the discourse on the introduction of quotas for supervisory boards, however, the years 2000–2013 evince a renaissance of the meaning of and emphasis on gender as a category. This can be seen in two lines of argument that dominated the discourse: (1) the rhetoric on waste of human capital; and (2) the emphasis on the particularity of women's qualifications. Before examining these discursive constructions in detail, a reflection of the developments in German equality politics related to access to leadership positions as well as their associated semantic and textual constructions as they relate to the categories of gender and work is useful.

From Equality to Gender Mainstreaming and Managing Diversity: The Legal and Political Discourse on the Under-Representation of Women in Leadership Positions, 1980–2005

The discussion about the *disadvantaging of* and *discrimination against* women in work contexts was stimulated by the second wave of the women's movement as well as by the way in which women's studies drew upon and critically reflected the women's movement. The initial focus was on the demand for equal opportunity and overcoming social inequality. One way in which these concerns were articulated was in the demand to make women financially independent of husbands through paid work (see Hericks 2011; Müller 2005). At the beginning of the 1980s, institutions focused on women's policy issues were founded in many of the German federal states. The first equality guidelines and statutes were issued at the state level, and large municipalities established equality bodies at the municipal level (Meuser and Riegraf 2010: 192f). The policies enacted at this time operated first under the label of 'women's policies' (*Frauenpolitik*) – a terminology that was ultimately discarded in favour of 'advancement of women' (*Frauenförderung*) – and they were focused on expanding programmes to improve women's qualifications (see Wetterer 2002: 130f). The concept of gender difference was thus fundamental for the conception of these programmes, for it classified women as less qualified for the demands of the labour market and for leadership positions in particular (ibid.).

Stimulated by critique undertaken within women's studies and feminist politics, the 1990s saw a reorientation in the field of women's policy. The policy of the advancement of women (*Frauen[förder]politik*) became equality policy (*Gleichstellungspolitik*). One line of critique concretely described the problematic nature of the so-called advancement of women, both on the level of semantics and as a framework for action, claiming that the advancement of women tended 'to want to dismantle women's supposed deficits and "handicaps" instead of examining the structures of gender relations that in many cases preform gender inequalities, even where no more deficiencies can be found' (Wetterer 2005: 6). It would thus be a false conclusion to assume that 'women's missing or "wrong" qualifications are the main obstacle to their integration and participation in the labour market' (ibid.). At the federal level, as well, 'advancement of women' became 'equality' (see DGleiG 2001). This change made it clear that women's deficient qualifications were no longer seen as the decisive factor in the persistence of vertical segregation; instead, the focus shifted to the structural reasons for women's under-representation in leadership positions (Müller 1999; Quack 1998; Wetterer 2002; Wimbauer 1999). This can be traced back to intensive studies on the subject of 'women in leadership positions' and 'women in organizations', in which the image of the 'glass ceiling' became a prominent rhetorical figure representing a structural obstacle on the way to the top. Yet from the mid 1990s there was hardly any discussion of quotas as a means of rectifying such structural injustice. Instead, two new concepts came to dominate the discourse when it came to questions surrounding gender-based inequality in the labour market: gender mainstreaming and managing diversity.

The concept of gender mainstreaming (GM) dates back in particular to the 1995 Fourth World Conference on Women in Beijing, and therefore arose in a decision-making context of women's policy (see Riegraf and Meuser 2010). The signing of the Amsterdam Treaty of 1997 ushered in a (renewed) primary law determination of the principle of equality as a result of which the member states pledged 'to make the equality of men and women an interdisciplinary task of politics' (Young 2005: 28). Since the signing of the Amsterdam Treaty, gender mainstreaming has been an obligatory policy for institutions in the public sector. In private enterprises, however, gender mainstreaming even today plays only a marginal role, if at all. At approximately the moment when gender mainstreaming became normative in the public sector, it was the concept of managing diversity that gained a foothold in the German private sector.

Managing diversity (MD) is a (business) strategy developed in the 1990s in the context of human resources management in the United States (see Krell and Wechter 2006). Diversity management was conceived as a 'concept for the productive utilization of social differences', for making businesses more successful by increasing their productivity and improving their market position (see Bruchhagen and Koall 2008). The category of gender[2] thus became a resource for improving corporate performance. This business-based model met with criticism, however, especially among gender researchers (Bereswill 2004; Hericks 2011; Stiegler 2008; Wetterer 2005). On the basis of economic rationales like those produced by MD, equality policies and gender justice only make sense 'if [they] pay for themselves' (Wetterer 2005: 9). Whereas the politics of women's equality draws attention to the historical roots of the situational inequalities of women, in the concepts of GM and DM, the category of social inequality is replaced by a semantics of cultural difference (see Riegraf and Meuser 2010), and diversity management furthermore conceives of gender as a human resource. Parallel to these displacements in the conceptualization of equality, however, a new discussion resumed also around the legal regulation of gender equality in the private sector.

When the Social Democratic Party (SPD) and Alliance 90/The Green Party took control of the government in 1998, the advancement of women in private sector enterprises was conceptualized for the first time as a concrete task of government. The 1998 coalition agreement between the SPD and Alliance 90/The Green Party thus introduced the generally formulated goal 'of decisively advancing women's equality in work and society' (KV 1998). In the autumn of 2000, Federal Minister for Family Affairs, Senior Citizens, Women and Youth Christine Bergmann presented key parameters for such an equality law. These key parameters were the result of negotiations that had taken place in a 'consensus roundtable' convened in 1999 and attended by representatives from government, science, private enterprise and advocacy groups (see Pfarr 2001: 5). This initiative to create a binding equality law for the German private sector failed, however: 'the economic resistance to a legal regulation, of whatever design, culminated in numerous public position statements' (ibid.: 6). Instead, in 2001 an agreement was reached according to which companies voluntarily pledged to foster the representation of women in leadership positions and to advance equality. At this point, a *semantic* shift in the discourse surrounding the under-representation of women in leadership positions was already underway. First and foremost, political actors (especially Alliance 90/The Green Party and the SPD) and representatives of German business (Bundesverband der Deutschen Industrie and Bundesverband der Deutschen Arbeitgeberverbände) argued that companies should acknowledge and support talented women. The agreement reads: 'The Federal Republic of Germany has at its disposal great potential in the form of well-trained female workers' (Vereinbarung 2001: 1f). The use of economic terminology to defend the equality of women in labour contexts is conspicuous. Women appear *as economic potential*, which is linked to the economic imperative of competition within Germany and to Germany's ability to compete internationally. The potential of 'qualified women' thus ought to be used 'to meet the challenges of national and international competition' (ibid.: 2). According to Hericks, this appeal to the potential of well-trained female workers creates a link between equality policy and the economy (Hericks 2011: 93).

Despite the criticism sparked by the measures proposed in the agreement as well as by its 'voluntary' and 'non-binding' character (see Holst 2005), the legal regulation of women's access to leadership positions was abandoned for the time being. In 2006, demands for a legal regulation arose once again, now with a focus on quotas for supervisory boards, but these were met with resistance, particularly from the side of business, as well as from the conservative parties of the Christian-Democratic Union and Christian-Social Union and the free-market liberal Free-Democratic Party. Nonetheless, from 2006, Alliance 90/The Green Party, who had adopted a vanguard role among political parties in pressing demands for gender equality, were joined by The Left and the social-democratic SPD in regularly introducing to parliamentary debate legislative drafts on the implementation of quotas, often with a focus on supervisory board positions. In 2015, with the support of the conservative CDU/CSU, quota legislation was finally passed. In order to trace the resistances and changes as well as the semantic developments in the categorizations of gender in the context of access to positions of power, an analysis of records of public consultations on the introduction of quotas was made. Here actors from many areas (politicians, experts, advocacy groups etc.) clashed in these hearings and struggled, armed with their respective strategies of legitimation, for discursive prerogative. Table 6.1 provides an overview of the public hearings and indicates the respective arenas from which experts were invited to speak as well as the number of experts invited to speak for each arena.

A Quota for Supervisory Boards: The Parliamentary Discourse, 2006–13

The parliamentary discourse of the years 2006–13 is best understood in terms of its roots in older discourses. The first step in the direction of quotas for supervisory board positions was taken by Alliance 90/The

Table 6.1 Public hearings on the introduction of a quota for supervisory boards, invited experts.

Year	Speakers/Actors (Arenas)
2008	business (3 experts), law (2 experts), science (1 expert) trade unions (1 expert), politics (1 expert), women's advocacy groups (0 experts).
2011	law (4 experts), business (3 experts), science (1 expert), women's advocacy groups (1 expert), trade unions (1 expert).
2013	law (5 experts), business (3 experts), science (1 expert), women's advocacy groups (1 expert), trade unions (0 experts).

Green Party with a motion put forward in the Bundestag demanding the introduction of a quota for supervisory committees in market-listed companies (DS 16/5279). This motion already contained several gendered patterns of argument that structured the discourse on the introduction of the quota. The motion begins with the following words:

> Germany has significant deficits when it comes to equality in the private sector. ... The persistence of discrimination against women is damaging to companies, to the economy, and to democracy. We are wasting our investments in education, companies are losing creative potential, and last but not least, we are failing to take advantage of the dynamism that a higher level of female employment would bring to the labour market. (DS 16/5279: 1)

On the one hand, this is a presentation of the fact that equality in the private sector is deficient and that discrimination against women still persists. It does not, however, present this fact as a disadvantaging of women, as a deficiency of justice, but instead as a waste of human capital. This interpretative scheme of human capital waste and of 'woman' as a location factor runs through the entire discourse and is applied across party lines and by various actors, impacting the classifications of gender in work contexts in a specific way. In the discourse on the introduction of supervisory board quotas, a renaissance in the meaning of and emphasis on the category of gender can be discerned. It is visible in two lines of argument that dominate the discourse: (1) in the rhetoric of human capital waste; and (2) in the emphasis on women's unique qualifications, as will be shown below.

Waste of Female Human Capital as a Legitimation Strategy

As shown above, in the 'Agreement between the federal government and representative associations of German business on the advancement of equal opportunity for women and men in the private sector' of 2 July 2001 (Vereinbarung 2001), the rhetoric of human capital waste was already in play in the context of calls for women's equal access to leadership positions. The above-cited motion on the introduction of a supervisory board quota, put forward by Alliance 90/The Green Party in 2006, followed the same rationale. An introductory argument states: 'The persistence of discrimination against women is damaging to companies, to the economy, and to democracy' (DS 16/5279: 1). The damage caused by discrimination is not inflicted upon women, but upon companies and the economy. This line of argument displaces the disadvantaging inherent to the construct of discrimination from the group of people affected – the group made up of women – onto companies and onto the economy, a supposedly autonomous entity for which discrimination against women generates disadvantages. From the perspective of the generation of meaningfulness, this line of argument interprets discriminatory behaviour against women as an economic disadvantage that society cannot afford. Both proponents and adversaries of the quota made use of this trope, albeit with differing recommendations as to the appropriate means of tapping women's human capital. At a 2008 public hearing to assess the Greens' motion to enact quotas for supervisory boards, Dr Beate Degen, an invited expert from the German section of Junior Chamber International (JCI Germany) and an opponent of the quota, argued:

> In the Federal Republic, women are trained as highly qualified specialists, but this is not reflected in a corresponding presence of women in leadership positions. This means that in today's economy, the women's knowledge is not being efficiently used, is being wasted. (Public hearing 2008, Degen: 3)

Here, too, the investments made in women – which are implied in their highly specialized training – are juxtaposed with the insufficient recovery of that investment, the deficient presence of women in leadership positions. In Beate Degen's speech, the wasted resource that had still been characterized vaguely as 'potential' in the 2001 agreement is now distinctly qualified. The resource 'knowledge', linked to women, is not utilized, but wasted. Degen then goes on to detail the consequences of this wastefulness:

> In an environment where diversity constitutes a significant, even critical success factor for guaranteeing innovation and the ability to compete, diversity management is becoming increasingly important for companies' ability to maintain or expand their market position. In future, access to highly qualified workers, coupled with the necessity of diversity, will play an ever-expanding and increasingly decisive role for companies competing globally. For companies, equality

> management, today and even more so in future, therefore doesn't merely mean opening up equal opportunities; it is also a tool for more efficiently utilizing the available female human capital as a competitive advantage. (Ibid.: 6)

The knowledge linked to women appears here as a component of diversity, which is in turn defined as a site factor. Diversity can be interpreted as the totality of differing characteristics, (species) variety or personal abilities, whereby Degen highlights that the knowledge linked to women is a specific knowledge classified through the category of gender. While the 'environment' in which such diversity is represented as a competitive factor and as innovation is not further defined, the managerial concept of diversity management, which applies the principle of diversity, is represented concretely as important for companies' market success. Degen here prognosticates that 'diversity' will grow in importance, not merely in the context of German enterprise, but also in that of global competition. In the semantics of her professional milieu, Degen uses the concept of 'equality *management*' to redefine the construct of equality – which was formed historically by law and women's politics – as an important task of private enterprise. In this vein, Degen also declares that equality management is not meant to serve 'merely' the opening up of equal opportunity, but also the efficient utilization of female human capital. The advancement of women in leadership positions becomes meaningful here at least in principle also via the creation of equal opportunity; but at the same time, the equal opportunity is not treated as an economic concession. Quite to the contrary: it results in business profits, which are classified in terms of 'efficiency' and 'competitive advantage'. It becomes obvious that the same line of argument, centred on the waste of human resources, is used both by those calling to implement a quota and by those such as Degen, who affirm that voluntary pledges and commitments on the part of companies would suffice.

Ansgar Gabrielsen is another central figure in the discourse who was also invited as an expert to speak at the public hearing on the quota in the Bundestag in 2008. In his position as Norway's Minister of Economy and Trade, he was responsible for getting the introduction of the quota in Norway off the ground. Gabrielsen presents Norway's project to set quotas for supervisory boards not as arising from a desire to prevent discrimination and implement equal opportunity, but as an economic undertaking for the better exploitation of resources. He first clarifies in the introduction to his statement:

> My original rationale was not based on equality, I was instead concerned with the creation of value in society and with the utilization of all of society's

> resources. That's why it was wrong to cling to a situation, like the one in Germany, in Great Britain and in other countries, where only 5 to 8% of the supervisory and executive board members are women.... So it was about a value creation initiative. At the time, I was Minister of Economy and Trade, and my job was to utilize the country's resources. (Public hearing 2008, Gabrielsen: 8)

Women are classified here again as national resources whose waste is interpreted per se as unjustifiable in respect of the national good, which is emphasized by the references to Germany and Great Britain. The former project, which was legitimated on grounds of prevention of discrimination and by demands for equality in order to improve women's access to top positions, has become a value creation initiative, an undertaking legitimated by national economic interests. The cognitive framework in which the discourse on the under-representation of women unfolds is set up here in a way that excludes concerns about equality. The rationales for setting a quota are thereby raised to the level of national economic calculations. This aspect was also highlighted by Annette von Alemann, another invited expert in 2008, but linked additionally to a constitutional argument:

> There are reasons to get behind a project like this. For politics, those reasons are making good on the equality mandate in Basic Law art. 3 par. 2 as well as national economic considerations, which tell us that it doesn't pay off when well-trained women remain stuck in inferior positions. (Public hearing 2008, Alemann: 4)

The fulfilment of the equality mandate long had a bearing on the legal discourse surrounding the introduction of quotas. It can be considered all the more significant that Jutta Glock, representative of the German Women Lawyers Association at the same 2008 hearing, did not present a single legal argument for the introduction of the quota, but instead based her argument on the independence of the demand for a quota from any issues of equality.

> The German Women Lawyers Association is of the view that the responsibilities placed upon supervisory boards, in particular by the Companies Act, are much too important for the economy than that enterprises could continue to leave them up to men alone. This has first of all nothing to do with gender justice.... In the USA ... it has already been researched and proven that gender diversity in top management positions and on supervisory boards correlates to businesses' economic success. (Public hearing 2008, Glock: 14)

It is clear that the production of meaning related to the advancement of women in leadership positions in the German economy takes places by way of various lines of argument and legitimation strategies. Meaningfulness can be produced by linking to the state's constitutional equality mandate according to Basic Law art. 3, to the prevention of discrimination against women, or to the safeguarding of equal opportunity. Yet none of these lines of argument can make do alone, without being coupled to arguments based on the prevention of economic disadvantages arising from wasted investments and resources and the resulting competitive disadvantages.

In the year 2011, as well, in which three parties (SPD, Alliance 90/The Green Party and The Left) demanded quotas to be set for supervisory boards, this pattern of argument remained a central component of their legitimation strategies. The rationale of the bill drafted by Alliance 90/The Green Party 'for the gender-equitable occupation of supervisory boards' reads:

> A greater proportion of women in leadership positions now means, and will in future continue to mean, a real competitive advantage for companies. In many sectors, the demographic shift is already clearly palpable. As these demographic changes take place, well-trained, experienced leaders are becoming a scarce resource. The active utilization of well-trained women's know-how, specialized skills and creativity is a hallmark of smart business policy. A binding quota will markedly accelerate the catching-up process relative to the companies in other European countries that are leading in this area. (DS 17/3296: 6)

In this rationale, it almost sounds as if companies would still – owing to the principle of voluntarism – require convincing of women's usefulness in leadership, even though it is the introduction of a legal regulation that is here at stake. The exploitation of women's accumulated human capital is referred to here as an economically rational activity, as 'smart business policy'. This activity becomes meaningful by reference to the interpretative scheme 'demographic shift', which in turn refers to the stock of knowledge that there is an increasingly severe lack of skilled workers and that this poses serious problems for the German economy. Additionally, there is the interpretative scheme 'international competition' and the implied struggle among states, which necessarily impacts their regulations. The implications a quota has for equality are not even mentioned here. In the hearing on this draft bill in 2011, this line of argument was used in particular by actors from the economic milieu in order to classify the introduction of a legal regulation as unnecessary. They consistently emphasized the existing consensus on the question of under-representation and on the necessity of exploiting women's resources for the economic milieu. Yvonne Beiertz, CEO of the personnel consulting firm Spencer Stuart, thus affirmed that, 'As long as women are under-represented, a substantial part of the available expertise goes unused' (Public hearing 2011, Beiertz: 2), suggesting that this alone is sufficient reason for companies to support women in the future. Such a fostering of talent, or such a flow of talent from bottom to top should, according to Daniela Weber-Rey – supervisory board member, member of the Commission on the German Corporate Governance Code, partner in a globally operating law firm, and expert at the 2013 hearing – explicitly not be based on the ideas of justice, but instead be undertaken in the name of economic necessity, that is to say for the sake of corporate interests (Public hearing 2013, Weber-Rey: 7). At the time of the third hearing on the introduction of quotas in 2013, however, significantly fewer legitimations can be found following the interpretative scheme of human capital waste. It can be conjectured that this interpretative scheme had by then established itself as a legitimate argument, and thus become a part of the latent stock of knowledge. This is further substantiated by a commentary put on the record by Gisela Notz, a researcher and politician active in the field of women's issues: The question of equality and quotas is not a legal or an economic question, but one that requires a political decision (Public hearing 2013, Notz: 10).

The question of the economic usefulness of women from an economic perspective here seems to have already been answered. In 2013, however, reference is also still made to the 'special' competencies of women, as will be shown below.

The Special Human Resource 'Woman' as a Legitimation Strategy

As has already been made clear, the notion of waste and the call to exploit resources refer to women's untapped skills and qualifications. In terms of diversity, this means an emphasis on differences among skills and qualifications, as demonstrated by a statement made by the representative of the German Women Lawyers Association:

> More importantly, it is scientifically proven that women and men demonstrate different approaches, different analyses, and different conclusions in economic contexts and when it comes to entrepreneurial decision-making. (Public hearing 2008, Glock: 14)

Just as gender difference was, at the turn of the nineteenth century, considered 'scientifically proven' in terms of women's and men's respective aptitudes and abilities, Glock likewise presents gender difference – their 'differing economic and social competencies and experiences' and their 'different approaches, different analyses and different conclusions in economic contexts and when it comes to entrepreneurial decision-making' – as scientific fact. This assumption of difference thereby becomes an inherent component of the call for diversity. The trade unionist Rainald Thannisch likewise stressed the scientific fact of gender difference at the public hearing of 2008:

> Furthermore, we know from scientific studies that increased plurality in supervisory boards, owing to female and male employees both having a voice, increases the boards' effectiveness. Women often stand for a different culture of leadership and a different leadership style, and bring to their work on the board different economic and social competencies and experiences as compared to men. A greater proportion of women will therefore increase the effectiveness of supervisory committees in an enduring way. (Public hearing 2008, Thannisch: 20)

This line of argument symbolizes a typical pattern in this discourse: it is no longer valid to negate the differences between men and women; instead, the positive potential of difference must be utilized.[3] But these standard thought patterns, as well as the notions that women have a different leadership style and are more conscientious, are also made use of on another level. Women's particular way of acting is additionally interpreted as a more moral way of behaving in business contexts, as a statement by Ansgar Gabrielsen shows in an exemplary way:

> I have read international articles, some articles from America, as well, and followed what happened there in the five hundred biggest corporations. I saw this also in relation to the impact on government customers. There were plenty of international scandals, and it was always the men who were caught up in these scandals. (Public hearing 2008, Gabrielsen: 15)

Here the construct of morality comes into play, which is historically associated with femininity (Gilligan 1992). It is also argued that the market will be stabilized by a higher proportion of women in leadership positions. The point of reference is, especially since 2007, the crisis of financial market capitalism in association with hegemonic masculinity (see Stückler 2011, among others), which is interpreted as having helped trigger the crisis. In this context especially, traditional classifications such as women's emotiveness, the ability to communicate and morality are emphasized, sometimes linked to the argument that women would contribute to companies' positive transformation. This is underscored also by Jutta Glock in her statement from 2008:

> Women generally think on a longer timeline than their male colleagues, who often appear to feel beholden only to immediate success. This has been scientifically proven in the USA, where, for example, banks generally score the creditworthiness of companies directed by women higher than that of companies directed by men. (Public hearing 2008, Glock: 6)

Glock connects up here with multiple legitimated public discourses. In opposition to risk-taking men, who are oriented only to the short term, women are presented as the gender dedicated to the dispositive of sustainability. This connects economic utility with gender stereotyping by way of creditworthiness, which is to say women's dependability and conscientious handling of resources. This discursive legitimation strategy puts the figure of the female board member – like the former figure of the female worker – 'on public display' as 'a problem in need of a solution' (Scott 1994: 451), in order to negotiate her right to existence in 'moral and categorical terms' (ibid.). The difference is that there is no discursive reference to the fact that there are problems *with* her (as was apparent in the negotiations on the handling of female workers), but only *without* her, and this, however, in both cases on account of her difference from the male gender. It is not the compatibility of being a woman and performing wage work that is the focus here; the point is rather that international competition lacks the specifically female competencies that would otherwise lead to greater success and efficiency in business and improve the work of supervisory boards in respect to quality, transparency and moral leadership. This argument was also taken up in 2013 by Thomas Sattelberger, an expert from Deutsche Telekom, who used it as a legitimation strategy for the introduction of a quota:

> This dual approach [quota plus bottom-up measures] also puts openly to the test something that is not often said aloud in the legal debate, namely the values of a masculine leadership culture. This culture is often marked – at least in the market-listed companies – by unconditional loyalty and an old-boy mentality, the willingness to work an unlimited number of hours, the will to succeed at almost any cost, and risk-seeking behaviour, sometimes without limits, gambler-like and not seldom without any commitment to values. It simultaneously raises the issue of a leadership culture with more cooperation, team orientation, fairness and risk awareness. (Public hearing 2013, Sattelberger: 14)

Sattelberger refers here in particular to scandals in the aftermath of the financial crisis in association with hegemonic masculinity (see Stückler 2011, among others), which, in turn, triggered demands for alternative 'female' competencies. Conversely, classifications formerly considered essential in leadership positions, such as perseverance and risk-taking, are devalorized.

What can we conclude from these developments about the classifications of gender in the context of work?

Transformation and Persistence in the Classifications of Gender

If we conclude by posing the question of a transformation of the interpretative schemes of gender in the context of work, we find that essential gender differences are no longer considered legitimate arguments for barring women access to (leadership) positions. Since the later 1980s, the reference to gender differences in the context of work has become questionable and has been increasingly delegitimized as a reference of differentiation and hierarchization (Heintz 2008; Heintz and Nadai 1998; Wilz 2002). In the 1990s, the focus was accordingly on structural reasons for the under-representation of women in leadership positions, and women were considered equally qualified to men. The process that led to the creation of a legal norm stipulating a quota for supervisory board positions, however, shows how schemes of difference can be reactivated, just as they were in this case at every level examined (law, business, EU). Nevertheless, the discussion about quotas unfolded according to a different paradigm of difference: the context of economic rationality, which conceptualizes both male and female individuals as carriers of human capital resources (see Wobbe and Renard 2017; Wobbe, Renard, and Müller 2017).

In the nineteenth century, the scientization of difference (Honegger 1991) functioned to legitimate the limited inclusion of women in the labour market. In the twentieth century, the figure of difference was delegitimized as an obstacle to inclusion and was replaced by the right of equal access to the employment system in connection with the individualization of women. The fundamental right of equal access to positions in the employment system is thus no longer in question in the discourse on quotas. In the discourse of the 2010s – as the results show – there has, however, been a formulation of competencies constructed as specific to professional women. Interestingly, these competencies draw on schemes of difference, such as sexual stereotypes (Hausen 2000), from the nineteenth-century discourse. The focus is on the difference between

Table 6.2 Scripts, promoters and interpretative schemes related to the German discourse on women's quotas.

	Scripts	Promoters	Interpretative scheme
1980s	Advancement of women (*Frauenförderung*)	Women's movement, women's studies	Difference – women need to be better qualified and given more opportunities in work contexts
1990s	Gender equality (*Gleichstellung*)	Women's studies, DJB (German Female Lawyers Association), actors of female politics	Equality – women's work skills are equal, structures cause inequality
From 2010	Quota, diversity (*Quotierung, Diversity*)	Parties (SPD, Greens, Left), science (law, politics, sociology) associations of women entrepreneurs/of women shareholders, DJB	Difference – women have specific skills needed in the labour market

genders, their heterogeneity, which is classified as a resource. Table 6.2 provides an overview of developments in the semantics and interpretations of gender.

The 'order of nature' postulated in the eighteenth century, whose classifications were based on the physiological structure of the human body, has now given way to an 'order of human capital'. If formerly it was biological-physiological classifications that justified gender difference and the allocation of woman and her responsibility to the area of reproduction, marriage and the family (Bublitz 1998: 17), now it is classifications of qualifications and specific competencies constructed as valuable resources in private enterprise. These specific competencies were suddenly in high demand in the wake of the contingent event of the financial crisis. Whereas soft skills such as forcefulness, competitiveness, risk-taking and so on have come to be viewed as scandalous traits that helped to bring about the current crises, supposedly feminine competencies such as teamwork, communicative skills, caution and restraint and a sense of responsibility now appear as indispensable resources in international competition. Owing to distinctions and individuations that produce particularly feminine competencies as positive for the labour market and the economy, emphasizing difference has thus once more become capable of legitimation.

Nonetheless, the potential of women is also cast as not yet fully activated, or underdeveloped. This circumstance is in turn a phenomenon of the unequal and asynchronous inclusion of men and women in the employment system. The yet-to-be-developed potential and uniqueness of women are thereby understood to be competitive factors.

Furthermore, in the 1980s and 1990s, the formerly dominant schemes of legitimation for the introduction of a women's quota, such as social inequality, justice and overcoming discrimination (social rationales), became less important. To be sure, the discourse presents the deficient equality of women in the private sector and ongoing discrimination against women as facts. It does not, however, present them as failures of justice, but casts them instead in terms of human capital waste. On the one hand, the arguments are made with recourse to the state's constitutional equality mandate according to Basic Law art. 3, to the reduction of gender inequalities, the prevention of discrimination against women and the guaranteeing of equal opportunity. Yet none of these lines of argument can make do without being coupled to arguments based on the prevention of economic disadvantages arising from wasted investments and resources and the associated competitive market disadvantages (economic rationales).

This is one of many explanations for the developments in the semantics and interpretations of gender and for creating consensus in the question of introducing a quota in Germany. But what happened to the share of women on supervisory boards after imposing the quota?

Table 6.3 gives an overview of the increase of women in the highest decision-making bodies of the largest listed companies in Germany and France.

After the introduction of a gender quota in France in 2011, the share of women on the corporate boards of major listed companies increased from 12% in 2010 to 22% in 2012. This is an increase of 10% in two years. In Germany, the impact of the quota seems to be much less. From January 2016, when the quota was introduced, up to May 2017, there was an increase of only 3.1%. It remains to be seen whether this is an indication of the weakness of the German quota and the continued opposition

Table 6.3 Women in decision-making bodies.

	2010	2011	2012	2013	2014	2015	2016	2017
GER	13%	15%	16%	20%	22%	25%	**27% q.i.***	**28.1% Up to May 2017**
FRA	12%	**17% q.i.***	**22%**	**27%**	**30%**	**33%**	**37%**	n.a.

***q.i.:** the quota was newly introduced in January of this year
Source: Deutsches Wirtschaftsinstitut (DIW): Managerinnen Barometer 2010–2017.

to women in decision-making bodies, or whether the development in Germany simply needs more time.

Katja Karolin Müller MA is a PhD candidate at the University of Potsdam (Germany) and Lecturer in Sociology and Gender Studies at Humboldt-Universität zu Berlin and at the University of Potsdam. Her research focuses on the sociology of gender and work and the major significance of gender categorization and ascription for institutional effects in the labour market. She worked for the project 'Metamorphoses of Equality II (1945–2010)' (Potsdam/CNAM-Lise Paris) co-founded by the Agence Nationale de la Recherche (ANR) and the Deutsche Forschungsgemeinschaft (DFG). She has recently published, with Theresa Wobbe and Léa Renard, 'Nationale und globale Deutungsmodelle des Geschlechts im arbeitsstatistischen sowie arbeitsrechtlichen Klassifikationssystem: Ein vergleichstheoretischer Beitrag (1882–1992)' in *Soziale Welt* (2017).

Notes

1. The data on which the study is based were derived from written documents incorporated in, or documenting, the legislative process in the period 2007–13: publications of the federal government, drafts of bills, party programmes, plenary minutes, agreements and expert position papers from the side of employers and employees, legal, political and economic experts, the input of various associations and societies as well as EU documents such as directives, Commission decisions and strategy papers.
2. Alongside other categories of difference such as ethnicity, sexual orientation, generational belonging and many others.
3. The EU Commission bases its argument to this effect on findings of studies conducted by businesses. McKinsey, one of the most important globally represented corporate and strategy consulting firms, has been studying the role of women in enterprise since 2007 and publishing annual or bi-annual reports entitled 'Women Matter'.

References

Primary Sources

Coalition Agreements

KV (1998). Aufbruch und Erneuerung – Deutschlands Weg ins 21. Jahrhundert. Koalitionsvereinbarung zwischen der SPD und Bündnis90/Die Grünen, Bonn, 20 October 1998.

Other Political Agreements

Vereinbarung (2001). 'Vereinbarung zwischen der Bundesregierung und den Spitzenverbänden der deutschen Wirtschaft zur Förderung der Chancengleichheit von Frauen und Männern in der Privatwirtschaft', 2 July 2001.

Laws

DGleiG (2001). Gesetz zur Durchsetzung der Gleichstellung von Frauen und Männern (Gleich stellungsdurchsetzungsgesetz – DGleiG), 30 November 2001.

Draft Laws and Applications

DS 16/5279 Antrag Fraktion BÜNDNIS 90/DIE GRÜNEN - Quote für Aufsichtsratsgremien börsennotierter Unternehmen einführen (DS 16/5279).

DS 17/3296 Gesetzentwurf 3296 Bündnis 90/DIE GRÜNEN – Entwurf eines Gesetzes zur geschlechtergerechten Besetzung von Aufsichtsräten (DS 17/3296).

Expert Opinion

Public hearing, 7 May 2008

- Alemann, Annette von: Universität Bielefeld.
- Degen, Dr Beate: Wirtschaftsjunioren Deutschland e.V. Berlin.
- Gabrielsen, Ansgar: Wirtschaftsminister a.D. Oslo.
- Glock, Prof. Dr Jutta: Rechtsanwältin, Deutscher Juristinnenbund e.V. Berlin.
- Solaro, Dr Patrica C.: Bayer AG Berlin.
- Thannisch, Rainald: Deutscher Gewerkschaftsbund Bundesvorstand, Berlin.
- Windbichler, Prof. Dr Christine: Humboldt Universität zu Berlin, Berlin.
- Zimmermann, Dr Anne: Deutscher Industrie- und Handelkammertag, Berlin.

Public hearing, 11 May 2011

- Beiertz, Yvonne: Partnerin Spencer Stuart Associates GmbH, Frankfurt.
- Dammann, Dr Angelika: SAP AG, Vorstandsmitglied Personal, Arbeitsdirektorin, Walldorf.
- Falkenhausen, Jutta Freifrau von: FidAR Frauen in die Aufsichtsräte e.V. Berlin.
- Hirte, Prof. Dr Heribert: Universität Hamburg, Rechtswissenschaft, Hamburg.
- Holst, Dr Elke: DIW Berlin.
- Laskowski, Prof. Dr Ruth: Universität Kassel, Wirtschaftsrecht, Kassel.
- Pfarr, Prof. Dr Heide: Direktorin Wirtschafts- und Sozialwissenschaftliches Institut und Mitglied der Geschäftsführung Hans-Böckler-Stiftung, Düsseldorf.
- Sacksowski, Prof. Dr Ute: Johann Wolfgang Goethe-Universität, Öffentliches Recht, Frankfurt Main.
- Schmidt, Prof. Dr Marlene: Deutscher Juristinnenbund e.V. Berlin.

Public hearing, 16 January 2013

- Bauer, Prof. Dr Jobst-Hubertus: Rechtsanwalt, Stuttgart.
- Glock, Prof. Dr Jutta: Rechtsanwältin, Deutscher Juristinnenbund e.V. Berlin.
- Hirte, Prof. Dr Heribert: Universität Hamburg, Rechtswissenschaft, Hamburg.
- Körner, Prof. Dr Marita: Universität der Bundeswehr München, Wirtschafts- und Arbeitsrecht, Munich.
- Notz, Dr Gisela: Wissenschaftlerin und Autorin, Berlin.
- Ostermann, Marie-Christine: Die Familienunternehmer – ASU e.V. und Der Jungen Unternehmer – BJU, Berlin.
- Sattelberger, Thomas: Stiftungsvorstand ZU, ehemaliger Personalvorstand Deutsche Telekom AG, Munich.
- Weber-Rey, Daniela: Rechtsanwältin, Frankfurt am Main.
- Willems, Dr Heiko: Bundesverband der Deutschen Industrie e.V. Berlin

Secondary Sources

Achatz, J. 2008. 'Die Integration von Frauen in Arbeitsmärkten und Organisationen', in S. Wilz (ed.), *Geschlechterdifferenzen – Geschlechterdifferenzierungen: Ein Überblick über gesellschaftliche Entwicklungen und theoretische Positionen.* Wiesbaden: VS Verlag, pp. 105–38.

Aulenbacher, B. 2007. 'Vom fordistischen Wohlfahrts- zum neoliberalen Wettbewerbsstaat: Bewegungen im gesellschaftlichen Gefüge und in den Verhältnissen von Klasse, Geschlecht und Ethnie', in C. Klinger, G.-A. Knapp, and B. Sauer (eds), *Achsen der Ungleichheit: Zum Verhältnis von Klasse, Geschlecht und Ethnizität.* Frankfurt: Campus, pp. 42–55.

Barlösius, E. 1997. 'Was ist Armut? Über den "Kampf um Klassifikationen"', in E. Barlösius, E. Kürsat, and H.P. Waldhoff (eds), *Distanzierte Verstrickungen: Die schwierige Bindung soziologisch Forschender an ihr Objekt.* Berlin: edition sigma, pp. 89–105.

Bereswill, M. 2004. '"Gender" als neue Humanressource? Gender Mainstreaming und Geschlechterdemokratie zwischen Ökonomisierung und Gesellschaftskritik', in M. Meuser and C. Neusüß (eds), *Gender Mainstreaming: Konzepte, Handlungsfelder, Instrumente.* Bonn: Bundeszentrale für Politische Bildung, pp. 52–70.

Berkovitch, N. 1999. *From Motherhood to Citizenship: Women's Rights and International Organizations.* Baltimore, MD: Johns Hopkins University Press.

Bruchhagen, V., and I. Koall. 2008. 'Managing Diversity: Ein (kritisches) Konzept zur produktiven Nutzung sozialer Differenzen', in R. Becker, and B. Kortendiek (eds), *Handbuch Frauen- und Geschlechterforschung: Theorie, Methoden, Empirie.* Wiesbaden: VS Verlag für Sozialwissenschaften, pp. 931–938.

Bublitz, H. (ed.). 1998. *Das Geschlecht der Moderne: Genealogie und Archäologie der Geschlechterdifferenz.* Frankfurt: Campus.

_______. 2000. 'Zur Konstitution von Kultur und Geschlecht um 1900', in H. Barlösius, C. Hanke, and A. Seier (eds), *Der Gesellschaftskörper: Zur Neuordnung von Kultur und Geschlecht um 1900.* Frankfurt: Campus, pp. 19–87.

Frey, M., et al. (eds). 2010. *Perspektiven auf Arbeit und Geschlecht: Transformationen, Reflexionen, Interventionen.* Munich: Rainer Hampp Verlag, pp. 248–77.

Fuchs, G., and S. Berghahn. 2012. 'Recht als feministische Politikstrategie? Einleitung', *Femina Politica* 2: 11–24.

Gilligan, C. 1982. *In a Different Voice.* Cambridge, MA: Harvard University Press.

Gottschall, K. 1995. 'Geschlechterverhältnis und Arbeitsmarktsegregation', in R. Becker-Schmidt and G.-A. Knapp (eds), *Das Geschlechterverhältnis als Gegenstand der Sozialwissenschaften.* Berlin: Campus, pp. 125–62.

_______. 2010. 'Arbeit, Beschäftigung und Arbeitsmarkt aus der Genderperspektive', in F. Böhle, G.G. Voß, and G. Wachtler (eds), *Handbuch Arbeitssoziologie.* Wiesbaden: VS Verlag, pp. 671–98.

Hausen, K. 1976. 'Die Polarisierung der "Geschlechtscharaktere"': Eine Spiegelung der Dissoziation von Erwerbs- und Familienleben', in W. Conze (ed.), *Sozialgeschichte der Familie in der Neuzeit Europas: Neue Forschungen.* Stuttgart: Klett, pp. 363–93.

_______. 'Arbeit und Geschlecht', in J. Kocka and C. Offe (eds), *Geschichte und Zukunft der Arbeit.* Frankfurt: Campus, pp. 343–61.

Heintz, B. 2008. 'Ohne Ansehen der Person? De-Institutionalisierungsprozesse und geschlechtliche Differenzierung', in S. Wilz (ed.), *Geschlechterdifferenzen – Geschlechterdifferenzierungen: Ein Überblick über gesellschaftliche Entwicklungen und theoretische Positionen.* Wiesbaden: VS Verlag, pp. 231–51.

Heintz, B., and E. Nadai. 1998. 'Geschlecht und Kontext: De-Institutionalisierungsprozesse und geschlechtliche Differenzierung', *Zeitschrift für Soziologie* 27(2): 75–93.

Hericks, K. 2011. *Entkoppelt und Institutionalisiert: Gleichstellungspolitik in einem deutschen Konzern.* Wiesbaden: Springer-VS.

Holst, E. 2005. 'Frauen in Führungspositionen: Massiver Nachholbedarf bei großen Unternehmen und Arbeitgeberverbänden', *DIW Wochenbericht* 72(3): 49–56.

Holst, E., and A. Kirsch. 2016a. 'Corporate Boards of Large Companies: More Momentum Needed for Gender Parity', *DIW Economic Bulletin* 3: 13–24.

_______. 2016b. 'Financial Sector: Share of Women on Corporate Boards Increases Slightly but Men Still Call the Shots', *DIW Economic Bulletin* 3: 27–37.

Honegger, C. 1991. *Die Ordnung der Geschlechter: Die Wissenschaften vom Menschen und das Weib 1750–1850*. Frankfurt: Campus.

_______. 2011. 'Die kognitiven Prinzipien der neuen Wissenschaften vom Menschen und die Genese einer weiblichen Sonderanthropologie in Frankreich', in T. Wobbe, I. Berrebi-Hoffmann, and M. Lallement (eds), *Die gesellschaftliche Verortung des Geschlechts: Diskurse der Differenz in der deutschen und französischen Soziologie um 1900*. Frankfurt: Campus, pp. 93–113.

Krell, G., and H. Wächter (eds). 2006. *Diversity Management: Impulse aus der Personalforschung*. Munich: Rainer Hampp Verlag.

Laqueur, T. 1992. *Auf den Leib geschrieben: Die Inszenierung der Geschlechter von der Antike bis. Freud*. Frankfurt: Campus.

Meuser, M., and B. Riegraf. 2010. 'Geschlechterforschung und Gleichstellungspolitik: Von der Frauenförderung zum Diversity Management', in B. Aulenbacher, M. Meuser, and B. Riegraft (eds), *Soziologische Geschlechterforschung: Eine Einführung*. Wiesbaden: Springer VS, pp. 189–209.

Müller, U. 1999. 'Zwischen Licht und Grauzone: Frauen in Führungspositionen', *Arbeit* 8(2): 137–61.

_______. 2005. 'Ein Geschlechterkampf in vier Runden: Rückblick auf fünfunddreißig Jahre Frauenbewegung und Frauenpolitik', *Beiträge zur feministischen Theorie und Praxis* (66/67): 67–86.

Nunner-Winkler, G. 1994. 'Eine weibliche Moral? Differenz als Ressource im Verteilungskampf', *Zeitschrift für Soziologie* 23(6): 417–33.

Pfarr, H. (ed.). 2001. *Ein Gesetz zur Gleichstellung der Geschlechter in der Privatwirtschaft*. Düsseldorf: Edition der Hans Böckler Stiftung.

Quack, S. 1998. 'Karrieren von Frauen in Glaspalästen: Weibliche Führungskräfte in europäischen Banken'. *Handelsblatt* 23/24 (February): 55.

Rehbinder, M. 2009. *Rechtssoziologie*. Munich: C.H. Beck.

Scott, J. 1994. 'Die Arbeiterin', in G. Fraisse and M. Perrot (eds), *Geschichte der Frauen, Bd. 4: 19. Jahrhundert*. Frankfurt: Campus, pp. 451–80.

Stiegler, B. 2008. 'Gender Mainstreaming: Fortschritt oder Rückschritt in der Geschlechterpolitik?', in R. Becker and B. Kortendiek (eds), *Handbuch Frauen- und Geschlechterforschung: Theorie, Methoden, Empirie*. Wiesbaden: VS Verlag, pp. 925–30.

Stückler, A. 2011. 'Hegemoniale Männlichkeit im Finanzmarkt-Kapitalismus', *gender...politik... online*, August. www.fu-berlin.de/sites/gpo/pol_theorie/Zeitgenoessische_ansaetze/stuecklerhegmaennlichkeit/Stueckler.pdf.

_______. 2014. 'Diskursanalytische Rechtsnormgeneseforschung: Zur diskursanalytischen Untersuchung von Rechtsentstehungsprozessen', *Journal for Discourse Studies* 3: 287–315.

Wecker, R. 1996. '"Weiber sollen unter keinen Umständen in der Nachtarbeit eingesetzt werden...": zur Konstitutierung von Weiblichkeit im Arbeitsprozess', in C. Eifert et al. (eds), *Was sind Frauen? Was sind Männer?* Frankfurt: Suhrkamp Verlag, pp. 196–239.

Wetterer, A. 2002. 'Strategien rhetorischer Modernisierung: Gender Mainstreaming, Managing Diversity und die Professionalisierung der Gender Expertinnen', *Zeitschrift für Frauenforschung und Geschlechterstudien* (3): 129–48.

_______. 2005. 'Gleichstellungspolitik und Geschlechterwissen – Facetten schwieriger Vermittlungen', genderKompetenzZentrum. Retrieved 8 January 2018 from www.

genderkompetenz.info/veranstaltungs_publikations_und_news_archiv/genderlectures/gl_wetterer_gleichstellungspolitik_und_geschlechterwissen_140205.pdf.

Wilz, S.M. 2002. *Organisation und Geschlecht: Strukturelle Bindungen und kontingente Kopplungen*. Opladen: Leske + Budrich.

Wimbauer, C. 1999. *Organisation, Geschlecht, Karriere: Fallstudien aus einem Forschungsinstitut*. Opladen: Leske + Budrich.

Wobbe, T. 2012. 'Making Up People: Berufsstatistische Klassifikation, geschlechtliche Kategorisierung und wirtschaftliche Inklusion um 1900 in Deutschland', *Zeitschrift für Soziologie* 41(1): 41–57.

Wobbe, T., and I. Biermann. 2009. *Von Rom nach Amsterdam: Die Metamorphosen des Geschlechts in der Europäischen Union*. Wiesbaden: VS Verlag.

Wobbe, T., and L. Renard. 2017. 'Gendered Boundaries between Household and Market as a Globalized Distinction: The Category of 'Family Workers' in International Statistics (1930s–1980s)', *Journal of Global History* 12(3): 340–360.

Wobbe, T., L. Renard, and K. Müller. 2017. 'Wirtschaften mit der Differenz: Deutungsmodelle des Geschlechts im Spiegel arbeitstatistischer und -rechtlicher Kategorisierungsprozesse von Arbeit (1882–1994)', *Soziale Welt* 68: 63–85.

Young, B. 2005. 'Widersprüche zwischen der europäischen Makroökonomie und Gender Mainstreaming: Unüberwindbare Widersprüche?', in A. Jünemann and C. Klement (eds), *The Policy of Gender Equality in the European Union*, 2nd edn. Baden-Baden: Nomos, pp. 27–45.

II

Transnational Interplay of Categorization

Chapter 7

Dynamics of Gendered Employment Regimes in France and Germany Over the Last Two Decades
How Can They Be Explained?

Arnaud Lechevalier

Introduction

For a long time, German society has been seen as an ideal type of conservative gender regime with a strong degree of 'familiarization', based on a traditional and non-egalitarian male breadwinner model in a conservative welfare state. However, over the last two decades the position of German women has dramatically changed in terms of access to employment, with a global employment rate much higher than that in France, and close to the EU average. At the same time, family policy has also been the subject of major reform carried out to improve the work and family life balance. With the objective of improved access to the labour market for women and a strategy of social investment in the field of the family, public policies have officially aimed at promoting the life conditions of women and have called into question the traditional model of social role sharing.

For its part, France has long been recognized in relevant literature as a modernized and original variant of the male breadwinner model, with higher activity rates for women as well as a comprehensive family policy which, despite its pro-natal objectives, aimed to guarantee a strong horizontal redistribution of income and an all-encompassing public system of childcare facilities. However, in recent years the employment of women in full-time equivalents has stagnated and family policy reforms have mainly aimed at individualizing and increasing the flexibility of 'choices' available to parents, including encouraging withdrawals for mothers from the labour market.

Against this background, this chapter aims to analyse how gender regimes in France and Germany have changed over the past two decades and how these changes can be explained. In comparison with the usual conceptualization and content of the gender regime (Betzel 2007), this chapter uses a more restricted definition. I propose the notion of an *employment gendered regime*, which is conceived as a set of interdependent variables concerning, first, the situation of women/mothers on the labour market – here mainly the rates of employment and working time – which aim to grasp the financial autonomy of women in particular; second, the role of the state concerning the regulation of gender relations, mainly through the objectives and instruments of employment and family policies, which convey, reproduce and fuel lasting differences in the gendered division of work and family (Lemière 2014); and third, social norms regarding the prevailing familial arrangements in a society with a focus on the fertility behaviour of women in order to understand the prevailing tensions between work and family.

The chapter will first provide an overview of employment in both countries since 1945, especially over the last twenty years. Second, it will explore how women's employment has grown in Germany and France and point out the role played by employment policy in each country. Third, the demographic context in both countries since 1945 will be analysed with a focus on the contrasting behaviour patterns of French and German women concerning fertility. In addition, on the basis of the inversion of the correlation between employment rates and fertility indicators within the Organisation for Economic Cooperation and Development (OECD) countries since the mid 1980s, the analysis will consider the reforms displayed in family policy in both countries over recent decades. Next, the chapter summarizes the main changes, with a focus on the activity of mothers and on familial configurations by employment status as a result of employment and fertility behaviours as well as predominant family social norms. Finally, the chapter aims to explain these changes by analysing the arguments made, the driving forces, as well as the actors at their root. The analysis mainly uses data from Eurostat (Labour Force Survey) and from the national accounts for long-term time series on employment and other data on employment, demography and the family from the OECD.

Women's Activity and Employment in Germany and France since 1945

In Germany the growth of both total and women's employment was strong at the beginning of the *Wirtschaftswunder*: from 1950 and 1962 the number of female employees increased by 2.3 million to reach 7.1 million. This growth was mainly due to part-time jobs for mothers, who looked for a supplementary income (von Oertzen 1999: 213). After this first period, the evolution of employment patterns in West Germany became more irregular due to stagnation in the 1960s and as a response to the first and second oil shocks. The employment of women aged fifteen to sixty-four, representing 37% of total numbers employed in the late 1950s, also stagnated between 1960 and 1975, before rising from 9.3 to 10.7 million from 1975 to the fall of the Berlin Wall in 1989.

Looking at the activity rates, the huge gap of forty points between men and women at the beginning of the 1960s was only reduced to thirty points at the end of the 1980s. We can therefore speak of a certain overall stagnation in West German society in relation to the increase in women's employment, even if an upward trend emerged until the late 1970s, thanks to a new development phase of part-time work (Maier 1993).

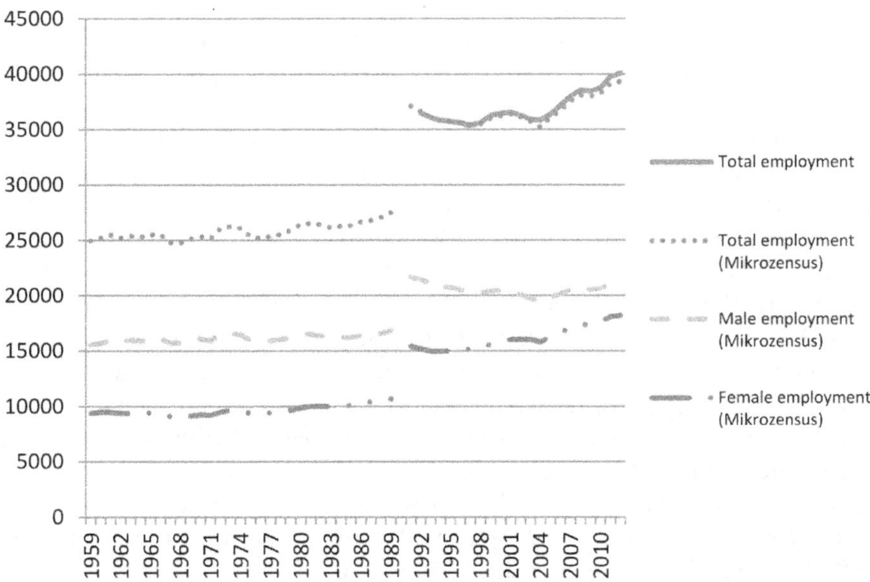

Chart 7.1 Total employment in Germany of persons aged fifteen to sixty-four years from 1959.

Source: Statistisches Bundesamt, Mikrozensus.

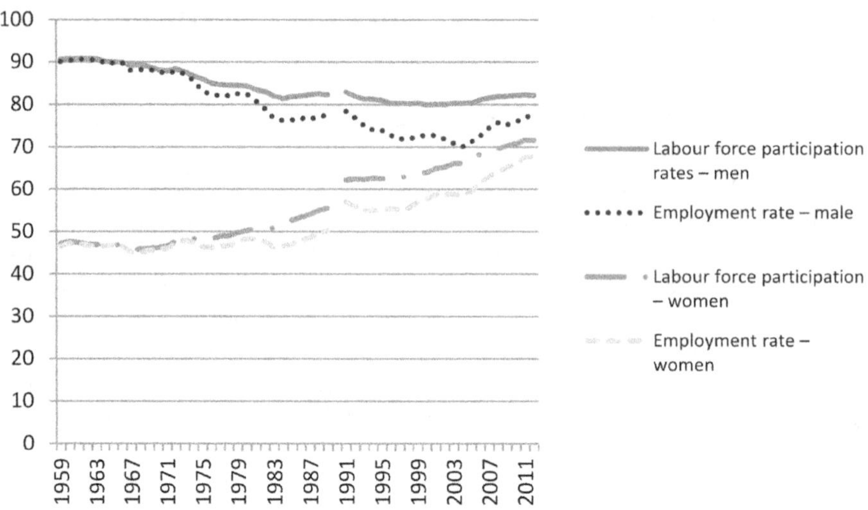

Chart 7.2 Labour participation rates and employment rates by sex in Germany (1959–2012). Source: Statistisches Bundesamt, Mikrozensus.

After the fall of the wall, the level of activity and employment of German women underwent profound transformations, which are still ongoing. The first increase took place at the turn of the century, but the real breakaway occurred up to 2005, with a spectacular rise of nine percentage points (from 59.6% to 68.8%) in just a few years; this leap was barely affected by the recession of 2009. Female employment increased by nearly 2.2 million between 2005 and 2013, a rise close to 14%.

In France, contrary to the received wisdom, we know from Maruani and Méron (2012: 31) that the share of women in the workforce followed 'a chaotic curve and not a downward slope' throughout the first half of the twentieth century, fluctuating between 34% and 40% (36% on the eve of World War I; see Marchand and Thelot 1991, 50). World War I had only a transitory impact. During the interwar period, France was a frontrunner among the developed countries. Only the change in registration in the status of family helpers in 1954 concealed this fact. Thus, the labour force behaviour of French women has to be considered in the very long term. The immediate post-war period marked a pause in female participation. Yet from the early 1960s onwards, the female participation rate gradually rose again: for the period 1962–68 alone, it increased from 40.5% to 43.1%. The push came mainly from women returning to work after pregnancy (Roux 1970).

From this point onwards, thanks to the dissemination of employed status in the services, women's employment experienced structural

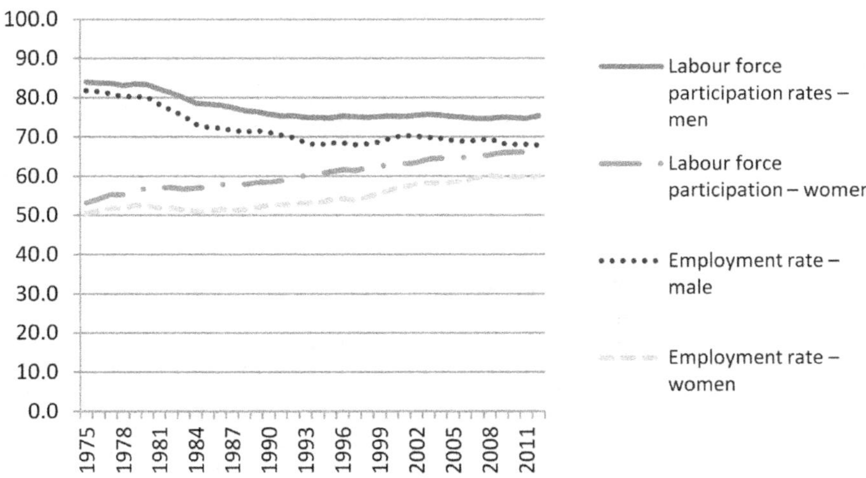

Chart 7.3 Labour participation rates and employment rates by sex in France (1975–2012). Source: Insee, LFS.

growth. According to the series on employment compiled by the Office for National Accounts (Les Comptes Nationaux),[1] the figures for male employment were the same in 2012 as in 1970. Since the male population aged between fifteen and sixty-four increased at the same time by more than 20%, this implies a decline in male employment rates of nearly fourteen percentage points since 1975. Overall, the rate of activity of women increased from 53% in 1975 to 67% in 2012, and the five million jobs created from 1970 to 2008 in France are all women's jobs – an increase of two-thirds, in spite of the decrease in activity rates of young and older women.

How Has Women's Employment Grown?

We begin with a comparison of the evolution and share of the overall volume of work in the economy to highlight the uniqueness of the German employment trajectory, before examining the consequences in terms of work time distribution, especially for women, in both countries. It is important to distinguish two clear periods in Germany. The first phase, from 1995 to 2005, was characterized by economic stagnation after the turn of the century. The second stage, from 2006 onwards, has been marked by strong economic growth only interrupted by the 2009 global recession. The volume of work in the economy, that is the number of hours worked, has more or less followed this trend, with a stagnation in

Chart 7.4 Variation of total employment by sex in France.

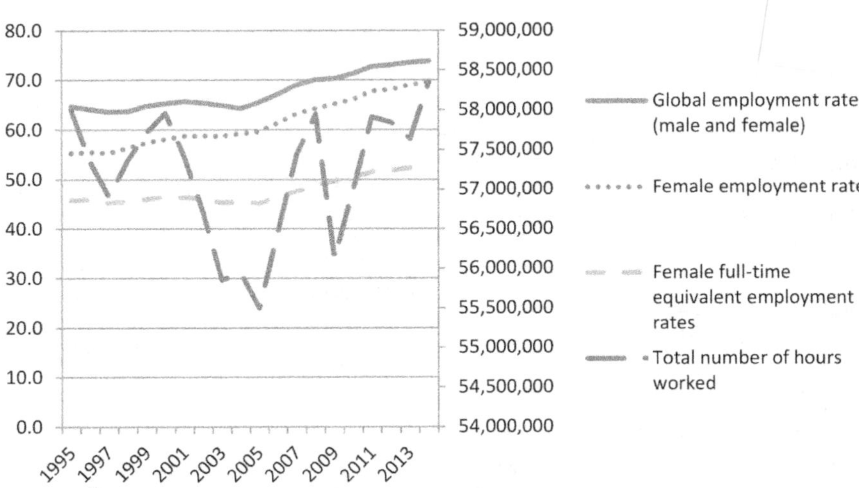

Chart 7.5 Global employment rate, female full-time equivalent employment rates (left-hand scale) and total number of hours worked in the economy (right-hand scale) in Germany. Source: OECD and Eurostat.

the second part of the 1990s, a decrease (of 4%) from 2000 to 2005 and an upturn of 6% since then. Yet all in all, the volume of work in 2015 is only 2% higher than in 1995 and still has not returned to its level of 1992. In other words, the growth in the employment rates in Germany over the last two decades has been mainly due to a redistribution of almost the same volume of work between more workers. A look at the kinds of jobs created, differentiated by working time and sex, allows us to understand the gendered dimension of this development. From 1995 to 2015, male employment stagnated, with growth of a mere 1.6% over twenty years. Moreover, there are fewer male full-time jobs now than twenty years ago; half of the male jobs created between 2005 and 2015 were part-time. Of equal significance is the fact that women's full-time employment stood at the same level in 2015 as it was twenty years ago. This means that the 3.7 million new jobs created between 1995 and 2015 are indeed the result of a balance between the destruction of more than one million full-time jobs – mainly male – and the creation of 4.8 million part-time jobs, three out of four of which are female jobs.[2]

This contrasts sharply with the development of the French labour market. The number of hours worked in the French economy grew almost continuously from 1995 to the onset of the financial and then the Eurozone crisis, yet it remained below its level of 2008 up to the end of 2015. At the same time, from 2008 to 2015, both the female employment rate and the global employment rate stagnated. Thus, the growth in

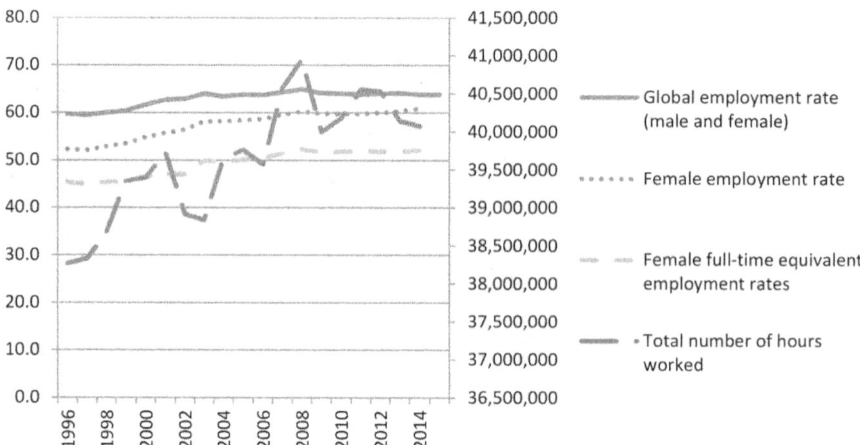

Chart 7.6 Global employment rate, female full-time equivalent employment rates (left-hand scale) and total number of hours worked in the economy (right-hand scale) in France.
Source: OECD and Eurostat.

employment of about 20% or 4.3 million new jobs took place before 2008. Two-thirds of this increase is due to female employment and two-thirds of these new jobs were full-time jobs. This corresponds with an increase of more than 25% in female full-time jobs. In sum, whereas 85% of new jobs in Germany over the last two decades were female part-time jobs, in France 50% of jobs created from 1995 to 2008 were female full-time jobs.

The role of female part-time jobs in the global employment dynamic in Germany can be better understood when compared with some other relevant European countries, with regards to the level and changes of the female Full-Time Equivalent Employment Rate (FTEER)[3] and of the FTEER gap – that is, the difference between the male and female FTEER. Despite a rise of almost fifteen percentage points in 'raw' female employment rates since 1995 (ten points since 2005) and a decrease in the raw employment gap by nineteen percentage points over this period, the FTEER gap has reduced less in Germany than in France or the United Kingdom. In other words, German women's FTEER has undergone an increase and reached a level that is in fact close to those of France and the UK and remains clearly below the Swedish one, which nonetheless has stagnated during the last decade.

A look at the variation in female employment by working time *and* age provides supplementary information on the relevant developments.[4] In Germany, the global stagnation of *full-time* employment between 1995 and 2015 is the result of the creation of 1.2 million full-time jobs for women aged *over fifty* and a loss of 1.3 million full-time workplaces

Table 7.1 Changes in male and female FTEER and gender gap over the last twenty years.

		1995	2002	2007	2014	2014/1995
France	FTEER Male	69.6	67.7	71.2	67.8	-1.8
	FTEER Female	45.3	47.1	51.5	52.1	6.8
	Gender Gap	24.3	20.6	19.7	15.7	-8.6
Germany	FTEER Male	75.3	72.8	75.8	77.0	1.7
	FTEER Female	45.7	46.1	47.6	53.0	7.3
	Gender Gap	29.6	26.7	27.1	24	-5.6
Sweden	FTEER Male	–	75.5	74.0	72.9	-2.6*
	FTEER Female	–	63.0	61.0	62.9	-0.1*
	Gender Gap	–	12.5	13	10	-2.5*
United Kingdom	FTEER Male	84.5	84.3	82.2	79.6	-4.9
	FTEER Female	48.0	51.8	52.1	53.7	5.7
	Gender Gap	36.5	32.5	30.1	25.9	-10.6

* 2014/2002
Source: OECD. See endnote 2.

for women *under fifty*. As concerns *part-time* employment, it is mainly the part-time work of women aged from twenty-five to forty-nine that explains the increase between 1995 and 2005. From 2006 onwards, the 3.5 million female part-time jobs created have been driven both by women over fifty years, which contributed to 50% of the total increase, and by women of childbearing age. Against this background, how can we explain the rise in *employment rate* of females aged twenty to forty-nine by twelve percentage points from 2005 to 2015, in spite of the stagnation of employment in this age category? The explanation lies in the changing shape of the age pyramid: the population aged twenty-five to forty-nine dropped over this period by 14%. On the other hand, the growth in employment of women aged fifty to sixty-four is the product of two factors: first, the rise of the population of this age category by seventeen percentage points, due to the first wave of German baby boomers (1955–65), who reached the age of fifty after 2005; and second, the surge in the employment rate by thirty percentage points over the overall period 1995–2015, partly because of the increase in the legal retirement age for women (Knuth 2014). This trend was mainly due to (highly) qualified women having children. Indeed, Germany belongs to the countries in which the duration of female working life (35.6 years in 2012, 31.2 in France) showed the most rapid rise from 2000 to 2014 (almost five years compared to 3.5 years in the EU, as well as in France).

In France, the 30% increase in *full-time* jobs between 1995 and 2015 is mainly due to women over fifty years of age. Three-quarters of the increase in *part-time* employment in the overall period is due to women over fifty, and one-quarter to women of childbearing age. There has been the same demographic push as in Germany, yet with the added temporal effect of an earlier baby boom wave in France, starting in 1942, and lasting longer than in Germany. The increase is primarily due to the arrival of the first wave of the baby boomers in the age group 55–59, for which the activity and employment rates are much higher than those in the 60–64 age group. The changes in activity and employment rates after 2008 reflect, in turn, the impact of recent pension reforms (Conseil d'Orientation des Retraites [COR] 2016). Concretely, the number of women aged fifty to sixty-four began to grow up to the mid 1990s and reached an increase of 50% over the overall period 1995–2015.

If the increase in older employees has played a key role in both countries, the growth of mothers' employment rates in Germany over the last ten years has been the other main change. Indeed, Germany has been catching up with France. While in 2005 the employment rates of women with one or two children were still higher by respectively 7.6 and 11 percentage points in France than in Germany, in 2015 the employment rate of German mothers with one child had become higher by two points than in France. For mothers with two children, the difference in employment rates between the two countries has significantly reduced, despite a slight rise in France over the last ten years. The reduction has been the strongest for mothers with upper secondary and post-secondary, non-tertiary, levels of qualification. The uniqueness of the change in Germany compared to other European countries has to be pointed out.

A look at both countries and what is known in the literature as the '(employment) motherhood penalty'[5] confirms these changes: in 2015 the penalty still remained higher in Germany (twenty-two points) than on average in Europe (fourteen points) or in France (12.7) – partly because of a still rising employment rate for childless women. However, this rate has declined by eleven percentage points in Germany over the last ten years, whereas it has more or less stagnated in France. A significant difference between the two countries has persisted: working mothers with young children tend to work part-time in Germany whereas a clear majority of them have full-time activity in France.[6] Moreover, one-fifth of all female employees are in marginal part-time jobs with monthly earnings of up to €450.

Against this background, it is important to look at the causes of changes in part-time work from 2006 to 2015. In France, more than ever before, it is mainly (40%) the impossibility of finding a full-time job, particularly for young women, and the necessity to care for a child or a frail

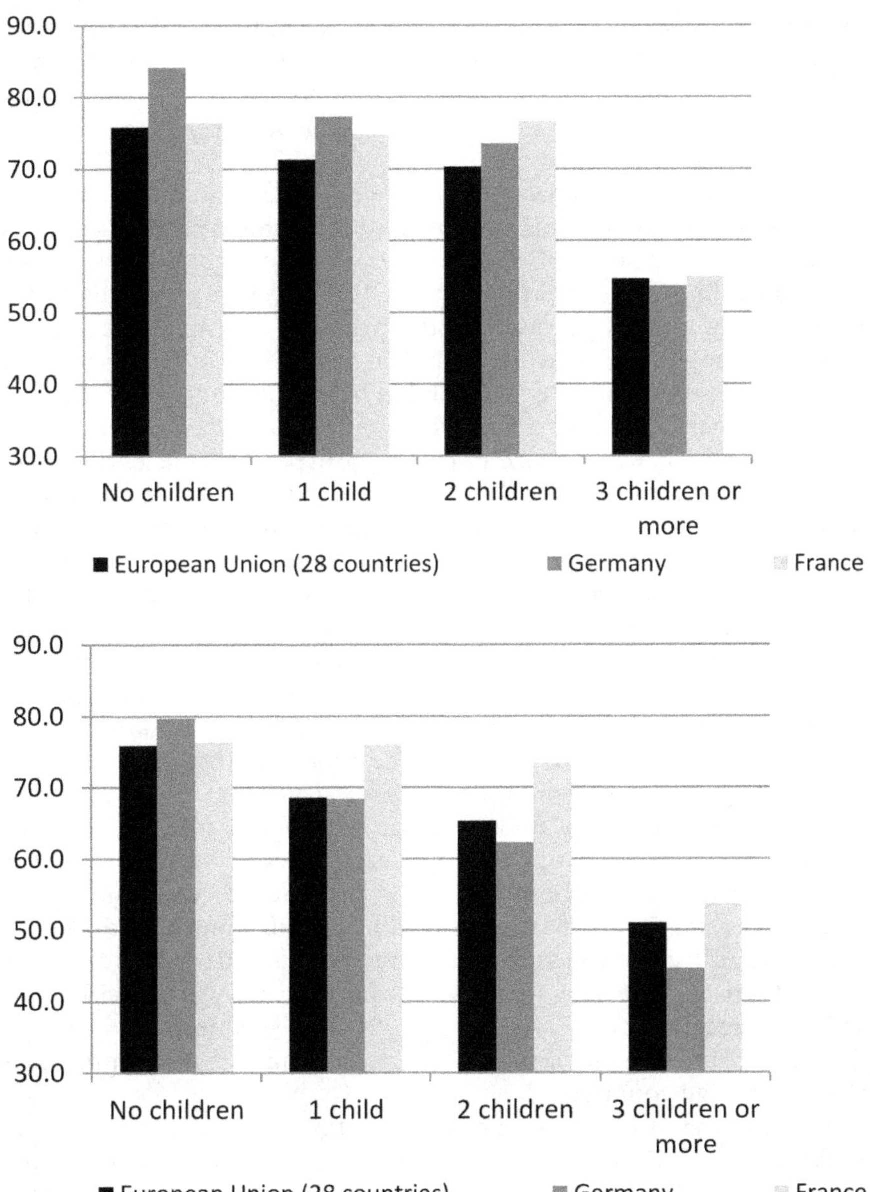

Chart 7.7 Employment rates of mothers with children younger than six years for 2015 (top) and 2005 (bottom). Germany has been catching up with France.

Source: Labour Force Survey, Eurostat.

person (40%) that have remained the main reasons for working part-time. In Germany, in 2015 only around 10% (20% in 2006) of women working part-time claimed the impossibility of finding a full-time job, whereas the need to provide assistance to children or adults in need of support concerned one out of two women.

This observation is indicative of a more general issue regarding the global redistribution of working time in both national economies. If the weekly working time of all employees was almost identical in Germany and France in 2013 (34.5 hours, the EU-15 average), the number of hours usually worked per week in the main job by employees is much more polarized in Germany between men and women as well as between women themselves, and the situation has been worsening for years.

The standard of working time for French women has remained the 35–39-hour week, which concerns nearly one in two women; less than one-fifth of employees work more than forty hours per week, compared to one-third in Germany, while 20% of women work less than twenty hours. This trend towards an increased polarization of working time among German employees has been reinforced over the past years (when comparing the period 2012 to 2000), while in France the distribution of weekly working time among women has remained stable since the turn of the century.

The main explanation for this lies in the way in which working time has been regulated – or not – over the last two decades. In Germany, two major developments have occurred. The first is the derogations to the collective agreements at the industry level (Lallement 2012; Lehndorf 2014), and the second has to do with the kinds of new jobs created. With regards to the first issue, one can say that changes to the labour market, including the consequences of the Hartz laws, and the weakening of the unions' bargaining power have resulted in only one out of two German employees (60% in the west and 48% in the east in 2012) being covered by a collective agreement, vis-à-vis two-thirds on average in the EU and 90% in France (Bispinck and Schulten 2009). This decrease in collective agreement coverage has caused a deregulation of working time, as in other European countries.

Second, the distribution of working time in Germany must be explained by the dissemination of atypical employment (short part-time, mini-jobs, Ich-AG[7]), seen mainly among women in the 1990s and immediately after the implementation of the Hartz legislation (Brenke 2011; Wanger 2006).

However, since 2006 the growth in employment has been triggered exclusively by (mainly part-time) jobs, which are subject to statutory social security. Moreover, in France in 2015 the standardized average annual working time of part-time workers (981 hours) amounted to 60%

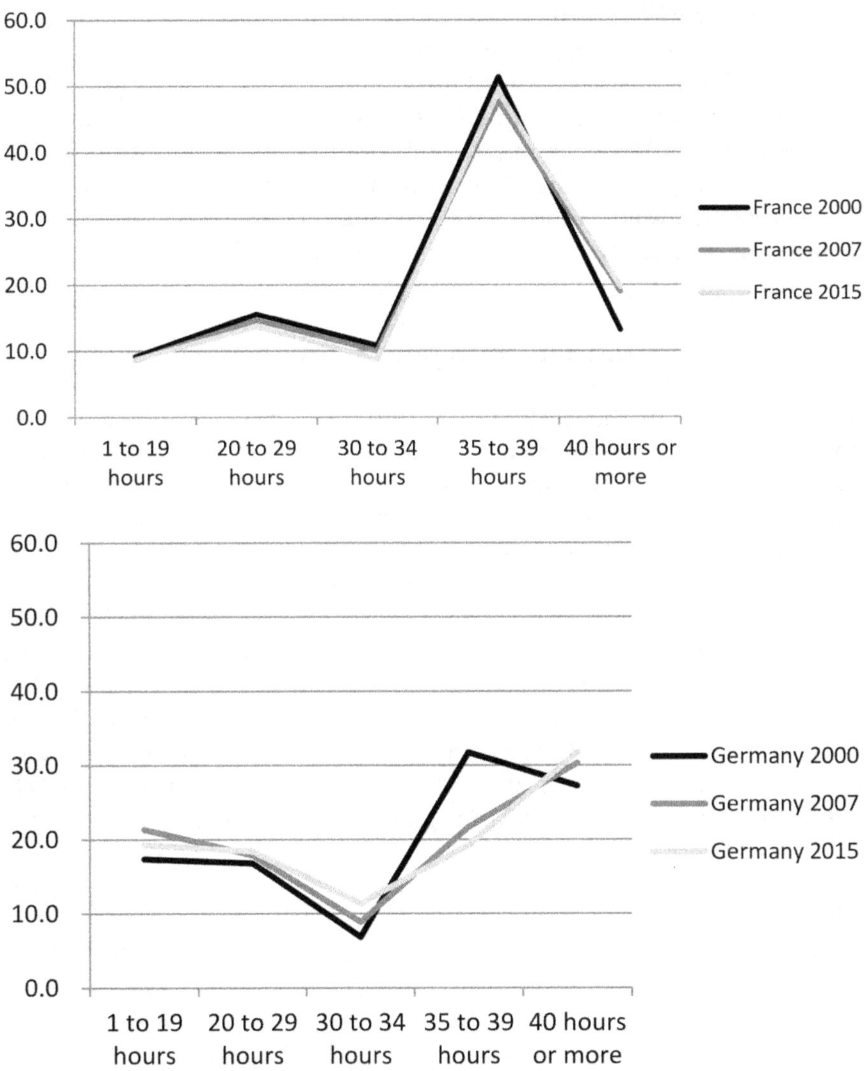

Chart 7.8 Distribution of weekly working time among women (salaried employees) in France and Germany (2000–2015).
Source: OECD.

of a full-time job – 6% above the European average – but only to 47% in Germany (Coe-Rexecode 2016).

Overall, the collective reduction of working time in France triggered by the thirty-five hours legislation, which has subsequently been challenged by conservative governments, has led to less dispersion of work time in France; the main gap is between qualified and non-qualified workers (Lehndorff, Wagner, and Christine 2011). The collective reduction of working time has reduced the share of part-time jobs by accelerating the frequency of transitions from (long) part time jobs to full-time jobs (Askenazy 2013). If a majority of parents reported a positive impact of the time reduction on their work/family balance, the inequalities between female wage earners have grown according to the management of working time at the business level (Letablier and Fagnani 2014).

Fertility and Demographic Growth since 1945

The magnitude of the decline in fertility rates has run parallel in both countries. In France, it reached 1.78 children per woman in the early 1990s, while starting at a higher initial level (2.9 in 1964), meaning that since 1945 French women have had 'half a child' more than German women on average (Pison 2012).

It should be noted that there has been a (new) increase in fertility rates in most OECD countries since 1995 (Luci and Thévenon 2011). France has had one of the strongest rises since the Total Fertility Rate (TFR) climbed from 1.78 to more than 2 in 2010. There has been also a slight increase in Germany after the lowest point in the early 1990s. Due to the construction of the TFR indicator and the timing of births now associated with prolonged education and delayed marriages (Lebras 1991), completed fertility[8] has remained slightly higher: 2.1 in France and 1.6 in

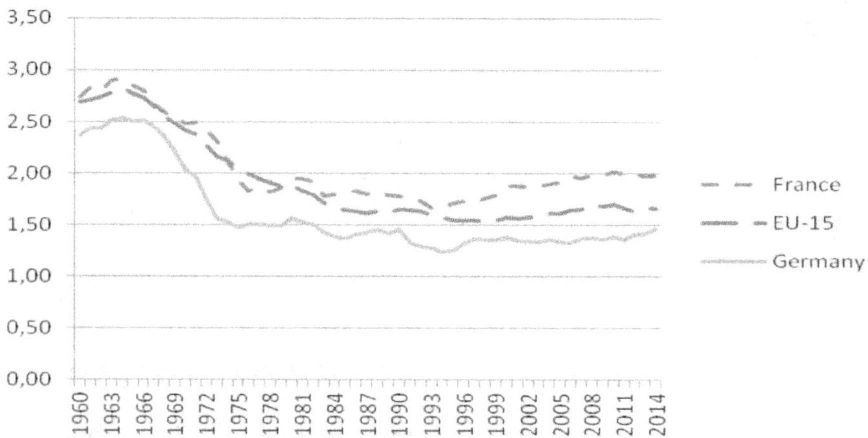

Chart 7.9 Change in the total fertility rate.

Source: OECD. http://www.oecd.org/els/family/database.htm.

Germany over the last past years. This birth revival has been mainly due to the policy of 'reconciliation' between work and family life for women (Luci and Thévenon 2011 and below). However, four main differences between France and Germany have to be pointed out as they are useful to help us understand the difference in the fertility behaviour of women in both countries, as well as illustrating some key aspects of the predominant family model.

The first concerns the desire to have children. There is no simple relation between the wish to have children and recorded fertility (Toulemon and Testa 2005). On average in OECD countries women wish to give birth to 2.28 children during their reproductive life, regardless of their age. France stands out here with 2.58 children per woman, placing France in the top ranks of OECD countries. According to OECD data, the ideal number of children for German women is only 1.96, one of the lowest among OECD countries. Data from the European Barometer show a decline in the number of children desired by German women, from 2.15 in 1988 to 1.75 in 2005, as well as a recent recovery (Prognos 2013: 48). If the child is valued both in France and Germany as a major contribution towards a successful life, in Germany the preference for freedom (living without having a child) is more frequent. Moreover, the high costs of children and the high duties attached to motherhood may explain why more women renounce having children or decide to limit their number (Letablier and Salles 2013b).

The second fact to be noted is the difference in the proportion of women who remain childless, especially among the most qualified. France and Germany were two polar cases among OECD countries for the 1965 cohort and infertility has a high correlation with completed fertility (Breton and Prioux 2009). The share of German women who have no children at the end of their reproductive life increased from 14% for the cohort in 1931 to 21% for the 1962–66 cohorts. In France, for all cohorts born between 1946 and 1960, the proportion of childless women at age forty-five has remained the same, at 13% (Masson 2013). In Germany, among the most highly educated women (*Akademikerinen*), this proportion reached around 30% (Schmitt and Wagner 2006). These differences are linked to the weight of the traditional family model in the different nations. For now, 'where the family is strong, the fertility is low' (Lebras 2007, 150) because the potential costs for professional career opportunities are higher. In Germany, the most important reasons put forward by women are fears regarding employment opportunities. More generally, there is a universal rule: the higher the mother's level of education, the lower the fertility. However, the orders of magnitude differ significantly in both countries: in Germany, low-skilled women have 1.7 children on average and the most qualified have only one child. The gap is lower in France, and has been reduced over recent years: qualified women born in 1965 have had on average 2.2 children, and non-graduate women 2.5.

Another indicator of the 'modernity' of the familial model is provided by the proportion of births outside of marriage. There is a strong correlation at the international level between the average fertility rate and the proportion of births outside marriage. In this respect, France is at the forefront with the Scandinavian countries and the UK, with more than one in two children born out of wedlock, while Germany and Spain, for example, stay below the OECD average with less than one-third of births outside marriage. More specifically, as shown by Letablier and Sales (2013b), the concept of marriage appears to be a prerequisite for the formation of families in Germany, while in France – including the PACS (Pacte Civil de Solidarité) – it is rather a way of legitimizing the childbirths ex-post.

Finally, the fourth significant difference between the countries is represented in the proportion of large families. In Germany, the proportion of women with three or more children has declined significantly between the cohorts born in the 1930s and those born during the 1940s (13%), before stabilizing at this level. On the other hand, the proportion of women with two children has remained stable from one cohort to another (approximately 37–40%). In contrast, in France, the proportion of women with exactly three children remained stable for women born between 1931 and 1959, at around 30%.

Reforms in Family Policy during Recent Years

On average in the OECD countries the total fertility rate decreased from 2.7 children per woman in 1970 to 1.6 in 2000, even if there is a strong heterogeneity between them. In line with the approach taken by the New Home Economics, this drop was explained by the rise in women's employment. Yet the major development here has been the apparent reversal of the correlation between the fertility rate and the employment rate of women. Until the mid 1980s, the countries with the highest fertility rates also had the lowest levels of employment. In fact, since then, two types of country patterns seem to have emerged: a first group of countries that combine high fertility rates and high employment rates of women, and another group characterized by low fertility rates and lower employment rates for women (Kögel 2004; Thévenon 2009). This fact has been interpreted as a change in the institutional context and in the social norms, which are assumed to have facilitated the balance between work and family. The development of childcare facilities for young children and a major change in attitude towards women's work, as a result of women's aspirations or employment opportunities in services, have led to a change in preferences and terms of arbitration (Brewster and Rindfuss 2000; Castels 2003). In this context, what were the main characteristics of family policies in Germany and France, keeping in mind that public policy may reproduce and encourage the traditional gender division of roles in two distinct ways: some measures and forms of financial support are familiarized (come into effect at the level of the couple or the family), while others can reproduce or reinforce gender inequalities on the labour market (Lemière 2014)? Traditionally, Germany was characterized by a high level of universal child benefits, regardless of the rank of the child, which households could set off to benefit from even greater tax reductions. The country has a joint mode of taxation (marital quotient), which discourages the activity of a second earner. Germany has had a long-term yet low-paid parental leave scheme and was characterized by the underdevelopment of its collective childcare facilities for young children. Comparatively, France has been known for a long time for its generous benefits for large families and young children, the 'family quotient' of its tax system, as well as its expenditure on services (childcare facilities). As a result, these combined benefits have led to a redistribution form with a U profile in respect to the distribution of income. Parental leave is long and poorly paid, which encourages low-skilled women to reduce their activity. Finally, if, for a very long time, the French exception has rested on the *crèches*, childcare options for children under three years old are relatively diversified, but of uneven quality and affordability.

According to the OECD, benefits in cash and tax breaks as a percentage of GDP are high and at a close level in both countries. Yet by calculating the structure and level of family benefit packages for a range of family configurations, it appears that levels of financial support to parents of one or two children are higher in Germany than in France, regardless of income level (Fagnani and Math 2010). However, expenditure in kind devoted to childcare and early education services is higher in France.

Nonetheless, over the last two decades in Germany a new political discourse on family policy has emerged (see below) and major reforms have been established concerning parental leave, the development of childcare facilities for young children and the promotion of gender equality. For decades, the development of childcare services had remained underdeveloped in West Germany, not only because of the weight of the Catholic tradition but also as a result of the decentralized federal structure and the multiplicity of stakeholders (Fagnani and Math 2010). Several initiatives at the local and regional level were progressively supported and financed by federal-level authorities (Giraud and Lucas 2014). After the first

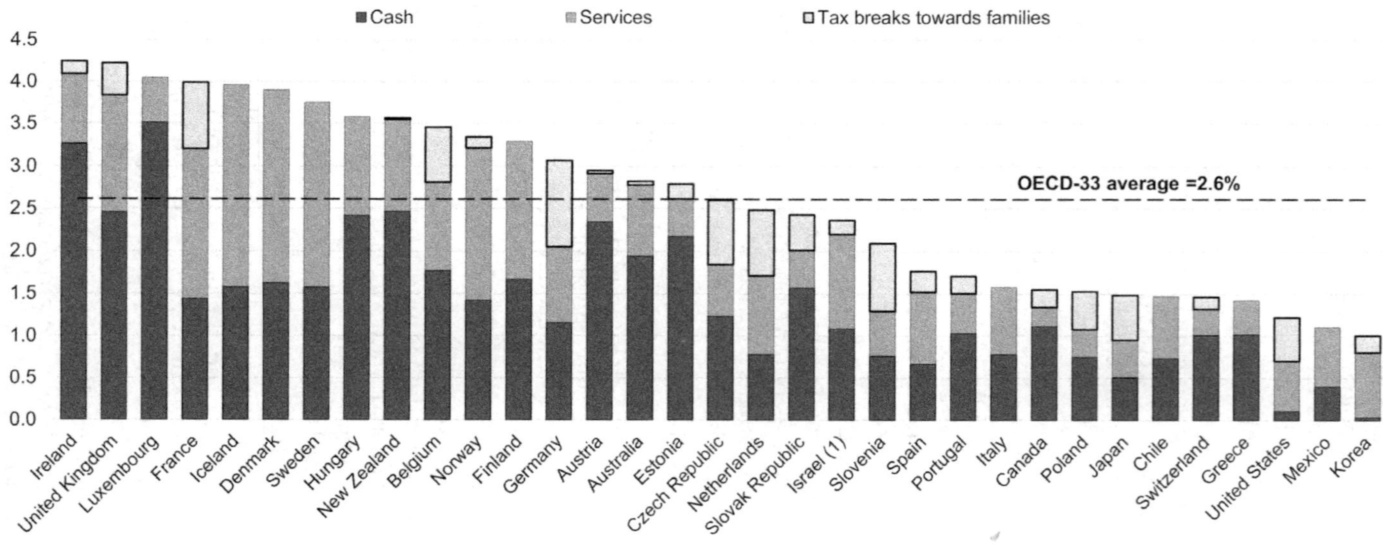

Chart 7.10 Public spending on family benefits in cash, services and tax measures (% of GDP).
Source: OECD, family database. http://www.oecd.org/els/family/database.htm.

developments inspired by the 'alliance for the family' launched in 2003 by Renate Schmid to expand childcare facilities at the local level, new legislation was adopted, and the law on the development of childcare facilities (*Tagesbetreuungsausbaugesetzt*) entered into force in 2005. Moreover, in 2008 the law for the promotion of children (*Kinderförderungsgesetzt*) was designed to implement the entitlement of parents to a care place before 2013 (providing a concrete coverage rate of 35% for children under three). Meanwhile, financing of this measure at the federal level has improved. The commitment at the federal level to quantitative objectives has eased the rise in young children waiting for childcare facilities, in spite of still ambivalent public opinion in the former West Germany. Moreover, the Bund has encouraged companies to become a *Familienfreundlicher Betrieb* (family friendly busines) by providing several tools, but with mixed results so far (Klammer and Letablier 2008).

Parental leave was reformed in 2007. Inspired by the Swedish model, its main characteristics are a relatively high replacement rate, a limited duration (ten months) – to avoid an overly long period out of the labour market for mothers – which can be extended to twelve months if the father also takes leave.[9] This new leave has achieved its main objectives by improving the income of the households concerned and increasing the female participation rate after the period of parental leave, while a quarter of fathers now interrupt their careers to care for their children (Wrolich et al. 2012).[10] Yet one-third of the recipients are only entitled to the minimum payment (up to €300 per month). The new parental leave scheme provides several advantages, first and foremost for parents with medium and high incomes, while parents with low incomes or none at all do not benefit (Henninger, Wimbauer, and Dombrowski 2008). Moreover, there are growing inequalities between skilled women, who worked full-time before taking leave and who return quickly to their job, and low-skilled mothers, who often stay away from the labour market for more than three years (Veil 2010). The 'Elterngeld Plus' reform, concerning children born since 2015, has aimed to ease the cumulation of the benefit with a part-time job.

Over the last twenty years, family policy in France has undergone two main shifts. If redistribution[11] and selectivity have always been a principle of French family policies, since the early 1970s it has become progressively more important to improve the vertical redistribution of the benefits system. This trend intensified up until the late 1990s (Martin 2010). Otherwise, family policy has become driven above all by the unemployment issue (Dang and Monnier 2011; Martin 2010), which has led to a change in the categorization of 'reconciliation' between family and jobs. The *Allocation de garde d'enfant à domicile* (AGED) was introduced in

1985–87 for mothers with three children, and then extended in 1994 to mothers with two children and followed in 1991 by the *Aide pour l'emploi d'une assistante maternelle* (AFEMA). Both measures aimed to increase employment in the service sector (nannies) and to boost the retirement of (low-skilled) mothers out of the labour market, and were very successful in this regard, with a high decline in participation levels for married women with two children, at least one of whom was aged under three (Piketty 1998). They were merged in 2004 into a single new benefit by the *Prestation d'accueil du jeune enfant* (PAJE), which includes a universal basic allowance until a child reaches the age of three, as well as a *complement de libre choix du mode de garde*, which is supposed to enlarge the freedom of choice in childcare for the parents as well as their choice regarding working time. Parents of a young child are given the opportunity to work only part-time – increasing the inequalities between women on the labour market (Lemière 2014) – or to limit their activity, a device that has proven to be successful (Marical, Minonzio, and Nicolas 2007).

The rhetoric of free choice has led to a shift from Kitas (daycare facility for children) towards benefits in cash ('cash for care'); more broadly it has led to a system that is primarily aimed at the solvency of families, enabling them to purchase services on the market (Letablier 2009). Consequently, the number of places in all types of care facilities has increased slowly over fifteen years, with only 15% of children under the age of three cared for by Kitas (Observatoire National de la Petite Enfance, 2012). At the same time, the number of children aged two and under who visit the *écoles maternelles* has declined sharply. If the collective care facilities have grown, it is largely due to the promotion of child minders (*assistante maternelle*), whose cost has become heavily subsidized since the reform implemented in 2004, which welcomed over a quarter of young children, for varying durations.

If the theoretical coverage of public care facilities is close to a total of 50% for children under three years of age, significant differences remain according to activity status and income levels. Indeed, the diversification of childcare facilities is contradicted by the logic of free choice because low-income households cannot afford to use registered childcare providers (Martin 2010). Thirty per cent of children under three now benefit from childcare facilities in Germany; it was less than 10% ten years ago. Yet 62% of children under three are mainly cared for by their parents, compared to 50% in France. Thus, the proportion of children attending formal childcare services has remained lower in Germany than in France, but equally the time spent in childcare facilities is notably longer in France (Letablier and Salles 2013b).

From the Male Breadwinner to Contrasting Household Configurations in Both Countries

What kind of picture can be drawn from these developments in employment and fertility behaviours in both countries over the past years regarding the composition of households by employment status and the changes it has seen? This can be taken from the EU-SILC (Statistics on Income and Living Conditions) and OECD data on household employment status.[12]

In relation to the proportion of children (aged 0–14) in jobless households, both countries have experienced contradictory developments in line with the global evolution of employment. In Germany the proportion slightly diminished from 2003 to 2013 from 10.6% to 9.2%, whereas it rose in France from the OECD average (8.8%) to 11.3%. Yet the striking fact concerning Germany is the spread of the 'one and a half' earners model of employment within housholds.

At the beginning of the 1990s, one household in the working-age population out of two was still composed of one parent working full-time with the other remaining inactive. Since then, the main change has concerned the shift from this traditional male breadwinner model to a new predominant model of households composed of one parent working full-time and the other part-time, rising by twenty-three percentage points, whereas the proportion of households with both parents working full-time decreased by almost five percentage points.

Table 7.2 Employment status of households (2008).

	Households with children						
	Both parents full-time	One parent full-time/ one parent part-time	One parent full-time/one adult not working	**Part-time/ part-time**	Part-time/one adult not working	**Both adults not working**	**Total**
GER	14.5	46.6	30.8	1.4	3.2	3.4	100
FRA	43.4	27.1	23.0	1.0	2.0	3.5	100

	Households without children			
	Full-time	**Part-time**	**Inactive**	**Total**
GER	35.6	34.9	29.5	100
FRA	58.4	18.6	22.9	100

Source: Bahle, Göbel and Hubl 2013.

Table 7.3 Children aged 0–14 by parental employment status, from 1994 to 2010: the growth of the 'one and a half' earners model in Germany.

Both parents full-time				One parent full-time/one parent part-time				One parent full-time/the other inactive			
1994	2007	2013	2013/ 1994	1994	2007	2013	2013/ 1994	1994	2007	2013	2013/ 1994
20.6	19.6	16.1	-4.5	21.6	34.7	45	23.4	47.1	31.8	28	-19.1
37.1	38.4	36.5	-0.6	16.7	21.8	26.9	10.2	38.5	29.6	25.8	-12.7

Source: OECD family database, 2010.

Table 7.4 Model of employment among households (in percentages) in 2011.

Men/Women	Households without children	Households with children
Full-time/full-time	45.0	22.2
Full-time/part-time	21.9	45.3
Full-time/inactive	13.5	19.9
Part-time/full-time	2.7	1.6
Part-time/part-time	2.4	2.1
Part-time/inactive	1.3	1.3
Inactive/full-time	4.6	1.7
Inactive/part-time	3.0	2.0
Inactive/inactive	5.6	3.9

Note: Households are persons, aged sixteen to sixty-four, who report cohabitation with their partners.
Source: IAB (Mikrozenzus).

Complementary data confirm the clear line of cleavage between German households with and without children concerning the frequency of the full-time/full-time and full-time/part-time configuration.

In France, the traditional male breadwinner model is no longer dominant. Instead, one can identify two distinct trends. First, since the 1970s, France has experienced a sharp increase in the number of single parents, representing 9.4% of families with children at home under the age of twenty-five in 1975 and 21.8% in 2008. Second, both partners working full-time has become the most common pattern among couples aged twenty to forty-nine wherein at least one partner has a job.

Changes in the Gendered Employment Regimes in Germany and France over the Last Twenty Years: Arguments, Driving Forces, Actors and Scales

According to this book's general grid of analysis, I will seek to explain these transformations in gendered employment regimes by analysing the arguments implied for both countries and therefore the cognitive and linguistic categories used, the driving forces as well as the main actors of the change. Where relevant, I will also pay attention to the rearrangements of the scales of power at which the recompositions have taken place and gained legitimacy. In order to put the last two decades in Germany and France into perspective, we will look at both countries' long-term backgrounds.

The male breadwinner model and the assignment of women to the private sphere were deeply anchored in German society. In the 1896 Civil Code, women were legally bound to the responsibility for homework and they were with few exemptions forbidden to seek employment. The economic dependence of women was legally established and remained almost unchanged until the 1970s. In the former West Germany, this role division was encouraged by public policies. First introduced in Prussia at the time of the Civil Code and then reintroduced by the Nazi regime in 1934 with the explicit goal of keeping women away from the labour market, the splitting income taxation – which provides an advantage for couples with unequal incomes – was enshrined in legislation in 1958 and though it has been amended since then, it has never been abolished (Wersig 2013). According to the subsidiarity principle, the kind of federalism at work in West Germany rested on the delegation of gender regulation onto private actors and at the local and regional (Länder) levels, even if some key policy areas such as matrimonial law, abortion legislation or the Bismarckian welfare state were under federal jurisdiction (Giraud and Lucas 2014). The underdevelopment of childcare facilities at the local level and school opening hours remained additional issues for the labour participation of women.

A series of obstacles have held back the modernization of the gender regime in Germany for a long time. These include the influence of Catholic tradition and the already mentioned central place of the subsidiarity principle as a key founding rule of the non-intervention of the federal state in that matter (Giraud and Lucas 2014), the weight of conservative forces in a political system that requires large political majorities, the cultural prevalence of the male breadwinner/women care-giver model, and the central importance of industry (Fleckenstein 2011; Giraud and Lucas 2009; Marry 2012). Yet in the aftermath of World War II, the non-intervention of the state in the familial sphere was also supported by feminist movements, which have for a long time considered – against the background of the late nineteenth-century institutional legacy and those of the Nazi era – the state as an agent of oppression for women (Ferre 2012). The 'counter-model' of the former German Democratic Republic, where the state controlled feminist movements and formerly promoted gender equality as well as female employment, was also important for explaining the search for the autonomy of the familial sphere vis-à-vis the federal state (ibid.).

However, thanks to the claims of the feminist movement, the modernization of women's rights started in the 1970s. At the same time, women profited from the *Bildungsexpansion* (Marry et al. 1998) and from the gradual process of the generalization of wage earners. The improvement in women's political representation, boosted by the emergence of the 'green party', the first initiatives on gender equality opportunities at the local level as well as the first women and gender research programmes, began to change the situation. The progressive conversion of the dominant political parties during the 1980s shows the gradual de-privatization of gender relations in the federal public sphere as shown by the support by federal-level authorities of local women's policy agencies (Giraud and Lucas 2014). Yet, as we have seen, the growth of employment remained limited in the former West Germany.

Just as for other issues concerning contemporary German society, the fall of the Berlin Wall caused a significant break. Reunification revealed how West German gender legislation was outdated compared to that of the new *Bundesländer.* It led to reform of the basic law regarding the concrete realization of the equality of rights for women and men and all elements hindering this equality. Several legislative areas were therefore concerned: marital and parental legislation granting formal equality to men and women (1997), legislation on abortion (1998) and on domestic violence (2001).

From an economic point of view, in the 1990s new arguments progressively appeared with the debate on the *Standort Deutschland* – Germany as a location for business and investment – and on the prospects of an ageing population. In the wake of reunification, the rise of public deficit and the deterioration of industrial competitiveness became predominant issues (Streeck 2009). At the same time, the long-term sustainability of public pension systems and of long-term care insurance was placed at the forefront of concerns by experts (Rürup commission, Hartz commission etc.), who marginalized the traditional expertise from the social partners (*Sozialbeirat*, managers of the statutory pension insurance) by pointing out the threats associated with the law fertility and the future decrease in the active population (Bundesministerium für Gesundheit und soziale Sicherung [BGSS] 2003). This demographic concern was deepened by worries regarding the poor results of the PISA (Programme for International Student Assessment from OECD), which raised the issue of pre-school childcare facilities (Salles and Letablier 2013). The main arguments made were in relation to the ageing population and the necessity to increase women's employment rates, in order to make the labour market more flexible and to improve the long-term sustainability of pension systems, as well as the macroeconomic performance jeopardized by concerns about the shrinking workforce.

With the new discourse, a paradigm shift in employment and family policies appeared against this background, which gradually changed the categories of thinking and acting: first, the promotion of flexible working hours for women; second, the development of childcare services; and third, substantial reform of childcare leave (Lewis et al. 2008). From the mid 1990s onwards, in the new context of the European Monetary Union, a twofold answer to these issues appeared. First, a strategy of supply side reforms, which consisted of a long-lasting wage moderation and an agenda for reforms of the labour market and the welfare state, was carried out by the red-green coalition, when it rallied 'the third way' after the turn of the century (the so-called 'Agenda 2010') (Giraud and Lechevalier 2012). Second, employers' associations and more generally business (*die Wirtschaft*) began to promote the entry of women into the labour market, aiming at developing low-cost service providers for the industry (Carlin and Soskice 2009) to make the labour market more flexible and to tackle the anticipated issue of labour shortage (*Arbeitskraftmangel*).

Under the overall influence of the EU framework, which had already begun to have an influence with the early gender directives in the 1970s (MacRae 2006), and in line with the guidelines of the European Employment Strategy, including gender streamlining and requirements due to the strategy of maximizing employment rates (Giraud and Lechevalier 2012, 2013), public policies regarding gender issues began to change. The EU's influence has been direct in such domains as employment discrimination, gender stereotypes and sexual harassment, and indirect in domains such as gender quotas in decision-making (European Parliament 2015a), but it has remained weak concerning the implementation of gender equality in the area of employment policy, as shown by street-level analyses (Letablier and Perrier 2008; Perrier 2015). The 'deadlock of privacy preserving federalism' has been gradually overcome (Giraud and Lucas 2014). The Federal Equality Law of 2001 introduced the principles of gender mainstreaming into the administration. In 2006, the General Equal Treatment Act (AGG) implemented, among others, two European directives: the Gender Equality Directive for goods and services and the Employment Gender Equality Directive. The AGG covers discrimination in employment and social legislation, private law and civil service law. After 2005, however, the policy of gender equality at the European level, which had always remained ambiguous (Jonsson and Perrier 2009), came to a halt and was mainly reduced to the maximization of employment rates (Maier 2015) and no longer pursued effectively at the national level in Germany (European Parliament 2015b).

The key actors of the new deal have become the Christian Democratic Party (CDU) and the employer's union (Henninger and Von Wahl 2014; Veil 2011; Von Wahl 2008). In fact, the appointment of Renate Schmidt (SPD, Social Democratic Party) at the beginning of the 2000s as a federal minister for the family during Schroeder's second term played an important role in creating the 'alliance for the family'. This alliance with business has placed the issue of women's participation in the labour market onto the agenda (Giraud and Lucas 2009). Schmidt commissioned two important reports (the Rürup and Gruescu report from 2003; the Bertram Rosler and Ehlert report in 2005) that triggered a debate about a 'sustainable family policy', in which both the labour force participation of women and the birth rate were increasingly formulated as new family policy objectives. Later, in 2005, the SPD manifesto included the expansion of nurseries for the youngest children and proposed the introduction of earnings-related parental leave. After the formation of the grand government coalition in 2005, the new CDU family minister, Ursula von der Leyen, commissioned new expertise, which attested to the ideological turn of the Christian Democratic Party and to the 'new alliance' between family and business.[13] This saw female employment as a means to ease the long-term financing of the pension system and to overcome the anticipated labour shortage, rather than a turn towards more gender equality (Fagnani 2009; Henninger et al. 2008). The CDU-CSU (Christian Democratic Union) and SPD (Social Democratic Party) government accelerated this progressive convergence between both parties in this domain, as well as the departure from the male breadwinner model in line with the Hartz reforms. As we have seen, the main reforms implemented concerned the labour market, parental leave and childcare facilities. This change was also eased by other actors, namely a 'new' conservative, 'elitist' and neoliberal feminism, which prioritized the policy of conciliation between work and family, which was seen more as an economic empowerment of (skilled) women rather than a global strategy of gender and social equality (Klaus 2010). The activating welfare state promoted by the Hartz legislation was, however, not linked with any consistent individualization of social and fiscal law or any significant measures towards defamiliarization. Demographically, the new policy course did not reward a general increase in birth rate, but rather its increase among highly qualified women (Henninger et al. 2008). The fertility behaviour of women has remained constrained by the choice between career and children (Marry 2013). At the same time, female employment's norm has become diversified, as shown by the polarization of working times; both changes have led to the dissemination among households of the 'one and a half' income earners model.

Despite the controversies within the CDU-CSU, the imperative for the mobilization of women voters and the competition between political parties are key factors (Blome 2014). Nonetheless, this competition has to be understood more accurately in regard to the coalition dynamic within the grand coalition (Henninger and von Wahl 2014): the 'social-democratization' of the family policy followed from 2005 to 2009 was undertaken by the CDU in order to pull as many votes as possible away from the SPD. This strategy was successful in view of the female vote in 2009. It was also supported by the German Employers' Associations, which saw in the generous earnings-related parental leave and the expansion of childcare facilities effective means for reconciling work and family, and for reintegrating women after child rearing (Fleckenstein 2011). The same logic prevailed within the CDU-FDP (Free Democrats) coalition after 2009. It explains the shift to the right in family and gender equality policy from 2009 to 2013 (Henninger and von Wahl 2014) as well as the failure of the implementation of the quota system for leadership positions in private business, which was eventually implemented by the new grand coalition in December 2014.

In France, the image of the full-time working mother had already become rooted during the nineteenth century. The belated nature of rural exodus and urbanization undoubtedly contributed to the social acceptance of the double figure of mother *and* worker (Marry 2012; Maruani and Méron 2012). The early development of the *salles d'asile*, replaced after 1848 by the *école maternelle* (nursery school), as an engine for the development of care services for young children is well documented. Children have always been an *affaire d'Etat* that legitimizes the intervention of the secular state in the norms of education as well as the care infrastructure (Veil 2011). Yet many aspects of government policy remained closed to the norms of gender segregation, even when it provided improved conditions for working women (White 2009). In 1892, night work was banned (see Lallement's chapter in this book) and in 1909 the first maternity legislation was passed, whereas other measures were adopted to help women working in the industry. The interwar period was a time of intense struggle. First, tools aimed to 'reconcile' work and family (maternity leave provisions and a private system of family allowance) were implemented in the private sector at the business level. With the Matignon Accords, the issue of reconciliation 'shifted from being a policy frame to extant norms regarding gender roles and became the principle around which future policies developed' (White 2009: 393). In contrast, the *mouvement familial* (especially the *Union féminine civique et sociale* from 1925 onwards) campaigned from the end of the nineteenth century for public intervention to help mothers to stay at home and claimed for an allowance that rewards the 'profession of mother'; the work of women is supposed to explain the drop in fertility and a perceived social decline.

Indeed, the French state has developed an explicitly interventionist family policy with its own institutions – as an autonomous field of the social security system – and financing. With the *Code de la famille* (1939), the state ousted business from the definition and implementation of the family policy. In terms of actors, however, another singularity of French family policy lies in the strong commitment of non-governmental organizations (NGOs), both in the policy decision process and in the implementation of policy measures. 'Family Unions' (UNAF), as an intermediate corps between the state and families, have remained powerful and influential in defining the objectives of family policy (Letablier 2008). This form of unified representation of families, rooted historically in pro-fertility and pro-family lobbies, has always coloured the debate, as there has been a weak counterforce in this field from the feminist side (ibid.). Nevertheless, in the 1970s and 1980s, women's movements fought for the development of childcare facilities to accompany and to ease the growth of participation in the labour force with some success, alongside the 'modernizers' of the Fourth and the Fifth Republic, which began to promote childcare services. Simultaneously, from 1965 onwards, a series of civil law and family policy reforms began to change the situation (Dang and Monnier 2011). At the same time, the long-standing alliance of academic and administrative actors stopped functioning, with the development of independent research programmes at the CNRS (Centre National de la Recherche Scientifique), whereas high-ranking civil servants developed their own expertise. They have continued to play a major role since the early 1980s, cushioning more broadly the family policy projects of political actors and referring to a common set of ideas, mainly at the *Commissariat général au Plan* (CGP), followed by the creation of the *Haut conseil de la famille* in 2009 (Martin 2010). Academic research bound to the feminist movement has had more success in influencing the policy of gender equality than the content of family or employment policies.

In retrospect, the immediate aftermath of World War II can be seen as a long phase of the 'male breadwinner model', symbolized by the implementation of the *quotient familial* (see above) implemented in 1945 as part of the fiscal redistribution system and of the 'allowance for women raising children at home' (*allocation de salaire unique*, which superseded the *Allocation de mère au foyer* put into force in 1938 under the influence of the *mouvement familial*). From 1932 onwards, the *code de la famille* established two central principles for the amount of child benefit: the birth rank of the children and the increase of benefit with the number of children. These principles were set out for the *allocation de salaire unique* (ASU), created in 1941 for pro-birth policy reasons by the Vichy regime, and were reformed after World War II in 1946. It played a crucial role in explaining women's labour force behaviour until its termination in 1978 (Martin 1998). Indeed, the scheme was renewed and extended by the 1946 law and the ASU became the masterpiece of family policy – far more important than child benefits.[14] Yet, from 1946 onwards, the ASU was only price-indexed, and its relative level declined gradually compared to the 'wage of reference'. For a long time, however, it remained a strong incentive for mothers to stay at home, according to the number of children and the period of time (ibid.: 1137–38). In fact, the development of activity rates of mothers from 1946 to the very beginning of the 1980s can be explained rather well by the variation in the level of the ASU. The rise in women's activity after 1968, especially that of mothers with two children, took place when the level of the benefit began to decline sharply (ibid.).

This growth in female employment up to the late 1960s was eased by the development of service activities and the public sector. Under the influence of the European Union, the gradual and piecemeal institutionalization of the principles of equal pay and equal opportunity – from the Roudy law at the beginning of the 1980s to the Genisson law in 2001 – has accompanied this growth in female employment (see Ricciardi's and Giraud's chapters in this book). Another key driving force has been the issue of work and family balance and therefore the kinds of interactions between family and employment policies. More precisely, as pointed out by White (2004, 2009), a consensus was made possible *peu à peu* among the relevant actors with contrasting interests (the women's movement, modernizers and employers but also pro-natalists, familists and others) on a main, yet ambiguous, argument: the reconciliation between work and family life, which has mainly been seen as gendered regarding the categories used or the content of public policies (Périvier and Silvera 2010; White 2004). This argument can be traced back to earlier debates, but it became central in the 1960s 'when both progressive and conservative actors were persuaded that it was in their interests to encourage women to be workers and mothers without having to accept a principle of gender equality' (White 2004: 258–59). Since women's employment has been identified as a major cause of the fall in the birth rate, the demographic issue has provided a link between employment and family policy. This argument not only helped as a focal point around which actors' interests converged, but it was progressively institutionalized by public policies through a process of normalization (White 2009).

Nonetheless, two different periods of reconciliation policies ought to be distinguished (Martin 2010; 2012). During the first one, from the 1970s to the late 1980s, priority was given to quality of childcare in collective facilities in order to encourage full-time work for mothers. The availability of childcare structures (crèches, nursery schools) improved, the proportion of two-year-old children visiting the *écoles maternelles* rose (up to one-third), childcare became more professionalized and, as a consequence, female employment increased regularly. The second period, from the late 1980s onwards, has been characterized – as mentioned above – by greater selectivity in family policy as well as by the diversification of reconciliation options between employment and family. Categories of thinking about the issue of reconciliation have in fact changed. Indeed, the fight against massive and persistent unemployment and the necessity to reduce the public deficit have become overarching arguments in the public debate, with far-reaching consequences for the content of family and employment policies. The use of family policy as part of employment policies has been reliant upon the development of new childcare provisions based on a rhetoric of 'free choice'. Since 2004, with the new PAJE benefit, parents should have a free choice in childcare, but also the choice (in fact the incentive) to reduce working time or to stop working when caring for their young children (Marical, Minonzio, and Nicolas 2007). Otherwise, the development of the domestic and caring services sector has increased female employment and has provided an incentive for them to enter the labour market. The work/family balance issue – reconsidered under the rhetoric of free choice – has been pushed to the forefront by the conservative parties in answering the family NGOs' claims, which support the pro-family ideology.

As a result, over the past two decades several developments have been less favourable to French women. First, the growth of the global female employment rate has weakened; this mainly concerns women over forty-five years of age. Second, the wage and employment gender gap as well as occupational segregation (Lemière and Silvera 2014) have ceased to reduce. Third, the number as well as the proportion of women living alone has sharply risen and inequalities among women have increased. This background may present a clue to understanding why female part-time employment has not increased since the turn of the century in France in spite of structural push factors,[15] and why therefore the two

Table 7.5 Changes in gendered employment regimes in Germany and France over the last two decades: a synthesis.

	Germany	**France**
Arguments and categories	*Standort Deutschland* and wage moderation. Maximizing the employment rate (flexibilization of working time for women). Demography: labour shortage and long-term sustainability of the social insurance system.	An ambiguous consensus in favour of reconciliation between work and family, which reshaped the interests of the main actors. Fighting unemployment and reducing public deficits. 'Free choice' for mother between work and family
Scales	Influence of the European Employment Strategy (maximization of employment rates) as well as EU gender mainstreaming. Better collaboration between scales within the federal system (childcare facilities). Growing role for the business at the local level (employment and family policies).	Influence of the European Employment Strategy as well as gender mainstreaming. Still strong ability of the central state to give the impetus but growing decentralization of public policies.
Driving forces	Long-term transformation of labour market (salaried employment, flexibilization) and of the employment policy. Conversion of the SPD to the third way and modernization of Christian and conservative parties. Weakening of the unions. Shrinking working-age population.	Long-term transformation of labour market (salaried employment, flexibilization). Change in family and employment policy in the context of massive unemployment. Modernization of the rights of women and resistance of the full-time employment norm for women.
Main actors	First, initiatives at the local level under the influence of the women's movement, then state and political forces at the federal level: 'Alliance for family', Christian Democratic Union and business. Experts: mainly from the business (Hartz Commission) and/or from the administration (Rürup Commission). Influence of the university on gender equality (*Gleichstellungsbericht*) policies.	Central state for public policies. 'Family Unions' (UNAF) and conservative parties. Weak influence of the feminist movement on family policy but improvement of gender equality policies. Experts: high-ranking civil servants and family policy (*Commissariat général au Plan, Haut conseil de la famille)*; academic research and gender equality.

earners household model has been so resilient. Two main complementary hypotheses are possible. The first relies on French women's commitment to full-time employment as shown by the high proportion of involuntary part-time jobs, viewed as a source of emancipation, although depending on the level of the total household income and the number of children (Bourreau-Dubois, Olivier, and Jankeliowitch-Laval 2001). As noticed before, this commitment has been eased by the collective reduction of working time at the turn of the century. This has led to a new norm of working time for women (with a median between thirty-five and thirty-nine hours a week) as well as to a partial substitution of (long) part-time through full-time jobs.[16] The reduction of working time has had a positive yet uneven impact on the work/family balance among women (Fagnani and Letablier 2004). A second explanation might concern the development of a substantial framework on gender equality in France from the 1970s onwards up to the new 'Law on real gender equality' in 2014. However, the implementation of gender equality policies has often been heterogeneous and has varied over time, depending on the political will of the respective government as well as on the content and means (voluntary *versus* obligatory) of the legislation (European Parliament 2015b). Yet the (unequal) progress achieved regarding the representation of women in the political as well as in the economic spheres has all in all contributed to the strengthening of their citizenship as workers (see Ricciardi's chapter in this book).

Conclusion: Towards Growing Inequalities between Women

In sum, we can synthesize the kinds of dynamics of 'gendered employment regimes' that have been at work over the last twenty years in both countries. In Germany, a series of changes to the labour market, amplified by the Hartz reforms and eased by the structural rise in women's qualification levels, as well as the modernization of family policy, have caused a sharp increase in employment rates of mothers and women aged over fifty. The fertility rate remains narrowly connected to the different levels of qualifications and one-third of highly qualified women remain childless. At the same time, in a context of growing employment rates it is mainly the medium-skilled mothers who have experienced the largest increases in employment. These trends are even more pronounced when one looks at mothers with children under six. The persistent deficit in care facilities for young children (i.e. lack of full-time school or childcare facilities in the afternoon), but also the enhanced polarization of working time (an increasing dispersion of weekly working time), has significantly … inequalities among women, while hindering any real de-differentiation of the social roles between men and women. The heterogeneity between women regarding employment and fertility has widened. The resilience of the traditional family model is still strong, consolidating a kind of gender regime, characterized by structurally low fertility, the dissemination of part-time jobs and of in-work poverty, which is ultimately leading to an extended version of the male breadwinner model through extra female pay. The Gender Equality Index ranks Germany lower than the EU average; only in the areas of work, money and time has Germany achieved better results than the EU average (European Parliament 2015a).

The French case remains transitional, situated somewhere between the 'state care-giver' and the 'marketized care-giver' model, even though the latter is being highly subsidized by the state. Full-time employment has remained the dominant employment norm in France, and thanks to the thirty-five hours legislation, implemented at the turn of the century, the dispersion of working time has remained more limited than in Germany. But the gradual institutionalization of the discourse on reconciliation between work and family, which has allowed the emergence of a consensus among actors with divergent interests, has remained ambiguous. In a context of persistent high unemployment and growing employment precariousness, it has been reinvested with the rhetoric of parental 'choice', showing the traditional gender division still underlying French family policy. Since the reform of 2004, the priority given to the cash-for-care model in family policy has increased inequalities between highly qualified women, for whom the presence of children has little effect on participation in the labour market because they can outsource some domestic tasks, and low-skilled women, who cannot do so to the same extent and who are forced to decrease their activity.

One of the main conclusions to be drawn suggests that the transformation of the labour market, reforms in family policy and the changes to the prevailing familial models have led both countries to a growing polarization as well as to growing inequalities among women. In Germany, this has even led to a fallback in the egalitarian two earners model; the proportion of households with two full-time breadwinners has decreased, whereas in France both partners working full-time has become the most common pattern among households with children.

Arnaud Lechevalier is an assistant professor in economics at the University Paris 1 Panthéon-Sorbonne. As a researcher at the Lise (CNAM-CNRS) and at the Center Marc Bloch (Humboldt University), he has worked on

European integration and Social Europe, comparative analysis of employment systems and welfare states in France and Germany, as well as on gender and public policies. From 2007 to 2013, he was Gastprofessor at the Europa University Viadrina in Germany.

Appendix

Table 7.A1 Full-time and part-time employment by sex, 1995–2005, 2005–15, 1995–2015.

	Germany		France	
	Thousand	Index	Thousand	Index
	2005/1995			
	Total			
Total	383.8	101.1	3060.5	114.0
Male	–836.2	95.9	1175.4	109.7
Female	1219.9	108.1	1885.1	119.5
	Full-time			
Total	–2329.2	92.2	2192.2	111.9
Male	–1545.6	92.2	1017.7	108.8
Female	–783.7	92.1	1174.6	117.0
	Part-time			
Total	2713.0	147.7	868.2	125.7
Male	709.4	208.5	157.7	127.1
Female	2003.6	139.8	710.5	125.5
	2015/2005			
	Total			
Total	3331.4	109.3	1205.4	104.8
Male	1172.2	106.0	164.1	101.2
Female	2159.2	113.3	1041.2	109.0
	Full-time			
Total	1233.8	104.5	664.7	103.2
Male	606.6	103.3	–90.3	99.3
Female	627.2	106.8	755.0	109.3
	Part-time			
Total	2096.6	125.0	540.7	112.7
Male	565.4	141.5	254.4	134.3
Female	1531.3	121.8	286.3	108.2

	2015/1995			
	Total			
Total	3715.2	110.5	4295.7	119.7
Male	336.0	101.6	1357.2	111.2
Female	3379.1	122.5	2938.4	130.3
	Full-time			
Total	-1095.4	96.3	2881.5	115.7
Male	-939.0	95.3	944.6	108.2
Female	-156.5	98.4	1937.0	128.1
	Part-time			
Total	4809.6	184.6	1414.9	142.0
Male	1274.8	295.0	413.5	171.0
Female	3534.9	170.3	1001.4	135.9

Source: LFS (Eurostat); own calculations.

Table 7.A2 Female full-time employment.

	Index			Contribution to total growth of employment (%)		
	2005/1995	2015/2005	2015/1995	2005/1995	2015/2005	2015/1995
Germany						
15–24 years	82.2	85.0	69.9	41.0	41.0	346.4
25–49 years	89.3	96.9	86.6	87.4	87.4	549.2
50–64 years	112.6	151.7	170.9	-28.4	-28.4	-795.6
15–64 years	92.1	106.8	98.4	100.0	100.0	100.0
France						
15–24 years	120.7	90.7	109.5	9.9	9.9	2.8
25–49 years	105.6	103.7	109.5	24.6	24.6	25.5
50–64 years	169.1	132.5	224.1	65.5	65.5	71.7
15–64 years	117.1	109.3	128.1	100.0	100.0	100.0

Source: Eurostat.

Table 7.A3 Female part-time employment.

	Index			Contribution to total growth of employment (%)		
	2005/ 1995	2015/ 2005	2015/ 1995	2005/ 1995	2015/ 2005	2015/ 1995
Germany						
15–24 years	221.6	122.8	272.1	11.6	6.3	9.3
25–49 years	137.3	102.6	140.9	64.5	8.0	40.1
50–64 years	134.8	171.0	230.5	23.8	85.7	50.6
15–64 years	139.9	121.8	170.3	100.0	100.0	100.0
France						
15–24 years	108.5	102.1	110.8	3.6	2.5	3.3
25–49 years	116.3	96.7	112.5	45.6	–26.6	24.9
50–64 years	174.6	141.8	247.6	50.8	124.1	71.7
15–64 years	125.6	108.2	135.9	100.0	100.0	100.0

Source: Eurostat.

Table 7.A4 Total female employment.

	Index			Contribution to growth (%)		
	2005/ 1995	2015/ 2005	2015/ 1995	2005/ 1995	2015/ 2005	2015/ 1995
Germany						
15–24 years	95.6	93.4	89.3	–7.2	–5.8	–6.3
25–49 years	106.2	99.5	105.6	49.9	–2.4	16.5
50–64 years	122.4	161.0	197.0	57.4	108.2	89.8
15–64 years	108.1	113.3	122.5	100.0	100.0	100.0
France						
15–24 years	116.4	94.4	109.9	7.6	–5.4	3.0
25–49 years	108.6	101.6	110.3	32.5	12.2	25.3
50–64 years	170.8	135.4	231.2	59.9	93.2	71.7
15–64 years	119.6	109.0	130.3	100.0	100.0	100.0

Source: Eurostat.

Notes

1. https://www.insee.fr/fr/accueil (last accessed 21 November 2018).
2. See Table 7.A1 in the appendix.
3. Full-time equivalent employment is the number of full-time equivalent jobs, defined as total hours worked divided by average annual hours worked in full-time jobs.

4. See Tables 7.A2 to 7.A4 in the appendix.
5. That is the difference in employment rates between women aged twenty to forty-nine without a child or with a child aged less than six years.
6. In 2015, two-thirds of active women with a child younger than six years had a part-time job in Germany, compared to less than one-quarter in France. Three-quarters of German mothers with two or more children under six worked part-time; only two out of five did so in France (Eurostat).
7. 'Ich-AG' (Me Inc.): a new benefit introduced by the Hartz legislation to help unemployed to become self-employed.
8. The average number of children born to women belonging to the same cohort once they have reached the end of their reproductive lives (in practice at the age of fifty).
9. See Henninger et al. 2008 for details.
10. Since 2011, the Elterngeld can no longer be combined with long-term unemployment benefit or with social assistance or family benefit. These cost-saving measures are driven by a workfare logic that has impoverished 16% of recipients (Kahmann 2015).
11. At first with the *code de la famille* in 1939, according to the number and rank of the children within the family and a progressive scale of benefits (Martin 1998).
12. We use three main sources: OECD family database, EU-SILC and the German Mikrozensus. The statistical classification is not exactly the same according to each source and the considered reference year. The indicator from the OECD database presents information on children in different types of households (couple families, sole-parent families and other 'complex families'). The EU-SILC allows us to distinguish between households with and without children.
13. 'Local alliance for families from an economical point of view', 'The expansion of child care: an investment to strengthen the Standort', and so on (see Veil 2011).
14. In 1946, the ASU increased from 25% to 40% for the second child (in comparison, child benefits increased from 10% to 20%) and from 30% to 50% for the third child (30% for child benefits) of a 'reference wage', that is the wage earned by workers in the metal industry in the Paris area. When mothers with two children remained or became inactive, the sum of benefits reached 60% of the reference wage, and 80% with three children (Martin 1998: 1131).
15. That is the growth of the services sector (mainly cleaning, accommodation and restaurants, retail, education and health care).
16. This highlights, from a gender perspective, the debate in France in 2016 on the 'law on labour' (the so-called El Komeri law). One of its main aims is to allow the working time regulation (to be less favourable for workers) at the company level.

References

Askenasy, P. 2013. 'Working Time Regulation in France from 1993 to 2012', *Cambridge Journal of Economics* 37: 323–47.

Bahle, T., C. Göbel, and V. Hubl. 2013. 'Familiäre Risikogruppen im europäischen Vergleich', *WSI Mitteilungen* 3: 192–200.

Betzel, S. 2007. 'Gender Regimes: ein ertragreiches Konzept für die komparative Forschung', *ZeS-Arbeitspapier* 12.

Bispinck, R., and T. Schulten. 2009. 'Re-Stabilisierung des deutschen Flächentarifvertragssystems', *WSI Mitteilungen* 4: 201–9.

Blome, A. 2014. 'Das Werden einer Wende: Einstellungen, Parteienwettbewerb und Familienpolitik im Wandel (1990–2008)', *WZB Mitteilungen* 143: 6–9.

Bourreau-Dubois, C., G. Olivier, and E. Jankeliowitch-Laval. 2001. 'Le travail à temps partiel et ses déterminants', *Economie et statistique* 349–50: 41–62.

Brenke, K. 2011. *Solo-Selbständige in Deutschland: Strukturen und Erwerbsverläufe*, Untersuchung für das Bundesministerium für Arbeit und Soziales – Endbericht.

Breton, D., and F. Prioux. 2009. 'Analyse de l'infécondité en France et en Allemagne: des lectures différentes d'un phénomène de plus en plus fréquent?', European Association for Population Studies (EAPS), Marrakesh, September.

Brewster, K.L., and R. Rindfuss. 2000. 'Fertility and Women's Employment in Industrialized Nations', *Annual Review of Sociology* 26: 271–96.

Bundesministerium für Gesundheit und soziale Sicherung (BGSS). 2003. Rürup-Bericht. *Nachhaltigkeit in der Finanzierung der sozialen Sicherungssysteme.*

Carlin, W., and D. Soskice. 2009. 'German Economic Performance: Disentangling the Role of Supply-Side Reforms, Macroeconomic Policy and Coordinated Economy Institutions', *SocioEconomic Review* 7(1): 67–99.

Castel, F.G. 2003. 'The World Turned Upside Down: Below Replacement Fertility, Changing Preferences and Family-Friendly Public Policy in 21 OECD Countries', *Journal of European Social Policy* 13(3): 209–23.

Coe-Rexecode. 2016. *La durée effective annuelle du travail en France et en Europe*, Document de travail no. 59.

Conseil d'Orientation des Retraites (COR). 2016. *Les âges de départ à la retraite en France: évolutions et déterminants.* Paris: COR.

Dang, A.T., J.M. Monnier. 2011. 'Gender Regimes and Welfare States in France: A Historical Perspective'. EconomiX, Working Paper 2011–40.

European Parliament. 2015a. *The Policy on Gender Equality in Germany: In-Depth Analysis for the FEMM Committee.* Directorate-General for Internal Policies.

———. 2015b. *The Policy on Gender Equality in France: In-Depth Analysis for the FEMM Committee.* Directorate-General for Internal Policies.

Eurostat. Retrieved 21 November 2018 from https://ec.europa.eu/eurostat/fr/data/database.

Fagnani, J. 2004. 'Schwestern oder entfernte Kusinen? Deutsche und französische Familienpolitik im Vergleich', in W. Neumann (ed.), *Welche Zukunft für den Sozialstaat: Reformpolitik in Frankreich und Deutschland.* Wiesbaden: Verlag für Sozialwissenschaften, pp. 181–204.

———. 2009. *Les réformes de la politique familiale en Allemagne: L'enjeu démographique*, Note du Comité d'études des Relations Franco-Allemandes no. 67.

———. 2011. 'The Predicament of Childcare Policy in France: What Is at Stake?', *Journal of Contemporary European Studies* 19(4): 517–61.

Fagnani, J., and M.T. Letablier. 2004 'Work and Family Life Balance: The Impact of the 35-Hour Laws in France', *Work Employment & Society* 18(3): 551–572.

Fagnani, J., and A. Math. 2010. 'Recent Reforms in French and German Family Policies: Similar Challenges, Different Responses', *Sociologia, Problemas e Práticas* 64: 11–35.

Ferre, M.M. 2012. *Varieties of Feminism: German Gender Politics in Global Perspective.* Stanford, CA: Stanford University Press.

Fleckenstein, T. 2011. 'The Politics of Ideas in Welfare Stage Transformation: Christian Democracy and the Reform of Family Policy in Germany', *Social Politics* 18(4): 543–71.

Giraud, O., and A. Lechevalier. 2012. 'L'évolution des modèles d'emploi depuis quinze ans: Des segmentations différenciées', in M. Dupré, O. Giraud, and M. Lallement (eds), *Trajectoires des modèles nationaux: Etat, démocratie et travail en France et en Allemagne.* Brussels: P.I.E. Peter Lang, pp. 291–312.

———. 2013. 'Les femmes au cœur de l'éclatement de la norme d'emploi en Allemagne', *Travail, Genre et Sociétés* 30: 189–94. English version: 'Women at the Center of the Break-Up of Employment Norms in Germany'. Retrieved 1 July 2018 from https://www.cairn-int.info/article-E_TGS_030_0189--women-at-the-center-of-the-break-up.htm.

Giraud, O., and B. Lucas. 2009. 'Le renouveau des régimes de genre en Allemagne et en Suisse: bonjour "néo maternalisme"?', *Cahiers du genre* 1(46): 17–46.

_______. 2014. 'Overcoming Privacy Preserving Federalism: A Multiscalar Approach to the Swiss and German Shifts in Gender Regime', *Fédéralisme Régionalisme* 14. Retrieved 21 November 2018 from https://popups.uliege.be/1374-3864/index.php?id=1392.

Henninger, A., and A. von Wahl. 2014. 'Grand Coalition and Multi-Party Competition: Explaining Slowing Reforms in Gender Policy in Germany (2009–2013)', *German Politics* 23(4): 386–99.

Henninger, A., C. Wimbauer, and A. Dombrowski. 2011. 'Demography as a Push toward Gender Equality? Current Reforms of German Family Policy', *Journal of Contemporary European Studies* 19(3): 393–407.

Jonsson, A., and G. Perrier. 2009. 'Les politiques de conciliation de l'Union européenne: dépassement ou déplacement de la dichotomie genrée public-privé?', in R. Sénac-Slawinski and P. Muller (eds), *Genre et action publique: la frontière public-privé en questions*. Paris: L'Harmattan, Logiques politiques, pp. 57–99.

Kahmann, M. 2015. 'La conciliation, de la marge au cœur des enjeux des politiques publiques', *Chronique internationale de l'IRES* 152: 64–85.

Klammer, U., and M.-T. Letablier. 2008. 'Les entreprises face à la conciliation travail et vie familiale: une comparaison Allemagne et France', *Recherches et Prévisions* 92: 73–85.

Klaus, E. 2010. 'Antiféminisme et féminisme élitiste en Allemagne: les termes du débats', *Travail, genre et sociétés* 2(24): 151–65.

Knuth, M. 2014. 'Arbeitsmarktreformen und "Beschäftigungswunder" in Deutschland', *WSI Mitteillungen* 3: 173–81.

Kögel, T. 2004. 'Did the Association between Fertility and Female Employment within OECD Countries Really Change Its Sign', *Journal of Population Economics* 17(1): 45–65.

Lallement, M. 2009. 'La régulation du temps de travail en France', *Informations sociales* 153: 56–64.

_______. 2012. 'Temps et nouvelles frontières du travail en Allemagne et en France: Entre évolutions transverses et idiosyncrasies nationales', in M. Dupré, O. Giraud, and M. Lallement (eds), *Trajectoires des modèles nationaux: Etat, démocratie et travail en France et en Allemagne*. Brussels: Peter Lang, pp. 229–48.

Lebras, H. 2007. *Les quatre mystères de la population francaise*. Paris: Fayard.

Lehndorff, S. 2014, 'It's a Long Way from Norm to Normality: The 35-Hour Week in France', *Industrial Labor Relations Review* 67(3): 838–63.

Lehndorff, S., A. Wagner, and F. Christine. 2011. 'Arbeitszeitentwicklung in Europa', in T. Händel and A. Troost (eds), *Bericht für die Fraktion der Vereinigten Europäischen Linken*. European Parlament.

Lemière, S. 2014. 'Le partage entre emploi et famille et entre femmes et hommes: Une question de politiques', *Regards croisés sur l'économie* 2: 230–44.

Lemière, S., and R. Silvera. 2014. 'Où en est-on de la ségrégation professionnelle?', *Regards croisés sur l'économie* 2(15): 121–36.

Letablier, M.-T. 2008. 'Why France Has High Fertility: The Impact of Policies Supporting Parents', *The Japanese Journal of Social Security Policy* 7(2): 41–56.

_______. 2009. 'Travail professionnel et travail domestique: Quelle articulation dans différents régimes d'État-Providence en Europe?', *European Journal of Economic and Social Systems* 22(2): 117–31.

Letablier, M.-T., and J. Fagnini. 2014. 'Work and Family Life Balance: The Impact of the 35-Hour Laws in France', *Work, Employment and Society* 18(3): 551–72.

Letablier, M.-T., and G. Perrier. 2008. 'La mise en œuvre du *gender mainstreaming* dans les politiques locales de l'emploi', *Cahiers du genre* 44(1): 165–84.

Letablier, M.-T., and A. Salles. 2013. 'Labour Market Uncertainties for the Young Workforce in France and Germany: Implications for Family Formation and Fertility', Document de travail du Centre d'Economie de la Sorbonne.
Lewis, J., et al. 2008. 'Patterns of Development in Work/Family Reconciliation Policies for Parents in France, Germany, the Netherlands and the UK in the 2000s', *Social Politics* 15(3): 261–86.
Luci, A., and O. Thévenon. 2011. 'La fécondité remonte dans les pays de l'OCDE: est-ce dû au progrès économique?', *Population et sociétés* 481.
MacRae, H. 2006. 'Rescaling Gender Relations: The influence of European Directives on the German Gender Regime', *Social Politics* 13(4): 522–50.
Maier, F. 1993. 'Zwischen Arbeitsmarkt und Familie: Frauenarbeit in den alten Bundesländern', in G. Helweig and M.N. Hildegard (eds), *Frauen in Deutschland 1945–1992*. Bundeszentrale für politische Bildung, pp. 257–80.
________. 2005. 'Europäische Politiken zur Gleichstellung: nur noch schöne Worte?', *WSI Mitteilungen* 1: 5–12.
Marchand, O., and C. Thelot. 1991. *Deux siècles de travail en France*. Paris: Insee.
Marical, F., J. Minonzio, and M. Nicolas. 2007. 'La PAJE améliore-t-elle le choix des parents pour un mode de garde?', *Recherches et Prévisions* 88(1): 5–20.
Marry, C., A. Kieffer, H. Brauns, and S. Steinmann. 1998. 'France-Allemagne: inégales avancées des femmes: Évolutions comparées de l'éducation et de l'activité des femmes de 1971 à 1991', *Revue française de sociologie* 39(1): 353–389.
________. 2012. 'Les comparaisons France/Allemagne au prisme du genre: Pour une critique des modèles nationaux', in M. Dupré, O. Giraud, and M. Lallement (eds), *Trajectoires des modèles nationaux: Etat, démocratie et travail en France et en Allemagne*. Brussels: Peter Lang, pp. 137–56.
________. 2013. 'Le modèle allemand est-il désirable pour les femmes?', *Travail, Genre et Sociétés* 30(2): 83–188.
Marry, C., et al. 1998. 'France-Allemagne: inégales avancées des femmes. Evolutions comparées de l'éducation et de l'activité des femmes de 1971 à 1991', *Revue Française de Sociologie* 39(2): 353–89.
Martin, C. 2010. 'The Reframing of Family Policies in France: Processes and Actors', *Journal of European Social Policy* 20(5): 410–20.
Martin, J. 1998. 'Politique familiale et travail des mères de famille: perspective historique 1942–1982', *Population* 53(6): 1119–53.
Maruani, M., and M. Méron. 2012. *Un siècle de travail des femmes en France: 1901–2011*. Paris: La découverte.
Masson, L. 2013. 'Avez-vous eu des enfants? Si oui, combien?', in *France, portrait social*. Paris: Insee édition, pp. 93–109.
OECD. Retrieved 21 November 2018 from https://data.oecd.org/fr/.
Observatoire National de la Petite Enfance. 2012. *L'accueil du jeune enfant en 2012*. Données statistiques.
Périvier, H., and R. Silvera. 2010. 'Maudite conciliation', *Travail, genre et sociétés* 24(2): 25–27.
Perrier, G. 2013. 'Le gender mainstreaming, entre objectivation institutionnelle et apprentissage de l'égalité', *Lien social et Politiques* 69: 35–61.
________. 2015. 'L'objectif d'égalité des sexes dans la mise en œuvre des politiques d'emploi à Berlin', *Politix* 209(1): 111–33.
Piketty, T. 1998, 'L'impact des incitations financières au travail sur les comportements individuels: une estimation pour le cas français', *Economie & prévision* 132(1): 1–35.
Pison, G. 2012. 'France-Allemagne: Histoire d'un chasse-croisé', *Population et sociétés* 487.
Prognos, A.G. 2013. *Geburten, Kinderwünsche in Deutschland: Bestandaufnahme, Einflusskfaktoren und Datenquellen*.

Roux, C. 1970. 'Tendances récentes de l'activité en France', *Population* 25(1): 179–94.

Salles A., and M.-T. Letablier. 2013a. 'La raison démographique dans les réformes de politiques familiales en France et en Allemagne', *Politiques sociales et familiales* 112: 73–83.

Schmitt, C., and G. Wagner. 2006. 'Kinderlosigkeit von Akademikerinnen überbewertet', *DIW-Wochenbericht* 21.

Streeck, W. 2009. *Re-forming Capitalism: Institutional Change in the German Political Economy.* Oxford: Oxford University Press.

Sylvera, R. 2010. 'Temps professionnel et temps familial: de nouvelles configurations européennes?', *Travail, genre et sociétés* 24(2): 63–88.

Thévenon, O. 2009. 'Increased Labour Participation in Europe: Progress in the Work-Life Balance or Polarization of Behaviours?', *Population-E* 64(2): 235–72.

Toulemon, L., and M.R. Testa. 2005. 'Fécondité envisagée, fécondité réalisée: un lien complexe', *Population et Société* 415.

Veil, M. 2010. 'Politiques familiales contre politiques de l'égalité des sexes? Le cas de l'Allemagne', *Travail, genre et sociétés* 24(2): 89–110.

_______. 2011. 'Familienpolitik in den Zwängen konservativer und neoliberaler Logiken: ein deutsch-französischer Vergleich', in R. Casale and E. Forster (eds), *Ungleiche Geschlechtergleichheit: Geschlechterpolitik und Theorien des Humankapitals.* Opladen: Budrich, pp. 95–111.

Von Oertzen, C. 1999. *Teilzeitarbeit und 'die Lust am Zuverdienen': Geschlechterpolitik und gesellschaftlicher Wandel in Westdeutschland 1948–1969.* Göttingen: Vandenhoeck und Ruprecht.

Von Wahl, A. 2008. 'From Family to Reconciliation Policy: How the Grand Coalition Reforms the German Welfare State', *German Politics* 26(3): 25–49.

Wanger, S. 2006. *Erwerbstätigkeit, Arbeitszeit und Arbeitsvolumen nach Geschlecht und Altersgruppen: Ergebnisse der IAB-Arbeitszeitrechnung nach Geschlecht und Alter für die Jahre 1991–2004.* IAB-Forschungsbericht no. 2.

Wersig, M. 2013. *Der lange Schatten der Hausfrauenehe: zur Reformresistenz des Ehegattensplittings.* Opladen: Budrich.

White, L.A. 2004. 'Ideas and Normative Institutionalization: Explaining the Paradoxes of French Family and Employment Policy', *French Politics* 2(3): 247–71.

_______. 2009. 'Explaining Differences in Child Care Policy in France and the USA: Norms, Frames, Programmatic Ideas', *International Political Science Review* 30(4): 385–405.

Windebank, J. 2012, 'Reconciling Work and Family Life for French Mothers in the Sarkozy Era: Working More to Earn More?', *International Journal of Sociology and Social Policy* 32(9/10): 576–88.

Wrolich, K., et al. 2012. *Elterngeld Monitor.* Berlin: DIW.

Chapter 8

'The Family's Economic Charm'

Recent Reclassifications of Maternity, Employment and Family in German Policy from a Historical-Sociological Perspective, 1900–2010

Theresa Wobbe, Maike Bussmann, Carolin Höroldt and Léa Renard

Introduction

In her book *Mères seules*, Anne-Laure Garcia (2013) uses the example of unmarried mothers in French and German policies to explore the meaning of motherhood over the twentieth century. In the early twentieth century, these policies were entangled in broader structural transformations such as emerging welfare states, disparate regulations of social security for mothers and 'national degeneration' together with imperial concerns. Even though the declining birth rates were to be noticed everywhere (in Sweden, Britain, Wales, Norway, Italy, Spain and Germany), in France the decrease manifested earlier (Bock 2002: 164). In France, unmarried mothers were seen first and foremost with respect to the declining birth rate, which was understood as a menace to the nation and a weakening of its military prowess vis-à-vis the German Empire (Cova 1997). Children of single mothers were thus more than welcome in the support of the nation. Whereas demographic and pronatalist discourses set the tone in France early, in Germany it was social discourses that gained relevance (Bock 2002; Garcia 2013; Garcia and Wobbe 2011).

Concerns about low fertility and the 'degeneration' of the population were not only related to the nation, but also to the empire, since motherhood was considered a decisive basis and resource for both (Davin 1978; Lindner 2014; Wildenthal 1997). While welfare measures for maternity and childcare were put on the national agenda around 1900, maternity and child health care provisions were transferred to the colonial territories during the interwar period (cf. Lindner 2014).

Furthermore, French and German policies were embedded in a broader framework of feminist demands for maternity protection throughout Europe (Bock and Thane 1991). In contrast to the controversies about the ban on night work (see Lallement's chapter and Wobbe and Müller's chapter in this book), the women's movements called for state intervention to improve the situation of mothers (Bock 2002: 162; Wikander, Kessler-Harris, and Lewis 1995). Even before 1914, mothers' rights in the sense of maternity protection (*protection des meres*; *Mutterschutz*) had already become a common topic thanks to the transnational women's movement. After 1919, feminists lobbied the League of Nations (LoN) in Geneva and the International Labour Organization (ILO) to put maternity protection on the agenda of international organizations (Berkovitch 1999; Bock and Thane 1991; Boris, Hoehtker, and Zimmermann 2018; Miller 1994; Zimmermann 2016). However, most of these efforts became fractured during the 1930s.

French pronatalist family politics have endured over the course of the twentieth century until today. By contrast, the continuity of German politics was broken by the antinatalist and racial policies established during the early stages of the National Socialist regime (Bock 1991: 235; Bock 2002: 206–18). Also, Germany shows further frictions due to the divided political systems after World War II. One German state strove for a socialist and population policy approach to the family, whereas the other one followed the reasoning that a 'pronatalist' population family policy was unacceptable. While Social Democrats, feminists and the Green Party 'had for long strictly resisted any family policy that could have been interpreted as "pro-natalist"', Christian Democrats 'followed the line "neither NAZI nor GDR"' (Ostner 2010: 212). Both the German Democratic Republic (GDR) state-regulated childcare policy and the Nazi state family and population policy were connoted as pronatalism.

During the late 1990s, German post-unification family policy became embedded in the field of the newly established European Union's employment strategy (EES) (European Commission 1997, 2003; Lewis 2006; Lewis and Giullari 2005). Since then, a significant shift has taken place from a 'familial' work/family reconciliation frame to a more economic one (European Council 1998; Lewis 2006). The altering focus on 'active employability' measures (European Council 1998: preamble, C 30/2) also covers family policy, connecting it to a more economically oriented rationale (Lewis 2006: 423). Within this so-called activation paradigm, previously connected themes such as maternity, demography rates in ageing and fertility, tax policy, paid work for mothers and childcare become a politics of interrelated policy fields (Lewis and Giullari 2005; Pascall and Lewis 2004).

According to welfare state research (Esping-Andersen 1990; for a comparative debate, cf. Mätzke and Ostner 2010a, 2010b; Pettit and Hook 2009; Pfau-Effinger 2004), German family policy persisted after 1945 as the conservative model *par excellence*, in opposition to the French model. This chapter broadens that focus by exploring the historicity of the controversies around maternity, family and employment that generated family policy in the first place. We aim to identify both the long-term entanglements and short-term configurations (Zimmermann 2006: 256) that reframed the categorizations of maternity, employment and family. We are inquiring after the cognitive options, driving forces and scaling that made reclassifications possible. This chapter also asks how and to what extent the new approach could emerge despite the understanding of German family policy as conservative in welfare research.

As discussed in the introduction to this volume, we understand categories as the result of contested processes of cultural attribution within a particular classification system, which are socially and historically contingent (cf. Lallement et al. 2015). Our approach is closely linked to investigating the historicity of the objects classified. Understanding 'how concepts gain and lose their currency and legitimacy is a task that entails reconstructing their making, resonance, and contestedness over time' (Somers 1999: 135). Theories of historical processes have generated a shift from crisis as manifested for instance in revolutions 'to multidimensional understandings of emergence and destabilization' (Clemens 2007: 529). They are interested in shifting configurations of factors (Zimmermann 2015: 128) rather than in the ordering of sequences. Since categories such as family or maternity refer to various scales simultaneously, they generate different levels of interrelations, possibilities, translations and feedback looping (Hacking 1995). By elaborating on this literature, we explore in which respect previously 'conservative' German family policy has lost its currency. As much as the other chapters, we explore the extent to which reconfigurations of actors in the national space are embedded in a transnational environment, in particular related to the EU policy field of the EES.

Against this backdrop, the chapter is based on a case study of the newly established parental leave measures in German family policy. The source materials consulted include legal documents, legal cases, parliamentary hearings, ministry reports and recommendations from public actors such as employer organizations, trade unions, feminist lawyers and so on. We also draw on historical research on the feminist movement, the interwar years, National Socialist race policy, the European Community law, European litigation and the ILO.

The chapter is organized in four parts. The first section focuses on shifting classifications from the discourses around 1900 and the 1920s to the National Socialist institutionalization of a new taxonomy. Next, we discuss East and West German pre-unification family policy with respect to part-time work. The third section addresses the post-1989 reframing of maternity, employment and family in the context of the EES. In the summary, we relate the findings to driving forces, cognitive options, public action and scaling.

Controversial Classifications of Maternity in the Early Twentieth Century and in National Socialist Racial Policy

From the late nineteenth century, central issues of the women's movement were social security for women, restrictive legislation of women's wage-work, and social security legislation for wage-earning and non-wage-earning mothers. These issues turned on the core questions of support for the working mothers of newborns, insurance against the risk of female poverty during motherhood, and the possibility of combining paid work and family work (Bock 2002: 157ff.). The fact that these demands were raised meant that mothers' work and employment were discussed as interrelated issues in the formation of the welfare state. Simultaneously, this debate became entangled throughout Europe with discourses about 'national degeneration' (cf. Wikander, Kessler-Harris, and Lewis 1995).

The decline in birth rates was perceived and dramatized as a threat to national greatness as well as European supremacy. In France, the declining birth rates had been recognized as a social problem since the nineteenth century, particularly after France's defeat at the hands of more populous Germany in the Franco-Prussian War of 1870/71. The birth rate in France was '21 per one thousand, in Sweden, England, Wales and Norway between 27 and 29, in Italy, Spain and Germany between 33 and 36 with a downward trend everywhere' (Bock 2002: 164). In France, feminists' demands for paid maternity leave and maternity insurance also encountered pronatalist debates such as those that arose in the National Alliance against Depopulation (Alliance Nationale contre la Dépopulation) (Garcia 2013).

After World War I, the world saw the creation of new kinds of international organizations, among which the ILO became the first special agency for labour standards. From the start, the ILO strove for the international standardization of 'women-specific labour protection' (Boris, Hoehtker, and Zimmermann 2018: 6). During its first conference in Washington in 1919, two women-specific labour protections from before the war were reaffirmed and adopted with further measures as international conventions. Preceding this decision and parallel with the International Labour Conference (ILC), an international Women's Labour Congress took place, resulting in a set of resolutions (Cobble 2018: 33ff.). Therein, women demanded, among other things, paid maternity benefits, prohibition of night work for men and women, a women's bureau in the ILO and an amended ILO constitution with voting rights and proportional representational guarantees for women (ibid.: 35). When the ILO adopted the Maternity Protection Convention (ILO-C-003) as its third international treaty in 1919, paid maternity benefits became fixed. Due to women's lobbying, and despite the scepticism of the predominant male delegates, the final convention adopted six weeks' leave with paid benefits before and after childbirth, including 'free attendance by a doctor or certified midwife' (Art. 3, c).

Women's remarkable impact on the Maternity Convention (Cobble 2018: 39) is also indicated in the universalist wording of Article 2. It is the first international legal document to address both married and unmarried women and both legitimate and illegitimate children. The category 'woman' is used insofar as 'the term *woman* signifies any female person, irrespective of age or nationality, whether married or unmarried, and the term *child* signifies any child whether legitimate or illegitimate' (Art. 2, emphasis in the original). The convention, thus, groups (employed) female persons as similar social units together in the distinct cluster 'woman'. This classification is irrespective of further attributions such as age, nationality and marital status. With this, maternity protection was introduced as a standard into international labour law for the first time. We have, however, to be aware of the fact that ILO conventions comprised particularistic limits. Following the 'colonial clause' in Article 19 of the ILO constitution, the imperial powers could preserve their right to modify labour standards for countries 'in which climate conditions, imperfect development of industrial organization or other special circumstances make industrial conditions substantially different'.[1] Thus, the metropolitan powers were authorized to exclude the colonial territories from the ratification of labour norms.

During the interwar period, general and state-funded family allowances were established in France, where the family wage – bonus payment by companies, mostly on their own initiatives – became prominent. After the Family Assistance Law of 1932, employers were required to join the equalization funds, and in 1939 the disparate regulations were systematized in the *Code de la famille* (Bock 2002: 170; cf. Cova 1997). In Germany, early steps were taken to adopt women and family as an object of social policy. The Weimar constitution was the first document to enshrine in law the civil equality of men and women (Art. 109) as well as maternity protection (Art. 119). The Maternity Protection Law of 1927 (Art. 139) provided six weeks' leave with paid benefits before and after childbirth, the duration of which could be prolonged in case of illness due to the childbirth with a medical certificate. Together with this legislation, Germany ratified the ILO Maternity Convention No. 3 and, hence, was among the first ILO member states to implement the respective measures (Reichsgesetzblatt (RGBl.), 1927 II, 497).

As the following section shows, the regime change of 1933 in Germany would usher in an entirely new approach that was unheard of before or after.

National Socialist Antinatalism: 'Unequal Value, Unequal Rights' (*ungleicher Wert, ungleiche Rechte*)

Over the last 120 years, the characteristics and models of maternity policies have varied in relation to the voluntariness of maternity, the forms of state intervention and their pro- or antinatalist orientations. Eugenics, antisemitism and race hygiene were an international phenomenon widespread throughout Europe, and an international movement since the turn of the twentieth century. From this perspective, maternity and birth were placed in the scientific context of the positive or negative characteristics of inheritance, that is, preventing the reproduction of the 'inferior' (*Minderwertigen*) in the interests of the 'superior' (*Höherwertigen*) (Schmuhl 1987; Weingart, Kroll, and Bayertz 1988). 'Scientific' eugenics formed an international movement of which the US, during the interwar period, was a global leader (Whitman 2017).

During the 1930s, anti-Jewish laws were issued in Italy, Hungary, Romania, Sweden, Norway, Finland, Estonia, Iceland and Denmark, while in Austria, German laws were in force (Bock 1986). For the Making of Nazi laws, the US served as a model to which Nazi lawyers referred for their racial legislation (Whitman 2017). As regards racial-based immigration, second-class citizenship and miscegenation, the US 'was indeed "the classic example" of a country with highly developed, and harsh, race law in the early 1930s' (ibid.: 12ff.). National Socialism was fundamentally different, however, because it made 'race' (*Rasse*) into a political category and institutionalized it as a state policy of 'racism in its form of antinatalism'

(Bock 1991: 234). Only in Nazi Germany was forced sterilization applied as an instrument of ethnic and eugenic racism, becoming part of the new 'population policy' and its guiding classification system of race.

As early as June 1933, Reich Minister of the Interior Wilhelm Frick made clear the new classification of the population and its respective vocabulary. According to his estimation, '20 per cent of the German population, i.e. another 11 million, were undesirable as mothers and fathers . . . in order to increase the number of hereditarily healthy progeny, we have first of all the duty to prevent the procreation of the hereditarily unfit' (Bock 1991: 235). On 14 July 1933, the law requiring the forced sterilization of so-called inferior life was introduced (Law for the Prevention of Hereditarily Diseased Offspring, *Gesetz zur Verhütung erbkranken Nachwuchses*, RGBl. 1933 I, 529). At the same time, voluntary sterilization was prohibited. The female and male victims were selected by physicians, psychiatrists, anthropologists, human geneticists and lawyers, who decided with their expertise upon forced sterilization.

The forced sterilization policy was embedded in a new classificatory scheme, which sorted individuals according to assumed 'inferior' or 'superior' characteristics with respect to the reproduction of the 'race'. Forced sterilization was a part of the law to protect German blood and German honour (RGBl. 1935 I, 1146). By 1939, approximately 150,000 women had been sterilized against their will. Beginning in 1939, approximately 100,000 Jewish and non-Jewish women were murdered as part of the 'euthanasia' action against hospitalized handicapped. Hundreds of thousands of the more than two million foreign prisoners in German forced labour camps, mostly from Poland and the Soviet Union, were forced to have abortions or were sterilized against their will (Bock 2002: 207).

Before World War I, in the German colonial context, family policy had already been connected to marriage law and citizenship. Furthermore, 'mixed marriages' (De Hart 2015) between people from the colonial territories and European people became regulated (Wildenthal 1997). In the 1930s, Nazi policy connected this regulation to both the racial classification system and the nation. Since the seizure of power, the regime had also been planning measures to prevent undesirable births. These culminated in the marriage prohibition laws (*Eheverbotsgesetze*, 1935) contained in the law to protect German blood and German honour (RGBl. 1935 I, 1146). These laws prohibited marriages as well as extramarital sexual relations between Jews and 'people of German blood' (*Deutschblütige*), which the language of the National Socialists called 'racial defilement' (*Rassenschande*) (Gosewinkel 2001). The Law for the Protection of the Hereditary Health of the German People (*Ehegesundheitsgesetz*, RGBl. 1935 I, 1246) furthermore prohibited marriages between the 'hereditarily healthy' (*Gesunden*) and the 'hereditarily diseased' (*Erbkranke*). It was the prerogative of the marriage licensing officials to decide whether a proposed marriage was 'undesirable for the national community' (*für die Volksgemeinschaft unerwünscht*), in which case the bride and groom would be reported to the sterilization authorities (Bock 2002: 209).

Also in 1935, the general law prohibiting abortion was repealed and replaced by the enshrinement of eugenically indicated abortion in the sterilization law. Thirty thousand women were forced to have abortions on eugenic grounds. Between 1933 and 1942, the same number of women (as well as approximately twelve thousand men) were prosecuted for having voluntary abortions (ibid.: 209). National Socialism installed a new order opposed to the social protection of mothers, maternity protection, and men's and women's desire for children. The frame of reference was no longer the individual, but the higher-order 'biological unity' of the anticipated *Volkskörper* (Süß 1998). The law prohibited sterilization for the 'valuable' of both sexes, whereas for the 'inferior' of both sexes it became 'obligatory' (Bock 1991: 237). The guiding distinction was no longer related to individual females and males, but to 'valuable' versus 'inferior' following the category of race. In 1942, following the regulation of the Maternity Protection Law, these measures were only applicable to women of 'German nationality', from which 'Jews were excluded' (RGBl. 1942 II, 324f.).

Traditional pronatalism, which aimed at protecting maternity, but also at supporting mothers and fathers, was trumped by a modern antinatalism that treated (potential) mothers and fathers unequally according to racist and eugenic criteria and also intervened in their bodies and lives. As Gisela Bock (1991: 238; 1986: 278ff.) demonstrates on the basis of letters, thousands of women and men protested against forced sterilization, and many women tried to get pregnant before they could be sterilized ('protest pregnancies').

To sum up, Nazi pronatalist measures were conditioned by racial and eugenic parameters. Excluded were 'parents or children who were considered eugenically or ethnically "unfit" – Jews (to whom even family-related tax rebates were denied), Gypsies, the physically, emotionally and mentally handicapped (particularly, but not only sterilized), "asocials", political opponents, labourers from eastern Europe' (Bock 1991: 246–47).[2]

German Family Policies: One Tradition, Two Versions

The differences between family policy in the Federal Republic of Germany (FRG) and the German Democratic Republic (GDR) were long dramatized in terms of the Cold War. Leaving that aside, their similarly problematic situations should not be overlooked, specifically the engagement with the genocide of the European Jews. Both East and West Germany were confronted with economic and social destruction after the war, albeit in different ways.

Equality between women and men was incorporated into the constitutions of both countries (see, for the following, Helwig 1987). The Basic Law of the FRG sees it as a fundamental right connected to personal dignity and human rights as anchored in the article prohibiting discrimination 'on the basis of sex, ancestry, race, language, home and origin, faith, religious or political views' (Art. 3). The 1949 constitution of the GDR also incorporated equality, though without protecting it as a fundamental right or giving it the weight of a universal human right independent of citizenship.

Both constitutions treat the protection of the family and of mothers. The constitution of the GDR aims to guarantee 'that women can reconcile their tasks as citizens and producers with their duties as wives and mothers' (Art. 18), meaning that women are required as citizens and as workers to combine family life and working life. In the Basic Law of the FRG, marriage and the family are placed 'under particular state protection' (Art. 6 (1)), whereby 'The care and upbringing of children are the natural right of the parents and their most important duty' (Art. 6 (2)). While the latter article is targeted at parents and the family space, the former addresses women individually as citizens and producers with respect to the reconciliation of work and family.

Both constitutions incorporate maternity protection and equality between children born in and out of wedlock. Whereas the GDR strove for a socialist orientation in its family policy, the FRG was focused on parliamentary democracy and market economics. Yet both states fostered families and children, although the GDR was explicitly pronatalist at an earlier stage, particularly in offering free childcare outside the home. As the 1950 Law for the Protection of Mothers and Children and the Rights of Women makes clear (Gesetzblatt der Deutschen Demokratischen Republik, GBl. 1950 I, 1037), East German policy was formulated as population policy from the very beginning, whereas in West German politics the linking of family and population planning remained taboo across all political parties into the 2000s (Klammer and Letablier 2007; Ostner 2010). In the Bonn Republic, this consensus remained – against the background of National Socialism, on the one hand, and the GDR's version of socialism, on the other – a shared policy foundation for nearly five decades.

Historical research on working mothers furthermore shows that the long-held notion that, when it came to working mothers, the two

German systems developed in diametrically opposite directions, needs to be requalified. In the 1950s, the labour force participation rates for women in East and West Germany drifted apart more quickly than is shown by the increase in their absolute numbers (Oertzen 2007; Oertzen and Rietzschel 1997). At the beginning of the 1960s, the proportion of dependently employed females among all employed persons was, at 34.3%, the highest for any country in Western Europe. It is interesting that in East and West Germany, it was the number of women who were employed part-time that was decisive (see Lechevalier's chapter in this book).

In this respect as well, research needs to make nuanced distinctions. The debate after 1945 was by no means a new one. Since the outbreak of the war, the Nazi regime had intensified the introduction of part-time work and succeeded in the mobilization of female industrial workers (Hachtmann 1993: 338–39, 347) in a kind of 'modernization against will' (ibid.: 332). In 1939, the female employment quota in the German Empire was higher than in the United States and the United Kingdom (Hachtmann 1989, 1993; Siegel 1989: 173–74). Since 1925, the share of married women and mothers had increased (Siegel 1989: 173–74) and this tendency continued after 1945, but did not start then. Women could now be found in manufacturing, agriculture, family businesses and many so-called side jobs (Oertzen 2007). In the course of the rationalization of industrial enterprises and the structural transformation of small businesses in agriculture and craft trades, the number of mothers working in the family businesses decreased (cf. Renard's chapter in this book; Willms-Herget 1983).

Following Oertzen (2007; Oertzen and Rietzschel 1997) and Rietzschel (1999), between 1946 and 1948 debates on half-day employment started in the four zones of occupation. In the FRG and GDR, later discussions about part-time working were stimulated by labour shortage because of the growth economy in the West and the demographic problematic in the East. By the late 1950s, part-time work for mothers had been discussed in the FRG by employers' associations, evaluated by the Federal Institute for Labour Placement and Employment Insurance (*Bundesanstalt für Arbeitsvermittlung und Arbeitslosenversicherung*, BAVAV) and treated with ambivalence by the trade unions (Oertzen 2007: 27ff). The Ministry of Labour feared that by institutionalizing part-time work as an earning model for women, there might be the risk of 'workers leaving full-time employment for part-time positions' (ibid.: 46), with a resulting decrease in the total working time of wives/mothers. But companies were nonetheless already offering mothers individualized (reduced) working hours in order to prevent them from quitting (ibid.: 43–45).

The stocktaking of the BAVAV's department for women's affairs conceptualized part-time work as a labour reform (Oertzen 2007: 43). Accordingly, this could occur by means of the 'apparent synthesis' of the opposition between easing the (health) burden of full-time working mothers, and 'tapping the silent labour reserve' (ibid.: 44) of married mothers and women. Female trade unionists for their part feared increased performance expectations, but also the dumping of men's wages. In the media, the impression arose 'that by the early sixties, it was no longer a taboo for married women to go out to work even if they did not strictly "need" the money' (ibid.: 47). It was now considered a legitimate form of paid employment with which the mothers of older children, for instance, could 'keep boredom at bay' (ibid.), mothers who wanted to improve the lives of their family, or pay for their husbands' advanced training, or mothers who simply wanted money they would be 'allowed' to spend on themselves. The young mothers of small children were in turn 'allowed' to work for the sake of their 'awareness of life' (ibid.: 47–48).

The Social Democratic Party (SPD) was overall the first to succeed in reacting to the new societal dynamics while also associating itself with conservative family concepts and tying these in with older socialist models of emancipation such as that which stated that women 'have a right to paid employment and to decide freely whether they wanted to work or not'. The husband's provider's salary was thus all the more important for guaranteeing that the woman's decision would be 'free'; at the same time, for the party executive's secretary for women's affairs, there was no question 'that the increasing employment of wives and mothers' must not imply 'to turn their backs on their maternal sphere of duties' (ibid.: 52). The change of thinking of the Christian-Democratic Union (CDU) began in 1964 as a reaction to the SPD's rapidly developing competence in fundamental gender political questions.

Turning to part-time work as a Western model, the government's report of 1966 (Oertzen 2007: 58) referred to the bestsellers of the 1950s (Simone de Beauvoir, Margaret Mead, Elisabeth Pfeil, Alwa Myrdal and Viola Klein), concluding that the 'model of woman is not something that exists a priori, but rather develops historically' (ibid.). Beyond the two Germanys, part-time work must be put in the broader context of paid female work and the transformation of the labour market. Since the turn of the twentieth century, the number of female employees has risen, and since 1945 it has done so increasingly also for women with small children (cf. Willms-Herget 1985). On the basis of data for the US labour market, Claudia Goldin (2006) argues that the economic position of women has passed through four phases since the 1880s. While characterizing the first three phases as evolutionary (1880–1920, 1930–50; 1950–70), she portrays the fourth phase, beginning with the take-off of part-time work in the 1970s, as a silent revolution: 'The availability of part-time work by firms led to an increase in those working less than 35 hours per week from 18 percent of the female labor force in 1940 to 28 percent in 1960 and from 14 percent of the female sales sector in 1940 to 40 percent in 1960' (ibid.: 6).

Mothers' part-time work also arose as a topic for the United Nations (UN) and the ILO in the early 1950s. In association with the ILO, the UN drafted a legal definition of part-time work in 1953 that became the authoritative reference and has been used ever since. It specifies a contractually secured occupation of indefinite duration voluntarily shortened to between twenty-four and thirty-five hours per week (UN 1953). The debate in the ILO lasted into the 1980s, however, when the organization included part-time work explicitly in its understanding of employment and issued labour standards. The discussion during the 1950s and 1960s proceeded similarly to the way it had in the German debate. The representatives of the trade unions feared wage dumping for male workers. Along with many representatives from post-colonial states, they campaigned for the retention and reinforcement of the male breadwinner model (Reichel 2014: 150ff). Differently from the German context, ILO women's labour experts demanded full-time employment for both men and women, suspecting that part-time work would be stigmatized as 'woman's work' even while no other appropriate economic basis would be provided for women (ibid.).

In the GDR and the FRG, part-time work of married women and mothers gained societal acceptance by the 1960s, although the meaning differed remarkably. In terms of hours worked in the FRG, a new type of employment evolved between twenty-four and thirty hours a week, including full insurance coverage and permanent contracts. But an increasing number of women worked in marginal positions, 'frequently without benefits' (Oertzen 2007: 206), up to twenty hours. Women in the GDR, in turn, worked thirty and more hours a week in permanent positions with full social security benefits (ibid.). In the FRG, part-time work referred 'mainly to half-time work subject to social insurance', while in the mid 1960s it meant 'housewives' work that failed to qualify for social insurance payments' (Oertzen 2007: 5), or simply a 'side job' (see Lechevalier's chapter in this book).

Overall, part-time work increased in both states between the 1950s and 1970s. The share of part-time workers among female employees in the FRG increased from about 8% in 1960 to 19.3% in 1970, while in the GDR it rose from 9% in 1958 to 15% in 1960 and 30% in 1970 (Oertzen 2007: 205). Yet Oertzen points to the fact that, on the hand, the numbers do not allow for a direct comparison, and on the other, the numbers themselves are the result of complex selection processes. With respect to West Germany, before 1964 no official statistics were available at all. Part-time work became a statistically relevant category in the 1970s (ibid.: 82–102). It remained a fragmented category depending on the selected labour tasks, the branches and the inclusion of family workers. But in comparison with the employment statistics around 1900, part-time work was established as a statistical category of work by the 1970s. The German occupational census in 1880 defined gainful work (*Erwerbstätigkeit*) as 'principal' or 'full-time' work (see Wobbe 2012), excluding shorter working times from the tables. During the 1960s and 1970s, part-time work became included both in the statistical representation of work and in the legal regulation. Before 1939, working hours had been individually negotiated and during World War II they were sanctioned by the Nazi state. During the post-war decades, part-time work, for the first time, became 'a right to regular paid employment with reduced working hours' (Oertzen 2007: 6).

Recent German Family Policy: Arguing about 'Freedom of Choice'

In 2003, Chancellor Gerhard Schröder's launch of 'Agenda 2010' aimed at reforming the German labour market (see Hegelich, Knollmann, and Kuhlmann 2011). It stood under the sign of unemployment in Germany and was conceptually linked to the EES. Ever since, a significant shift has taken place from a 'familial' work/family reconciliation frame to a more economic one (European Council 1998; Lewis 2006). The altered focus on 'active employability measures rather than passive support measures' (European Council 1998: preamble, C 30/2) also touches on family policy 'as a means of addressing a whole variety of problems from low fertility rates, to improving competitiveness and growth, and achieving gender equality' (Lewis 2006: 423). In turn, work/family reconciliation is increasingly connected to the quality and productivity of work. The EES aimed to improve the EU's competitiveness by means of full employment and changing workplace culture, which in turn require two adult working persons.

'Agenda 2010', which was made possible by various reforms of labour, pension and tax law, also incorporated the expansion of public childcare offerings (for the international development of maternity and parental provisions, see ILO 2014). In 2003, the German government had already launched the programme 'Future of Education and Care', which was financed with a sum of four billion euros to expand day care centres.

In this broader context, German family policy turned to a convergence with the evolution of EU member states that transcends the (former) male breadwinner model (Hohnerlein and Blenk-Knocke 2009), which is considered a paradigm shift (Henninger, Wimbauer, and Dombrowski 2008; Ostner 2006). Moreover, it is argued that, compared to the EU context, the previously 'conservative' German family policy reveals the most extensive change of objectives and instruments supporting the adult worker model (Lewis et al. 2008: 270). Notwithstanding, we have to bear in mind various preceding measures in order to contextualize the recent transformations.

The introduction of a statutory maternity leave entitlement (*Mutterschaftsurlaub*) responding to women's increasing labour market participation took place in 1979 (for an overview, see Figure 1 in Gangl and Ziefle 2015). Whereas the 1953 Maternity Law provided fourteen weeks before and after childbirth, the 1979 law introduced for the first time an additional maternity leave benefit replacing earnings of up to 750 Deutschmark (Gangl and Ziefle 2015: 522; Gerlach 2010: 255–73). Employers were prohibited from dismissing workers on parental leave. By 1986, a statutory parental leave entitlement (*Erziehungsurlaub*) was introduced up to ten months after childbirth. The eligibility was addressed to parents and its duration was extended to thirty-six months until 1992. The parental leave was complemented by a 'child-raising benefit' (*Erziehungsgeld*) for non-working parents of 600 Deutschmark up to twenty-four months (Gangl and Ziefle 2015: 522f.). Against this backdrop, the 2006 Federal Law on Parental Benefits and Parental Leave (*Bundeselterngeld- und Elternzeitgesetz*, BEEG) indicates a shift, because it alters the policy of compensation via transfers to an earning replacement. Parental benefit is granted up to 67% of income (calculated on the basis of the income in the year preceding childbirth), capped by 1,800 euros months and limited to twelve months (Art. 2, BEEG). Its main objective was to meliorate families' financial basis through the prevention of financial risk, by offering families more 'freedom of choice' when it came to reconciling family with employment (Drucksache 16-1889). In this regard, the legislation reflected the shifting conditions of work and life as well as declining birth rates (ibid.; Drucksache 16-2785: 2).

The BEEG constitutes a key event given the *longue durée* of family policy in Germany. It manifests the temporal dimension of the shift from a sequence model, in which the care of children is only possible at the cost of interrupting mothers' occupations, to a more flexible model. At the programme level, the rationale was to provide state support to allow both sexes flexibility to perform paid work during a postnatal family phase (Pfahl and Reuß 2009: 20).

The first amendments to the law were made just two years later in 2008. The planned amendments provided for the introduction of a minimum benefit period of two months to encourage free choice and support 'a more intensive bonding with the child also for the second parent' (Drucksache 16-9415: 5, 6), implying both fathers and mothers, although it suggested that fathers also 'could' take a single month (ibid.: 6). For good reason, the sunset clause specifies two months rather than 50% of the total available time (Trappe 2013). Furthermore, grandparents are also supposed to be granted the possibility of taking parental leave if their own children are still minors or in the last two years of an apprenticeship (Drucksache 16-9415). These amendments are meant to serve two aims: first, to increase the 'freedom of choice' among various life plans for families with children; and second, to make family and career more compatible (ibid.).

A family policy supplement was added in 2013 with the introduction of the childcare subsidy (*Betreuungsgeld*) whose rules are likewise laid out in the BEEG. Its implementation can be understood as an 'equity measure' for parents who do not make use of their right to a spot in publicly funded childcare centres subsequent to their receipt of the parental benefit (*Elterngeld*). However, this compensatory payment of around 100–150 euros by no means offsets the funds provided by the state for childcare or the earnings from even the lowest-paying job (including lost social security contributions). To legitimate this, the federal government argued, on the one hand, that it is a way to guarantee that the parents of small children are free to choose their care-giver, and, on the other hand, that it is a way to recognize and support the parenting work done by the parents of small children.

The childcare subsidy is thus based once again on the sequence model, as the receipt of childcare subsidies necessarily means prolonging the work interruption of the childcare subsidy beneficiary, since presumably it is only in rare cases that parents have an intra-familial network of which they can avail themselves, or the money for comprehensive private childcare. It must be assumed that this model will be chosen by parents who are not employed, since the incentive is certainly real at a sum of 100 euros. This is why the parental benefit (*Elterngeld*) has also been interpreted as redistribution from poorer families to wealthier ones (Klammer and Letablier 2007; Ostner 2010). The real financial incentives for the adult worker model are provided by spousal income splitting (*Ehegattensplitting*) in combination with state steering in the area of minor employment (*geringfügige Beschäftigung*). In this context, the childcare subsidy can be understood as simply an additional extra, which might, in constellations that anyway conform to the former model (and with low-skilled mothers) give the decisive stimulus to return at least to a single-earner model. The significance of the tax and social security systems for family earning models in Germany becomes especially clear in light of the above-mentioned examples.

An analysis of the law and the documents used in drafting the legislation shows how parenting tasks were ascribed to women and men, which actors were relevant and which categories and classificatory schemes were used to reconfigure family policy issues (cf. the introduction to this volume; Lallement et al. 2015). The reconfiguration of the principal distinctions of maternity (*Mutterschaft*) or parenthood (*Elternschaft*), familial duties or 'freedom of choice', for example, which are instructive for understanding the reformulation of the compatibility of work and family, is interesting. Also, the parliamentary hearings in 2006 and 2008 revealed that different statements were presented, but they did not result in a principle dispute. Whereas in 2006 and 2008 a (relative) consensus emerged between legislators and experts, as well as among the experts themselves, the introduction of the childcare subsidy in 2013 had a highly polarizing effect on opinion.

The experts from economics, legal studies, educational studies, medicine, the church, the administration and civil society organizations share the same basic terms, whereas they differ in their framing. The representative of the Bavarian Catholic Family Association, for instance, attributes 'freedom of choice' to the possibility of childcare at home (Drucksache 17(13)188c: 3), whereas the representative of the local umbrella organizations identifies 'true freedom of choice' with the supply of public care facilities (Drucksache 17(13)188a: 1f). The legal experts, for instance, do not agree about the status of the childcare subsidy according to German constitutional law. While various legal experts argue that the subsidy breaches the German constitution's equal opportunity measure and the protection of the family measure (Art. 2, Art. 6) (cf. Drucksache 17(13)188f: 1; Drucksache 17(13)188k: 2), according to others, the childcare subsidy successfully implements state neutrality regarding parents' scope of freedom (Drucksache 17(13)188j: 13). Experts from education and conservative family civil rights organizations also emphasize the welfare of the child and competing educational concepts and norms. From their perspective, care at home appears to be the most appropriate education for children up to three years (Drucksache 17(13)188d; Drucksache 17(13)188g). On the other hand, the reconciliation of family and work is the central rationale of economics experts, who argue on the basis of the efficiency of an employment-oriented family policy (Drucksache 17(13)188h).

The introduction of the BEEG was shaped by the notion of 'freedom of choice' and the observation that the societal context and the structure of employment, as well as the social forms of family and partnership, had fundamentally changed (Drucksache 16-1889). The legislation therefore emphasized infrastructural improvements for care facilities, a family-sensitive work culture, and sustainable financial support for families (ibid.). Contrary to the BEEG, the 2012 draft placed 'freedom of choice' in the EU context, namely the choice between public childcare and childcare at home. The childcare subsidy, on the contrary, emphasized the 'recognition of education' at home, which should 'be valued' (Drucksache 17-9917). Accordingly, a shift took place which has since generated disputes about the category of 'freedom of choice'. However, in 2015, it was annulled by the Federal Constitutional Court.

The debate manifests different views about family policy and its reorientation, pointing to more extensive structural transformations. It was worries about demographic trends in ageing and fertility that provided the original impetus for the reconceptualization of family policy (Klammer and Letablier 2007: 675). But the question arises as to why the policy shift began around 2000. The old either-or between either birth rate growth or female employment was now supposed to be reconciled by means of state programmes. In connection with this, 'five indicators' were 'offensively' applied as future measures of an efficient family policy, namely 'birth rate, compatibility, poverty risk, level of education and parenting competency' (Ristau 2005: 18).

The new guiding principle of sustainability encompasses 'durability' based 'on demographic population safeguarding', education and parenting at home to 'expand human resources', which are the basis of economic growth. At the same time, the 'security of the resource "commitment and care"' (Ristau 2005: 18) is to be ensured. As Malte Ristau, the department head relevant for the policy shift in the Federal Ministry for Families, Senior Citizens, Women and Youth (BMFSFJ), emphasizes: 'The new charm of the family is, as far as its effectiveness goes, in large part an economic charm' (ibid.: 19). Childcare is cast as an economic factor whose benefit, according to economists, can now be empirically demonstrated for the first time (ibid.).

Since the 1990s, the efficacy of family policy has become measurable by means of an international template, with reference to EU member states, on the one hand, and, on the other hand, with reference to members of the OECD as units of comparison (for the EU, see Gerlach 2010: 357–413). These contexts have become decisive not only for EU employment policy, but also for German employment, population and family policy. They created a new framework for viewing maternity, employment and family through the lens of economic efficiency together with demographic change, public spending and future viability. This constitutes a shift from a family-centred to a child-centred policy, foregrounding such issues as education, health and demography.

In the course of this reorganization, the meaning of family policy and its ministry has also changed. This field has become a machinery covering 148 family-related and eight marriage-related instruments and providing a budget of €200 milliard in 2010 (Prognos-Stiftung 2014). Family policy is also linked to both the 'activating' labour and population policy, with respect to human resources and behavioural changes. The role of the ministry itself is changing in relation to other ministries and social actors, namely from wealth redistributor to regulator and moderator. This is indicated by various alliances with employers' associations, companies, foundations and scientific consultants (see contributions in Gerlach 2017; Klammer and Letablier 2007; Ostner 2010). As opposed to previous expertise from within the ministry and from family organizations, in particular Catholic umbrella organizations, the requested expertise for the change in family policy relies on external consultancy such as that from the Prognos Foundation (cf. the resumé of the Prognos-Stiftung 2014). Ultimately, family policy altered from a focus on the family associations and their social-moral arguments to a focus on economic expertise and macroeconomic models (Gruescu and Rürup 2005: 3).

Discussion of the Findings

As the results show, the displacement of scales and rationales opened the way for new connections in the twentieth century. In the course of this, interactions and changes in scale ensued, as manifested in the correlation between the European Employment Strategy and family policy: previously disparate topics, namely the birth rate decline, employment and parenting competency, were set in relation to one another and integrated under the roof of economic efficiency and sustainability. This also resulted in cooperation between economists and social actors in German family policy. Henninger, Wimbauer, and Dombrowski (2008: 288) argue that the demographic push provided a window of opportunity for the reconciliation of employment and family, while 'pronatalist objectives' gain no policy evidence without equal opportunity. Moreover, the respective incentives favour middle-class parents with high income, while disadvantaging those with low or no income (ibid.). This merging of equal rights, economic rationales, individualization and socially segmented family policy points to an intersection between class, gender, maternity and paternity. Accordingly, the recent policy shift indicates altering configurations of the welfare policy as it has evolved since the turn of the twentieth century when the women's movement discussed maternity and employment as interrelated issues. In those days, maternity insurance for employed mothers (together with unemployment insurance) formed the centrepiece of protection against risks.

In this regard, National Socialism's policy represents an upheaval in the wake of which a radical new framework was put in place. The understanding of maternity, employment and family was thus subject to a fundamental reclassification, such that the individuals affected were observed and classified according to their 'racial value'. This measure determined the framework of meaning of National Socialist policy, which no longer saw the primary distinction in gender relations, but in race relations. This represents a break with traditional notions of the family. It constituted a modern family policy based on scientific racism and was implemented by scientific experts and administrators who intervened in the private sphere as well as in the bodies and lives of those affected.

After 1945, National Socialism and the East-West conflict determined family policy in both German states. In the FRG, the taboo against pronatalist family measures (as a supposedly Nazi feature) and the need to strike a contrast to the socialist version resulted in deadlock. In the socialist framework of family policy in the GDR, an attempt was made to 'break free' from the fetters of National Socialism, while at the same time the GDR implemented its own mode of state control over the family. The part-time working debate, however, points, due to labour shortage, to the necessity to tap the 'silent' resource of mothers. That scarcity, to be sure, was rooted in different conditions, on the one hand in the growth economy, and in the demographic problematic on the other. Notwithstanding, it generated a turning point by which 'the meaning of paid employment for married women was redefined and permanently entrenched in society' (Oertzen 2007: 210).

The post-unification framework of family policy since the 1990s reflects an entirely different configuration, that is, the disappearance of the post-war order and the displacement of the growth economy together with a recomposition of family and employment. For its part, it geared towards increasing the efficiency of the family and of both parents for the sake of society. With this, there emerged a new entanglement of maternity protection (*Mutterschutz*) and parental leave (*Elternzeit*), of 'activating' labour and population policy together with a shift from a family-centred to a market-oriented model. The primacy of improving efficiency is also clear in the framing: 'demographic population safeguarding' (generative reproduction) on the one hand and 'expanding human resources' (economic growth and full employment) on the other. In this, we encounter pronatalist principles, which combine family policy, population policy and economic growth to secure the sustainability of society. This implies a 'new social policy agenda', namely 'how to achieve social solidarity through enabling individuals and families to support themselves' (OECD 2007: 4). Overall, family members have to acquire 'time competence' and 'time sovereignty' (Drucksache 17-9000). This focus increases the societal expectations of parents (parenting competence, flexibility etc.) to the end of making society viable for the future.

Conclusion

At the beginning of this chapter, we asked how recent German family policy became possible given its supposed conservatism, as compared to France. Before this background, the chapter explored the historicity of the controversies that generated family policy. To this end, we were interested in identifying both the long-term entanglements and short-term configurations. This historical contextualization of concepts, resonances and conflicts was intended to shed light on 'which things crystallized at a given time and are today made available, or not, for action' (Zimmermann 2015: 122). We took up the discourses on maternity, employment and family with a view to their formation and put them into the context of social questions and conditions.

On the basis of this historical-sociological perspective, we are able to weight recent recompositions. The entanglements between maternity, employment and family, which were institutionalized during the formation of the welfare state and strengthened after 1945, underwent two frictions in the first instance. Due to the principles of 'unequal value, unequal rights', the Nazi policy made race into a political category and the racialized nation-state by which the former entanglement of family and maternity became shattered. That policy established a new taxonomy, which classified individuals according to their presumed 'inferiority' or 'superiority'. Herewith, political and social rights of mothers and fathers became undermined and dissolved.

As the debates in East and West Germany show, part-time work came to be the response to the structural transformation of the labour market and to women's aspirations as well. Part-time work was negotiated in the cognitive scheme of 'women's two roles' and in the frame of motherhood together with employment, indicating long-term entanglements as instituted during the early twentieth century. The recent shift in family policy points to another frame. The coordination of parents' employment became negotiated together with fertility and family responsibilities regarding 'flexibility' and 'time competence'. What was reflected now was the restructuring of the labour market within the context of globalization, the deregulation of previously achieved labour standards, demographic concerns, tax policy and economic competitiveness. In this new framework, the EU lends itself as a transnational reference system that triggers those dynamics of which it is a result. Connected to this, the 'family' has become a resource of mobilization and (time) flexibility schemes within which parents are expected to make their choices among various 'incentives'. Simultaneously, family policy itself has been made a measurable object of economic calculus and steady evaluation.

When we look back in conclusion at the period under investigation, it becomes clear that a cultural change in expectations accompanied the shift towards individualization and equality between women and men, mothers and fathers. This long-term transformation generates a gain in individual leeway for mothers and fathers even with a view in societal challenges as to their increased personal contributions. For gender relations, this shift implies that in the twentieth century, more equity or equality was involved in structural formats that required effective exploitation of individuals' 'human resources' without sufficiently accounting for the societal problematic of social reproduction.

The dynamic of the neoliberal model characterized here is not obvious, however, and not an effect of a so-called historical necessity or determination. Certain concepts only gain currency under specific conditions. World Wars I and II were just as much the result of contingent historical processes and social conditions as were the Great Depression and decolonization after 1945. This also holds true for the cognitive options. The microeconomic behaviourist theory of human capital was not yet available in the early twentieth century, and macroeconomics had only just emerged in the 1930s. The regulation of family policy, thus, falls back on a body of knowledge that is, historically speaking, a relatively new product of the upheavals of the twentieth century. Today, we do not know the extent to which another twist will alter the 'economic charm of the family'.

Theresa Wobbe is Professor Emerita of Sociology at the University of Potsdam, and fellow of the Margherita von Brentano Centre for Gender Studies at the Free University of Berlin. She specializes in historical sociology, sociology of knowledge, institutionalist gender analysis, and sociology of classification and comparison in world society. Her research focuses on long-term transformations of gender and work, international statistics as an instrument of globalization, and the making of gender as a global category of comparison. Her current projects deal with the ILO discontinuities in the notion of forced labour, 1919–2017, and the conceptional history of gender in global political institutions.

Maike Bussmann received her Diploma in Sociology from the Technical University of Dresden. She spent her study abroad at the University de Vest, Timişoara (Romania) within the European ERASMUS programme in International Relations and Gender Studies. Her research interests include the theory and history of the German women's movement and gender-based wage inequality. She worked with the Chair of Sociology of Gender. As a member of the Agence Nationale de la Recherche (ANR) and the Deutsche Forschungsgemeinschaft (DFG) project 'Metamorphoses of Equality II (1945–2010)' (Potsdam/CNAM-Lise Paris), she focused on the equal pay concepts of the ILO and German labour law and labour policy.

Carolin Höroldt studied Sociology at the University of Leipzig (BA), and at the University of Potsdam (MA); she spent her study abroad within the European ERASMUS programme at the University of Karlstad, Sweden. She worked with the Chair of Sociology of Gender, and for the project 'Metamorphoses of Equality II (1945–2010)' (Potsdam/CNAM-Lise Paris), co-founded by the Agence Nationale de la Recherche (ANR) and the Deutsche Forschungsgemeinschaft (DFG), on ILO equality concepts. Currently, she is preparing her PhD proposal.

Léa Renard is a PhD candidate in sociology and political science at the University of Potsdam (Germany) and the University of Grenoble Alpes (France). She worked for the project 'Metamorphoses of Equality II (1945–2010)' (Potsdam/CNAM-Lise Paris), co-founded by the Agence Nationale de la Recherche (ANR) and the Deutsche Forschungsgemeinschaft (DFG), on family workers and statistical classification. Her PhD project explores shifting statistical categories of immigration and nationality in France and Germany over time (1880–2010).

Notes

1. See the ILO constitution at ILO NormLex: http://www.ilo.org/dyn/normlex/en/f?p=1000:62:0::NO:62:P62_LIST_ENTRIE_ID:2453907:NO. (retrieved 12 May 2018). For ILO-C-003, see Article 6.
2. It was antinatalism that led from the policies of the 1930s to genocide in the 1940s. Sterilization was extended to forced labourers, to Polish and Russian women, and sterilization

experiments were conducted in concentration camps. The first use of gas as an instrument of killing was seen in 1939, for the 'annihilation of unworthy life' ('euthanasia' or 'action T4'). Many of the administrative and political actors of the sterilization programme were active in action T4. Above all, the doctors among them 'played an important role in the genocide of the Jews' (Bock 1991: 248).

References

Primary Sources

2006–2014: Federal Law on Parental Benefits and Parental Leave (and its revision)

Draft Law

Drucksache 16-1889-2006 Gesetzentwurf der Fraktionen der CDU/CSU und SPD. Entwurf eines Gesetzes zur Einführung des Elterngeldes (Draft Law of the Christian-Democratic/Christian Social and the Social-Democratic faction. Draft of a law for parental leave).

Drucksache 16-9415-2008 Gesetzentwurf der Fraktionen der CDU/CSU und SPD zur ersten Änderung (Draft Law of the Christian-Democratic/Christian-Social and the Social-Democratic faction. First amendment).

Report and Recommendation Parliamentary Committee (*Ausschuss für Familie, Senioren, Frauen und Jugend*)

Drucksache 16-2785-2006 Beschlussempfehlung und Bericht des Ausschusses FSFJ zu den Gesetzentwürfen.

2012: Childcare Subsidy (*Betreuungsgeld*)

Draft Law

Drucksache 17-9917-2012 Gesetzentwurf Betreuungsgeld (childcare subsidy).

Experts statements at the Parliamentary Committee (*Ausschuss für Familie, Senioren, Frauen und Jugend*)

Drucksache 17(13)188a Freese, Jörg, Offer, Regina, and Ursula Krickl. 2012. Bundesverband der Kommunalen Spitzenverbände, Berlin.

Drucksache 17(13)188c Schroeter, Johannes. 2012. Landesvorsitzender des Familienbundes der Katholiken in Bayern.

Drucksache 17(13)188d Böhm, Rainer. 2012. Leitender Arzt, Sozialpädiatrisches Zentrum Bielefeld.

Drucksache 17(13)188e Viernickel, Susanne. 2012. Alice Salomon Hochschule, Berlin.

Drucksache 17(13)188f Wieland, Joachim. 2012. LL.M., Deutsche Universität für Verwaltungswissenschaften, Lehrstuhl für Öffentliches Recht, Finanz- und Steuerrecht. Speyer.

Drucksache 17(13)188g Kelle, Birgit. 2012. Vorsitzende von Frau 2000plus e. V., Kempen.

Drucksache 17(13)188h Plünnecke, Axel. 2012. Institut der deutschen Wirtschaft, Köln.

Drucksache 17(13)188k Sacksofsky, Ute. 2012. Goethe-Universität, Institut für Öffentliches Recht. Frankfurt am Main.

Drucksache 17(13)188j Kluth, Winfried. 2012. Martin-Luther-Universität Halle-Wittenberg, Lehrstuhl für Öffentliches Recht, Halle an der Saale.

Family Reports by the Federal Ministry for Family and Youth (*Familienberichte*)

Drucksache 17-9000 Achter Familienbericht Zeit für Familie – Familienzeitpolitik als Chance einer nachhaltigen Familienpolitik. Bundesministerium für Familie, Jugend und Senioren. Berlin 2012.

Secondary Sources

Berkovitch, N. 1999. *From Motherhood to Citizenship: Women's Rights and International Organizations.* Baltimore, MD: John Hopkins University Press.

Bock, G. 1986. *Zwangssterilisation im Nationalsozialismus. Studien zur Rassenpolitik und Frauenpolitik.* Opladen: Westdeutscher Verlag.

________. 1991. 'Antinatalism, Maternity and Paternity in Nation Socialist Racism', in G. Bock and P. Thane (eds), *Maternity and Gender Policies: Women and the Rise of the European Welfare States 1880s–1950s.* London: Routledge, pp. 233–55.

________. 2002. *Women in European History*, trans. Allison Brown. Oxford: Blackwell.

Bock, G., and P. Thane (eds). 1991. *Maternity and Gender Policies: Women and the Rise of the European Welfare States 1880s–1950s.* London: Routledge.

Boris, E., D. Hoehtker, and S. Zimmermann. 2018. 'Introduction: A Century of Women's ILO', in E. Boris, D. Hoehtker, and S. Zimmermann (eds), *Transnational Networks, Global Labour Standards and Gender Equity, 1900 to Present.* Leiden: Brill, pp. 1–23.

Clemens, E.S. 2007. 'Toward a Historicized Sociology', *Annual Review of Sociology* 33: 527–49.

Cobble, D.S. 2018. 'The Other ILO Founders: 1919 and Its Legacies', in E. Boris, D. Hoehtker, and S. Zimmermann (eds), *Transnational Networks, Global Labour Standards and Gender Equity, 1900 to Present.* Leiden: Brill, pp. 27–49.

Cooper, F., and A.L. Stoler (eds). 1997. *Tensions of Empire: Colonial Culture in a Bourgeois World.* Berkeley: University of California Press.

Cova, A. 1997. *Maternité et droits des femmes en France, XIXe–XXe siècles.* Paris: Anthropos, coll. Historiques.

Davin, A. 1978. 'Imperialism and Motherhood', *History Workshop* 5: 28–31.

De Hart, B. 2015. 'Regulating Mixed Marriages through Acquisition and Loss of Citizenship', *The ANNALS of the American Academy of Political and Social Science* 662: 170–87.

Esping-Andersen, G. 1990. *The Three Worlds of Welfare Capitalism.* Cambridge: Polity Press.

European Commission. 1997. 'Commission Adopts Guidelines for Member States Employment Policies for 1998', I?/97/1069, Brussels, 12 December.

________. 2003. *Scoreboard on Implementing the Social Policy Agenda*, COM (2003) 57 final, Brussels.

European Council. 1998. Council Resolution of 15 December 1997 on the 1998 Employment Guidelines, *Official Journal of the European Communities* C 30/1-5.

Gangl, M., and A. Ziefle. 2015. 'The Making of a Good Woman: Extended Parental Leave Entitlements and Mothers' Work Commitment in Germany', *American Journal of Sociology* 121(2): 511–63.

Garcia, A.-L. 2013. *Mères seules: Action publique et identité familiale.* Rennes: Presses Universitaires de Rennes.

Garcia, A.-L., and T. Wobbe. 2011. 'Maternité, Mutterschaft, Mütterlichkeit: Familienpolitische Codierung im deutschen und französischen Kontext', in T. Wobbe, I. Berrebi-Hoffmann, and M. Lallement (eds), *Die gesellschaftliche Verortung des Geschlechts: Diskurse der Differenz in der deutschen und französischen Soziologie um 1900.* Frankfurt: Campus Verlag, pp. 114–41.

Gerlach, I. 2010. *Familienpolitik*, 2nd edn. Wiesbaden: VS Verlag.

________. (ed.). 2017. *Elternschaft: Zwischen Autonomie und Unterstützung.* Wiesbaden: Springer.

Giraud, O., and B. Lucas. 2014. 'Overcoming Privacy Preserving Federalism: A Multiscalar Approach to the Swiss and German Shifts in Gender Regime', *Fédéralisme et Regionalism* 14. http://popups.ulg.ac.be/1374-3864/index.php?id=1392.

Goldin, C. 2006. 'The Quiet Revolution that Transformed Women's Employment, Education, and Family', *The American Economic Review* 96: 1–21.

Gosewinkel, D. 2001. *Einbürgern und Ausschließen: Die Nationalisierung der Staatsangehörigkeit vom Deutschen Bund bis zur Bundesrepublik Deutschland*. Göttingen: Vandenhoeck & Ruprecht.

Gruescu, S., and B. Rürup. 2005. 'Nachhaltige Familienpolitik: Essay', *Aus Politik und Zeitgeschehen* 23–24: 3–6.

Hachtmann, R. 1989. *Industriearbeit im 'Dritten Reich': Untersuchungen zu den Lohn- und Arbeitsbedingungen in Deutschland 1933–1945*. Göttingen: Vandenhoeck & Ruprecht.

———. 1993. 'Industriearbeiterinnen in der deutschen Kriegswirtschaft 1936 bis 1944/45', *Geschichte und Gesellschaft* 19(3): 332–66.

Hacking, I. 1995. 'The Looping Effect of Human Kinds', in D. Sperber et al. (eds), *Causal Cognition: A Multidisciplinary Debate*. Oxford: Clarendon Press, pp. 351–83.

Hegelich, S., D. Knollmann, and J. Kuhlmann. 2011. *Agenda 2010: Strategien, Entscheidungen, Konsequenzen*. Wiesbaden: VS Verlag für Sozialwissenschaften.

Helwig, G. 1987. *Frau und Familie: Bundesrepublik Deutschland DDR*. Berlin: Landeszentrale für Politische Bildung.

Henninger, A., C. Wimbauer, and R. Dombrowski. 2008. 'Demography as a Push toward Gender Equality? Current Reforms of German Family Policy', *Social Politics: International Studies in Gender, State & Society* 15(3): 287–314.

Hohnerlein, E.M., and E. Blenk-Knocke. 2009. 'Eigenständige Existenzsicherung von Frauen im Sozial- und Familienrecht: Rollenleitbilder von Männern und Frauen im europäischen Vergleich'. Retrieved 25 July 2016 from https://www.mpg.de/386412/forschungsSchwerpunkt.pdf.

International Labour Office. 2014. *Maternity and Paternity at Work: Law and Practice across the World*. Geneva: ILO. http://www.ilo.org/wcmsp5/groups/public/---dgreports/---dcomm/---publ/documents/publication/wcms_242615.pdf.

Klammer, U., and M.-T. Letablier. 2007. 'Family Policies in Germany and France: The Role of Enterprises and Social Partners', *Social Policy & Administration* 41(6): 672–92.

Lallement, M., T. Wobbe, I. Berrebi-Hoffmann, and O. Giraud. 2015. 'Kategorien des Geschlechts in der Arbeitswelt/Catégories de genre et mondes du travail', *Trivium* 19: 2–10.

Lewis, J. 2006. 'Work/Family Reconciliations, Equal Opportunities, and Social Policies: The Interpretation of Policy Trajectories at the EU Level and the Meaning of Gender Equality', *European Journal of Public Policy* 13: 420–37.

Lewis, J., and S. Giullari. 2005. 'The Adult Worker Model Family, Gender Equality and Care: The Search for New Policy Principles and the Possibilities and Problems of a Capabilities Approach', *Economy and Society* 34: 76–104.

Lewis, J., T. Knijn, C. Martin, and I. Ostner. 2008. 'Patterns of Development in Work/Family Reconciliation Policies for Parents in France, Germany, the Netherlands, and the UK in the 2000s', *Social Politics* 15(3): 261–86.

Lindner, U. 2014. 'The Transfer of European Social Policy Concepts to Tropical Africa, 1900–50: The Example of Maternal and Child Welfare', *Journal of Global History* 9(2): 208–31.

Mätzke, M., and I. Ostner. 2010a. 'The Role of Old Ideas in the New German Family Policy Agenda', *German Policy Studies* 6(3): 119–62.

———. 2010b. 'Postscripts: Ideas and Agents of Change in Time', *Journal of European Social Policy* 20(5): 268–76.

Miller, C. 1994. 'Geneva – The Key to Equality: Inter-war Feminists and the League of Nations', *Women's History Review* 3(2): 219–45.

OECD. 2007. *Babies and Bosses – Reconciling Work and Family Life: A Synthesis of Findings for OECD Countries*. Paris: OECD Publishing.

Oertzen, C. von. 2007. *The Pleasures of Surplus Income: Part-Time Work, Gender Politics, and Social Change in West Germany, 1955–1969*. New York: Berghahn Books.

Oertzen, C. von, and A. Rietzschel. 1997. 'Comparing the Postwar Germanies: Breadwinner Ideology and Women's Employment in the Divided Nation 1945–1970', *International Review of Social History* 42: 175–96.

________. 2006. 'Paradigmenwechsel in der (west)deutschen Familienpolitik', in P. Berger (ed.), *Der demographische Wandel: Chancen für die Neuordnung der Geschlechterverhältnisse*. Frankfurt: Campus Verlag, pp. 165–99.

Ostner, I. 2010. 'Farewell to the Family As We Know It: Family Policy Change in Germany', *German Policy Studies* 6(1): 211–44.

Pascall, G., and J. Lewis. 2004. 'Emerging Gender Regimes and Policies for Gender Equality in a Wider Europe', *Journal of Social Policy* 33: 373–94.

Pedersen, S. 1993. *Family, Dependence, and the Origins of the Welfare State: Britain and France, 1914–1945*. Cambridge: Cambridge University Press.

Pettit, B., and J.L. Hook. 2009. *Gendered Tradeoffs: Family, Social Policy, and Economic Inequality in Twenty-One Countries*. New York: Russell Sage Foundation.

Pfahl, S., and S. Reuß. 2009. *Das neue Elterngeld: Erfahrungen und betriebliche Nutzungsbedingungen von Vätern. Eine explorative Studie*. Düsseldorf: Hans-Böckler-Stiftung.

Pfau-Effinger, B. 2004. *Development of Culture, Welfare States and Women's Employment in Europe: Theoretical Framework and Analysis of Development Paths*. Aldershot: Ashgate.

Prognos-Stiftung. 2014. *Endbericht: Gesamtevaluation der ehe- und familienbezogenen Maßnahmen und Leistungen in Deutschland. Auftraggeber Bundesministerium der Finanzen und Bundesministerium für Familie, Senioren, Frauen und Jugend*. Berlin, 2 June.

Reichel, K. 2014. *Dimensionen der (Un)Gleichheit: Geschlechtsspezifische Ungleichheiten in den sozial- und beschäftigungspolitischen Debatten der EWG in den 1960er Jahren*. Stuttgart: Franz Steiner Verlag.

Rietzschel, A. 1999. 'Teilzeitarbeit in der Industrie: Ein Störfaktor auf dem Weg zur Gleichberechtigung?', in P. Hübner and C. Tenfelde (ed.), *Arbeiter in der SBZ/DDR*. Essen: Klartext, pp. 169–84.

Ristau, M. 2005. 'Der ökonomische Charme der Familie', *Aus Politik und Zeitgeschehen* 23–24: 6–23.

Schmuhl, H.-W. 1987. *Rassenhygiene, Nationalsozialismus, Euthanasie: Von der Verhütung zur Vernichtung 'lebensunwerten Lebens', 1890–1945*. Göttingen: Vandenhoeck & Ruprecht.

Siegel, T. 1989. *Leistung und Lohn in der nationalsozialistischen 'Ordnung der Arbeit'*. Opladen: Westdeutscher Verlag.

Somers, M.R. 1999. 'The Privatization of Citizenship: How to Unthink a Knowledge Culture', in V.E. Bonnell and L. Hunt (eds), *Beyond the Cultural Turn: New Directions in the Study of Society and Culture*. Berkeley: University of California Press, pp. 121–64.

Süß, W. 1998. 'Gesundheit', in H.G. Hockerts (ed.), *Drei Wege deutscher Sozialstaatlichkeit NS-Diktatur, Bundesrepublik und im Vergleich*. Munich: R. Oldenbourg Verlag, pp. 50–100.

Trappe, H. 2013. 'Väter mit Elterngeldbezug: Nichts als ökonomisches Kalkül?', *Zeitschrift für Soziologie* 42: 28–51.

UN. 1953. Economic and Social Council, Commission of the Status on Women, 7th Session, Part-Time Employment. *Preliminary Report, prepared by the International Labour Office*, ILO E/CN.6.222, 12 February.

Weingart, P., J. Kroll, and K. Bayertz. 1988. *Rasse, Blut und Gene*. Frankfurt: Suhrkamp.

Whitman, J.Q. 2017. *Hitler's American Model: The United States and the Making of Nazi Race Law*. Princeton, NJ: Princeton University Press.

Wikander, U., A. Kessler-Harris, and J. Lewis (eds). 1995. *Protecting Women: Labour Legislation in Europe, the United States, and Australia, 1880–1920*. Champaign: University of Illinois Press.

Wildenthal, L. 1997. 'Race, Gender, and Citizenship in the German Empire', in F. Cooper and A.L. Stoler (eds), *Tensions of Empire: Colonial Culture in a Bourgeois World.* Berkeley: University of California Press, pp. 263–83.

Willms-Herget, A. 1983. 'Grundzüge der Entwicklung der Frauenarbeit zwischen 1880–1980', in W. Müller, A. Willms, and J. Handl (eds), *Strukturwandel der Frauenarbeit 1880–1980.* Frankfurt am Main: Campus, pp. 25–46.

_______. 1985. *Frauenarbeit: Zur Integration der Frauen in den Arbeitsmarkt.* Frankfurt am Main: Campus Verlag.

Wobbe, T. 2012. 'Making Up People: Berufsstatistische Klassifikation, geschlechtliche Kategorisierung und wirtschaftliche Inklusion um 1900 in Deutschland', *Zeitschrift für Soziologie* 41: 41–57.

Zimmermann, B. 2006. *Arbeitslosigkeit in Deutschland: Zur Entstehung einer sozialen Kategorie.* Frankfurt am Main: Campus Verlag.

_______. 2015. '*Socio-Histoire* and Public Policy Rescaling Issues: Learning from Unemployment Policies in Germany (1870–1927)', in S. Börner and M. Eigmüller (eds), *European Integration, Processes of Change and the National Experience.* Basingstoke: Palgrave Macmillan, pp. 121–46.

Zimmermann, S. 2016. 'The International Labour Organization, Transnational Women's Networks, and the Question of Unpaid Work in the Interwar World', in C. Midgley, A. Twells, and J. Cartier (eds), *Women in Transnational History: Connecting the Local and the Global.* London: Routledge, pp. 33–53.

_______. 2018. 'Globalizing Gendered Labour Policy: International Labour Standards and the Global South, 1919–1947', in E. Boris, D. Hoehtker, and S. Zimmermann (eds), *Transnational Networks, Global Labour Standards and Gender Equity, 1900 to Present.* Leiden: Brill, pp. 227–54.

CHAPTER 9

FROM PARTICULAR PROTECTION TO UNIVERSAL PRINCIPLES

Shifting Classifications of Employment Rights in the ILO, the EU and German Labour Law, 1919–88

Theresa Wobbe, Carolin Höroldt and Maike Bussmann

Introduction

In her research on women's lobbying in the League of Nations, Carol Miller demonstrates that the quest for equality was seen as a locus for vibrant transnational feminist groups. Their efforts during the interwar years resulted in the 'campaign for an equality treaty that represented one of the most important feminist initiatives' of that period (Miller 1994: 220). Even feminist groups that did favour gendered differential labour protection became attracted to the international initiative to improve women's equal status. Ultimately, the League decided to conduct an inquiry into women's civil and political status, and asked the International Labour Organization (ILO) to conduct a survey on women's economic status.

Following Miller, this activism challenged the idea that the question of women's status belonged in the national domain exclusively. The time was ripe for feminists to expand from the national to the international level 'and to endeavour to obtain by international agreement, what national legislation had failed to accomplish' (Miller 1994: 221). In lieu of restrictive measures, they aimed at establishing the equal rights principle through an international treaty. Against this background, Miller refers to the Geneva headquarters during the interwar years as the 'key to equality' (ibid.). At the same time, according to Susan Zimmermann, the years between the late 1920s and World War II even indicate a 'new phase in the history of the struggle over gender-specific labour legislation' (Zimmermann 2016a: 395).

From a long-term and global perspective, this chapter considers the interwar years as a transitional period from the national to the transnational level of regulation, from protective measures for particular categories of employees to universal principles of equal treatment irrespective of attributed social categories. During the interwar period, the international women's movement operated in a new environment of international bodies on which they, at the same time, 'conferred legitimacy ... and thus helped to institutionalize their centrality' (Berkovitch 1999b: 109).

The chapter aims at further expanding the existent research by exploring this transformation with respect to the classification of categories such as 'women', 'work' and 'rights', from the interwar period to the late twentieth century. The configuration of fundamental change that occurred in the interwar years came about over the course of the nineteenth century. In Europe, distinct labour legislation for children, juveniles and women with regard to certain jobs, time and sectors appeared in the 1840s, albeit focusing on different aspects of protection (Berkovitch 1999a: 43ff.; Kessler-Harris, Lewis, and Wikander 1995: 5ff.). From the 1880s, gendered differential labour protection and women's wage work became a prominent and contested issue on national political agendas. As a series of international governmental and feminist congresses between 1890 and 1914 indicate, the regulation of wage work became a highly controversial phenomenon at an international scale (Wikander 1995). These debates touched on the complexities, paradoxes and 'hard choices' women had to make (Kessler-Harris, Lewis, and Wikander 1995: 2). The International Convention Respecting the Prohibition of Night Work for Women in Industrial Employment was the first inter-state convention to be adopted as the so-called Berne Convention in 1906.

International cooperation formed a part of nation-states' concern with the reassessment of free market liberalism and the regulation of competition rules. Labour came to be considered a special market (Desrosières 2010) that had to be protected by safeguarding male wageworkers against illness and unemployment. In this framework, protective legislation for women appears to have been part of the effort to hedge the wages of male workers against the 'cheaper' wages of female factory workers with many allowed exemptions, whereas household servants, family workers, agricultural workers and home-based workers were not incorporated therein. In the wake of the welfare state, the national state's responsibility was expanded to protect 'the mothers of the next generation' against the dangers of industrial labour (Berkovitch 1999a; Bock 2002; Lewis and Rose 1995; Wikander, Kessler-Harris, and Lewis 1995), although not all men agreed on the same reasons for government interventions (Kessler-Harris, Lewis, and Wikander 1995: 10).

After World War I, the newly established International Labour Organization (ILO) in Geneva added protective labour legislation for women to its agenda, institutionalizing it as an international standard. In the late 1920s, this policy was increasingly challenged by the campaign for an equality treaty to push equality between men and women forward (see the contributions in Boris, Hoehtker, and Zimmermann 2018).

Equal employment rights for women, after 1945, gained prominence in various settings and at different levels. In 1951, the ILO set the stage for equal treatment and non-discrimination with the Equal Remuneration Convention (ILO C100), and seven years later the Discrimination in Employment and Occupation Convention (ILO C111).[1] These ongoing actions served both as a prototype and as a script for the European Economic Community's (EEC) equal pay provision and European national law as well (Hoskyns 1996; Wobbe 2003). In this configuration, the German constitution (1949) offers an interesting example, with the status of equal gender rights anchored in Article 3. Against the backdrop of National Socialism, the new German constitution enshrined fundamental rights as universal human rights (Art. 1).

The aim of this chapter is to explore these transitional dynamics from protective, namely women-specified measures to equality principles, in particular with regard to the meaning of rights and equality over time. What concepts of 'women' and 'work' are embodied in legislation and litigation? What do 'protection' and 'non-discrimination' mean, and how does it affect women's and men's rights? How did the diverse legal settings touch on one another in the years to come?

As the introduction to this book outlined, we understand categories such as equality or difference as the result of contested processes of interpretation und cultural models (Berger and Luckmann 1966/1991). Legal categorization works as a distinct mode of classification, since it generates certain scopes of abstraction and generality. Like statistical categories, juridical ones create new relations of equivalence and terminologies 'that transcend the singularities of individual situations' (Desrosières 1998: 8) through law, norms and standards. They create entities that back 'our descriptions of the world and the ways we act on it' (ibid.: 3). In order to explore the dynamics of legal decisions, circulations and conversions, this chapter will reconstruct the sociohistorical contexts in which notions of equality and difference are created, translated and challenged.

The chapter is organized into two parts. The first part discusses the transitional period from the interwar years to the aftermath of World War II with regard to the ILO. Then, the meaning of equal pay and equal treatment is examined with regard to the EEC. Which problematic was at stake and through which lens was women's and men's paid work understood as being equally remunerated and made comparable at this point of history? The second part deals with litigation, legal mobilization and the tariff practices of the social partners. Two significant cases of the Federal German Labour Court (*Bundesarbeitsgericht*, BAG) regarding 'women's wage groups' will exemplify how, during the post-war years, equal remuneration became legally negotiated in litigation connected to the wage-setting tariff system. The two cases shed light on how actors argued on categories of equality in the national legal system, which is embedded within European supranational legal norms. The concluding remarks discuss the findings.

Shifting Equality Classifications of the ILO and EU Law

The ILO was the first international organization to address social problems, particularly post-World War I labour relations and labour standards at the international level. Founded in 1919, together with the League of Nations and under its umbrella in part XIII of the Paris Peace Treaties (Arts. 387–427),[2] the ILO was created as a permanent international organization on the principle that 'lasting peace can only be established if it is based on social justice' (ILO Constitution 1919: Preamble). In support of this mission, the constitution stipulated a means to foster international cooperation, including 'the collection and distribution of information on all subjects relating to the international adjustment of conditions of industrial life and labour', in particular 'with a view to the conclusion of international conventions, and the conduct of such special investigations' (ibid.: Art. 396; Kott and Droux 2013). By monitoring and reformulating national labour law, the ILO devised instruments to spur international legislation.

Due to its universal and imperial strands, the ILO's notion of international standards was fairly precarious and restricted. The constitution provided a 'colonial clause', which granted the metropolitan powers the right to exclude the colonial territories from ratification. In the late 1920s, the ILO instituted a 'Native Labour Code' that separated the colonies, as a particular realm from the 'International Labour Code' comprising the international conventions that only applied to Western legal-political systems. In the following, we have to keep in mind this fractured meaning of the 'international' (Maul 2007: 480f.; Wobbe 2019; Zimmermann 2016a, 2016b).

Contesting Gender-Coded Labour Protection and Strict Equality in the Interwar Years

The ILO standard-setting system has provided conventions, recommendations and declarations utilized to this day. As opposed to the practices of other international organizations, the ILO tripartite structure exceeds usual intergovernmental cooperation by bringing together state representatives and those of employers and workers, all of them being conferred with voting rights (ILO constitution 1919: Art. 389; Rodgers et al. 2009: 19ff.). Although from its start the ILO was interested in women-specific protective standards, it was not the 'Women's ILO' (Boris, Hoehtker, and Zimmermann 2018). While the ILO formed a focal point for transnational feminist activism during the interwar period, women's organizations had no formalized access to its tripartite structure (Cobble 2018; Zimmermann 2016b: 33). However, parallel with the first International Labour Conference (ILC), an international Women's Labour Congress took place. It resulted in a set of resolutions demanding, among other things, the prohibition of night work for men and women (Cobble 2018: 33ff.). Due to the feminist lobbying, two provisions were incorporated in the 1919 ILO constitution (Wikander 2010). As far as 'questions specially affecting women' were concerned, one of the two permitted advisers of delegations 'should be a woman' (Art. 389). In addition, the principle that 'women and men should receive equal remuneration for work of equal value' was listed under the general principles of the constitution, like the right of association, the eight-hour day and the abolition of child labour (Art. 427).

At first, the ILO did not refer to the idea of equal treatment but aimed its politics at gender-based, differential labour protection. The Maternity Protection (C03) and the Women's Night Work Convention (C04)[3] belonged to the very first legal instruments that were adopted in 1919. By classifying women workers, foremost, with respect to their role as mother and wife, and, thus, as a particular category of the labour market, both conventions connected to the pre-war discourse on protecting wage-working women (Wikander 1995). They also have to be considered in the context of the labour market reintegration processes of male soldiers after the war (Nielsen 1980). By introducing protective legislation, the ILO also created an international framework for organizing previously scattered protective measures into a global standard (Zimmermann 2016a, 2016b).

Feminist activists themselves were divided over the issue of protective measures. One strand of activism – mainly, but not exclusively, trade union women – aimed at sustaining women's 'special conditions' as workers, wives and mothers, and thus fought for paid maternity leave and restricted working hours. Gertrud Hanna, a member of the German workers' delegation, strove for the principle of equal protection of female and male workers, which she considered to be a gradual process. From the early 1920s she successfully incorporated the inclusion of previously excluded categories such as agricultural workers in protection schemes (for Hanna, see Scheiwe and Artner 2018: 76–86). The other strand – mainly liberal, but not only middle-class women – sought to strengthen women's market positions via an international equality treaty that provided civil, social and economic equality status between the sexes (Berkovitch 1999a: ch. 2; Eisenberg 2013: 10; Määttä 2008: 67ff.; Miller 1994: 220ff.; Zimmermann 2016a, 2016b, 2018).

At the turn of the 1930s, the quest for women's equality status accelerated. In 1929 and 1930 respectively, Equal Rights International and Open Door International (ODI) were founded, with both strictly opposing the ILO protective labour conventions. Then, ten of the more moderate, largest women's organizations formed the Liaison Committee of Women's International Organisations in 1931 (Berkovitch 1999b: 110; Miller 1994: 224). As the 1930 International Labour Conference elucidated, ILO Director Albert Thomas found the organization to be under attack through equal rights feminists, 'obtaining absolute equality of conditions of work for the two sexes' (ILC 1930: Report of the Director, 67). Their continued 'opposition to any policy of special protection' (ibid.) was felt as a severe threat to the ILO gender-specific conventions. Although many women activists argued for a 'flexible approach' (Miller 1994: 226), the stricter equality politics resulted in an enormous stimulation of feminist activism around 1930.

At the same time, the global economic crisis, with its consequences for women, played a decisive role in shifting focus onto women's equality status. Against this background, Eugenia Wasniewska, the workers' adviser of the Polish delegation, requested 'a thorough study of the existing conditions of the employment of women, with a view to promoting effective international action to improve those conditions' (ILC 1931: 474). To this end, she recommended that 'an advisory Committee for the question of women's work' should be set up, comprising 'representatives of Governments, employers and workers, and including women representatives' (ibid.). Preceding this conference, French feminist Marguerite Thibert of the ILO Women's and Young Workers' Division initiated an intensive communication about this recommendation (see Thébaud 2018). She recommended to the governing body another format. After 'a stormy exchange of views' (Natchkova and Schoeni 2013: 57) in discussions among the governing body, a Correspondence Committee on Women's Work was established at the ILO Office in 1932 (ibid.: 58).

Finally, the League of Nations decided to launch an inquiry into the worldwide political and civil status of women, while the ILO was to examine women's economic status. The ILO was asked that it 'undertake an examination of those aspects of the problem within its competence – namely, the question of equality under labour legislation – and that it will, in the first place, examine the question of legislation which effects discriminations, some of which may be detrimental to women's rights to work' (ILO 1939: VII; Eisenberg 2013: 12; Miller 1994: 232). Interestingly, this request included the matter of discrimination related to women's rights to work, so that protective provisions could also be studied with respect to the issue's unjust implications.

Marguerite Thibert worked with the help of the Correspondence Committee on the requested inquiry, resulting in a first data collection and analysis of *The Law and Women's Work* (ILO 1939). Covering women's working conditions in forty countries, the study offered the first tentative steps towards collecting data regarding the status of women under labour legislation. Whereas the ILO study *Women's Work under Labour Law* (ILO 1932) did not even mention discrimination, the 1939 survey references the term around fifty times. In this regard, the 1939 report reflects a more inclusive approach by addressing gendered differential labour protection, in addition to equality status. In particular with regard to women's legal position as 'professional workers', as well as the liberal professions, the issue of equal remuneration and the status of married women were considered from the perspective of discrimination (ILO 1939: 433). Meanwhile, the ILO had endorsed 'that women should have full opportunity to work and should receive remuneration without discrimination' (resolution (7) ILC 1937: 785) while confirming the 'principle of equality of pay' two years later (resolution (8) ILC 1939: 785).

The League's Committee to Study the Legal Status of Women, between 1938 and 1939, outlined a set of questions to be elaborated on by three international institutes.[4] The legal experts for these institutes, however, 'quickly discovered problems interpreting non-Western law' (Eisenberg 2013: 13) and had to delay their inquiry to 1941, when the work of the League had been put down due to the war in Europe.

The Language of Human Rights and Equality after World War II

In the transition from war to peace economy, principles of full employment, economic growth and social justice came to prevail in the world's economic reconstruction (Arndt 1987; Clavin 2014; Rodgers et al. 2009). Instead of a language of difference, non-discrimination and equality became the terminology of the day.

The ILO Declaration of Philadelphia (1944) reflects this paradigmatic change, stating: 'All human beings, irrespective of race, creed, or sex, have the right to pursue both their material well-being and their spiritual development in conditions of freedom and dignity, of economic security and equal opportunity' (Declaration of Philadelphia 1944: II). Philadelphia marks the fundamental shift that occurred in the ILO when labour was connected to the new human rights framework, including *all* human beings in the language of universalism and equality, addressing both the sexual difference and the colonial difference (Wobbe 2015). Accordingly, all human beings were to be incorporated into humankind on an equal footing, irrespective of their socially classified differences and independent of their individual citizenship status (Berkovitch 1999a: 117).

Within this framework, the interwar inquiry into women's status provided a fundamental foundation for the establishment of the United Nations Commission on the Status of Women (1946) (Eisenberg 2013; Miller 1994: 239). The main function of the new body was to provide 'recommendations ... on urgent problems requiring immediate attention in the field of women's rights' (UN E/90, E/84 para. 6)[5] in order to prepare UN conventions.

The ILO reconfigured its former protective measures in a dramatically changing global environment in which the productivity of labour 'appears to be one of the important and challenging issues in the world today', thus, the 'real need in almost every sector is for increased production' (ILC 1950b: 2). From this shifting perspective, women's employment rights are reconsidered in a revised frame. As the preparatory report for the Equal Remuneration Convention states, after 1919 the issue of equal pay was 'primarily considered as that of protecting men's wages and of preventing their being levelled down by the employment of women at lower rates' (ILC 1950a: 2). Now, protective politics are understood, rather, as a social injustice against women, and also as an obstacle to the new economic reasoning of productivity, namely the 'rational utilization of the available labour supply' (ibid.). Equal pay, at this moment of history, is explicitly reflected regarding post-war rationales: 'Non-discrimination should be achieved not only as a measure of social justice but to promote labour mobility and efficient utilisation of the labour force.' (ibid.: 7)

As opposed to the interwar period, women are now conceived of as a 'substantial part of the labour force' (ILC 1950a: 2; Whitworth 1994). Due to post-war reconstruction, the efficient use of female workers and full employment became instrumental for economic growth and social justice as a means to peace and security. Thus, Convention No. 100 endorses the rationale of individual performance, namely that 'measures shall be taken to promote objective appraisal of jobs on the basis of the work to be performed' (C 100, Art. 3a). Instead of assumptions concerning the gender of the worker, the convention points to the identification of the performed work (Hericks and Wobbe 2016). As a result, the ILO seeks to shift 'emphasis in wage-setting from valuing the person to valuing the job' (Hoskyns 1996: 53).

Similar developments were reflected in the debate on the Equal Remuneration Convention during the International Labour Conference (ILC 1951). The adviser of the French trade union pointed to productivity and 'well-being', for which equal pay would serve as 'a fresh source of economic development' (ibid.: 340). The Finnish government adviser considered equal treatment between the sexes as a means for the removal of 'unfair competition' (ibid.: 343), leading to higher productivity for women and the selection of the 'best workers available' (ibid.). Unlike the interwar years, women as human resources and their impact on the labour market became a factor in its own right.

This twin of social justice and economic efficiency also holds true for the endeavour of European integration, which eventually evolved, foremost, as an economic endeavour during the early 1950s. Facing the task of international reconstruction and the decline of their empires in a Cold War Europe, the six founding member states strove for a common market 'to ensure the economic and social progress of their countries by common action in eliminating the barriers which divide Europe' (Treaty Establishing the European Economic Community: preamble; hereafter EEC).[6] This included 'the establishment of a system ensuring that competition shall not be distorted in the Common Market' (ibid.: Art. 3f). Due to the incremental environment, the treaty negotiations were embedded in a framework of global expectations. Consider the Code of Liberalization (1949) of the European Organization for Economic Cooperation (OEEC) and the General Agreement for Tariffs and Trade (GATT) principles regulating competition as obligatory conditions of the common market. The ILO international labour standards provided in addition the regulatory framework for social justice. Thus, ILO representatives participated in the preparatory negotiations, so as to feed the discussions with their expertise on a variety of issues, including employment rights for women (Hoskyns 1996: 53ff.; Wobbe 2003; Wobbe and Biermann 2009: 61).

Since equal pay was introduced in the French constitution in 1946, during the treaty negotiations the French delegation demanded that it be adopted by all member states in order to prevent competitive disadvantages (Hoskyns 1996; Van der Vleuten 2007; Wobbe and Biermann 2009). Eventually, a compromise was reached, and the provision became written into the treaties under EEC Article 119. Unlike the ILO formula of equal remuneration for work of equal value (C 100, Art. 1b), the EEC Article reads 'equal pay for equal work' (Art. 119). There appear to have been at least two considerations for this wording. On the one hand, it became obvious that this wording was intended 'to compare a wider range of jobs – if it could be argued that the value was the same' (Hoskyns 1996: 53). On the other hand, the comparability of performances created an issue of commensuration that concerned the experts. How were different jobs to be compared with respect to their value? Given the lack of standardized job classifications and procedures for the sexes, and of statistical data, this was by no means a minor question (see Ricciardi's chapter in this book).

The conclusion of this section will necessitate a brief discussion of the rationales shaping the ILO's and the EEC's considerations in introducing the equal pay principle into law. Both of them aligned with the rationales of economic growth and social justice, even if they focused on different aims. The ILO connected both imperatives to the promotion of international labour standards in the context of inter-state cooperation. On the other hand, the EEC focused on fair competition rules in the common market while establishing, to this end, a distinct supranational legal system together with the European Court of Justice (ECJ), thus making legal decisions on 'European law'. As a result, treaty provisions like Article 119 could be litigated as an individual right.

It was in this normative framework that the ECJ ruling in three cases, Defrenne v. Sabena, formed a landmark in European employment rights. This case resulted from the case that flight attendants brought against the Belgian airline Sabena. They were 'extremely angry about their terms of work' (Hoskyns 1996: 69). Even though direct discrimination in pay had ended in 1966, female flight attendants had to retire at forty while their male colleagues could work until the age of fifty-five. In 1968, Belgian feminist lawyers Marie-Thérèse Cuvelliez and Eliane Vogel-Polsky initiated the case of Gabrielle Defrenne, in order to test the applicability of Article 119. According to Sabena's terms, Defrenne was forced to resign as flight attendant at age forty. The ECJ stated in Defrenne I (case 80/70) that Article 119 did not include social security plans, while making clear that member states 'are required to ensure the application' of the equal pay principle (ibid.: 451). In Defrenne II (case 43/75), the court put equal pay into the context of the EEC social and economic aims, forming 'a part of the foundations of the Community' (ibid.: 12). In other words, member states were obliged to convert the equal pay principle to national law, while women could enforce Article 119 in national courts irrespective of domestic law. Hence, the equal pay article conferred subjective rights to individuals and was fully enforceable before national courts (Cichowski 2007: ch. 3). In Defrenne III, the judgement pointed to the 'respect for the fundamental personal rights' as 'one of the general principles of Community law', and, resulted in the judgement that 'the elimination of discrimination based on sex formes part of those human rights' (case 149/77: no. 26, 27), which the ECJ had to ensure. The frame of equal pay was, thus, expanded from an economic meaning of competition to the universal principle of human rights.

These ground-breaking Defrenne cases, together with the Equal Treatment Directive (76/207/EEC),[7] set the terms for converting the equal remuneration provision of Article 119 into a general principle of equal treatment covering access to employment, including promotion, vocational training and work conditions (76/207/EEC: Art. 1). Since then, the meaning and scope of equal treatment is 'that there shall be no discrimination whatsoever on grounds of sex either directly or indirectly by reference in particular to marital or family status' (Art. 2). Thus, the relevance of equality has been expanded from a narrow focus on remuneration to now include the more general and far-reaching goal of equal treatment requiring equality in procedures such as hiring and job evaluation. As the frequency distribution of ECJ norm references in gender equality cases shows, 87.5% of them have referred to Article 119 and the Equal Treatment Directive between 1971 and 2013 (see Chart 9.1). As opposed to the ILO Equal Pay Convention, the European principle of equal treatment is enforceable as an individual right.

This section has attempted to explore the altering classification of categories, such as 'woman', 'work' and 'rights', with regard to the ILO and the EEC from the interwar to the post-war period. Feminist activism for women's equality status in employment had dismantled gender differential protective measures since the late 1920s in the midst of the economic depression. From a long-term perspective, it becomes clear that, even though the outbreak of war disrupted further actions, these efforts offered a significant foundation for post-war women's equality rights. Likewise, post-war reconstruction generated a configuration in which the human rights framework and the quest for both economic growth

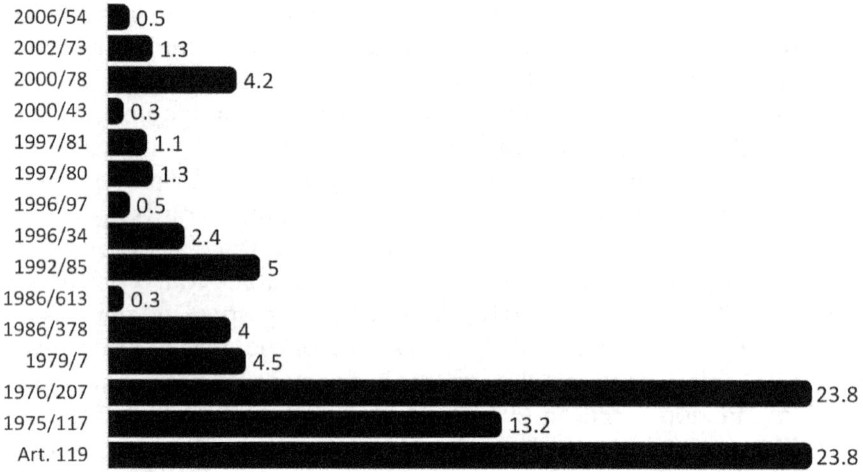

Chart 9.1 Percental frequency of norm references of ECJ decisions with respect to Article 119/Article 141, 1971–2013.

Source: Own calculations according to EurLex (see also Wobbe and Biermann 2009: 100).

and social justice created altering cultural models. By doing so, the concepts of 'women' and 'work' circulated between the European and the ILO international level. The next section turns to national litigation in Germany. Beginning with a court decision in 1955, this section examines a further decision in 1988 to explore pervasive arguments in the wage-setting tariff system.

Legal Mobilization of Equality in German Labour Law and the Wage-Setting System after 1945

In Germany after 1945, women's employment growth revived during the 1950s, continuing the increase in women's paid work since the late nineteenth century (Hachtmann 1993; Stockmann 1985). Among other factors, the growth is due to part-time jobs of mothers, although this pattern did not constitute a new historic phenomenon in the 1950s. From 1938, the National Socialist regime introduced part-time work as a modernization measure of the war economy to stimulate women's employment (Hachtmann 1993: 338).[8] From 1925 to 1939, the number of married women workers in the industry and handicraft business grew from 21.4% to 41.3% (ibid.: 336, 363 Tab. 2). As Arnaud Lechevalier demonstrates in his chapter in this book, employment growth (1959–2001) dropped in Germany between the 1960s and 1970s, to rise once again from 9.3 to 10.7 million after 1975, and to fall once again in 1989. Compared to women's employment participation rates in France (1975–2001), women's participation rates in Germany were diminished in low socioeconomic fields, and there were different patterns and reasons for growth in each country. French women displayed a constant standard of work time of 35-39 hours per week, for 50% of women, while 20% of women in Germany worked less than twenty hours (see Lechevalier's chapter in this book).

Historically, the *Wirtschaftswunder* together with changing consumer expectations appears to be linked to the pattern of part-time work (Oertzen 1999) and 'women's rates', as well as to migration in post-war Germany. In her book on women migrant workers, Monika Mattes directs her argument to this connection. According to Mattes (2005: 22), while part-time work was established for German women, female migrants were recruited to answer the shortage of low-wage sector workers and stabilize the preferred family model. While skilled male migrants received 'male-type' jobs, unskilled women migrants were recruited for 'female-type' jobs (ibid.: 205). This constellation of part-time work and low-wage sector employment with women's rates was affected but not changed through a 1955 court decision.

A female unskilled worker (*Hilfsarbeiterin*) litigated against a chair factory where she worked stapling wood. The wage distribution for the staff provided for four wage groups, of which three were dedicated to skilled, semi-skilled and unskilled workers (*Facharbeiter*, *Angelernte*, *Hilfsarbeiter*). A separate section of the wage determination contained the so-called 'women's wage groups', according to which women should receive 80% of men's wages. By arguing that she performed the same job that the men did, the claimant demanded to receive the pay differential for the other wage group, for the period of her employment. In this first instance, the District Court in Hameln sued the employer to pay the wage difference. This decision was struck down by the Provincial Court of Appeal in Hannover, arguing that contrary to the claimant's allegation, women and men were employed in different work operations: whereas men were machining the raw wood and forwarding it, only some women were assisting men, but women were concerned predominantly with the stapling of the material. In conclusion, the court determined that differentials in remuneration were not based on 'the different treatment of the sex' but were a result of the different economic valuation for the performed work.

In the next step, the claimant brought the suit before the BAG, so as to overrule the first decision. Now, she referred her suit to the German constitution, stating that the wage differentials violated the gender equal rights Article 3.2. The BAG decided that women's wage groups violated the constitutional article. The decision represented a turning point in German labour litigation in two respects. The first involves the relationship between the German constitution and the constitutional principle of the tariff autonomy (Art. 9) and the respective prevalence. Both the employer and the National Association of Employers argued that Article 3.2 of gender equal rights was not applicable to the tariff wage settlements. The second turning point concerns the implementation of equal pay and its operative aspect with regard to the determination of individual work performance.

The BAG decision of 15 January 1955 (1 AZR 305/54) states the following: 'The equal pay principle as a constitutional right is not only binding state authority but also the tariff contractual parties' (AZR 305/54). In other words, the constitution's equality principle was attributed not only a vertical but also a horizontal obligation. In addition, the court clarified that the equality principle provides direct and subjective rights, since the constitutional gender equal rights principle confers 'genuine legal norms instead of mere programmatic qualities [*Programmsätze*]' (Leitsatz 1). During this period, several legal suits in the domain of equal pay refer to this 1955 BAG decision.[9]

At the same time, the BAG decision enacted the prohibition of the women's wage groups and gender-related rates, stating 'that the sexual difference principally was forbidden to play a role for the legal treatment of men and women' (AZR 305/54: 3). Put differently, the decision prohibited direct and overt discrimination, namely a direct reference to women as a source for their disadvantages. Thus, the second statement (Leitsatz 2) reads: 'The equal pay principle and anti-discrimination include the principle of equal remuneration for equal work of men and women'. How did its statements affect both women's wages and the practices of employers and trade unions?

Practices of Tariff Systems

As has been previously demonstrated, the BAG decision shifted to an equality focus. While deciding that the constitutional equal rights article includes equal pay, the court even claimed the issue's prevalence with regard to the constitutional article of the tariff autonomy. Thus, the social partners had to determine the appropriate method to ensure the application of the equal remuneration principle, while accounting for the constitutional principles (AZR 365/54:16). Three practical strategies for tariff conversion are identified across the metal industry in various German states, namely: (1) the de facto retention of women's wage

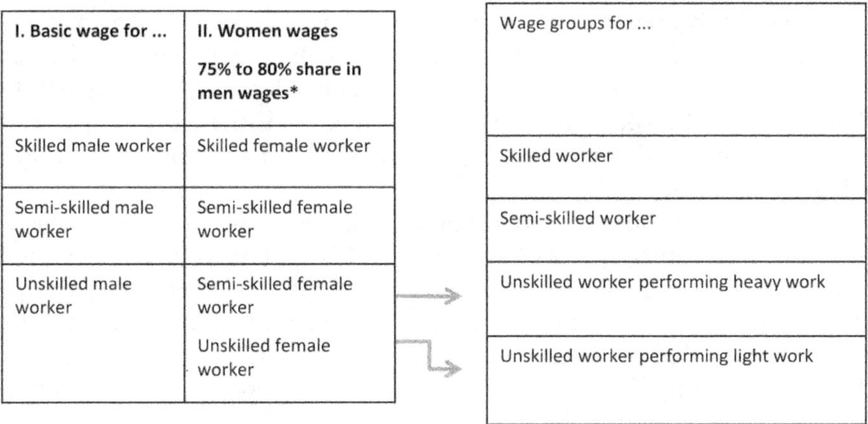

Graph 9.1 Job classification. Graph created by the author.

groups (practices of *ignoring the law*); (2) the establishment of 'light wage groups' (*rhetorical* practices); and (3) the formation of two or three 'light wage groups' (additional differentiation).

The practices of ignorance were employed in widely ranging fields in the metal industry in the states of Hessen, Bavaria and Northern Westphalia. There, women's wage rates were held constant until 1972, without even evaluating job schemes and positions. As Graph 9.1 indicates, women's basic wages were 75% to 80% of men's wages, irrespective of the women's jobs. The social partners followed the concept of incommensurability between women' and men' work performance, assuming 'that there would not exist job comparability, and, therefore they had not to respond to the quest for equal pay' (Müller-Hagen 1959: 44). This reasoning reinforced the sexual job segregation at hand. Since work tasks were already attributed to female and male labourers on the site, implying strictly different practices, there appeared to be no need to compare them.

The second rhetorical practices resulted in the introduction of the guiding distinction between heavy and light physical work, so as to replace the banned reference based on sex in the sweets industry. The example of the framework collective agreement within the wood-processing industry (see Graph 9.1) documents how the organizing category of the collective agreement became neutralized. By relabelling the existing female-male taxonomy, the categorization was labelled with a sex-neutral wording, including the new gender-coded distinction between 'heavy' and 'light' as the guiding classification. This renaming demonstrates a practice widespread across various fields, such as the metal and wood industry, both constructing and assuring the analogies between physical heaviness and masculinity, and physical lightness and femininity as a semantic demarcation (Berger and Luckmann 1966/1991). As a circular letter reads, 'the social partners [though] agreed, that those tasks were due to their peculiarity usually processed by female workers' (Müller-Hagen 1959: 44).

Finally, additional differentiation facilitated the incorporation of further distinctions in work categories. What was introduced, then, was an additional distinction between the segments of lower wage groups, that is, between more or less light work. As a consequence, unskilled work was supplemented through 'more difficult light work' and 'less difficult light work' (Müller-Hagen 1959: 42f.) according to workers with mainly heavy physical tasks and those with primarily lighter physical tasks. These jobs were attributed to the new grade D, while the new grade E should include 'all unskilled workers'. Since only wages in group D were upgraded, women were especially assigned to the E group. As these examples clarify, the binary opposition of more or less heavy was instrumental to both rename and introduce further distinctions, which appeared to be rhetorically neutral.

From a Gender-Coded Yardstick to the Comparability of Work

In 1988, the BAG decided that assumptions regarding physical differences – heaviness and lightness in particular – would no longer be legitimate categories from the view of shifting scientific expertise (AZR 707/87). By then, German courts had argued that assumed different muscular strength or muscular burden between men and women justified unequal pay. In 1988, the BAG decided that these criteria would no longer be legitimate as a measure of the wage classification system. Unlike the 1955 decision, the court now rejected the heavy/light dichotomy, resting its evaluation on scientific expertise, which had replaced physical criteria through the category of performance and 'normal bodily burden' (ibid.: 23, 28). The work task should be evaluated according to the individual resilience of the single female and male person (ibid.: 27) instead of an average value referring to men. The court referred to the ECJ decision in case 237/85 in which the European Court argued following the Equal Pay Directive (75/117 EEC).[10] It stated: 'the use of values reflecting the average performance of workers of one sex as a basis for determining the extent to which work makes demands or requires effort or whether it is heavy constitutes a form of discrimination on grounds of sex, contrary to the directive' (ECJ 237/85: 26). Collective negotiations, therefore, had to take into consideration the resilience of the human being (ibid.:

27) while considering further factors of working conditions. As a consequence, the performance of females was no longer evaluated on the basis of that of males, but referred to the human average, which in turn constituted the criteria for comparing the work of both sexes.

Unlike the ruling in 1955, the court's decision in 1988 was not merely grounded in constitutional equality rights. The first EEC directive (75/117/EEC) enforcing the application of the principle of equal pay for men and women expanded the meaning of the equal pay Article 119 by introducing the ILO notion 'work of equal value'. It pointed to 'the same work', not in the sense of identical tasks, but as 'work to which equal value is attributed' (ibid.). To this end, the 'job classification system' had to be based on the same criteria 'for both men and women and so drawn up as to exclude any discrimination on grounds of sex' (ibid.). Individual performance had to be the measure for the same job criteria. This provision exceeds the constitutional equality rights principle insofar as it forms a practical and operative scheme according to which procedures have to be organized. In contrast to the interwar period and the 1955 ruling, the court did not rely any longer on presumed difference. Instead, individual performance and the measurable normalcy of 'bodily burden' constitute the criteria.

Discussion of the Findings

This chapter has sought to illuminate the classifications and reclassifications that indicate the transitional dynamics from protective to equality measures over the interwar years and in the aftermath of World War II by exploring the categories at different scales. The first lesson learnt from our findings is that both periods followed the transformation from war to peace, resulting in altering social orders and cultural structures of work and gender. From this view, it becomes clear that the rise of global institutions and their universal principles was by no means a continuation of the past but a historically contingent and unforeseen institutional change, which manifests the deconstruction of interwar equality concepts.

During the interwar period, the incommensurability of male and female industrial workers became the guiding framework of international labour law. It was embedded in broader processes of the codification of labour law and precarious international social standards, predominantly dedicated to European male workers as distinct from 'colonial labour' (Wobbe 2015, 2019; Zimmermann 2016a, 2016b, 2018). During the 1930s, the binary opposition with respect to male/female, work/

family, difference/equality came under pressure through transnational feminism in a period of economic depression. After 1945, equality and anti-discrimination became the terminology of the day with a worldwide range. This broader shift was embedded in a configuration of fundamental change, namely the decline of European empires, the processes of decolonization, the emergence of human rights and the global spread of the nation-state model, accompanied by the rise of economic knowledge and technical expertise in international organizations (Berkovitch 1999a; Speich Chassé 2014).

Secondly, our findings suggest that the transition from former presumptions of incommensurability of females' and males' work to its commensurability is driven by both rationales of economic efficiency and social justice. The ILO Equal Pay Convention sheds light on the shifting meaning of 'women', 'labour' and 'rights' nested in altering conceptions of economic and social logics. Economic growth, maximum production and full employment, together with social standards, became the yardstick by which to consider women as a labour force and a human resource, just as men. Herewith, processes of individualization were set in motion embracing women's individual rights as workers and valuing their job instead of their person. As the EU gender equality directives and the case law show, these norms have addressed the evaluation of individual performance by enforcing respective taxonomies (direct and indirect discrimination, equal treatment, equal opportunity etc.) together with distinct procedures.

The third lesson learnt from our findings is that equality classifications are not just fixed legal doctrines and law in the books, but practically contested domains of shifting meaning, litigation and public disputes. As this chapter illustrates, the controversies between protective measures and principles of equality are complex, touching on the wicked problems of both women's labour and gender relations, and with this the problematic of social reproduction. According to the discussed case study, individual workers made their legal claims because constitutional and European law provisions were violated. From their practical experiences they compared the work performed by men and women and its respective pay while pushing legal reflections forward. The social partners' reaction to the 1955 court decision did not merely maintain former practices, but rather they created new kinds of classification, as the phenomenon of the 'light wage groups' demonstrates. By neutralizing the virtual sexually differentiated job classification, new wording and additional distinctions were introduced. Following the EU taxonomy, the 'light wage groups' manifest indirect discrimination by generating a job scheme that appears to be neutral, though disadvantaging one sex. Due to the collective power of the social partners, including their institutional safeguarding, the legal mobilization matters in particular.

Finally, the interplay between the ILO, EEC and litigations in Germany suggests that scales opened new spaces of social interaction and circulation of categories in litigation and court decisions. ILO and EEC legal norms of equality and anti-discrimination emerged within the context of global institutions in the post-war period while, at the national level; they were translated and brought before national courts and the ECJ and stimulated new interactions. Legal claims making enfolded. Whereas in 1955, before the foundation of the EEC, the wage-setting tariff system was challenged on the basis of the equality principle of the German constitution, in 1988 the European equal treatment principle (Equal Pay Directive) formed the imperative point of reference. German courts had to incorporate this principle, due to the binding quality of European law in the member states' legal systems. The 1988 decision, thus, translated and exploited the European legal scale, to abolish the 'light wage groups'. Therefore, various actors connected simultaneously or subsequently to different levels of action (Zimmermann 2015) by exploiting possibilities and conflicts in the complex field of European law-making, which constitutes the configuration for mobilization in a national space deeply embedded in transnational institutions.

Theresa Wobbe is Professor Emerita of Sociology at the University of Potsdam, and fellow of the Margherita von Brentano Centre for Gender Studies at the Free University of Berlin. She specializes in historical sociology, sociology of knowledge, institutionalist gender analysis, and sociology of classification. Her research focuses on long-term transformations of gender and work, international statistics as an instrument of globalization, and the making of gender as a global category of comparison. Her current projects deal with the ILO discontinuities in the notion of forced labour, 1919–2017, and the conceptional history of gender in global political institutions.

Carolin Höroldt studied Sociology at the University of Leipzig (BA), and at the University of Potsdam (MA); she spent her study abroad within the European ERASMUS programme at the University of Karlstad, Sweden. She worked with the Chair of Sociology of Gender, and for the project of the Agence Nationale de la Recherche (ANR) and the Deutsche Forschungsgemeinschaft (DFG) 'Metamorphoses of Equality II (1945–2010)' (Potsdam/CNAM-Lise Paris) on ILO equality concepts. Currently, she is preparing her PhD proposal.

Maike Bussmann received her Diploma in Sociology from the Technical University of Dresden. She spent her study abroad at the University de Vest, Timişoara (Romania) within the European ERASMUS programme in International Relations and Gender Studies. Her research interests include the theory and history of the German women's movement and gender-based wage inequality. She worked with the Chair of Sociology of Gender. As a member of the project of the Agence Nationale de la Recherche (ANR) and the Deutsche Forschungsgemeinschaft (DFG) 'Metamorphoses of Equality II (1945–2010)' (Potsdam/CNAM-Lise Paris), she focused on the equal pay concepts of the ILO and German labour law and labour policy.

Notes

1. See ILO NORMLEX: ILO C100 Equal Remuneration Convention, 29 June 1951 (No. 100); ILO C111 Discrimination (Employment and Occupation) Convention, 15 June 1958 (No. 111), http://www.ilo.org/dyn/normlex/en/f?p=1000:12000:::NO::: (accessed 6 June 2018).
2. The covenant of the League of Nations (Treaties of Versailles et al.) includes the ILO Constitution in Part XIII of the Treaties of Versailles (Arts. 387–427), Saint-Germain-en-Laye (rts. 332–372) and Trianon (Arts. 315–355), and Part XII of the Treaties of Neuilly (Arts. 249–289) and Sèvres (Arts. 374–414), signed between 28 June 1919 and 10 August 1920. It came into enactment on 10 January 1920. In this chapter, the numbering of articles is that of the ILO Constitution, including the Declaration of Philadelphia.
3. See ILO NORMSLEX: ILO C03 Maternity Protection Convention, 29 November 1919 (No. 3); ILO C04 Night Work (Women) Convention, 28 November 1919 (No. 4), http://www.ilo.org/dyn/normlex/en/f?p=1000:12000:::NO::: (accessed 6 June 2018).
4. The International Institute for the Unification of Private Law (Rome), the International Institute of Public Law, and the International Bureau for the Unification of Criminal Law (both in Paris) undertook the bulk of the work. Questions of Mohammedan and Hindu law were split between specialists in France and India after the fact, when difficulties in interpreting these 'foreign' laws were discovered (Eisenberg 2013: 13, fn 7).
5. ECOSOC, Resolution Establishing the Commission on the Status of Women (CSW), E/RE S/2/11, 21 June 1946.
6. The EUR-Lex resources only provide Dutch, French, German and Italian versions of the treaty: Treaty establishing the European Economic Community. Rome, 25 March 1957, https://eur-lex.europa.eu/legal-content/EN/TXT/?uri=celex:11957E/TXT
   For the English version see : University of Pittsburgh, Archive of European Integration http://aei.pitt.edu/37139/ (accessed 12 November 2018).
7. Council Directive 76/207/EEC of 9 February 1976 on the implementation of the principle of equal treatment for men and women as regards access to employment, vocational training and promotion, and working conditions. *Official Journal* L 039, 14 February 1976, pp. 0040–0042.
8. From 1938 to 1944, the working time of qualified and unqualified women workers decreased (Hachtmann 1993: 364, Tab. 3).

9. See the decisions BAG 246/54, BAG 64/56, BAG 203/56, BAG 326/56 affirming the equal pay's horizontal obligation. The last decision from March 1957 stated that the job of shop assistants in female and male departments does not legitimate different pay (BAG 246/54: 1).
10. Council Directive 75/117/EEC of 10 February 1975 on the approximation of the laws of the member states relating to the application of the principle of equal pay for men and women. *Official Journal* L 045, 19 February 1975, pp. 0019–0020.

References

Primary Sources

Rulings Bundesarbeitsgericht (German Federal Labour Court)
BAG 1 AZR 305/54 [15 January 1955].
BAG 1 AZR 246/54 [2 March 1955].
BAG 1 AZR 365/54 [6 April 1955].
BAG 4 AZR 398/65 [17 August 1966].
BAG 4 AZR 363/83 [17 April 1985].
BAG 4 AZR 707/87 [17 April 1988].
BAG 4 AZR 713/87 [17 April 1988].

Rulings European Court of Justice
Case C-80/70 Defrenne v. SABENA [1971] ECR 445.
Case C-43/75 Defrenne v. SABENA [1976] ECR 00455.
Case C-149/77 Defrenne v. SABENA [1978] ECR 01365.
Case C- 237/85 Rummler v. Dato-Druck GmbH [1986] ECR 02101.

Secondary Sources

Arndt, H.W. 1987. *Economic Development: The History of an Idea.* Chicago: University of Chicago Press.

Berger, P.L., and T. Luckmann. 1966/1991. *The Social Construction of Reality: A Treatise in the Sociology of Knowledge.* London: Penguin Books.

Berkovitch, N. 1999a. *From Motherhood to Citizenship: Women's Rights and International Organizations.* Baltimore, MD: Johns Hopkins University Press.

________. 1999b. 'The Emergence and Transformation of the International Women's Movement', in J. Boli and G.M. Thomas (eds), *Constructing World Culture: International Nongovernmental Organizations since 1875.* Stanford, CA: Stanford University Press, pp. 100–26.

Bock, G. 2002. *Women in European History*, trans. Allison Brown. Oxford: Blackwell.

Boris, E., D. Hoehtker, and S. Zimmermann. 2018. 'Introduction: A Century of Women's ILO', in E. Boris, D. Hoehtker, and S. Zimmermann (eds), *Transnational Networks, Global Labour Standards and Gender Equity, 1900 to Present.* Leiden: Brill, pp. 1–23.

Cobble, D.S. 2018. 'The Other ILO Founders: 1919 and Its Legacies', in E. Boris, D. Hoehtker, and S. Zimmermann (eds), *Transnational Networks, Global Labour Standards and Gender Equity, 1900 to Present.* Leiden: Brill, pp. 27–49.

Cichowski, R.A. 2007. *The European Court and Civil Society: Litigation, Mobilization and Governance.* Cambridge: Cambridge University Press.

Clavin, P. 2014. *Securing the World Economy: The Reinvention of the League of Nations, 1920–1946*. Oxford: Oxford University Press.

Declaration of Philadelphia. 1944. 'Declaration of Philadelphia: Declaration Concerning the Aims and Purposes of the International Labour Organisation', in *26th International Labour Conference Philadelphia Record of Proceedings*, Annex. Montreal: International Labour Office.

Desrosières, A. 1998. *The Politics of Large Numbers: A History of Statistical Reasoning*, trans. Camille Naish. Cambridge, MA: Harvard University Press.

_______. 2010. 'Words and Numbers: For a Sociology of the Statistical Argument', in A. Rudinow Sætnan, H. Lork Lomell, and S. Hammer (eds), *The Mutual Construction of Statistics and Society*. London: Routledge, pp. 41–63.

Eisenberg, J. 2013. 'The Status of Women: A Bridge from the League of Nations to the United Nations', *Journal of International Organizations Studies* 4(2): 8–24.

Hachtmann, R. 1993. 'Industriearbeiterinnen in der deutschen Kriegswirtschaft 1936 bis 1944/45', *Geschichte und Gesellschaft* 19(3): 332–66.

Hericks, K., and T. Wobbe. 2016. 'Ein Sieg des Fortschritts? "Gleichbehandlung" und "Leistung" aus der Perspektive der World Polity-Forschung', in M. Funder (eds), *Neo-Institutionalismus – Revisited: Bilanz und Weiterentwicklungen aus der Sicht der Geschlechterforschung*. Baden-Baden: Nomos, pp. 71–96.

Hoskyns, K. 1996. *Integrating Gender*. London: Verso.

International Labour Conference. 1930. *Proceedings of the 14th International Labour Conference*. Geneva: ILO.

_______. 1931. *Proceedings of the 15th International Labour Conference*. Geneva: ILO.

_______. 1937. Resolution (7) Concerning Women Workers, Submitted by Mr McGrady and Miss Abbott, Government Delegates of the United States of America, in *Proceedings of the 23th International Labour Conference*. Geneva: ILO, p. 785.

_______. 1939. 'Resolution (8) Concerning the Employment of Women, Submitted by Mr Jouhaux, French Workers' Delegate, and Mr Kupers, Netherlands Workers' Delegate', in *Proceedings of the 25th International Labour Conference*. Geneva: ILO, p. 792.

_______. 1950a. *33rd Session: Equal Remuneration for Men and Women Workers for Work of Equal Value*. Report V (1). Geneva: ILO.

_______. 1950b. *23rd Session: Report of the Director General*. Report V (1). Geneva: ILO.

_______. 1951. *34rd Session: Record of Proceedings*. Geneva: ILO.

International Labour Office. 1932. *Women's Work under Labour Law: A Survey of Protective Legislation*. Studies and Reports Series I (Employment of Women and Children) No. 2, Geneva. Published in the UK for the ILO (League of Nations): P.S. King & Son.

_______. 1939. *The Law and Women's Work: A Contribution to the Study of the Status of Women*. Studies and Reports Series I (Employment of Women and Children) No. 1, Geneva. Published in the UK for the ILO (League of Nations): P.S. King & Son.

International Labour Organization Constitution. 1919. 'Treaty of Paris, Part XIII Labour', in *Der Vertrag von Versailles (1919): Der Friedensvertrag zwischen Deutschland und den alliierten und assoziierten Mächten nebst dem Schlußprotokoll und der Vereinbarung betreffend die militärische Besetzung der Rheinlande. Amtlicher Text der Entente und amtliche deutsche Übertragung*. Auf Grund der endgültigen, neu durchgesehenen amtlichen Revision. Im Auftrage des Auswärtigen Amtes (Final and new reviewed official revision on behalf of the Foreign Office), 2nd edn, Berlin 1924, pp. 207–20.

Kessler-Harris, A., J. Lewis, and U. Wikander. 1995. 'Introduction', in U. Wikander, A. Kessler-Harris, and J. Lewis (eds), *Protecting Women: Labour Legislation in Europe, the United States, and Australia, 1880–1920*. Urbana: University of Illinois Press, pp. 1–28.

Kott, S., and J. Droux (eds). 2013. *Globalizing Social Rights: The International Labour Organization and Beyond*. Geneva: ILO.

Lewis, J., and S.O. Rose. 1995. '"Let England Blush": Protective Labour Legislation,

1820–1914', in U. Wikander, A. Kessler-Harris, and J. Lewis (eds), *Protecting Women: Labour Legislation in Europe, the United States, and Australia, 1880–1920*. Urbana: University of Illinois Press, pp. 91–124.

Määttä, P. 2008. *The ILO Principle of Equal Pay and Its Implementation*. Tampere: Tampere University Press.

Mattes, M. 2005. *'Gastarbeiterinnen' in der Bundesrepublik: Anwerbepolitik, Migration und Geschlecht in den 50er bis 70er Jahren*. Frankfurt: Campus.

Maul, D. 2007. 'The International Labour Organization and the Struggle against Forced Labour from 1919 to the Present', *Labour History* 48(4): 477–500.

Miller, C. 1994. 'Geneva – The Key to Equality: Interwar Feminists and the League of Nations', *Women's History Review* 3(2): 219–45.

Müller-Hagen, D. 1959. 'Die Verwirklichung des Lohngleichheitsgrundsatzes und die dabei auftretenden Probleme', Ph.D. dissertation. Frankfurt: Johann Wolfgang Goethe-Universität.

Natchkova, N., and C. Schoeni. 2013. 'The ILO, Feminists and Expert Networks: The Challenges of a Protective Policy (1919–1934)', in S. Kott and J. Droux (eds), *Globalizing Social Rights: The International Labour Organization and Beyond*. Genf: Palgrave, pp. 49–64.

Nielsen, H. Karl. 1994. 'The Concept of Discrimination in IlO Convention no.111', *International and Comparative Law Quarterly* 43(4): 827–856.

Oertzen, C. von. 1999. *The Pleasure of Surplus Income: Part-Time Work, Gender Politics, and Social Change in West Germany, 1955–1969*, trans. P. Selwy. New York: Berghahn Books.

Rodgers, G., et al. 2009. *The International Labour Organization and the Quest for Social Justice, 1919–2009*. Geneva: ILO.

Scheiwe, K., and L. Artner. 2018. 'International Networking in the Interwar Years: Gertrud Hanna, Alice Salomon and Erna Magnus', in E. Boris, D. Hoehtker, and S. Zimmermann (eds), *Transnational Networks, Global Labour Standards and Gender Equity, 1900 to Present*. Leiden: Brill, pp. 75–96.

Speich Chassé, D. 2014. 'Technical Internationalism and Economic Development at the Founding Moment of the UN System', in M. Frey, S. Kunkel, and C.R. Unger (eds), *International Organizations and Development, 1945–1990*. Basingstoke: Palgrave Macmillan, pp. 23–45.

Stockmann, R. 1985. 'Gewerbliche Frauenarbeit in Deutschland 1875–1980: Zur Entwicklung der Beschäftigtenstruktur', *Geschichte und Gesellschaft* 11(4): 447–75.

Thébaud, F. 2018. 'Difficult Inroads, Unexpected Results: The Correspondence Committee on Women's Work in the 1930s', in E. Boris, D. Hoehtker, and S. Zimmermann (eds), *Transnational Networks, Global Labour Standards and Gender Equity, 1900 to Present*. Leiden: Brill, pp. 50–74.

Van der Vleuten, A. 2007. *The Price of Gender Equality: Member States and Governance in the European Union*. Aldershot: Ashgate.

Whitworth, S. 1994. 'Gender, International Relations and the Case of the ILO', *Review of International Studies* 20(4): 389–405.

Wikander, U. 1995. 'Some "Kept the Flag of Feminist Demands Waving": Debates at International Congresses on Protecting Women Workers', in U. Wikander, A. Kessler-Harris, and J. Lewis (eds), *Protecting Women: Labour Legislation in Europe, the United States, and Australia, 1880–1920*. Champaign: University of Illinois Press, pp. 33–43.

________. 2010. 'Demands on the ILO by Internationally Organized Women in 1919', in J. Van Daele et al. (eds), *ILO Histories: Essays on the International Labour Organization and Its Impact on the World during the Twentieth Century*. Bern: Peter Lang, pp. 67–89.

Wikander, U., A. Kessler-Harris, and J. Lewis (eds). 1995. *Protecting Women: Labour Legislation in Europe, the United States, and Australia, 1880–1920*. Champaign: University of Illinois Press.

Wobbe, T. 2003. 'From Protecting to Promoting', *European Law Journal* 9: 88–108.

_______. 2015. 'Das Globalwerden der Menschenrechte in der ILO: Die Umdeutung von Arbeitsrechten im Kontext weltgesellschaftlicher Strukturprobleme von den 1930er bis 1950er Jahren', in B. Heintz and B. Leisering (eds), *Menschenrechte in der Weltgesellschaft: Deutungswandel und Wirkungsweise eines globalen Leitwerts*. Frankfurt: Campus, pp. 283–316.

_______. 2019. '"*Hard to See, Harder to Count*": Deutungskontexte der Kategorie Zwangsarbeit in der International Labour Organization während der 1920er und 2000er Jahre', in H. Bennani, M. Bühler, S. Cramer, and A. Glauser (eds), *Beobachtung und Vergleich. Soziologische Untersuchungen zur Weltgesellschaft*. Frankfurt: Campus.

Wobbe, T., and I. Biermann. 2009. *Von Rom nach Amsterdam: Die Metamorphosen des Geschlechts in der Europäischen Union*. Wiesbaden: Verlag für Sozialwissenschaft.

Zimmermann, B. 2015. '*Socio-Histoire* and Public Policy Rescaling Issues: Learning from Unemployment Politics in Germany (1880–1927)', in S. Börner and M. Eigenmüller (eds), *European Integration, Processes of Change and the National Experience*. Basingstoke: Palgrave Macmillan, pp. 121–46.

Zimmermann, S. 2016a. 'Night Work for White Women and Bonded Labour for "Native" Women? Contentious Traditions and the Globalization of Gender-Specific Labour Protection and Legal Equality Politics, 1926 to 1939', in S. Kimble and M. Röwekamp (eds), *New Perspectives on European Women's Legal History*. New York: Routledge, pp. 394–427

_______. 2016b. 'The International Labour Organization, Transnational Women's Networks, and the Question of Unpaid Work in the Interwar World', in C. Midgley, A. Twells, and J. Cartier (eds), *Women in Transnational History: Connecting the Local and the Global*. London: Routledge, pp. 33–53.

_______. 2018. 'Globalizing Gendered Labour Policy: International Labour Standards and the Global South, 1919–1947', in E. Boris, D. Hoehtker, and S. Zimmermann (eds), *Transnational Networks, Global Labour Standards and Gender Equity, 1900 to Present*. Leiden: Brill, pp. 227–54.

Chapter 10

Negotiating the Boundaries of Equality at Work

Tensions about a Gendered Employment Norm in France and in the European Community, 1914–2014

Ferruccio Ricciardi

Introduction

The principle of equality between men and women was set forth in the Preamble of the French constitution of 1946 and then reintegrated into the constitution of 1958. In the fields of work and labour law, this principle has long been associated with a logic of protection (i.e. protection of family life and the national birth rate through a prohibition on women's night work) which sometimes became a logic of *exclusion* (until 1965, a husband's authorization was required before his wife could work). In a context of weak support for the citizenship rights of women workers, the battle for equality, in France as well as in Western Europe, was first waged as a battle for equal pay. Unable to rely upon full citizenship rights in the family sphere or the political sphere, it was therefore in the economic sphere that fundamental aspects of women's liberation played out, particularly in the post-World War I era, when women not only began to work in traditionally masculine sectors such as metallurgy, but began to weigh in on collective bargaining in those sectors as well. After World War II, the struggle against wage discrimination became more and more important to both labour union and feminist demands, while actors on the international level (like the International Labour Organization or the

European Economic Community) began elaborating on and diffusing the ideal of 'equal pay for equal work'.

Taking the affirmation of this principle as the starting point for a complex and difficult path towards emancipation, this chapter examines the modes of constructing and deconstructing gendered employment categories over the long term (from World War I to today), in France within the larger context of Europe (i.e. the European Economic Community space). If the principle of sexual differentiation in the division and organization of labour has been formally rejected, the practical reality remains quite different and presents multiple situations of more or less disguised discrimination. Thus, by looking at actual practices rather than normative texts, we may not only observe the fabrication of a gendered employment norm, but may also see its legitimacy called into question and its content effectively weakened during the period subsequent to the affirmation of the principle of equality between men and women at work. This principle was forged through struggle in the political sphere and the labour union sphere, as well as through debate among experts and technocrats, at both a local scale (in France) and an international scale (notably in Europe). Observation in the fields of collective bargaining, professional classification and legislative production allows us to account for the tensions that have, since the early twentieth century, accompanied this two-fold process. Relying on a vast corpus of archival sources (including notably the archives of the European Commission, of the European Trade Union Confederation, and of French labour unions) and integrating an interdisciplinary body of academic work devoted to the same topic, this chapter proposes to present the issues that arose in relation to the representation and the laborious implementation of what is known today as workplace equality.

'Equal Pay for Equal Work': An Illusory Principle?

Progressive implementation of the principle of equal pay must be situated within a long history of collective bargaining if the underlying mechanisms for elaborating employment categories and professional classifications capable of resisting discrimination are to be rendered visible. The starting point was World War I, which was the occasion for real change in the promotion and legitimation of women's work in France. However, this relative change effectively hid the elements giving rise to wage inequality, which would long persist thereafter.

State-sponsored industrial mobilization during the Great War was undoubtedly beneficial for the promotion of women's employment. For example, in the Parisian metallurgy sector, women accounted for up to 30% of the total employee population in 1917 (Omnès 1997a). At the beginning of the conflict, the tasks entrusted to women were generally manual tasks involving simple, low-intensity, highly repetitive operations. The professional qualifications of women workers climbed steadily. Their wages climbed too. Nonetheless, possibilities for promotion remained limited. Regardless of their level of work, women's salaries were subject to 15–20% reductions, which effectively institutionalized the hitherto disguised minimization of women's wages. Employers justified these measures by arguing that they covered costs arising from the new equipment and supervision necessary for the integration of inexperienced women workers. These additional costs were never taken into consideration, however, when it came to integrating equally inexperienced male workers. Although never explicitly stated, the perception that women's earnings constituted 'extra income' (*salaire d'appoint*) – derived from the perception that women did not need a 'real salary' because their needs were not as great as men's needs were – was pervasive in employer discourse, serving to justify a non-egalitarian wage structure that was sensitive to intangible 'natural' differences (Lee Downs 1995, 2006).

This approach was to be found in the collective agreement adopted by Parisian metallurgists, signed on 12 June 1936, during the period in which the French Popular Front (Front populaire), the left-wing coalition that emerged during the 1930s, controlled the government. This collective agreement would serve as a model for subsequent agreements reached in multiple other industries in France.

The wage schedule that emerged from negotiations distinguished thirteen generic categories based on qualification, age and gender, each of which could be identified and assessed within each of the three hundred feminine and masculine occupations. The new generic categories tended to attribute greater value to masculine qualities and jobs and lesser value to feminine qualities and jobs. For example, a new categorization of male and female semi-skilled workers (*ouvrier spécialisé*, or OS) appearing in the agreement divided the old unskilled worker category (*manœuvre spécialisé*) in two, dissociating the manual set-up work from work on the machines themselves. Minimum salaries were attributed to these two new categories which represented a reduction in remuneration for feminine set-up work. During the negotiations, feminine OS set-up work was enduringly devalued (Omnès 1997b). Additionally, by eliminating the possibility of gaining qualification through on-the-job practice and by referring instead only to each employee's level of certification (*Certificat d'aptitude professionnelle*, or CAP), the collective agreement contributed to excluding women from qualified work positions. No CAP for feminine work existed in metallurgy, which translated into a negation of qualification for the work carried out by women (jobs merely requiring manual labour were considered innately feminine both by employers and by unions) (Machu 2013). More generally, the collective agreement reinforced a sexual segregation of the workforce that was engendered by the rationalization of labour, and simultaneously contributed to undoing or erasing women's place in the dynamic of professionalization that began during World War I.

Following World War II, these job classification principles were reiterated by the French government, which, until 1950, assumed the power to fix salaries and to regulate labour relations. Minimum pay rates were determined through a centralized administrative process, which left companies with some discretion, notably with respect to individual salaries. By ministerial order (the *arrêtés* Parodi-Croizat of 1945–46), the government renewed the hierarchy of the job categories established in 1936 through collective bargaining with the metallurgist branch. These categories consisted of a wage coefficient, which in turn fixed wage-rate hierarchy.[1] If, during the construction of this kind of classification, the principle of 'equal pay for equal work' was formally respected, there were nonetheless multiple criteria, which could influence wage determination, especially for women. First, the minimum pay rate varied according to sex, to the extent that certain clauses refer to a sex-based categorization of jobs. For example, one ministerial order relating to Parisian metallurgy stipulated that under no circumstances could the minimum pay rate of women be more than 10% less than the minimum pay rate of men belonging to the same occupational category (Saglio 2007: 60).

A law passed on 11 February 1950, which allowed for a return to the practice of fixing pay rates through collective bargaining, made the 'equal pay for equal work' principle an obligatory element for collective agreements by making it a condition for their renewal. The suppression of that practice was accompanied by the guarantee that the minimum pay rates for women would be equal to the minimum pay rates of men belonging to the same occupational category, while the employer retained limited discretion to set the average maximum pay rate (notably through the payment of employee bonuses). And since only the minimum pay rate was the object of collective negotiation,[2] the actual pay rates were set at the company level (Lanquetin 2006). Employee qualification and job classification mechanisms could then be mobilized to justify a gender-differentiated use of the workforce, effectively making any detection of gender-based wage discrimination difficult to detect (Guilbert 1965).

While the formal principle of equal pay was instituted shortly after 1945, real equality remained evasive. The pay schedules that effectively differentiated between men's pay rate and women's pay rate were associated with the job classification schemes agreed upon through collective bargaining in 1936, which were taken up again after World War II, and which were not abandoned until 1968 (Eyraud 1978).

Article 119 of the Treaty of Rome, or Regulation through Persuasion

At the international and European levels, the principle of equal remuneration is codified by Convention No. 100 of the International Labour Organization (ILO), which was ratified in France in 1951, and then by the Treaty of Rome, which was signed in 1957 by the original member states of the European Economic Community (EEC). Article 119 of the Treaty of Rome provided that 'each Member State shall during the first stage ensure and subsequently maintain the application of the principle that men and women should receive equal pay for equal work'. This article was inserted into the treaty at France's request, for reasons relating to economic competition. French textile manufacturers were concerned that competitors located in other member states would engage in social dumping (the textile sector relied heavily on a female labour force). The principle of equality expressed here was therefore designed for the market, in the interest of preserving the freedom of contract and avoiding unfair competitive practices and protectionism (Jacquot 2009: 253).

Although seeming to make equal remuneration between men and women an exceptional circumstance required for economic integration, Article 119 of the Treaty of Rome nonetheless lays the groundwork for the principle of prohibiting sex discrimination (Hoskins 1996: ch. 3). Over the following years, equality of remuneration, far from becoming mere 'dead letter', would become the object of European initiatives. Throughout the 1960s and 1970s, the European Commission, along with the European Council and various commissions associated with the European Parliament, employed a variety of means (i.e. questionnaires, investigations, expert opinions, official recommendations) to incite EEC member states to translate principle into practice and notably to make collective actors more sensitive to the issue of assuring equal remuneration for equal work.

Beginning in 1959, multiple initiatives were undertaken to encourage adequate implementation of Article 119, notably through interaction between government experts and representatives of professional organizations (i.e. meetings, letters, official events at the national and international levels).[3] The implementation of wage equality gave rise to problems relating to the legal and technical aspects of bringing given instances of work into equivalence (through, for example, the use of occupational classification schemes) and still left room for effective discrimination. Thus an official recommendation issued by the European Commission on 20 July 1960 invited EEC member states to take necessary measures to assure the complete implementation of the principle of equality.[4] The next step consisted in a detailed examination of the status of implantation in each member state with the help of a special study group composed mainly of jurists and statisticians.[5] This group produced several reports, addressed either to the European Commission or to the European Parliament, as a means of building awareness among relevant actors, both by indirectly informing them of the group's findings and by indirectly soliciting measures intended to improve implementation.

Upon reading these reports, which were dedicated mostly to the industrial manufacturing context, it becomes apparent that there were essentially two groups of countries: one group including those member states that had legal instruments intended to allow women to avail themselves of the court system to protect their right to equal pay (France, Germany, Italy and Luxemburg), and another group composed of member states that still did not have any such instruments (Belgium and the Netherlands). With regard to collective agreements, however, gaps and insufficiencies were observed in most member states: the inexistence

Table 10.1 The negative gap (expressed in %) between the average hourly earnings of women compared to those of men belonging to the same group as defined by level of qualification (manufacturing industries).

	S	SS	US	OTH	GEN
Belgium	33.2	28.7	25.0	17.7	31.9
West Germany	26.8	25.6	21.8	25.9	30.3
France	25.8	19.4	15.6	18.1	27.5
Italy	29.4	24.0	9.1	–	24.8
Luxembourg	47.0	27.7	44.3	48.1	45.5
Netherlands	40.1	39.9	31.3	7.7	39.3

Note: The gap in question corresponds to the difference between men's average hourly earnings and women's average hourly earnings, divided by men's average hourly earnings.
S = skilled workers; SS = semi-skilled workers; US = unskilled workers; OTH = other workers; GEN = general result for the whole set.
Source: ETUC Archives, 2964, Commission des communautés européennes, *Rapport de la Commission au Conseil sur l'état de l'application au 31 décembre 1968 du principe d'égalité entre rémunérations masculines et féminines*, 18 June 1970, ch. 2, p. 7.

of any collective agreement in some sectors or sub-sectors; direct discrimination arising from specific dispositions regarding women's wages; indirect discrimination arising mostly from job classification schemes.[6]

Thus, if France and Germany saw lower gender-based wage gaps than other member states (Table 10.1), the aggregate data still hid structural effects arising from the use of professional qualifications or from the specificity of the industrial sectors in question. In Germany, for example, the presence of so-called 'light-wage groups' (*Leichtlohngruppen*) in the collective agreements of many branches of activity did not favour the detection of wage discrimination. In France, the numbers were misleading essentially because of the unequal valorization of 'masculine' versus 'feminine' qualities formalized in occupational classification schemes.

More generally, consensus arose among European civil servants that the legal implementation of Article 119 was insufficient in light of economic constraints:

> We attempted to 'level up' by raising feminine wages to the level of masculine wages. But we soon realized that on one hand, there were many ways to artificially circumvent the principle, and that on the other hand, the national legal systems had not relayed Article 119, which remained bogged down in economic considerations due to its insufficient legal buttressing, which undoubtedly reflected insufficient conviction with respect to the right to equality.[7]

A Seamstress on the Assembly Line: Occupational Classification in the Post-1968 Era

In May 1968, as the mobilization of a variety of groups (including groups in favour of equality for women) besieged France (Zancarini-Fournel and Artières 2015), the principle of wage equality was still far from being effectively implemented. In the report of one among many European studies dedicated to the issue, one can read the following observation:

> If the classification systems established under the collective agreements are not, in principle, applied any differently according to a worker's gender, in reality there is an observable trend toward under-qualifying, or toward qualification-based discrimination, which in a number of cases tends to undervalue women's work.[8]

The problem, which we have seen above, was not a new one and seemed even to re-emerge in a cyclical way from the 1930s onwards. The context of 1968, however, seemed particularly encouraging for demands for equality. Labour unions, including notably the Democratic Confederation of Labour (Confédération française démocratique du travail, or CFDT), adopted a new focus on women's issues, and opened up new perspectives on gender-based division of labour. Within the context of its self-management (*autogestion*) project, the CFDT effectively proposed a tight link between class struggle and sexual conflict, quickly making the fight for employee equality a priority (Le Brouster 2010).

A law passed on 22 December 1972, concerning equal remuneration between men and women, increased an institutional and normative framework for this combat; however, the law did not seem to sufficiently meet the demands of union activists, nor did it satisfy the experts. Rather, it fell into step with the reformist vision advocated at the time by the Gaullist Prime Minister Jacques Chaban-Delmas, which involved strengthening 'contractual policy' in such a way as to accommodate some of the demands being made by the labour and feminist movements (the Prime Minister's advisor on labour matters was Jacques Delors). After a long incubation period – the initial draft had been submitted in 1963 – the law transcribed the main provisions of ILO Convention no. 100 into the French labour code, including notably the principle of equal pay for equal work and the definition of remuneration structured around the notion of 'minimum' pay.

Before the law could even be approved, worker criticism was already strong. In October 1972, Jeannette Laot, who was in charge of women's policy matters at the CFDT, characterized a draft of the law as being poorly adapted to the situation, which it claimed to modify. While the situation was better than it had been during the war, during which time collective agreements seemed to naturally accept cases of gender-based wage discrimination, these cases had since become increasingly subtle and were increasingly perceived as the 'dupery' of characterizations through which feminine work was arbitrarily distinguished from masculine work.[9] The CFDT's major concern was the meaning attributed to the notion of 'same work', which was derived from a system that linked remuneration to cadence of work or to output, and not for example to the amount of knowledge acquired (through a degree programme or an apprenticeship), or to the nature of the work itself, or to the amount of responsibility assumed, and so on.[10]

Implementation studies conducted by the Women's Labour Committee (Comité du travail féminin), an advisory organism created in 1965 as part of the French Ministry of Labour and which has been heavily involved in the struggle for gender equality since that time, all pointed in the same direction (Revillard 2007). By mobilizing external expertise and member activism, mostly arising from the non-profit, academic and union communities, the Committee quickly became the leading authority on a particular kind of 'state feminism' that involved struggling against discrimination while also diffusing knowledge about women's work. During meetings of the *ad hoc* commission on remuneration, which was in charge of informing the Committee on that subject, the notion of a 'work station' – and the ways in which work stations were attributed – was often called into question. According to Jacques Duraffourg, Professor of Ergonomics at the Conservatoire National des Arts et Métiers, who was invited to address the Committee on this very topic, a number of work station studies in sectors involving mass production effectively allowed researchers to determine the characteristics of the work stations that were most often occupied by women. The work in question was often highly fragmented with low cycle duration and heavy time constraints. Remuneration was linked to output goals or established productivity norms, and the effective dissociation of design functions from implementation functions was often most pronounced. In short, these jobs bore the trace of a postulate implicit in Taylorism, which was that the remuneration of workers was endlessly adaptable. However, according to Duraffourg, nothing proved that women were more adaptable than men when it came to monotonous and repetitive work.[11]

Other variables were at play in the Taylorization of feminine industrial work, which were related to the structure of the labour market. For example, another report from the Women's Labour Committee underscored the way in which, paradoxically, the earnings gap between men and women persisted among industrial workers in spite of the fact that between 1968 and 1971 women working in industry had benefitted from larger pay raises than women working in the tertiary sector (+31% versus +27% approximately). In a situation where feminine employment was growing significantly in the industrial sector, feminine remuneration remained concentrated in lower steps of the pay scale. More generally, the average pay for women generally only exceeded the average pay of women manual workers by 27%.[12] All the studies commissioned by the Committee pointed to the persistence of situations of wage discrimination, whether of the direct or indirect variety; consequently, new emphasis was put on the need for occupational training, for example, to counter the effects of sex-based employment discrimination (Revillard 2007).

These multiple instances of observed disparity in the remuneration of men and women led the Women's Labour Committee to propose, in 1976, a highly critical evaluation of the law of 1972.[13] First, the Committee denounced the gender pay gap (which tended to be higher among manual workers), differences in career progression (which had been increasing over the previous fifty years) or even differences in socio-occupational category (discrimination being strongest among upper management). Then the Committee pointed out the 'defects', or even the stereotypes, that were hastily attributed to feminine work to justify their lesser remuneration: their 'potential maternity', their 'absenteeism', their 'instability' at work, and of course the widespread idea that a woman's earnings were merely 'extra' income for her family. The Committee therefore hoped to open up discussion about 'work of equal value' as a way of reconceptualizing existing modalities of work evaluation in such a way as to better take account of the job-related qualities mobilized, including knowledge, skills, dexterity, physical strength and psychological resiliency, the use of which implied physical or intellectual effort.[14] While it is true that, as work inspectors at the time indicated, men and women often occupied different jobs, it was now the modalities of job attribution and the possibilities for promotion that were brought into question, rather than the simple comparison of pay levels attributed to workers who have the same coefficient.[15]

The Committee's reconceptualization effort built upon that which labour unions had already begun. It called job classification schemes into question to the extent that they gave rise to indirect discrimination – discrimination not against women directly, but against 'feminine' jobs, which were less advantageously classified than 'masculine' jobs requiring equivalent levels of qualification. Disadvantageous classification entailed lower coefficients, and thus lower pay. Furthermore, this recognition deficit could be observed further upstream as well, in relation to training. For example, the feminine CAP (*Certificat d'aptitude professionnelle*) was often less valued than its masculine counterpart. Such was the case for women manual workers employed in the electronics sector, who held a CAP qualification as a seamstress. While the seamstress CAP assured a high level of dexterity, it was not recognized as a qualification at all by the electronics branch. Rather, the seamstress CAP was seen as originating from a distinct and inferior branch, in recognition of dexterity which merely came naturally to women. Thus, while the seamstress CAP proved to be indispensable for hiring purposes, it was not taken into account for classification purposes. Instead it could even penalize women as they built their careers as qualified workers (Gallot 2012, ch. 3). In this type of situation, the new law for wage equality had no effect. Consequently, it became the object of heavy criticism.

In this respect, union leaders from the CFDT and the National Confederation of Work (Confédération nationale du travail, or CGT), the left-wing union, were among the law's most prominent critics. The devaluing of women's qualities for job classification purposes became the main target of a discourse that not only attacked the perverse effects of gender-based division of labour, but also attacked the technical and intellectual premises that justified the existing modalities of job evaluation and which penalized qualification levels by looking instead at job requirements as the operative criteria against which the quality of work should be measured. The language of the CFDT's denunciation of existing modalities of job classification deserves to be cited at length:

> Women mostly occupy the jobs figuring at the bottom of the classification grids. That positioning is determined by the characteristics of the jobs they hold.
>
> The so-called 'scientific' work-evaluation method, which is based solely upon time measurements and which is most frequently used to establish these classifications, is increasingly called into question.
>
> The too-exclusively educational frame of reference for evaluating the level of worker training is more directly problematic for the female workforce because women generally have lower levels of technical training.
>
> Numerous union organizations are raising issues relating to job classification schemes. But even the scheme set forth in the metallurgists' collective agreement cannot really change the situation for women, unless the larger power dynamic existing in many companies, and in the context of which these schemes are implemented, allows for implementation that is not strictly job-based.[16]

Within the CGT, opinions about the law of 1972 were no less severe, often integrating the CFDT's objections over the perverse effects that could arise when classifications were based on job characteristics rather than the professional skills of each individual person.[17] Since women and men most often occupied different posts, it was the modalities of job attribution and promotion possibilities, rather than the wages paid to the set of individuals working at any given level, that accounted for gender inequalities with regard to pay. The great complexity of such a mechanism for setting pay rates also made it difficult for employees to appeal to the work inspector over instances of violation of the law. Consequently, in 1976, the first official evaluation of the law's implementation noted that there had been only eighteen formal complaints.[18]

The Contribution Made by European Expertise: From the Notion of 'Same Work' to that of 'Equal Treatment'

On 8 April 1976, the European Court of Justice ruled in favour of a demand for compensation brought by Gabrielle Defrenne, a former flight attendant for Sabena Airlines, in light of her remuneration at a level that was unequal to that of male colleagues carrying out identical work. Through its ruling, the court recognized the general principle of equality, or non-discrimination, as the cornerstone of the European legal order.[19] The outcome of this legal battle, which, as Defrenne's attorney Eliane Vogel-Polsky pointed out, had lasted nearly fifteen years, showed that equivalence of pay, when considered in isolation, did not exist; rather, equivalence of pay could only exist within the larger framework for recognizing equal treatment (Gubin 2007: 91–97). From that perspective, the court reinterpreted the meaning of Article 119, emphasizing its dual purpose – both economic (as a measure to protect competition) and social (as a measure to improve the living and working conditions for the workforce) (Lanquetin 2006).

For the purposes of this chapter, the Defrenne-Sabena case is of particular interest because it established a distinction

> between, on the one hand, direct and overt discrimination susceptible to being observed through criteria relating to the identity of the work and to the equality of pay ... and, on the other hand, indirect and disguised discrimination which cannot be identified except as a function of more explicit European or national implementation measures.[20]

If the applicability of the principle of equal remuneration were to remain limited to 'direct and overt' cases of discrimination alone, the court suggested that full implementation of the objectives pursued by Article 119, through the elimination of both direct and indirect discrimination between male and female workers not only within individual companies but also within entire branches of industry or even within the global economy, would imply in some cases the intervention of adequate European and national measures.[21] In other words, the court's decision validated an expansive reading of the 'same work' element so that the job evaluation criteria and worker classification schemes, which were often sources of effective discrimination, could be considered as part of the issue and eventually revised.

It was precisely the definition of 'same work' that was at issue, to the extent that the ILO convention provided that equal remuneration was only applicable to work of equal value, and the EEC Directive of 10 February 1975 (the so-called Equal Pay Directive), seeking to harmonize implementation of the equal pay principle at the member state level, indicated that the principle would only apply to instances involving the 'same work'. The interpretation of this latter notion became a matter of jurisprudence, as nothing else specified any other common measure against which the remuneration of feminine work and masculine work could be measured.[22]

Again in 1979, in France, ambiguity with regard to the criteria for evaluating masculine and feminine jobs was pervasive. According to a study by the Centre for Studies and Research on Qualification (Centre d'études et de recherches sur les qualifications, or CEREQ), job classification depended less upon evaluation criteria that were difficult to comprehend than it did upon descriptions of the tasks to be carried out, which allowed the definition of qualifications to become rather arbitrary. For example, in the retail sector (department stores, etc.), which was normally quite feminized, job classification always set out definitions to determine the characteristics of the job (i.e. entry-level sales representative, qualified sales representative, highly qualified sales representative); however, these definitions did not refer to common criteria that could be evaluated (i.e. type of activity, degree of autonomy, level of knowledge) because in most instances they designate the tasks to be performed and the kinds of performance required. And whether job evaluation operations were actually carried out or merely envisioned, it seemed that reputedly 'feminine' qualities (dexterity, coordination, rapidity or interpersonal relations) were insufficiently valued.[23] Generally, in most European countries, the ambiguity of the exact meaning of 'equal value' (which could depend upon a variety of factors, including job-related knowledge, educational degree, skills acquired through experience, responsibilities, physical or psychological resiliency), and the very small number of court decisions taking up the issue of equal pay, could only hinder efforts to actually implement the equal pay principle.[24]

From the mid 1970s, prominent thinking about issues relating to equality between men and women at work related to concerns about the qualifications necessary to carry out feminine work. Expert opinions from the EEC were addressed to the major actors in the labour field of each member state, pleading for some deep rethinking of occupational classification schemes in order to prevent all forms of gender discrimination, including implicit forms. Among the measures envisioned were the following: the rejection of different qualification rules for men and women; the rejection of job evaluation criteria that had no relation to the concrete reality of the conditions under which work was being carried out; commitment to considering all of the job-related qualities required for all of the relevant tasks, particularly when determining the value of so-called 'feminine' work; and the refusal to push artificial classification differentiation too far, because it was often women who found themselves in the lowest subcategories all while assuming responsibilities that were practically identical to those assumed by men.[25]

The effort to revise job classification schemes fit into a larger movement of awakening to both the social and economic stakes of gender discrimination within the EEC, as seen from within the framework of the social action programme launched by the European Commission in 1974. A specialized agency in charge of women's issues was set up within the Commission in 1976 in order to promote workplace equality through new *ad hoc* legal instruments (Directives) or simply through the dissemination of information to member state institutions and collective actors, and even to the public at large (i.e. through pedagogical films).[26] This commitment gradually became formalized, as evidenced by Directive 76/206 of 9 February 1976, on the implementation of the principle of equal treatment for men and women as regards access to employment, vocational training and promotion, and working conditions, and by Directive 76/7 of 19 December 1978, on the progressive implementation of the principle of equal treatment for men and women in matters of social security.

Considering that the goal of equal pay had remained unattained despite multiple efforts undertaken at the national level and multiple European-level recommendations, European experts – most of whom were women – favoured widening the scope of intervention. Promoting 'equal treatment' effectively entailed eliminating the many differences in treatment that were manifest in working life, by addressing their root causes (i.e. occupational training, maternity, differentiated regulation relating to working hours, the need for work-life balance).[27]

A French Perspective on the Principle of Equality: The Roudy Law and Workplace Equality

Among the propositions brought forward in the early 1970s by the Women's Labour Committee in order to resolve the problem of wage equality was a new proposition to 'improve women's occupational training'.[28] Having observed the ineffectiveness of measures intended to close the wage gap between men and women directly, ministerial experts were thus leaning towards measures to improve the levels of qualification prevalent among women workers. This new policy orientation was relayed both via governmental representatives and via employers' associations which, since the 1960s, had promoted the feminization of certain jobs in the industrial sector in order to encourage the insertion, integration and professional growth of women. Furthermore, by following the lines of reflection laid out by European institutions, the ministerial experts were also able to move the debate gradually beyond mere wage equality and to consider instead the larger issue of equal treatment.

With an eye towards proposing a new law, Nicole Pasquier, who was the Minister of Women's Affairs under the right-wing Raymond Barre's government (during the presidency of Valery Giscard d'Estaing), began a consultation initiative in 1980 involving the leaders of certain companies. The companies in question provided the Ministry with specific indications about the measures they had adopted to promote women's employment. Their responses to the Ministry's questionnaire related mainly to the gap between the training already acquired by women job-seekers and the skills needed to be hired (the 'feminine' CAP certifications, as we saw above, were not recognized by many branches of industry) and to the relative absence of occupational training among women (and the fact that opportunities for the promotion of women appeared quite rare). A number of stereotypes figured among the obstacles evoked by respondent companies: women had less availability to work overtime; women habitually would only accept certain kinds of jobs; men resisted the devalorization of work that was progressively becoming feminized, and so on. These representations effectively reinforced a gender-based division of labour. Despite all of this, respondent companies still made efforts to promote women's employment, even if only for the purpose of increasing productivity and 'modernizing' labour relations. Thus, in 1974, Peugeot launched an internal investigation, through occupational physicians and psychologists, regarding the difficulties experienced by its women employees upon integrating into 'traditionally masculine' jobs (Gallot 2012: 320–27). These voluntary commitments taken by the respondent employers, and supported both by the government and by some workers' organizations, contributed to changing the focus by shifting the dominant discourse from the issue of wage equality to that of workplace equality (*égalité professionnelle*). The promotion expanded training and better qualifications for women became a preferred means for improving their classification and thus their remuneration.

It was in this context of both reflection and experimentation that France passed its law of 13 July 1983 on workplace equality, which became known as the Roudy law (*loi Roudy*) in honour of Yvette Roudy, Minister of Women's Affairs under the socialist government of Pierre Mauroy (during the presidency of François Mitterrand). The law prohibited employers from using gender as grounds for refusal to hire, to promote or to train potential or current employees. In the event of litigation between employer and employee, the employer would henceforth bear the burden of proof, which had been previously borne by the employee. In transposing Directive 76/207 into law, member states had to respect its anti-discrimination purpose. The French legal tradition, which upheld the principles of equality and protection as part of a larger pro-family or paternalist outlook, would consequently be modified. New opportunities for affirmative action (*actions positives*) as a means for accomplishing 'substantive' equality, and new recognition of indirect discrimination as a grounds for legal action, were indicative of a transformation in the legal paradigm of equality at work. As for implementation, the main provisions of the law imposed new measures of vigilance with respect to the working conditions, the remuneration, the training and the promotion of employees (evidenced by an annual company report) and the negotiation, among social partners, of 'equality plans' (*plans d'égalité*), which were to define the remedial measures to be taken to allow women employees to catch up with men employees (notably in the area of training) (Lanquetin 2004).

This latter measure – the 'equality plans' – was the Roudy law's most emblematic measure. By addressing issues relating to training and effective discrimination, the new law integrated elements that were responsive to the Women's Labour Committee's criticism of the law of 1972. The new law was also responsive to suggestions made by the CFDT, which was directly involved in its drafting and which integrated the content of contemporary European debates relating to discrimination into union discourse as well as into technocratic and civil service discourse. The idea, defended by the confederation, of addressing workplace inequality through remedial 'catch-up' measures (affirmative action) was consistent with the principle of equal opportunity (*égalité des chances*), which henceforth found new favour among labour unionists in Europe.[29] As of 1979, the European Trade Union Confederation, for example, widened the scope of its actions in favour of women workers via a programme for procuring rights and opportunities for women. In this programme, which was elaborated in Munich by the Confederation's third congress, access to employment and wage equality were not only part and parcel of a larger occupational training reform initiative, but also related to more general efforts to improve work-life balance (notably for reasons relating to maternity).[30]

By the end of 1992, only thirty company 'equality plans' had been formalized, to the benefit of fewer than five thousand women. No retail companies figured among the signatory parties, and only 30% of companies having more than fifty employees actually followed the law by drafting an annual report comparing the situation of workers (Jobert 1989: 79). Upon closer inspection, at the company level, the results were even more modest than reported. The historian Fanny Gallot studied the implementation of the first 'equality plan' at the Moulinex factory in Alençon in 1983 (specialized in the production of home appliances), the employees of which were mostly women. Her study revealed that the training initiatives adopted to help women in gaining access to better jobs were complicated by uncertainty with respect to the company's future need for qualified workers in light of increasingly automated modernization which mostly affected 'masculine' jobs (Gallot 2012: 333–36). Notwithstanding legal obligations and the corresponding risks of legal sanction (which were small), the mechanisms that were intended to assure the law's success only worked when there was voluntary commitment on the part of employer companies.

Despite these difficulties in implementing the Roudy law, it is important to emphasize that it did channel a significant change in discourse by leading the debate over equal pay into a larger and more politically ambitious debate over workplace equality. This cognitive adjustment involved moving beyond the simple question of pay to consider a plurality of larger questions about the different stages of women's career development, ranging from training to retirement, and including intermediary questions about the balance between family life and professional life. Thus, a new representation of gender relations in the working world was sketched out, fusing rights-based and opportunity-based guarantees against a regulatory backdrop encouraging the integration of women workers. This social-liberal orientation was itself validated by the discourse circulating among European institutions.

From Workplace Equality to Employment Diversity: Social Dialogue and the 'Modernization' of Social Relations

With the Roudy law falling short of expectations, legislative revision began in the late 1980s. Several initiatives were undertaken under the auspices of the Rocard government, and then the Chirac government (always during the presidency of Mitterand). These initiatives essentially went in one of two directions. The first was to encourage gender diversity in the workplace as a means of offsetting the risks of discrimination arising out of gender-based divisions of labour and the perverse effects of implementing occupational classification schemes. The second was to pursue the goal of workplace equality through collective negotiation. In the first scenario, by garnering labour union support notably from the CFDT, and by leveraging European-level recommendations to make equal opportunity into an essential and transversal element for all of the EEC's economic and social policy (so-called 'gender mainstreaming'), new 'diversity contracts' (*contrats de mixité*) were progressively being put into place beginning as early as 1987, especially within small and medium-sized firms.[31] These contracts, which were touted as being more responsive to company demands to protect their competitiveness, were intended to gradually replace existing workplace equality policies. In the second scenario, the goal of workplace equality continued to figure into the inter-professional accord concluded on 23 November 1989, which itself figured into larger agreements to promote the 'modernization' of business in times of rapid technological change and to adjust legal limitations on working hours and working conditions (Jobert 1989). In a context of heavy unemployment and a weakening of French unionism, these accords wagered on the success of an initiative simultaneously reforming the framework for a company's productive activities, organizational activities and labour relations. However, this initiative went forward without first gaining consensus from the CGT or the French Confederation of Catholic Workers (Confédération française des travailleurs chrétiens, or CFTC), for example, which opposed an emerging questioning of the existing prohibition on women's night work in the industrial sector. This prohibition would remain in place in France until 2001, when it was repeatedly condemned by the European Court of Justice.

The new policy based on voluntary commitment on the part of companies took form through a very rich and active round of collective bargaining, with successive initiatives moving forward throughout the 1990s and early 2000s. However, while these initiatives sometimes appeared to complement each other, they also appeared to be globally ineffective. The Genisson law (*loi Genisson*), adopted in France on 9 May 2001, established an obligation to negotiate at both the company and branch levels to reach the goal of workplace equality (we recognize here a certain degree of continuity with the Roudy law). A few years later, the inter-professional accord of 1 March 2004 followed along similar lines. It addressed equality and workplace diversity while also envisaging new initiatives in the areas of recruitment, ongoing training, promotion, professional mobility and of course equal remuneration. Upon renewing that accord, a law on equal remuneration, passed on 23 March 2006, obliged social partners to negotiate various matters at both at the branch and company levels. Among these matters were the measures to be undertaken to close the gender pay gap, to improve the relation between family life and work life, and to improve access to occupational training. Additionally, the law for real equality between men and women, adopted in France on 14 August 2014, insisted on reinforcing collective bargaining while providing new resources for the pursuit of equality (i.e. public guarantees to offset unpaid alimony, public information campaigns to combat sexual stereotypes). Generally, all of these efforts were focused on the social dialogue and effectively valorized it for the purpose of addressing the obstacles that impeded women from integrating into the workplace on an equal footing with men in terms of employment-related rights and career opportunities.

If, in the end, consensus among unionists for the triumvirate of 'equal pay', 'workplace equality' and 'employment diversity' might henceforth be legitimately posited as a given, the goals would nonetheless remain unattained. Certainly, more than fifty accords relating to these issues were signed in the years following 2001, especially among large corporate groups. The themes of workplace equality and equal remuneration nonetheless remained inadequately addressed at the branch level in spite of the fact that the 2006 law established 31 December 2010 as the deadline for negotiating measures to close the gender pay gap. The accords specifically addressing workplace equality often merely referred to previous negotiations to guide implementation efforts, particularly for matters concerning equal pay, which henceforth would be hinged to annual wage-specific rounds of collective bargaining. Today, the gradual institutionalization of the principles of workplace equality and equal opportunity is observable within an evolving legislative framework and within collective agreements; however, at the same time, implementation measures again seem to lack steam and are sometimes merely swallowed up by newer but only tangentially related policy mechanisms (human resource management, company-specific social policy measures, etc.) (Laufer and Silvera 2006). Yet nothing about the specific context of labour relations in France, or about the weakness of union representation in companies, would seem to put France into a position where it can effectively support an institutionalization of the principle of equality between men and women. Furthermore, gender-based discrimination – and especially gender-based pay discrimination – today remains perceived as a subject of marginal importance (Ardura and Silvera 2001). Finally, while attempting to reinforce the coercive dimension of its legal mechanisms, the state – acting as a *de facto* motor for equality policies since the post-war era – seemed to show more affinity for a diversity-toting company discourse focused on economic performance than it showed towards social justice objectives (Laufer 2014).

Conclusion

This chapter has sought to shed light upon the construction and deconstruction of gender-based employment categories adopted in France during the twentieth century by focusing its study upon such indicators as collective agreements, qualifications required of women seeking to integrate into the workplace, and the transformation of relevant legal mechanisms. A relevant change in the cognitive and institutional frames of reference for the notion of workplace equality can be observed. The demand for equal pay, which arose during the period immediately following World War II and which made use of the principle of 'equal pay for equal work' (*à travail égal, salaire égal*), gradually shifted towards larger frames of reference, such as the more comprehensive principles of 'equal treatment' and 'equal opportunity'. This shift is occurring in a context where arguments associating social protection with market-driven economic demands are cutting across national borders. This cognitive adjustment is effectively indebted not only to the commitment of unionists, political leaders and feminist activists (some of whom held positions of power within the cabinets and ministerial commissions of French government) but also to the commitment of authorities associated with the European Community, which has contributed to making policies that were once considered to be applicable as limited exceptions into more generally applicable norms (van der Vleuten 2007).

We are observing a paradoxical convergence between, on the one hand, an egalitarian discourse derived from the experience of May 1968, which targeted the supposedly technical and intellectual premises of Taylorist evaluation practices that were prejudicial for women, and, on the other hand, the liberal logic underpinning the construction of the European common market, which tends to equate equal rights with equal opportunity. Common criticism of job classification schemes and of systems of functional evaluation – particularly in the industrial sector – tended to reveal the sources of indirect or disguised discrimination, which was itself an expression of the contentious effects of a gender-based division of labour. When engaging in employee classification, the 'qualities' of women were often devalued, albeit merely owing to the fact that elements of qualification were not all recognized as having equal value (physical strength was valued in men, but rapidity was not valued in women).

In France, the trajectory of legislative mechanisms intended to counter or even to resolve the problems of gender inequality in the workplace, as well as the trajectory of certain heavily involved actors such as the CFDT, attests to the gradual redefinition of social issues and to the gradual redesigning of the legal and normative instrumentation mobilized by the state. The law of 1972 on equal remuneration was replaced by the Roudy law in 1983, which by transposing part of the European legal corpus, brought the challenge of defining equality into the French labour code. The Roudy law wagered on the success of efforts to improve women's level of occupational qualification when mobilizing a discourse with liberal characteristics, demanding that public agencies take charge of various relevant social variables (from training to maternity) for the purpose of favouring the insertion of women into the workplace. Similarly, the conversion of the CFDT into an organization in favour of remedial 'affirmative action' measures had the effect of affirming the principle of equal opportunity (for the purpose of improving women's working and living conditions) and drawing support from unionists throughout Europe.

If criticism of the system of work evaluation and remuneration is making it increasingly clear that there is a real need to rethink occupational qualifications (in such a way as to better account for acquired knowledge, the nature of the work undertaken, and the importance of the responsibilities assumed by the employee), there is also reason to observe that both the legislative solutions and the solutions derived through collective bargaining have adhered to a 'contractual policy' framework which essentially takes care to improve women's access to the labour market. The shift from formal equality to substantive equality, in other words, was accomplished by constructing a citizenship of women workers indexed on a complex logic of performance, employability and mobility.

Ferruccio Ricciardi is a research fellow (*chargé de recherche*) at the French National Center for Scientific Research (CNRS), affiliated to the Conservatoire National des Arts et Métiers (CNAM) of Paris. His research deals with history of work and management in a comparative and transnational perspective. Among his latest publications is *La Fracture gestionnaire: savoirs et techniques d'organisation en Italie (1948–1960)* (Classiques Garnier, 2016).

Notes

Special thanks to Catherine Marry for her comments on a preliminary version of this chapter, as well as to Daniel Hotard for its meticulous translation.

1. The occupational grid is based on qualifications, that is, vocational skills certified by a diploma or developed with experience; each category corresponds to a coefficient proportional to the hourly minimum wage defined by the collective agreement of the branch (Saglio 1986).
2. The minimum pay rate being understood as the rate of pay that could be sustained throughout the branch, regardless of disparities in productivity.
3. ETUC Archives (European Trade Union Confederation Archives, International Institute of Social History, Amsterdam), 2864, CEE-Commission, *Rapport de la Commission au Conseil sur l'état d'avancement des travaux relatifs à l'art. 119 CEE*, 12 October 1961.
4. ETUC Archives, 2865, Assemblée parlementaire européenne. Documents de séance, *Rapport intérimaire sur l'égalisation des salaires masculins et féminins*, 11 October 1961.
5. ETUC Archives, 2864, CEE-Commission, *Rapport de la Commission au Conseil sur l'état d'avancement des travaux relatifs à l'art. 119 CEE*, 12 October 1961.
6. ETUC Archives, 2864, Commission des communautés européennes, *Rapport de la Commission au Conseil sur l'état d'application au 31 décembre 1968 du principe d'égalité entre rémunérations masculines et féminines*, 18 June 1970.

7. ETUC Archives, 2864, Commission des communautés européens, *L'emploi des femmes et ses problèmes dans les états membres de la Communauté économique européenne*, July 1970, p. 177. The original French text states: 'on a choisi d'égaliser "par le haut" en relevant les salaires féminins au niveau des salaires masculins. Mais on s'aperçoit d'une part que par maints artifices on a tourné le principe, d'autre part que les droits nationaux n'ont pas relayé l'article 119, qui est demeuré englué dans l'économique par insuffisance d'armature juridique, et ceci, sans doute, par insuffisance de conviction dans le droit à l'égalité'.
8. ETUC Archives, 2865, Parlement européen. Documents de séance, *Rapport sur l'application du principe de l'égalité des rémunérations entre les travailleurs masculins et féminins*, 8 May 1968, p. 8. The original French text states: 'si les systèmes de classifications prévus par les conventions collectives ne sont pas en principe appliqués d'une manière différente aux travailleurs des deux sexes, on observe dans les faits une tendance à la sous-qualification ou à une discrimination dans la qualification tendant, dans un certain nombre de cas, à dévaloriser le travail effectué par les femmes'.
9. Archives CFDT (Archives de la Confédération française démocratique du travail, Paris), 8H 785, Déclaration de Jeannette Laot au CES du 30 octobre 1972.
10. Archives CFDT, 8H 652, Projet de rapport sur l'état d'application du principe d'égalité des rémunérations masculines et féminines, s.d. [1972].
11. Archives CFDT, 8H 652, Ministère du Travail. Comité du travail féminin. Compte rendu de la réunion de la Commission ad-hoc sur les salaires du 18 décembre 1975.
12. Archives CFDT, 8H 652, Ministère du Travail. Comité du travail féminin, *Les salaires féminins (1968–1970–1971). Les salaires des ouvriers et des ouvrières (1972–1973–1974)*, September 1974.
13. Archives CFDT, 8H 652, Ministère du Travail. Comité du travail féminin, *Bilan de l'application de la loi du 22 décembre 1972 sur l'égalité de rémunération entre hommes et femmes*, March 1976.
14. Ibid.
15. Archives CFDT, 8H 652, Ministère du Travail. Comité du travail féminin, Compte rendu de la réunion de la Commission ad-hoc sur les salaires du 10 février 1975.
16. ETUC Archives, 2832, CFDT, *Rapport sur l'état d'application de l'égalité de salaire en France*, 12 May 1977.
17. CGT, *Antoinette*, September 1971, no. 88.
18. ETUC Archives, 2832, CFDT, *Rapport sur l'état d'application de l'égalité de salaire en France*, 12 May 1977.
19. AHUE (Archives historiques de l'Union européenne, Florence), FDE 80, *Service juridique de la Commission des communautés européennes. Note aux membres de la Commission*, 15 June 1978.
20. Archives CFDT, 8H 652, Commission des Communautés européennes. Groupe spécial article 119. Groupe de travail paritaire ad hoc 'Egalité salariale et classifications professionnelles', *Discrimination indirectes par les biais des classifications professionnelles*, 10 March 1981, p. 2.
21. Ibid.
22. Archives CFDT, 8H 652, Confédération européenne des syndicats, *Projet de rapport sur l'égalité de salaire entre main-d'œuvre masculine et féminine*, 2 February 1978.
23. Archives CFDT, 8H 652, Centre d'études et de recherches sur les qualifications, *Rôle joué par les critères d'évaluation de postes dans les écarts de rémunération par sexe*, May 1979.
24. AHUE, FDE 101, Commission des Communautés européennes. Réseau d'experts sur l'application des directives relatives à l'égalité, *Rapport final de synthèse*, 1987, pp. 28–34.
25. Archives CFDT, 8H 652, Commission des Communautés européennes. Groupe spécial article 119. Groupe de travail paritaire ad hoc 'Egalité salariale et classifications professionnelles', *Discrimination indirectes par les biais des classifications professionnelles*, 10 March 1981, pp. 29–36.

26. AHUE, FDE 281, *Note de réflexion*, 28 June 1976; *Documents sur les actions communautaires dans le domaine de l'égalité homme/femme devant l'emploi*, 13 July 1976.
27. AHUE, FDE 64, Commission des Communautés européennes, *Egalité de traitement entre les travailleurs masculins et féminins*, 12 February 1975.
28. ETUC Archives, 2866, Commission des communautés européennes, *Projet de rapport de la Commission au Conseil sur l'état d'application au 31 décembre 1972 du principe d'égalité entre rémunérations masculines et féminines*, 22 November 1972, p. 29.
29. Archives CFDT, 8H 760, *Observations de la CFDT sur l'avant-projet de loi relatif à l'égalité professionnelle entre les hommes et les femmes*, 26 July 1982.
30. ETUC Archives, 2836, Confédération européenne des syndicats, *Programme pour l'obtention de l'égalité des droits et des chances des femmes*, 1979.
31. Archives CFDT, 8H 761, Bureau national, *Pourquoi la CFDT a-t-elle réclamé une loi-cadre pour assurer la mixité des emplois?*, 16–17 April 1980; see also Toutain (1992).

References

Primary Sources

European Trade Union Confederation Archives (International Institute of Social History, Amsterdam)

2832 Documents regarding the questionnaire of 22 February 1977 of the Working Party of women trade union leaders on the application of Article 119 of the Treaty of Rome on the principle of equal pay for men and women.

2864-2866 Documents regarding the application of Article 119 of the Treaty of Rome on the principle of equal pay for men and women.

Archives de la Confédération française démocratique du travail (Paris)

8H 652 Politique de la CFDT pour l'égalité professionnelle entre hommes et femmes.

8H 760 Position de la CFDT sur la loi du 13 juillet 1983 sur l'égalité entre hommes et femmes.

8H 761 Politique de la CFDT pour l'égalité professionnelle entre hommes et femmes.

8H 785 Interventions de Jeannette Laot, secrétaire nationale de la CFDT.

Archives Historiques de l'Union européenne (Florence)

FDE 64 Directive 76/207/CEE (emploi, formation et promotion professionnelle, conditions de travail).

FDE 80 Activités de la Cour de justice des communautés européennes.

FDE 101 Réseau européen d'experts sur la mise en œuvre des directives en matière d'égalité.

FDE 281 Actions communautaires dans le domaine de l'égalité hommes/femmes devant l'emploi.

Secondary Sources

Ardura, A., and R. Silvera. 2001. 'L'égalité hommes/femmes: quelles stratégies syndicales?', *Revue de l'IRES* 37(3): 93–118.

Eyraud, F. 1978. 'La fin des classifications Parodi', *Sociologie du travail* 3: 259–78.

Gallot, F. 2012. 'Les ouvrières, des années 1968 au très contemporain: pratiques et représentations', Ph.D. dissertation, Université Lumière Lyon 2.

Gubin, E. 2007. *Eliane Vogel-Polsky: Une femme de conviction*. Brussels: Institut pour l'égalité des femmes et des hommes.

Guilbert, M. 1965. *Les fonctions des femmes dans l'industrie*. Paris: Mouton.

Hoskins, C. 1996. *Integrating Gender: Women, Law, Politics in the European Union*. London: Verso.

Jacquot, S. 2009. 'La fin d'une politique d'exception: l'émergence du *gender mainstreaming* et la normalisation de la politique communautaire d'égalité entre les femmes et les hommes', *Revue française de science politique* 59(2): 247–77.

Jobert, A. 1989. 'L'égalité professionnelle dans la négociation collective en France', *Travail et emploi* 63: 77–87.

Lanquetin, M.-T. 2004. 'Une loi inappliquée', *Travail, genre et sociétés* 12(2): 182–90.

_______. 2006. 'Chronique juridique des inégalités de salaires entre les femmes et les hommes', *Travail, genre et sociétés* 15: 69–82.

Laufer, J. 2014. *L'égalité professionnelle entre les femmes et les hommes*. Paris: La Découverte.

Laufer, J., and R. Silvera. 2006, 'L'égalité des femmes et des hommes en entreprise: de nouvelles avancées dans la négociation?', *Revue de l'OFCE* 97: 97–271.

Le Brouster, P. 2010. 'La prise en charge par la CFDT de la question des femmes dans les années 1960 et 1970', in C. Guillaume and S. Pochic (eds), *Actes de la journée 'Genre et syndicalisme: regards croisés franco-anglais'*. Paris: EHESS, pp. 27–34.

Lee Downs, L. 1995. *Manufacturing Inequality: Gender Division in the French and British Metalworking Industries, 1914–1939*. Ithaca, NY: Cornell University Press.

_______. 2006. 'Salaires et valeur du travail: L'entrée des femmes dans les industries sous le sceau de l'inégalité en France et en Grande Bretagne (1914–1920)', *Travail, genre et sociétés* 15: 31–49.

Machu, L. 2013, 'Genre, conventions collectives et qualifications dans l'industrie française du premier XXe siècle', *Clio: Femmes, Genre, Histoire* 38: 41–59.

Omnès, C. 1997a. *Ouvrières parisiennes: marchés du travail et trajectoires professionnelles au XXe siècle*. Paris: Editions de l'EHESS.

_______. 1997b. 'Féminisation, qualification et salaires dans la métallurgie parisienne d'une guerre à l'autre', *Les Cahiers du Mage* 2: 35–47.

Revillard, A. 2007. *La cause des femmes au ministère du Travail: le Comité du travail féminin (1965–1984)*. Paris: L'Harmattan.

Saglio, J. 1986, 'Hiérarchie de salaires et négociations des classifications: France, 1900–1950', *Travail et Emploi* 27: 7–19.

_______. 2007. 'Les arrêtés Parodi sur les salaires: un moment de la construction de la place de l'Etat dans le système français de relations professionnelles', *Travail et Emploi* 111: 53–73.

Sellier, F. 1961. *Stratégie de la lutte sociale*. Paris: Editions ouvrières.

Toutain, G. 1992. *L'emploi au féminin: pour une méthode de la mixité professionnelle*. Paris: La documentation française.

Van der Vleuten, A. 2007. *The Price of Gender Equality: Member States and Governance in the European Union*. London: Ashgate.

Zancarini-Fournel, M., and P. Artières (eds). 2015. *68: une histoire collective (1962–1981)*. Paris: La Découverte.

Index

CPSIA information can be obtained
at www.ICGtesting.com
Printed in the USA
LVHW080308140919
631033LV00003B/43/P

9 781789 201871